Linux Service Management Made Easy with systemd

Advanced techniques to effectively manage, control, and monitor Linux systems and services

Donald A. Tevault

BIRMINGHAM—MUMBAI

Linux Service Management Made Easy with systemd

Group Product Manager: Wilson D'souza

Publishing Product Manager: Vijin Boricha

Senior Editor: Arun Nadar

Content Development Editor: Rafiaa Khan

Technical Editor: Nithik Cheruvakodan

Copy Editor: Safis Editing

Project Coordinator: Shagun Saini

Proofreader: Safis Editing

Indexer: Manju Arasan

Production Designer: Nilesh Mohite

First published: February 2022

Production reference: 2291221

Published by Packt Publishing Ltd.

Livery Place

35 Livery Street

Birmingham

B3 2PB, UK.

ISBN 978-1-80181-164-4

`www.packt.com`

I'd like to thank the good folk at Packt Publishing for making the publishing of this book such a smooth process. I'd also like to thank my cats and my opossum for graciously allowing me to use their names in the demos.

– Donnie

Contributors

About the author

Donald A. Tevault – you can call him Donnie – got involved with Linux way back in 2006 and has been working with it ever since. He holds the Linux Professional Institute Level 3 Security certification and the GIAC Incident Handler certification. Donnie is a professional Linux trainer, and thanks to the magic of the internet, teaches Linux classes all over the world from the comfort of his living room. He's also a Linux security researcher for an IoT security company.

About the reviewer

Steve Shilling has worked in the IT industry commercially since 1987 but started with computers back in 1982, writing basic programs and debugging games programs written by others at a very early age. Steve has a broad knowledge covering Unix, Linux, Windows, and mainframe systems, but primarily works in the Unix/Linux space and has worked across many industries, including finance, retail, and insurance. Today, Steve provides training and consultancy in DevOps, SRE, production support, and anything to do with Linux automation or the automation of processes.

He currently works at TPS Services Ltd, specializing in IT training and consultancy, life coaching, management training, and counseling. Steve is the author of *The Grass Is Greener - Linux as a Desktop* and has also reviewed Packt books in the past.

Table of Contents

3

Understanding Service, Path, and Socket Units

4

Controlling systemd Services

5

Creating and Editing Services

6
Understanding systemd Targets

7
Understanding systemd Timers

8
Understanding the systemd Boot Process

9
Setting System Parameters

10
Understanding Shutdown and Reboot Commands

Section 2: Understanding cgroups

11
Understanding cgroups Version 1

12
Controlling Resource Usage with cgroups Version 1

13
Understanding cgroup Version 2

Section 3: Logging, Timekeeping, Networking, and Booting

14
Using journald

15
Using systemd-networkd and systemd-resolved

16

Understanding Timekeeping with systemd

17

Understanding systemd and Bootloaders

18

Understanding systemd-logind

Index

Other Books You May Enjoy

Preface

Welcome, dear reader, to the world's first comprehensive book about systemd and its ecosystem. Although systemd has become the world's most prevalent Linux init system, not all that much has been written about it. There is, of course, the official systemd documentation that you can find online. But it's rather terse and doesn't give you much in the way of practical examples. There are also some good tutorials in the form of blog posts, but most of them just cover the basics. I've only been able to find two other books with `systemd` in the title. Both of them are outdated and also just cover the basics.

My goal in writing this book has been to take you beyond the basics, to show you how to be a more effective Linux systems administrator. In every chapter, we'll be looking under the hood to see how systemd actually works. Rest assured, there will be plenty of hands-on demos to show you how to make systemd sing and dance just the way you want it to.

Who this book is for

If you're a Linux systems administrator, or if you're studying to become one, you can benefit from this book. It can also be a good study aid if you're preparing to take a Linux certification exam, such as the ones from CompTIA, the Linux Professional Institute, or the commercial Linux distro vendors.

What this book covers

Chapter 1, Understanding the Need for systemd, explores the history of Linux init systems and explains why the legacy init systems needed to be replaced with something a bit more robust. We'll also briefly look at the controversy that has surrounded the shift to systemd.

Chapter 2, Understanding systemd Directories and Files, explores the various directories that contain systemd files. We'll also explore the various systemd unit files and configuration files, and will explain the purpose of each type. Finally, we'll briefly look at the executable files that are associated with systemd.

Chapter 3, Understanding Service, Path, and Socket Units, examines the inner workings of the service, path, and socket unit files. We'll examine the parts that are in each, and look at some of the parameters that you can set. Along the way, I'll give you some pointers about how to find information about what the various parameters are doing for you.

Chapter 4, Controlling systemd Services, explores how to control systemd services. We'll start by looking at how to list what services are on the system and what their states are. We'll then look at how to enable, disable, start, stop, and restart services.

Chapter 5, Creating and Editing Services, looks at how to use systemctl to create and edit systemd service files. For those of you who need to work with Docker containers, I'll show you a cool method for using the new `podman` Docker replacement to easily turn your containers into services. We'll also look at how to reload a service file once it's been either added or changed.

Chapter 6, Understanding systemd Targets, looks at the various systemd targets. We'll explain what they are and the structure of a target file. We'll then compare systemd targets to the old SysVinit runlevels, and then look at how to change a system from one target to another.

Chapter 7, Understanding systemd Timers, looks at how to create systemd timers. We'll also compare systemd timers to the old cron system, to see which we like better.

Chapter 8, Understanding the systemd Boot Process, looks at the systemd boot process and how it compares to the old SysVinit boot process.

Chapter 9, Setting System Parameters, looks at how to use systemd utilities to set certain system parameters. Once you see how it's done with systemd, you just might agree that systemd makes it easier.

Chapter 10, Understanding Shutdown and Reboot Commands, looks at how to use the `systemctl` utility to shut down and reboot a Linux system. After that, we'll see whether the old-fashioned `shutdown` command still works.

Chapter 11, Understanding cgroups Version 1, looks at what cgroups are and a bit about their history. We'll then look at how cgroups can help make a Linux system more secure.

Chapter 12, Controlling Resource Usage with cgroups Version 1, looks at using cgroups to control resource usage on a modern Linux system. This includes how to control memory and CPU usage, as well as how to allocate resources to users.

Chapter 13, Understanding cgroups Version 2, looks at cgroups version 2. We'll see how it's different from version 1 and how it improves upon version 1. After that, we'll take a brief look at how to work with it. As an added bonus, we'll look at how we can easily do things with cgroup version 2 that we can't easily do with version 1, such as creating `cpusets` and assigning CPU cores to the proper **non-uniform memory access** (**NUMA**) node.

Chapter 14, Using journald, looks at the basic usage of journald and how it differs from the legacy rsyslog. We'll also look at why we still need rsyslog. Most importantly, you'll learn how to extract and format the data you need from your system logs.

Chapter 15, Using systemd-networkd and systemd-resolved, shows you why you might want to use systemd-networkd and systemd-resolved instead of the default Network Manager, and how to go about doing so. We'll give you an in-depth look at how to set up systemd-networkd for various scenarios and how the procedure differs for the Ubuntu- and Red Hat-type distros.

Chapter 16, Understanding Timekeeping with systemd, looks at the various ways to maintain accurate time on systemd systems. We'll look at `ntp`, `chrony`, `systemd-timesyncd`, and the Precision Time Protocol. We'll discuss the pros and cons of each and how configure them.

Chapter 17, Understanding systemd and Bootloaders, looks at using both GRUB2 and systemd-boot to set up a machine to use EFI/UEFI mode for booting. We'll then look at installing Pop!_OS Linux on a machine that's set up to use UEFI boot mode, and will briefly discuss the Secure Boot feature.

Chapter 18, Understanding systemd-logind, looks at how to use and configure systemd-logind. We'll also learn how to use the loginctl utility to view information about user login sessions, to control the logind service, and to terminate sessions of troublesome users. We'll wrap up the chapter by taking a brief look at polkit, which is an alternate way of granting administrative privileges to certain users.

To get the most out of this book

To perform the demos in this book, you should have a good grasp of basic Linux command-line usage and should know how to create VirtualBox virtual machines. You can download VirtualBox from `https://www.virtualbox.org/` and find the download sites for the various Linux distros at `https://distrowatch.com/`. When you create the virtual machines, allocate enough memory for the machines to run efficiently, and enough drive space to hold everything you need for the demos. (I recommend at least 2 GB of memory for text-mode virtual machines, and at least 4 GB for graphical-mode virtual machines, unless I specify otherwise for specific demos. Set the virtual drive to about 20 GB.)

Software/hardware covered in the book	OS requirements
VirtualBox	Windows, macOS, or Linux (any)
An AlmaLinux 8 `.iso` image file	
An Ubuntu Server 20.04 `.iso` image file	
A Pop!_OS Linux `.iso` image file	

When you install an Ubuntu distro, you'll automatically be added to the `sudo` group, which gives you full `sudo` privileges. When you install AlmaLinux, you'll be given the chance to create a password for the root user. My recommendation is to not do that and instead just check the **Make this user administrator** box on the **Create User** screen of the installer.

Download the example code files

You can download the example code files for this book from GitHub at `https://github.com/PacktPublishing/Linux-Service-Management-Made-Easy-with-systemd`. If there's an update to the code, it will be updated on the existing GitHub repository. We also have other code bundles from our rich catalog of books and videos available at `https://github.com/PacktPublishing/`. Check them out!

Code in Action

Code in Action videos for this book can be viewed at `https://bit.ly/31jQdi0`.

Download the color images

We also provide a PDF file that has color images of the screenshots/diagrams used in this book. You can download it here: `https://static.packt-cdn.com/downloads/9781801811644_ColorImages.pdf`.

Conventions used

There are a number of text conventions used throughout this book.

`Code in text`: Indicates code words in text, database table names, folder names, filenames, file extensions, pathnames, dummy URLs, user input, and Twitter handles.

Any command-line input or output is written as follows:

```
donnie@ubuntu20-04:~$ sudo systemctl daemon-reload
[sudo] password for donnie:
donnie@ubuntu20-04:~$
```

Bold: Indicates a new term, an important word, or words that you see onscreen. For example, words in menus or dialog boxes appear in the text like this. Here is an example: *Click Flash from Etcher to write the image.*

> **Tips or important notes**
> Appear like this.

Get in touch

Feedback from our readers is always welcome.

General feedback: If you have questions about any aspect of this book, mention the book title in the subject of your message and email us at `customercare@packtpub.com`.

Errata: Although we have taken every care to ensure the accuracy of our content, mistakes do happen. If you have found a mistake in this book, we would be grateful if you would report this to us. Please visit `www.packtpub.com/support/errata`, selecting your book, clicking on the Errata Submission Form link, and entering the details.

Piracy: If you come across any illegal copies of our works in any form on the Internet, we would be grateful if you would provide us with the location address or website name. Please contact us at `copyright@packt.com` with a link to the material.

If you are interested in becoming an author: If there is a topic that you have expertise in and you are interested in either writing or contributing to a book, please visit `authors.packtpub.com`.

Share Your Thoughts

Once you've read *Linux Service Management Made Easy with systemd*, we'd love to hear your thoughts! Scan the QR code below to go straight to the Amazon review page for this book and share your feedback.

`https://packt.link/r/1801811644`

Your review is important to us and the tech community and will help us make sure we're delivering excellent quality content.

Section 1: Using systemd

Upon completion of Part 1, you will know how to control system services, set environment parameters, and create new systemd units.

This part of the book comprises the following chapters:

- *Chapter 1, Understanding the Need for systemd*
- *Chapter 2, Understanding systemd Directories and Files*
- *Chapter 3, Understanding Service, Path, and Socket Units*
- *Chapter 4, Controlling systemd Services*
- *Chapter 5, Creating and Editing Services*
- *Chapter 6, Understanding systemd Targets*
- *Chapter 7, Understanding systemd Timers*
- *Chapter 8, Understanding the systemd Boot Process*
- *Chapter 9, Setting System Parameters*
- *Chapter 10, Understanding Shutdown and Reboot Commands*

1 Understanding the Need for systemd

In this first chapter, we'll first briefly look at the history of Linux `init` systems. We'll then look at the shortcomings of the legacy `init` systems and why certain Linux engineers felt the need to develop a new type of `init` system. Finally, we'll look at the controversy that has surrounded `systemd`. For easy reference, here's a list of the topics:

- The history of Linux `init` systems
- The shortcomings of SysV `init` and upstart
- The advantages of `systemd`
- The `systemd` controversy

So, with the introductory comments out of the way, let's jump in.

Technical requirements

For this chapter, all you need is a Linux virtual machine that runs `systemd`. As you read through this chapter, you might want to look at some of the files on the virtual machine.

The history of Linux init systems

So, what is an `init` system? Well, `init` is short for *initialization*. An `init` system, then, initializes the operating system upon bootup. After the bootup has completed, the `init` system will continue working, managing system processes and services. Each system process is assigned a process ID number, or *PID*. The `init` process is always PID 1, and every other process that gets started on the system is either a child or a grandchild of the `init` process.

For many years, the **SysV Init** system was the primary `init` system for Linux-based operating systems (SysV is short for *System 5*. The *V* is the Roman numeral for 5). SysV `init` was originally developed by Bell Labs engineers for the Unix operating system, all the way back in the early 1970s. (At that time, I was a young pup in junior high school, and I still had a full head of hair.)

> **Note**
>
> There are actually a few more Linux `init` systems besides the ones that I'm mentioning here. But these were the most commonly used ones in the pre-`systemd` days.

SysV `init` worked well in its day, but it was never perfect. Nowadays, with new high-performance hardware, SysV `init` has shown both its age and its deficiencies. The first attempt to come up with something better occurred in July 2009, when Ubuntu engineers released the first version of the **upstart** `init` system. Although it was better than SysV, it still had its share of problems, especially the early versions which were quite buggy.

The shortcomings of SysV Init and upstart

The first problem with SysV is that of its rather lengthy boot-up times. When you boot up a SysV machine, all of its services have to start up in sequential order. That might not be so bad on a normal desktop machine, but it can be a bit problematic on a server that needs to run lots of services. In that case, each service would have to wait its turn to start, which could take a while.

The next problem with SysV is its complexity. Instead of simple, easy-to-understand configuration files, SysV does everything with complex Bash shell scripts. The `init` scripts that control system services all have to be assigned a priority number, so that services will start and stop in the proper order. Take, for example, the `init` script that starts the Apache web server on a CentOS 5 machine. First, we can see that it's a fairly lengthy script, as shown here:

```
[student@localhost init.d]$ pwd
/etc/init.d
[student@localhost init.d]$ ls -l httpd
-rwxr-xr-x 1 root root 3523 Sep 16  2014 httpd
[student@localhost init.d]$ wc -l httpd
131 httpd
[student@localhost init.d]$
```

You can see from the `wc -l` output that it consists of 131 lines. As you can see here, 37 of those lines are comments, which still leaves us with 94 lines of actual code:

```
[student@localhost init.d]$ grep ^# httpd | wc -l
37
[student@localhost init.d]$
```

Look inside, and you'll see that it's quite complex and convoluted. Here's just the first part of it:

```
#!/bin/bash
#
# httpd        Startup script for the Apache HTTP Server
#
# chkconfig: - 85 15
# description: Apache is a World Wide Web server.  It is used to serve \
#              HTML files and CGI.
# processname: httpd
# config: /etc/httpd/conf/httpd.conf
# config: /etc/sysconfig/httpd
# pidfile: /var/run/httpd.pid

# Source function library.
. /etc/rc.d/init.d/functions

if [ -f /etc/sysconfig/httpd ]; then
        . /etc/sysconfig/httpd
fi

# Start httpd in the C locale by default.
HTTPD_LANG=${HTTPD_LANG-"C"}

# This will prevent initlog from swallowing up a pass-phrase prompt if
# mod_ssl needs a pass-phrase from the user.
INITLOG_ARGS=""

# Set HTTPD=/usr/sbin/httpd.worker in /etc/sysconfig/httpd to use a server
# with the thread-based "worker" MPM; BE WARNED that some modules may not
# work correctly with a thread-based MPM; notably PHP will refuse to start.

# Path to the apachectl script, server binary, and short-form for messages.
apachectl=/usr/sbin/apachectl
httpd=${HTTPD-/usr/sbin/httpd}
prog=httpd
pidfile=${PIDFILE-/var/run/httpd.pid}
lockfile=${LOCKFILE-/var/lock/subsys/httpd}
RETVAL=0
STOP_TIMEOUT=${STOP_TIMEOUT-10}

# check for 1.3 configuration
check13 () {
        CONFFILE=/etc/httpd/conf/httpd.conf
        GONE="(ServerType|BindAddress|Port|AddModule|ClearModuleList|"
        GONE="${GONE}AgentLog|RefererLog|RefererIgnore|FancyIndexing|"
        GONE="${GONE}AccessConfig|ResourceConfig)"
        if LANG=C grep -Eiq "^[[:space:]]*($GONE)" $CONFFILE; then
                echo
                echo 1>&2 " Apache 1.3 configuration directives found"
                echo 1>&2 " please read /usr/share/doc/httpd-2.2.3/migration.html"
                failure "Apache 1.3 config directives test"
                echo
                exit 1
        fi
}

# The semantics of these two functions differ from the way apachectl does
# things -- attempting to start while running is a failure, and shutdown
# when not running is also a failure.  So we just do it the way init scripts
# are expected to behave here.
start() {
        echo -n $"Starting $prog: "
        check13 || exit 1
        LANG=$HTTPD_LANG daemon --pidfile=${pidfile} $httpd $OPTIONS
        RETVAL=$?
:|
```

Figure 1.1 – An old-fashioned SysV Init script

Toward the end of the script, you'll see the code that stops, starts, restarts, and reloads the Apache daemon, as shown here:

```
# See how we were called.
case "$1" in
  start)
        start
        ;;
  stop)
        stop
        ;;
  status)
        status -p ${pidfile} $httpd
        RETVAL=$?
        ;;
  restart)
        stop
        start
        ;;
  condrestart|try-restart)
        if status -p ${pidfile} $httpd >&/dev/null; then
                stop
                start
        fi
        ;;
  force-reload|reload)
        reload
        ;;
  graceful|help|configtest|fullstatus)
        $apachectl $@
        RETVAL=$?
        ;;
  *)
        echo $"Usage: $prog {start|stop|restart|condrestart|try-restart|force-reload|reload|status|fullstatus|graceful|help|configtest}"
        RETVAL=2
esac
```

Figure 1.2 – The start, stop, restart, reload section of an init script

This code, or code similar to this, has to be in every `init` script so that the human user can control the daemon. To complicate things even more, developers didn't always write this code consistently for different programs. So, for example, a status display for one daemon didn't always look the same as the status display for another daemon.

Then, there's the problem of inconsistent implementation across the different families of Linux distros. With SysV, there were at least three different methods of implementation. Red Hat-type distros used one method, Debian-type distros used another method, and Slackware-type distros use yet another. For example, the Red Hat way of controlling services required using the `service` and `chkconfig` commands. When working with Debian-type systems, I always used to have to look up the service management commands, because I could never remember them. With Slackware, you don't have any service management commands. To enable or disable a service on a Slackware machine, you just set or remove the executable permission from the appropriate `init` script.

Runlevels were also a source of confusion, because each family of distro had its own set of runlevel definitions. For example, here are the definitions for the graphical runlevel:

- The Red Hat family used runlevel 5.
- The Slackware family uses runlevel 4.
- The Debian family used no specific runlevel for either text mode or graphical mode. Instead, you enabled or disabled graphical mode by enabling or disabling the X server daemon.

So, you can see that this was all quite confusing, especially for anyone who worked in a mixed environment. It should be fairly obvious that we needed something that was a bit less confusing.

As if this weren't enough, there was also the issue of performance. SysV worked well in its day, when computing hardware was more primitive. But, on modern hardware with multiple CPUs that each have multiple cores, we need something a bit more robust. Ubuntu's upstart was supposed to fix this, but it didn't quite live up to its promise. Nowadays, Upstart is completely dead, but there are still some diehards who refuse to give up SysV. In the enterprise, `systemd` is king.

The advantages of systemd

We've just seen the problems with SysV and upstart. Now, let's look at what makes `systemd` better.

systemd's simplicity

In contrast to SysV, `systemd` is really quite simple to configure. For example, look at how short the Apache service file is on a CentOS 7 machine with `systemd`:

```
[donnie@localhost ~]$ cd /lib/systemd/system
[donnie@localhost system]$ ls -l httpd.service
-rw-r--r--. 1 root root 752 Jun 26  2018 httpd.service
[donnie@localhost system]$ wc -l httpd.service
22 httpd.service
[donnie@localhost system]$
```

There are only 22 lines, and 5 of those lines are comments, as you can see here:

```
[Unit]
Description=The Apache HTTP Server
After=network.target remote-fs.target nss-lookup.target
Documentation=man:httpd(8)
Documentation=man:apachectl(8)

[Service]
Type=notify
EnvironmentFile=/etc/sysconfig/httpd
ExecStart=/usr/sbin/httpd $OPTIONS -DFOREGROUND
ExecReload=/usr/sbin/httpd $OPTIONS -k graceful
ExecStop=/bin/kill -WINCH ${MAINPID}
# We want systemd to give httpd some time to finish gracefully, but still want
# it to kill httpd after TimeoutStopSec if something went wrong during the
# graceful stop. Normally, Systemd sends SIGTERM signal right after the
# ExecStop, which would kill httpd. We are sending useless SIGCONT here to give
# httpd time to finish.
KillSignal=SIGCONT
PrivateTmp=true

[Install]
WantedBy=multi-user.target
httpd.service (END)
```

Figure 1.3 – A systemd service file

I'll explain everything in the `systemd` files later. For now, I just want to show you that a `systemd` service file is much simpler than a SysV `init` script. (As we'll soon see in the upcoming chapters, it's easier to learn how to use the `systemd` directives than it is to learn how to write shell-scripting code for `init` scripts.)

systemd's consistency

The next `systemd` advantage is its consistency. Yes, boys and girls, you no longer have to remember multiple sets of system management commands for multiple families of Linux distros. Instead, you'll now use the same commands on all Linux distros that use `systemd`. So, this eliminates a major source of frustration for administrators, and for anyone who's studying to take a Linux certification exam.

systemd's performance

In contrast to SysV, `systemd` can start services in parallel, rather than just one at a time in sequence. This makes for much quicker boot-up times than for SysV. Once the machine is booted, performance is more robust than that of SysV.

With `systemd`, we have a much cleaner way of killing processes. For example, if you needed to use the `kill` command to forcefully terminate the Apache web server service on a SysV machine, you would only terminate the Apache process itself. If the web server process had spawned any child processes due to running CGI scripts, for example, those processes would continue on for a while longer as *zombie* processes. But, when you kill a service with `systemd`, all processes that are associated with that service will also get terminated.

systemd security

An added bonus is that you can configure `systemd` service files to control certain aspects of system security. Here are some of the things that you can do:

- You can create a `systemd` service that can restrict access to or from certain directories, or that can only access or be accessed from certain network addresses.
- By using namespaces, you can effectively isolate services from the rest of the system. This also allows you to create containers without having to run Docker.
- You can use `cgroups` to limit resource usage. This can help prevent certain types of denial-of-service attacks.
- You can specify which root-level kernel capabilities a service is allowed to have.

With all this, you can make `systemd` somewhat emulate a mandatory access control system, such as SELinux or AppArmor.

All the way around, `systemd` is much better than any `init` system that came before it. But it hasn't made everyone happy.

The systemd controversy

If you've been in the computer world for any length of time, you may have seen that we geeks can get quite passionate about our operating systems. In the early 1990s, I finally replaced my text mode-only 8088 machine with one that could run a graphical interface. I first gave Windows 3.1 a try, and quickly decided that I really hated it. So, I bought a copy of OS/2, which I liked much better and ran for quite a few years on my home-built 486 machine. But, all of my geek buddies at work were big Windows fans, and they kept arguing with me about how much better Windows is. I thought that they were all crazy, and we kept getting into some rather heated arguments.

Then, when I got into Linux, I quickly learned that you don't want to go into any Linux forum and ask which Linux distro is the best for a newbie to start with. All that does is start fights, leaving the poor newbie more confused than ever. And now, the fight is over whether or not `systemd` is a *good thing*. Here are some of the objections:

- By trying to do too much, `systemd` violates the Unix concept of having each utility just do one thing but having it do it well.
- It's controlled by a large corporation (Red Hat).
- It's a security problem.
- Its `journald` component saves system logs to a binary format, which some people believe is more easily corrupted than the plain-text files that `rsyslog` creates.

If you look at things objectively, you might see that the objections aren't so bad:

- Yes, the `systemd` ecosystem includes more than just the `init` system. It also includes network, bootloader, logging, and log-in components. But those components are all optional, and not all Linux distros use them in a default setup.
- It was created primarily by Red Hat, and the project leader is a Red Hat employee. But Red Hat released it under a free-as-in-speech software license, which means that no one company can ever take full control of it. Even if Red Hat were to suddenly decide that future versions of `systemd` were to be proprietary, the free code is still out there, and someone would fork it into a new free version.
- Yes, there have been some security bugs in `systemd`. But that's also true of OpenSSL, the Bash shell, and even the Linux kernel itself. To complain about `systemd's` security would only be valid if the bugs hadn't gotten fixed.
- The `journald` component does create log files in a binary format. But it's still possible to run `rsyslog` on `systemd` distros, and most do. Some distros, such as the Red Hat Enterprise Linux 8 family, use `journald` to gather system information and then just have `journald` pass the information to `rsyslog` in order to create normal text files. So, with RHEL 8, we have the best of both worlds.

Soon after the release of `systemd`, some people who had never even tried it put up blog posts that explained why `systemd` was pure evil and that they would never use it. A few years ago, I created a `systemd` tutorial playlist on my BeginLinux Guru channel on YouTube. The first video is called *Why systemd?*. Quite a few people left comments about why they would never use `systemd` and said that they would change to either a non-`systemd` Linux distro or to a FreeBSD-type distro in order to avoid it.

The bottom line is this: all enterprise-grade Linux distros now use `systemd`. So, I think that it might be here to stay.

Summary

In this first chapter, we've looked at the history of the most common Linux init systems. We've seen the ways in which the legacy init systems are deficient, and we've seen why `systemd` is a much better replacement. We wrapped things up by looking at the objections against `systemd`.

One of the challenges of learning `systemd` is that, until now, there hasn't been any real comprehensive documentation about it. There's basic usage documentation on the Red Hat website, but it doesn't even cover all components of the `systemd` ecosystem. There are only two `systemd`-specific books that I could find, which are a few years old. (One book is specific to Fedora, the other is specific to Ubuntu.) Even those books leave some things out. So, the challenge I've set for myself is to create a comprehensive, hands-on guide for all things `systemd`. In the chapters that follow, I'll do my best to accomplish that goal.

In the next chapter, we'll go on a quick tour of the `systemd` directories and files. I'll see you there.

Questions

1. Who created the original SysV `init` system?

   a. Bell Labs

   b. Red Hat

   c. Debian

   d. Ubuntu

2. Which of the following is true about SysV?

   a. It's a modern, robust `init` system.

   b. When booting a machine, it can start services in parallel.

   c. When booting a machine, it can only start services sequentially.

   d. It has security features that `systemd` doesn't have.

3. Which of the following is *not* true about `systemd`?

   a. It has security features that can somewhat emulate a mandatory access control system.

   b. It can start services in parallel.

   c. It can use `cgroups` to limit resource usage.

   d. It's a legacy system that needs to be replaced.

Answers

1. A
2. C
3. D

Further reading

- An overview of Linux `init` systems:

  `https://www.tecmint.com/best-linux-init-systems/`

- Why `init` needed to be replaced with `systemd`:

  `https://www.tecmint.com/systemd-replaces-init-in-linux/`

- Red Hat's `systemd` documentation:

  `https://access.redhat.com/documentation/en-us/red_hat_enterprise_linux/8/html/configuring_basic_system_settings/index`

- Some arguments against `systemd`:

  `https://textplain.net/blog/2015/problems-with-systemd-and-why-i-like-bsd-init/`

  `https://www.theregister.com/2014/10/21/unix_greybeards_threaten_debian_fork_over_systemd_plan/`

2
Understanding systemd Directories and Files

In this chapter, we'll explore the various `systemd` unit files and configuration files and explain the purpose of several types. We'll briefly look at some of the executable files that are associated with `systemd`. Along the way, we'll also look at the directories where these files live.

These are the topics we will cover in this chapter:

- Understanding the `systemd` configuration files
- Understanding the `systemd` unit files
- Understanding the `systemd` executables

The topics in this chapter comprise basic foundational knowledge of `systemd`. We'll be building upon this foundation in the chapters to come.

If you're ready, let's go.

Technical requirements

If you'd like to follow along with what I'm doing, you'll need a couple of **virtual machines** (**VMs**). Here, I'm using Ubuntu Server 20.04 for the Ubuntu side of things, and AlmaLinux 8 for the Red Hat side of things. (You'll also see me using Fedora to point out a couple of things, but you won't need a Fedora VM yourself.)

Check out the following link to see the Code in Action video: `https://bit.ly/3xL4os5`

Understanding the systemd configuration files

In this section, we'll look at the configuration files that control how the various components of `systemd` operate. If you want to follow along with your own VM, it won't much matter which distro you have because things will be mostly the same across all `systemd`-enabled distros. Okay—so now you're yelling at me, saying:

Mostly the same? Why, Donnie, you told us before that systemd is implemented consistently across all distros! What gives?

Well, it is consistent, in that the management and control commands are the same across all distros, but the `systemd` ecosystem includes several different components besides just the `init` system. These components are optional, and some Linux distros don't use all of them in a default configuration. Several of these components have configuration files in the `/etc/systemd/` directory, as you can see here:

```
[donnie@localhost systemd]$ pwd
/etc/systemd
[donnie@localhost systemd]$ ls -l *.conf
-rw-r--r--. 1 root root  720 May 31  2016 bootchart.conf
-rw-r--r--. 1 root root  615 Mar 26  2020 coredump.conf
-rw-r--r--. 1 root root 1041 Mar 26  2020 journald.conf
-rw-r--r--. 1 root root 1042 Mar 26  2020 logind.conf
-rw-r--r--. 1 root root  584 Mar 26  2020 networkd.conf
-rw-r--r--. 1 root root  529 Mar 26  2020 pstore.conf
-rw-r--r--. 1 root root  764 Mar 26  2020 resolved.conf
-rw-r--r--. 1 root root  790 Mar 26  2020 sleep.conf
-rw-r--r--. 1 root root 1762 Mar 26  2020 system.conf
-rw-r--r--. 1 root root  677 Mar 26  2020 timesyncd.conf
-rw-r--r--. 1 root root 1185 Mar 26  2020 user.conf
[donnie@localhost systemd]$
```

The `timesyncd.conf` file, which you see second from the bottom in the preceding code snippet, is one of those components that you won't see everywhere. It's for the service that synchronizes the machine's time to a trusted external source. You see it here, but you won't see it on either **Red Hat Enterprise Linux** (**RHEL**) or any of RHEL's free-of-charge derivatives. That's because RHEL-type distros use an alternate time-synchronization service called `chronyd`, and just because you see a configuration file here for a particular `systemd` component doesn't necessarily mean that that component is being used. On the Fedora machine from which I took the preceding code snippet, the `networkd`, `resolved`, and `timesyncd` components are all disabled. (As with the RHEL distros, Fedora uses `chronyd` for time-keeping, but it still has the `timesyncd` component installed.) On the other hand, if you look at the newest versions of Ubuntu Server, you'll see that these optional components are enabled by default. (We'll see later how to tell if a service is either enabled or disabled.)

Okay—let's talk about what's in these configuration files. We'll start by looking at the `system.conf` file, which sets the configuration for the `systemd init` process. (For space reasons, I can only show part of the file here. You can view the whole file on your VM by doing `less /etc/systemd/system.conf`.) Here's a snippet:

```
[Manager]
#LogLevel=info
#LogTarget=journal-or-kmsg
#LogColor=yes
#LogLocation=no
. . .
. . .
#DefaultLimitNICE=
#DefaultLimitRTPRIO=
#DefaultLimitRTTIME=
```

Now, I'm not going to explain this file line by line because I don't want you to hate me for boring you to death. But seriously, in normal circumstances, you might not ever have to change any of these configuration files. If you think that you might need to do anything with them, your best bet is to read their associated man pages, which will have a breakdown of what each of these parameters is doing for you. The trick is that for most of these files, you'll have to add the `systemd-` text string to the front of the filename to find its man page. For example, to look at the man page for the `system.conf` file, type the following:

```
man systemd-system.conf
```

Also, you might have noticed that in all of these configuration files, every line is commented out. That doesn't mean that those lines have no effect. Instead, it means that these are the default parameters that are compiled in. To change something, you would uncomment the line for the desired parameter and change its value.

> **Pro tip**
>
> You can use the `apropos` command to find all man pages with a specific text string in either the man page name or man page description. For example, to find all pages that match the `systemd` string, just type the following: `apropos systemd`.
>
> You can also type `man -k systemd`, which is a synonym for `apropos systemd`. (I got into the habit early on of always typing `apropos`, and I've never broken this habit.) If nothing comes up when you try this, you might have to rebuild the man page database, which you'll do by typing `sudo mandb`.

All right—I think we've talked enough about the configuration files. Next up, we'll talk about the `systemd` unit files.

Understanding the systemd unit files

Instead of using a set of complex Bash shell scripts, the `systemd init` system controls system and service operations with various types of *unit* files. Each unit file has a filename with a filename extension that describes which type of unit it is. Before we look at these files, let's see where they live.

The `/lib/systemd/system/` directory is the default location for unit files that either come with the operating system or come with any packages that you might install. There might be times when you'll either need to modify some of these unit files or even create your own, but you won't do that in this directory. Instead, you'll do that in the `/etc/systemd/system/` directory. Any unit files in this directory that have the same name as unit files in `/lib/systemd/system/` take precedence.

> **Tip**
>
> You can read about unit files by typing the following: `man systemd.unit`.
>
> At the bottom of this man page, you'll see where it refers you to other man pages for each specific type of unit file. You'll soon see that the trickiest part about this is having to search through the various man pages whenever you need to look up something about a particular unit-configuration parameter. To make things easier, you can look up a specific directive in the `systemd.directives` man page, which will direct you to the man page that contains information about that directive.

Now that you know where the unit files are, let's look at *what* they are.

Types of unit files

In the `/lib/systemd/system` directory, you'll see various types of unit files that each perform a different function. Here's a list of the more common types:

- `service`: These are the configuration files for services. They replace the old-fashioned init scripts that we had on the old **System V** (**SysV**) systems.
- `socket`: Sockets can either enable communication between different system services or they can automatically wake up a sleeping service when it receives a connection request.
- `slice`: Slice units are used when configuring `cgroups`. (We'll look at these in *Part 2, Understanding cgroups*.)
- `mount` and `automount`: These contain mount point information for filesystems that are controlled by `systemd`. Normally, they get created automatically, so you shouldn't have to do too much with them.
- `target`: Target units are used during system startup, for grouping units and for providing well-known synchronization points. (We'll cover these in *Chapter 6, Understanding systemd Targets*.)
- `timer`: Timer units are for scheduling jobs that run on a schedule. They replace the old cron system. (We'll work with these in *Chapter 7, Understanding systemd Timers*.)

- `path`: Path units are for services that can be started via path-based activation. (We'll cover service, path, and socket units in *Chapter 3*, *Understanding Service, Path, and Socket Units*.)
- `swap`: Swap units contain information about your swap partitions.

  That's about it for the basic description of our unit files. We'll go into the nitty-gritty details about them in subsequent chapters.

Understanding the systemd executables

Normally, we would search for a program's executable files in either a `bin/` or an `sbin/` directory, and you will indeed find some of the `systemd` utility executable files there, but most of the `systemd` executables are found instead in the `/lib/systemd/` directory. To save space, here's just a partial listing:

```
donnie@donnie-TB250-BTC:/lib/systemd$ ls -l
total 7448
-rw-r--r--  1 root root 2367728 Feb  6  2020 libsystemd-
shared-237.so
drwxr-xr-x  2 root root    4096 Apr  3  2020 network
-rw-r--r--  1 root root     699 Feb  6  2020 resolv.conf
-rwxr-xr-x  1 root root    1246 Feb  6  2020 set-cpufreq
drwxr-xr-x 24 root root   36864 Apr  3  2020 system
-rwxr-xr-x  1 root root 1612152 Feb  6  2020 systemd
-rwxr-xr-x  1 root root    6128 Feb  6  2020 systemd-ac-
power
-rwxr-xr-x  1 root root   18416 Feb  6  2020 systemd-
backlight
-rwxr-xr-x  1 root root   10304 Feb  6  2020 systemd-
binfmt
-rwxr-xr-x  1 root root   10224 Feb  6  2020 systemd-
cgroups-agent
-rwxr-xr-x  1 root root   26632 Feb  6  2020 systemd-
cryptsetup
. . .
. . .
```

You see that the executable for `systemd` itself is here, as well as the executables for the services that `systemd` runs as part of its own system. On some Linux distros, you'll see symbolic links in either the `/bin` or `/usr/bin` directories that point to some of the executable files here. For the most part, you won't directly interact with these files, so let's move on to something that you will interact with.

The `systemctl` utility is for controlling `systemd`, and you'll use it a lot. It's a multi-purpose tool that can do a lot of things for you. It lets you view the different units and the status of the units, and either enable them or disable them. For now, we'll look at some `systemctl` commands that allow you to view different types of information. Later, we'll talk about using `systemctl` to control and edit specific units. If you'd like to follow along, fire up a VM and start getting your hands dirty.

One thing to notice is that some `systemctl` commands require root privileges, and others don't. If you're just looking at system or unit information, you can do that with your normal user permissions. If you need to change a configuration, you'll need to assume the awesome powers of root. Okay—let's get started.

We'll first list the active units that `systemd` currently has in memory. We'll do that with the `systemctl list-units` command. It's a very long output, so I'll just show you the first few lines here:

```
[donnie@localhost ~]$ systemctl list-units
UNIT
LOAD   ACTIVE SUB       DESCRIPTION
proc-sys-fs-binfmt_misc.automount
loaded active waiting   Arbitrary Executable File Formats
File System Automount Point
sys-devices-pci0000:00-0000:00:17.0-ata3-host2-
target2:0:0-2:0:0:0-block-sda-sda1.device  loaded active
plugged   WDC_WDS250G2B0A-00SM50 1
sys-devices-pci0000:00-0000:00:17.0-ata3-host2-
target2:0:0-2:0:0:0-block-sda-sda2.device  loaded active
plugged   WDC_WDS250G2B0A-00SM50 2
sys-devices-pci0000:00-0000:00:17.0-ata3-host2-
target2:0:0-2:0:0:0-block-sda.device       loaded active
plugged   WDC_WDS250G2B0A-00SM50
sys-devices-pci0000:00-0000:00:1b.2-0000:02:00.1-sound-
card1.device                               loaded active plugged
GP104 High Definition Audio Controller
```

```
sys-devices-pci0000:00-0000:00:1b.3-0000:03:00.1-sound-
card2.device                                loaded active plugged
GP104 High Definition Audio Controller
. . .
. . .
```

This is the automount section, which shows the various devices that have been mounted. As you can see, this covers more than just storage devices.

Next, we have the mount, path, and scope units, as follows:

```
. . .
. . .
-.mount
loaded active mounted   /
boot.mount
loaded active mounted   /boot
dev-hugepages.mount
loaded active mounted   Huge Pages File System
dev-mqueue.mount
loaded active mounted   POSIX Message Queue File System
home.mount
loaded active mounted   /home
run-user-1000.mount
loaded active mounted   /run/user/1000
sys-fs-fuse-connections.mount
loaded active mounted   FUSE Control File System
sys-kernel-config.mount
loaded active mounted   Kernel Configuration File System
sys-kernel-debug.mount
loaded active mounted   Kernel Debug File System
tmp.mount
loaded active mounted   Temporary Directory (/tmp)
var-lib-nfs-rpc_pipefs.mount
loaded active mounted   RPC Pipe File System
cups.path
loaded active running   CUPS Scheduler
systemd-ask-password-plymouth.path
loaded active waiting   Forward Password Requests to
Plymouth Directory Watch
```

```
systemd-ask-password-wall.path
loaded active waiting   Forward Password Requests to Wall
Directory Watch
init.scope
loaded active running   System and Service Manager
session-1.scope
loaded active abandoned Session 1 of user donnie
session-3.scope
loaded active abandoned Session 3 of user donnie
session-4.scope
loaded active running   Session 4 of user donnie
. . .
. . .
```

Note here that there's a mount unit for each partition on your drive.

Keep scrolling down, and you'll see the same kind of display for the service, slice, socket, swap, target, and timer units. At the bottom, you'll see a brief explanation of the status codes and a short summary, as follows:

```
LOAD   = Reflects whether the unit definition was
properly loaded.
ACTIVE = The high-level unit activation state, i.e.
generalization of SUB.
SUB    = The low-level unit activation state, values
depend on unit type.

182 loaded units listed. Pass --all to see loaded but
inactive units, too.
To show all installed unit files use 'systemctl list-
unit-files'.
lines 136-190/190 (END)
```

Use the `--all` option to also see units that are not active, like so:

```
[donnie@localhost ~]$ systemctl list-units --all
  UNIT
LOAD      ACTIVE   SUB       DESCRIPTION
● boot.automount
not-found inactive dead      boot.automount
  proc-sys-fs-binfmt_misc.automount
loaded    active   waiting   Arbitrary Executable File
Formats File System A
```

```
  dev-block-8:2.device
loaded    active   plugged   WDC_WDS250G2B0A-00SM50 2
  dev-disk-by\x2did-ata\x2dWDC_
WDS250G2B0A\x2d00SM50_181202802064.device
loaded    active   plugged   WDC_WDS250G2B0A-00SM50
  dev-disk-by\x2did-ata\x2dWDC_WDS250G2B0A\
x2d00SM50_181202802064\x2dpart1.device
loaded    active   plugged   WDC_WDS250G2B0A-00SM50 1
  dev-disk-by\x2did-ata\x2dWDC_WDS250G2B0A\
x2d00SM50_181202802064\x2dpart2.device
loaded    active   plugged   WDC_WDS250G2B0A-00SM50 2
. . .
. . .
```

That was luck. We found an inactive unit right at the very top.

You can also view specific types of units with the `-t` option. For example, to see just the service units, run the following command:

```
[donnie@localhost ~]$ systemctl list-units -t service
UNIT
LOAD   ACTIVE SUB     DESCRIPTION
abrt-journal-core.service
loaded active running Creates ABRT problems from
coredumpctl messages
abrt-oops.service
loaded active running ABRT kernel log watcher
abrt-xorg.service
loaded active running ABRT Xorg log watcher
abrtd.service
loaded active running ABRT Automated Bug Reporting Tool
alsa-state.service
loaded active running Manage Sound Card State (restore
and store)
atd.service
loaded active running Deferred execution scheduler
auditd.service
loaded active running Security Auditing Service
avahi-daemon.service
loaded active running Avahi mDNS/DNS-SD Stack
. . .
. . .
```

You can view the other units in the same way.

Now, let's say that we just want to see the services that are dead. We can do that with the `--state` option, like so:

```
[donnie@localhost ~]$ systemctl list-units -t service
--state=dead
  UNIT                                       LOAD      ACTIVE
SUB  DESCRIPTION
  abrt-vmcore.service                        loaded
inactive dead Harvest vmcores for ABRT
  alsa-restore.service                       loaded
inactive dead Save/Restore Sound Card State
  auth-rpcgss-module.service                 loaded
inactive dead Kernel Module supporting RPCSEC_GSS
● autofs.service                             not-found
inactive dead autofs.service
  blk-availability.service                   loaded
inactive dead Availability of block devices
  dbxtool.service                            loaded
inactive dead Secure Boot DBX (blacklist) updater
  dm-event.service                           loaded
inactive dead Device-mapper event daemon
  dmraid-activation.service                  loaded
inactive dead Activation of DM RAID sets
  dnf-makecache.service                      loaded
inactive dead dnf makecache
  dracut-cmdline.service                     loaded
inactive dead dracut cmdline hook
. . .
. . .
```

By running `systemctl --state=help`, you'll see a list of all of the different states that you can view for the different unit types.

In addition to seeing the units that are currently in memory, you can also see the unit files that are installed on the system by running the following command:

```
[donnie@localhost ~]$ systemctl list-unit-files
UNIT FILE                                               STATE
proc-sys-fs-binfmt_misc.automount
static
```

```
-.mount
generated
boot.mount
generated
dev-hugepages.mount
static
dev-mqueue.mount
static
home.mount
generated
proc-fs-nfsd.mount
static
. . .
. . .
session-1.scope
transient
session-3.scope
transient
session-4.scope
transient
abrt-journal-core.service
enabled
abrt-oops.service
enabled
abrt-pstoreoops.service
disabled
abrt-vmcore.service
enabled
abrt-xorg.service
enabled
abrtd.service
enabled
. . .
. . .
```

Here, you see some things that may seem rather strange. At the top, you see some mount files that are in a `generated` state. These files live in the `/run/systemd/units/` directory and are automatically generated by `systemd`. To create these mount files, `systemd` reads the `/etc/fstab` file every time you either boot the machine or manually reload the `fstab` file.

Unit files in a `static` state are ones that you can neither enable nor disable. Rather, other units will call in these static units as dependencies.

Unit files in a `transient` state deal with things that are, well, transient. Here, we see three scope units that are managing three user sessions. When a user logs out of a session, one of these units will disappear.

And of course, units that are in an `enabled` state will automatically start upon booting the machine, and units that are in a `disabled` state won't.

To see if just one individual unit is either enabled or active, you can use the `is-enabled` and `is-active` options with `systemctl`. A while back, I told you that the `networkd`, `resolved`, and `timesyncd` services were all disabled on my Fedora machine. Here's how to prove that:

```
[donnie@localhost ~]$ systemctl is-enabled systemd-timesyncd
disabled
[donnie@localhost ~]$ systemctl is-enabled systemd-networkd
disabled
[donnie@localhost ~]$ systemctl is-enabled systemd-resolved
disabled
[donnie@localhost ~]$
```

And here's how to prove that they're not active:

```
[donnie@localhost ~]$ systemctl is-active systemd-timesyncd
inactive
[donnie@localhost ~]$ systemctl is-active systemd-resolved
inactive
[donnie@localhost ~]$ systemctl is-active systemd-timesyncd
inactive
[donnie@localhost ~]$
```

On the other hand, the `NetworkManager` service is enabled and active on my Fedora machine, as you can see here:

```
[donnie@localhost ~]$ systemctl is-enabled NetworkManager
enabled
[donnie@localhost ~]$ systemctl is-active NetworkManager
active
[donnie@localhost ~]$
```

Now, I'll leave it to you to verify all of this on the Ubuntu machine.

You can also see information about just one *type* of unit file. Here, we'll just look at information about the swap unit files:

```
[donnie@localhost units]$ systemctl list-unit-files -t swap
UNIT FILE                                                 STATE
dev-mapper-fedora_localhost\x2d\x2dlive\x2dswap.swap generated

1 unit files listed.
[donnie@localhost units]$
```

Just as it did with the mount unit files, `systemd` generated this file by reading the `/etc/fstab` file.

Earlier, I showed you the `/etc/systemd/system.conf` file, which sets the global configuration for `systemd`. With the `show` option, you can see the actual running configuration by doing `systemctl show`. Here's the partial output:

```
[donnie@localhost ~]$ systemctl show
Version=v243.8-1.fc31
Features=+PAM +AUDIT +SELINUX +IMA -APPARMOR +SMACK
+SYSVINIT +UTMP +LIBCRYPTSETUP +GCRYPT +GNUTLS +ACL +XZ +LZ4
+SECCOMP +BLKID +ELFUTILS +KMOD +IDN2 -IDN +PCRE2 default-
hierarchy=unified
Architecture=x86-64
Tainted=local-hwclock
FirmwareTimestampMonotonic=0
LoaderTimestampMonotonic=0
KernelTimestamp=Thu 2021-03-11 11:58:01 EST
KernelTimestampMonotonic=0
. . .
. . .
DefaultLimitRTPRIOSoft=0
DefaultLimitRTTIME=infinity
DefaultLimitRTTIMESoft=infinity
DefaultTasksMax=4608
TimerSlackNSec=50000
DefaultOOMPolicy=stop
```

Use the `--property=` option to view just one item, like so:

```
[donnie@localhost ~]$ systemctl show
--property=DefaultLimitSIGPENDING
DefaultLimitSIGPENDING=15362
[donnie@localhost ~]$
```

There is a man page for `systemctl`, and you're welcome to peruse it. But if you just need a quick reference, run `systemctl -h`.

All right—I think that's enough for now. So, let's wrap this chapter up and put a bow on it, shall we?

Summary

Okay—we've hit the ground running and have covered quite a few concepts. We covered the various types of configuration files and unit files and saw where they live. We ended by using the `systemctl` command to view information about our running system.

In the next chapter, we'll expand on this by showing you the inner workings of the service, path, and socket unit files. I'll see you there.

Questions

1. Which of the following commands tells you what the running `systemd` configuration is?

   a. `systemctl list`

   b. `systemctl show`

   c. `systemd show`

   d. `systemd list`

2. Which of the following statements is true?

   a. To configure your drive partitions, you need to hand-configure the mount units.

   b. The mount units for your drive partitions get generated automatically when `systemd` reads the `fstab` file.

   c. The mount units for your drive partitions are static units.

   d. No mount units are needed for your drive partitions.

3. Which of the following will tell you if the `NetworkManager` service is running?

   a. `systemctl active NetworkManager`

   b. `systemd active NetworkManager`

   c. `systemd enabled NetworkManager`

   d. `systemctl is-enabled NetworkManager`

   e. `systemctl is-active NetworkManager`

Answers

1. b
2. b
3. e

Further reading

`systemd` units and unit files:

`https://www.digitalocean.com/community/tutorials/understanding-systemd-units-and-unit-files`

3
Understanding Service, Path, and Socket Units

In this chapter, we'll examine the inner workings of the service, path, and socket unit files. We'll examine the parts that are in each and look at some of the parameters that you can set. Along the way, I'll give you some pointers about how to find information about what the various parameters are doing for you.

In this chapter, we will cover the following topics:

- Understanding service units
- Understanding socket units
- Understanding path units

At some point in your Linux administrator career, you could be tasked with modifying existing units or creating new ones. The knowledge in this chapter can help you with that. So, if you're ready, let's go.

Technical requirements

As always, I'll be doing the demos on an Ubuntu Server 20.04 virtual machine and an Alma Linux 8 virtual machine. Feel free to fire up your own virtual machines to follow along.

Check out the following link to see the Code in Action video: `https://bit.ly/2ZQBHh6`

Understanding service units

Service units are the equivalent of init scripts on old SysV systems. We'll use them to configure our various services, which we used to call *daemons* in the old days. A service can be pretty much anything that you want to start automatically and run in the background. Examples of services include Secure Shell, your web server of choice, a mail server, and various services that are required for proper system operation. While some service files can be short and sweet, others can be fairly lengthy, with more options enabled. To read about all of these options, just type the following:

```
man systemd.directives
```

The descriptions for all of the parameters that you can set are spread over several different man pages. This `systemd.directives` man page is an index that will direct you to the proper man page for each parameter.

Rather than trying to explain every parameter that service files can use, let's look through a few example files and explain what they're doing.

Understanding the Apache service file

We'll start with the service file for the Apache web server. On my Ubuntu Server 20.04 virtual machine, it is the `/lib/systemd/system/apache2.service` file. The first thing to note is that service unit files are divided into three sections. The top section is the `[Unit]` section, which contains parameters that can be placed in any type of unit file. It looks like this:

```
[Unit]
Description=The Apache HTTP Server
After=network.target remote-fs.target nss-lookup.target
Documentation=https://httpd.apache.org/docs/2.4/
```

Here, we see these three parameters:

- `Description=`: Okay, this one should be fairly self-explanatory. All it does is tell the human user what the service is. The `systemctl status` command pulls its description information from this line.
- `After=`: We don't want Apache to start until certain other things have happened. We haven't talked about `target` files yet, but that's okay. For now, just know that we want to prevent Apache from starting until after the network, any possible attached remote filesystems, and the Name Switch Service are available.
- `Documentation=`: Here's another one that's self-explanatory. It just shows where to find the Apache documentation.

To read about the options that you can place in the `[Unit]` section of any unit file, just type the following:

```
man systemd.unit
```

Next, we have the `[Service]` section, where things get a bit more interesting. It contains parameters that can only be placed in a service unit file, and looks like this:

```
[Service]
Type=forking
Environment=APACHE_STARTED_BY_SYSTEMD=true
ExecStart=/usr/sbin/apachectl start
ExecStop=/usr/sbin/apachectl stop
ExecReload=/usr/sbin/apachectl graceful
PrivateTmp=true
Restart=on-abort
```

In this particular file, we see these parameters:

- `Type=`: There are several different service types that you'll see described in the `systemd.service` man page. In this case, we have the `forking` type, which means that the first Apache process that starts will spawn a child process. When Apache startup is complete and the proper communication channels have been set up, the original process—the *parent* process—will exit and the child process will carry on as the main service process. When the parent process exits, the `systemd` service manager will finally recognize the service as having fully started. According to the man page, this is the traditional behavior for Unix services, and `systemd` just carries on the tradition.

- `Environment=`: This sets an environmental variable that affects the behavior of the service. In this case, it tells Apache that it was started by `systemd`.
- `ExecStart=`, `ExecStop=`, and `ExecReload=`: These three lines just point the way to the Apache executable file, and specify the command arguments for starting, stopping, and reloading the service.
- `PrivateTmp=`: Many services write temporary files for various reasons, and you're probably used to seeing them in the `/tmp/` directory that everyone can access. Here though, we see a cool `systemd` security feature. When set to `true`, this parameter forces the Apache service to write its temporary files to a private `/tmp/` directory that nobody else can access. So, if you're concerned that Apache might write sensitive information to its temporary files, you'll want to use this feature. (You can read more about this feature, as well as other security features, on the `systemd.exec` man page.) Also, note that if you leave this parameter out altogether, it will default to `false`, which means that you won't have this protection.
- `Restart=`: Sometimes, you might want a service to automatically restart if it stops. In this case, we're using the `on-abort` parameter, which just means that if the Apache service were to crash with an unclean signal, `systemd` would automatically restart it.

Okay, that's it for the `[Service]` section. Let's move on to the `[Install]` section, which looks like this:

```
[Install]
WantedBy=multi-user.target
```

The nomenclature for this seems a bit weird because it doesn't seem like we're installing anything here. What this actually does is control what happens when you enable or disable a unit. In this case, we're saying that we want the Apache service to be enabled for the `multi-user.target` unit, which will cause the service to automatically start when the machine boots into the multi-user target. (We'll cover targets and the boot-up process later. For now, just understand that the multi-user target is when the machine is fully booted and ready for use. For you SysV veterans, the target in this case is akin to a SysV runlevel.)

Understanding the Secure Shell service file

For something a bit different, let's look at the service file for the Secure Shell service, which on this Ubuntu machine is the `/lib/systemd/system/ssh.service` file. Here's the `[Unit]` section:

```
[Unit]
Description=OpenBSD Secure Shell server
Documentation=man:sshd(8) man:sshd_config(5)
After=network.target auditd.service
ConditionPathExists=!/etc/ssh/sshd_not_to_be_run
```

In the `[Unit]` section, we see the `ConditionPathExists=` parameter, which we didn't see before. It checks for either the existence or non-existence of a file. In this case, we see an exclamation point (`!`) in front of the path to the file, which means that we're checking for the non-existence of the named file. If `systemd` finds it there, it won't start the Secure Shell service. If we were to remove the exclamation point, then `systemd` would only start the service if the file *were* there. So, if we wanted to prevent the Secure Shell service from starting, all we'd have to do is create a dummy file in the `/etc/ssh/` directory, like so:

```
sudo touch /etc/ssh/sshd_not_to_be_run
```

I'm not sure how useful this feature really is, because it's just as easy to simply disable the service if you don't want it to run. But, if you think that you might ever need this, it's there for you.

Next up is the `[Service]` section:

```
[Service]
EnvironmentFile=-/etc/default/ssh
ExecStartPre=/usr/sbin/sshd -t
ExecStart=/usr/sbin/sshd -D $SSHD_OPTS
ExecReload=/usr/sbin/sshd -t
ExecReload=/bin/kill -HUP $MAINPID
KillMode=process
Restart=on-failure
RestartPreventExitStatus=255
Type=notify
RuntimeDirectory=sshd
RuntimeDirectoryMode=0755
```

In the `[Service]` section, we see a few new parameters:

- `EnvironmentFile=`: This parameter causes `systemd` to read a list of environmental variables from the specified file. The minus sign (`-`) in front of the path to the file tells `systemd` that if the file doesn't exist, don't worry about it and start the service anyway.
- `ExecStartPre=`: This tells `systemd` to run a specified command before it starts the service with the `ExecStart=` parameter. In this case, we want to run the `sshd -t` command, which tests the Secure Shell configuration to ensure that it's valid.
- `KillMode=`: I've already told you that one of the beauties of `systemd` is its ability to stop all processes of a service if you have to send a kill signal to it. That's the default behavior if you don't include this parameter in your service file. Sometimes though, you might not want that. By setting this parameter to `process`, a kill signal will only kill the main process for the service. All other associated processes will remain running. (You can read more about this parameter on the `systemd.kill` man page.)
- `Restart=`: This time, instead of automatically restarting a stopped service `on-abort`, it will now restart it `on-failure`. So, in addition to restarting the service because of an unclean signal, `systemd` will also restart this service because of an unclean exit code, a timeout, or a watchdog event. (A watchdog, in case you're wondering, is a kernel feature that can restart a service upon some sort of unrecoverable error.)
- `RestartPreventExitStatus=`: This prevents the service from automatically restarting if a certain exit code is received. In this case, we don't want the service to restart if the exit code is `255`. (For more information about exit codes, see the `$EXIT_CODE, $EXIT_STATUS_` section of the `systemd.exec` man page.)
- `Type=`: For this service, the type is `notify`, instead of `forking` as we saw in the previous example. This means that the service will send a notification message when the service has finished starting. After it sends the notification message, `systemd` will continue loading the follow-up units.
- `RuntimeDirectory=` and `RuntimeDirectoryMode=`: These two directives create a runtime directory under the `/run/` directory, and then set the permissions value for that directory. In this case, we're setting the `0755` permission on the directory, which means that it will have read, write, and execute permissions for the directory's owner. Everyone else will only have read and execute permissions.

Finally, here's the `[Install]` section:

```
[Install]
WantedBy=multi-user.target
Alias=sshd.service
```

In the `[Install]` section, we see the `Alias=` parameter, which can be quite handy. That's because certain services can have different names on different Linux distros. For example, the Secure Shell service is `sshd` on Red Hat-type systems and just `ssh` on Debian/Ubuntu systems. By including this `Alias=sshd.service` line, we can control the service by specifying either name.

Understanding the timesyncd service file

For the last example, I want to show you the service file for the `timesyncd` service. This is the `/lib/systemd/system/systemd-timesyncd.service` file. First, the `[Unit]` section:

```
[Unit]
Description=Network Time Synchronization
Documentation=man:systemd-timesyncd.service(8)
ConditionCapability=CAP_SYS_TIME
ConditionVirtualization=!container
DefaultDependencies=no
After=systemd-sysusers.service
Before=time-set.target sysinit.target shutdown.target
Conflicts=shutdown.target
Wants=time-set.target time-sync.target
```

For this file, I mainly just want to focus on the security-related parameters. In the `[Unit]` section, there's the `ConditionCapability=` parameter, which I'll explain in a moment. The `Wants=` line, which isn't security-related, defines the dependency units for this service. If these dependency units aren't running when this service gets started, then `systemd` will attempt to start them. If they fail to start, this service will still go ahead and start anyway.

Next, we'll look at the `[Service]` section, where we'll see more security-related parameters. (For space reasons, I can only place part of the file here, so feel free to view it on your own virtual machine.):

```
[Service]
AmbientCapabilities=CAP_SYS_TIME
CapabilityBoundingSet=CAP_SYS_TIME
ExecStart=!!/lib/systemd/systemd-timesyncd
LockPersonality=yes
MemoryDenyWriteExecute=yes
. . .
. . .
ProtectSystem=strict
Restart=always
RestartSec=0
RestrictAddressFamilies=AF_UNIX AF_INET AF_INET6
RestrictNamespaces=yes
RestrictRealtime=yes
RestrictSUIDSGID=yes
RuntimeDirectory=systemd/timesync
StateDirectory=systemd/timesync
SystemCallArchitectures=native
SystemCallErrorNumber=EPERM
SystemCallFilter=@system-service @clock
Type=notify
User=systemd-timesync
WatchdogSec=3min
```

The `AmbientCapabilities=` and the `CapabilityBoundingSet=` parameters are all set to `CAP_SYS_TIME`, as is the `ConditionCapability=` parameter in the `[Unit]` section. Toward the end of the `[Service]` section, we see the `User=systemd-timesync` line, which tells `systemd` to run this service under a non-privileged account. But, setting the system time requires root privileges, which the `systemd-timesync` user doesn't have. We can fix that by assigning a root-level kernel capability to this user. In this case, we're allowing this user to set the system time, but nothing else. Some systems though, might not be able to implement the `AmbientCapabilities=` directive. So, the double-exclamation points (`!!`) in the `ExecStart=` line tell `systemd` to run the indicated service with minimum privileges. Be aware that this double-exclamation point option only takes effect if the system can't deal with the `AmbientCapabilities=` directive.

> **Note**
>
> You can read more about kernel capabilities by typing `man capabilities`. An important thing to understand about kernel capabilities is that they can vary across different CPU architectures. So, the set of capabilities that can be used with an ARM CPU won't be the same as the set of capabilities on an x86_64 CPU.

Read down through the rest of the `[Service]` section, and you'll see a lot of parameters that are obviously for enhancing security. I'm not going to go over all of them, because for most of them, you can tell what they're doing just by looking at their names. For the few that aren't so obvious, I would encourage you to consult the man pages. These security settings are a powerful feature, and you can see here that they're pretty much doing the same job as a mandatory access control system.

And finally, we have the `[Install]` section:

```
[Install]
WantedBy=sysinit.target
Alias=dbus-org.freedesktop.timesync1.service
```

The main thing to see here is that this service is wanted by the `sysinit.target`, which means that it will come up during the system initialization process.

We've only scratched the surface for what we can do with service files. But there are so many different parameters that scratching the surface is all we can reasonably expect to do. Your best bet is to skim over the man pages to get a good feel for things and to consult the man pages whenever you have questions.

Next, we'll cover socket units. (Fortunately, that section won't need to be quite as long.)

Understanding socket units

The socket unit files are also in the `/lib/systemd/system/` directory, and their filenames end with `.socket`. Here's a partial list of them on one of my Ubuntu Server machines:

```
donnie@ubuntu20-10:/lib/systemd/system$ ls -l *.socket
-rw-r--r-- 1 root root  246 Jun  1  2020 apport-forward.socket
-rw-r--r-- 1 root root  102 Sep 10  2020 dbus.socket
-rw-r--r-- 1 root root  248 May 30  2020 dm-event.socket
-rw-r--r-- 1 root root  197 Sep 16 16:52 docker.socket
-rw-r--r-- 1 root root  175 Feb 26  2020 iscsid.socket
-rw-r--r-- 1 root root  239 May 30  2020 lvm2-lvmpolld.socket
-rw-r--r-- 1 root root  186 Sep 11  2020 multipathd.socket
-rw-r--r-- 1 root root  281 Feb  2 08:21 snapd.socket
-rw-r--r-- 1 root root  216 Jun  7  2020 ssh.socket
. . .
. . .
-rw-r--r-- 1 root root  610 Sep 20 10:16 systemd-udevd-kernel.
socket
-rw-r--r-- 1 root root  126 Aug 30  2020 uuidd.socket
donnie@ubuntu20-10:/lib/systemd/system$
```

The socket units can do a couple of things for us. First, they can take the place of the legacy `inetd` and `xinetd` *superserver* daemons that were on the old SysV systems. This means that instead of having a server daemon run full-time, even when it isn't needed, we can leave it shut down most of the time, and only start it when the system detects an incoming network request for it. For a simple example, let's look at the `ssh.socket` file on an Ubuntu machine:

```
[Unit]
Description=OpenBSD Secure Shell server socket
Before=ssh.service
```

```
Conflicts=ssh.service
ConditionPathExists=!/etc/ssh/sshd_not_to_be_run

[Socket]
ListenStream=22
Accept=yes

[Install]
WantedBy=sockets.target
```

Even though this socket file gets installed by default, it's not enabled by default. On a default configuration of Ubuntu, the Secure Shell service runs all the time. In the `[Unit]` section, we see these two interesting directives:

- `Before=ssh.service`: This tells `systemd` to start the socket before starting the Secure Shell service.
- `Conflicts=ssh.service`: This tells `systemd` to not allow the Secure Shell service to run normally if this socket is enabled. If you were to enable this socket, the normal SSH service would get shut down.

In the `[Socket]` section, we see that the socket listens on port `22/tcp`, which is the default port for Secure Shell. The `Accept=yes` line is a bit deceiving because it doesn't mean exactly what you would think. It really means that the service will spawn a new instance for every incoming connection. According to the `systemd.socket` man page, this setting should only be used for services that were designed to work under the old `inetd` and `xinetd` schemes. For better performance, new services should be designed to not behave like this.

To demonstrate how this works, I first want to show you that the `ssh` service on my Ubuntu VM is running normally:

```
donnie@ubuntu20-10:~$ sudo systemctl is-active ssh
active
donnie@ubuntu20-10:~$
```

So, it's `active`, which means that it's running as a normal daemon. Now, let's enable `ssh.socket`, and then look at the difference:

```
donnie@ubuntu20-10:~$ sudo systemctl enable --now ssh.socket
Created symlink /etc/systemd/system/sockets.target.wants/ssh.
socket → /lib/systemd/system/ssh.socket.
```

```
donnie@ubuntu20-10:~$ sudo systemctl is-active ssh
inactive
donnie@ubuntu20-10:~$
```

So, as soon as I enable this socket, the `Conflicts=` line automatically shuts down the `ssh` service. But I can still connect to this machine because the socket will automatically start the SSH service just long enough to service the connection request. When the service is no longer needed, it will automatically go back to sleep.

Secondly, note that this socket doesn't mention which service to start, or where its executable file is. That's because the socket, when activated, will just pull that information from the `ssh.service` file. You don't have to tell it to do that, because the default behavior for any socket file is to get its information from a service file that has the same prefix in the filename.

Finally, socket units can enable communication between operating system processes. For example, a socket can take messages from various system processes and pass them to the logging system, as we see here in this `systemd-journald.socket` file:

```
[Unit]
Description=Journal Socket
Documentation=man:systemd-journald.service(8) man:journald.
conf(5)
DefaultDependencies=no
Before=sockets.target
. . .
. . .
IgnoreOnIsolate=yes

[Socket]
ListenStream=/run/systemd/journal/stdout
ListenDatagram=/run/systemd/journal/socket
SocketMode=0666
PassCredentials=yes
PassSecurity=yes
ReceiveBuffer=8M
Service=systemd-journald.service
```

We see here that instead of listening to a network port, this socket listens for TCP output from `/run/systemd/journal/stdout`, and for UDP output from `/run/systemd/journal/socket`. (The `ListenStream=` directive is for TCP sources, and the `ListenDatagram=` directive is for UDP sources. The `systemd.socket` man page doesn't make that clear, so you have to do some DuckDuckGo searching to find this out.)

There's no `Accept=yes` directive here, because, unlike the Secure Shell service that we saw earlier, the `journald` service doesn't need to spawn a new instance for every incoming connection. By leaving this setting out, it defaults to a value of `no`.

The `PassCredentials=yes` line and the `PassSecurity=yes` line cause the sending process to pass security credentials and security context information to the receiving socket. These parameters also default to `no` if you leave them out. To enhance performance, the `ReceiveBuffer=` line sets aside 8 MB of buffer memory.

Finally, the `Service=` line specifies the service. According to the `systemd.socket` man page, this can only be used if `Accept=no` is set. The man page also says that this usually isn't needed, because by default the socket will still reference the service file that has the same name as the socket. But if you do use this, it might pull in some extra dependencies that it might not otherwise pull in.

Understanding path units

You can use a path unit to have `systemd` monitor a certain file or directory to see when it changes. When `systemd` detects that the file or directory has changed, it will activate the specified service. We'll use the **Common Unix Printing System** (**CUPS**) as an example.

In the `/lib/systemd/system/cups.path` file, we see this:

```
[Unit]
Description=CUPS Scheduler
PartOf=cups.service

[Path]
PathExists=/var/cache/cups/org.cups.cupsd

[Install]
WantedBy=multi-user.target
```

The `PathExists=` line tells `systemd` to monitor a specific file for changes, which in this case is the `/var/cache/cups/org.cups.cupsd` file. If `systemd` detects any changes to this file, it will activate the printing service.

Summary

All right, we've made it through another chapter, which is a good thing. In this chapter, we examined the structure of the service, socket, and path unit files. We saw the three sections of each type of unit and looked at some of the parameters that we can define for each of those sections. Of course, it's pretty much impossible to explain every single available parameter, so I've just shown you a few examples. And I'll show you more examples in the next few chapters.

An important skill for any IT administrator is knowing how to look up things that you don't know. That can be a bit of a challenge with `systemd`, because things are spread out over quite a few man pages. I've given you some tips on how to use the man pages to find what you need, which will hopefully be of some help.

The next skill you'll want to acquire is that of controlling service units, which is the topic of the next chapter. I'll see you there.

Questions

1. Which kind of unit monitors files and directories for changes?

   a. system

   b. file

   c. path

   d. timer

   e. service

2. A socket unit can:

   a. automatically notify the user if a network request comes in

   b. automatically set up communication between Linux and Windows machines

   c. listen for network connections, and act as a firewall

   d. automatically start a network service when it detects a connection request for that service

3. What is the purpose of the `[Install]` section?

   a. It defines what other packages are to be installed when you install a service.

   b. It defines what happens when you enable or disable a unit.

   c. It defines parameters that are specific to an install unit.

   d. It defines parameters that are specific to a service unit.

Answers

1. c
2. d
3. b

Further reading

`Systemd` socket units:

`https://www.linux.com/training-tutorials/end-road-systemds-socket-units/`

The difference between `ListenStream=` and `ListenDatagram=`:

`https://unix.stackexchange.com/questions/517240/systemd-socket-listendatagram-vs-listenstream`

Monitoring paths and directories:

`https://www.linux.com/topic/desktop/systemd-services-monitoring-files-and-directories/`

4
Controlling systemd Services

Now that we've seen what `systemd` services are, it's time to learn how to control them. In this chapter, we're going to do just that. Specifically, we'll cover the following skills:

- Verifying the status of a service
- Starting, stopping, and reloading services
- Enabling and disabling services
- Killing a service
- Masking services

These are good skills to have, because you'll be practicing them a lot in your routine as a Linux server administrator. So, if you're ready, let's get started.

Technical requirements

All you need for this chapter is a virtual machine of some sort, with full sudo privileges for your own user account. For my demos, I'll be using the brand-new AlmaLinux 8 for the Red Hat (RHEL) side of things and Ubuntu Server 20.04 for the Ubuntu side.

Check out the following link to see the Code in Action video: `https://bit.ly/3oev29P`

> **A word about CentOS Linux**
>
> I know, you're probably used to seeing CentOS Linux for these demos. But, at the end of 2020, the Red Hat company announced that they would end support for the enterprise-ready version of CentOS 8 at the end of 2021. Its replacement, CentOS Stream, is a rolling-release distro that you might not want to use in the enterprise. Fortunately, there are suitable enterprise-ready replacements for CentOS 8 from other organizations, which include Oracle Enterprise Linux 8, Springdale Linux 8, and Alma Linux 8. At the time of writing, Rocky Linux 8 is in the planning stages and will eventually be released by a founder of the original CentOS project. At this point, it's impossible to know which one will become the most popular replacement for CentOS. (Of course, there's also **Red Hat Enterprise Linux 8** (**RHEL 8**), but you'll need to purchase a subscription in order to do anything meaningful with it.)

This is going to be hands-on, folks. So, if you're feeling spry, fire up a virtual machine and follow my lead.

Verifying the status of a service

I'll be using Alma Linux for this first demo, for a reason that will become clear in just a moment. First, let's install the Apache web server by doing the following:

```
sudo dnf install httpd
```

Before you can start using Apache, you'll want to know whether it's enabled, so that it will automatically start when you reboot the machine. You'll also want to know whether it's active, which just means that it's running.

To see whether it's enabled, do the following:

```
[donnie@localhost ~]$ systemctl is-enabled httpd
[sudo] password for donnie:
disabled
[donnie@localhost ~]$
```

Here, you see why I'm using a RHEL-type distro for this. When you install a service on any RHEL-type machine, it's normally `disabled` by default. When you install a service on Ubuntu, it's normally `enabled` by default. So, by doing this on Alma Linux, I can give you more to look at.

Next, let's see whether Apache is running, by doing the following:

```
[donnie@localhost ~]$ systemctl is-active httpd
inactive
[donnie@localhost ~]$
```

Okay, it isn't. Now, let's look at both things at once:

```
[donnie@localhost ~]$ systemctl status httpd
 httpd.service - The Apache HTTP Server
   Loaded: loaded (/usr/lib/systemd/system/httpd.service;
disabled; vendor preset: disabled)
   Active: inactive (dead)
     Docs: man:httpd.service(8)
[donnie@localhost ~]$
```

There are a couple of things that I want you to note about these commands. Firstly, if you just want to view information about services, you don't need sudo privileges. Secondly, if you want to do anything with a service, you don't need to append the `.service` filename extension. I mean, you can if you want to, and it won't hurt anything, but you don't have to. If there are multiple types of unit files with the same name, `systemctl` will always invoke the `.service` unit by default. For example, the **Common Unix Printing System** (**CUPS**) has a `.service` unit, a `.path` unit, and a `.socket` unit, as you can see here:

```
[donnie@localhost ~]$ ls -l /lib/systemd/system/cups.*
-r--r--r--. 1 root root 142 Aug 27  2020 /lib/systemd/system/
cups.path
-r--r--r--. 1 root root 248 Aug 27  2020 /lib/systemd/system/
cups.service
-r--r--r--. 1 root root 136 Aug 27  2020 /lib/systemd/system/
cups.socket
[donnie@localhost ~]$
```

Without a filename extension, `systemctl` will show information about `cups.service`, as shown next:

```
[donnie@localhost ~]$ systemctl status cups
cups.service - CUPS Scheduler
   Loaded: loaded (/usr/lib/systemd/system/cups.service;
enabled; vendor preset: enabled)
   Active: active (running) since Tue 2021-03-30 16:37:18 EDT;
33min ago
     Docs: man:cupsd(8)
 Main PID: 989 (cupsd)
   Status: "Scheduler is running..."
    Tasks: 1 (limit: 11274)
   Memory: 3.2M
   CGroup: /system.slice/cups.service
           └─989 /usr/sbin/cupsd -l
Mar 30 16:37:18 localhost.localdomain systemd[1]: Starting CUPS
Scheduler...
Mar 30 16:37:18 localhost.localdomain systemd[1]: Started CUPS
Scheduler.
Mar 30 16:38:14 localhost.localdomain cupsd[989]: REQUEST
localhost - - "POST / HTTP/1.1" 200 362 Create-Printer-
Subscriptions successful-ok
[donnie@localhost ~]$
```

This shows a lot more information about a running service than what the `is-active` option does. The `cups.service - CUPS Scheduler` line at the top comes from the `Description=CUPS Scheduler` line in the `[Unit]` section of the `cups.service` file, and information about the man page comes from the `Documentation=man:cupsd(8)` line. The `Main PID:` line shows that the main CUPS process has a **Process Identification Number** (**PID**) of `989`. Verify that with this handy `ps aux` command:

```
[donnie@localhost ~]$ ps aux | grep 'cups'
root        989  0.0  0.5 340316 10196 ?        Ss   16:37
0:00 /usr/sbin/cupsd -l
donnie     8352  0.0  0.0 221904  1072 pts/1    R+   18:02
0:00 grep --color=auto cups
[donnie@localhost ~]$
```

Yes indeed, it is PID `989`.

Don't worry about that `CGroup:` line for now. We'll talk about cgroups later.

The final thing you see is system log entries that got created when the service started. On a RHEL-type system, you'll see them in the `/var/log/messages` file. On Debian and its offspring, such as Ubuntu, you'll see them in the `/var/log/syslog` file.

To see information about the other types of units, you'll need to append the filename extension, as shown:

```
[donnie@localhost ~]$ systemctl status cups.path
 cups.path - CUPS Scheduler
   Loaded: loaded (/usr/lib/systemd/system/cups.path; enabled; vendor preset: enabled)
   Active: active (running) since Tue 2021-03-30 16:37:12 EDT; 1h 16min ago
Mar 30 16:37:12 localhost.localdomain systemd[1]: Started CUPS Scheduler.
[donnie@localhost ~]$
```

This makes for a shorter display, since there's less to show about `.path` units.

All right, we're off to a good start. Let's get back to that Apache service and see what we can do with it.

Starting, stopping, and reloading services

We've already seen that when you install a service on a RHEL-type distro, such as Alma Linux, the service is normally disabled and not active by default. So now, I'll give you three guesses about what the command is to start a service.

Give up? Okay, here's how we start Apache:

```
[donnie@localhost ~]$ sudo systemctl start httpd
[sudo] password for donnie:
[donnie@localhost ~]$
```

Well, that's easy enough. Let's take a look at the status. Here's the first part of the command output:

```
[donnie@localhost ~]$ sudo systemctl status httpd
 httpd.service - The Apache HTTP Server
   Loaded: loaded (/usr/lib/systemd/system/httpd.service; disabled; vendor preset: disabled)
```

```
   Active: active (running) since Tue 2021-03-30 18:35:05 EDT;
1min 8s ago
     Docs: man:httpd.service(8)
 Main PID: 8654 (httpd)
   Status: "Running, listening on: port 80"
. . .
. . .
```

You see here that the service is active, but that it's also still disabled. This means that if I were to reboot the machine, the service won't automatically start. To see more information, use the `ps aux` command, as follows:

```
[donnie@localhost ~]$ ps aux | grep httpd
root        8654  0.0  0.6 275924 11196 ?        Ss   18:35
0:00 /usr/sbin/httpd -DFOREGROUND
apache      8655  0.0  0.4 289796  8160 ?        S    18:35
0:00 /usr/sbin/httpd -DFOREGROUND
apache      8656  0.0  0.5 1347588 10032 ?       Sl   18:35
0:00 /usr/sbin/httpd -DFOREGROUND
apache      8657  0.0  0.5 1347588 10032 ?       Sl   18:35
0:00 /usr/sbin/httpd -DFOREGROUND
apache      8658  0.0  0.6 1478716 12080 ?       Sl   18:35
0:00 /usr/sbin/httpd -DFOREGROUND
donnie      8924  0.0  0.0 221904  1044 pts/1    R+   18:39
0:00 grep --color=auto httpd
[donnie@localhost ~]$
```

The first process listed here as PID `8654` belongs to the root user and is the main process that we see in the `systemctl status` output. The next four processes, with PIDs `8655` through `8658`, are used whenever someone connects to a website on this server and belong to the non-privileged `apache` user. This is a security feature that's been built into Apache for pretty much forever and has nothing to do with `systemd`. Running these processes under a non-privileged user account helps prevent attackers from taking over the system for their own nefarious purposes.

> **Note**
>
> If you want to see what the rest of the `ps` output means, view the `ps` man page by doing:
>
> `man ps`

To stop the Apache service, just do `sudo systemctl stop httpd`. (Yeah, I bet you didn't see that one coming.)

If you change the configuration of a running service, you'll need to reload it. You can do that with the `restart` option, which will restart the service and cause the new configuration to be reloaded. Certain services, such as Apache, also have the `reload` option. This will read in the new configuration without interrupting the running service. Be aware, though, that you can't always use `reload`. With Apache, for example, you can use `reload` to reload changes to website configuration files, but you'll need to use `restart` to read in certain changes to the Apache configuration, such as when you enable or disable an Apache module. To see whether `reload` works for any particular service, try consulting the documentation for that service.

The specific commands to start, stop, restart, or reload a service can be defined in its associated `.service` file. Here are the relevant lines from the `httpd.service` file on the Alma machine:

```
[Service]
. . .
. . .
ExecStart=/usr/sbin/httpd $OPTIONS -DFOREGROUND
ExecReload=/usr/sbin/httpd $OPTIONS -k graceful
. . .
. . .
```

For now, don't worry about what the start and reload options you see here mean, because that knowledge is specific to Apache, rather than to `systemd`. What I do want you to notice is the `ExecReload=` line. We see here that Apache has its own built-in way of reloading its configuration. Contrast that with what you see in this `sshd.service` file, which is also from the Alma machine:

```
[Service]
. . .
. . .
ExecStart=/usr/sbin/sshd -D $OPTIONS $CRYPTO_POLICY
ExecReload=/bin/kill -HUP $MAINPID
. . .
. . .
```

Here, we see that the Secure Shell service doesn't have its own internal mechanism for reloading its configuration. Instead, it relies on the old-fashioned `kill` utility that's been in Linux almost forever. Realize though that `kill` doesn't always mean *to kill*. When you use the `kill` utility, it sends a signal to a process to make it do something. Normally, you would send a signal that really would kill the process. But you can also use it to send the `HUP` signal to a service, which will cause the service to reload its configuration without service interruption. (In case you're wondering, `HUP` is an acronym for *Hang Up*. The original purpose of this signal was to inform running programs when a serial line was dropped. However, the purpose of the `HUP` signal has since been changed to what it is now.) The `$MAINPID` instance that you see is an environmental variable that `systemd` uses to access the PID number of the main Secure Shell process.

Optionally, you can have a line that defines what happens when you issue a `stop` command. You don't see that here on Alma Linux, but you do see it in the `apache2.service` file on Ubuntu as shown here:

```
[Service]
. . .
. . .
ExecStart=/usr/sbin/apachectl start
ExecStop=/usr/sbin/apachectl stop
ExecReload=/usr/sbin/apachectl graceful
. . .
. . .
```

You haven't seen an `ExecRestart=` parameter, because there isn't one. Restarting a service just consists of stopping it, and then starting it again.

Next up, we'll look at how to enable and disable services.

Enabling and disabling services

It's all well and good that we have Apache running, but if we were to reboot our Alma Linux machine, Apache won't start until you start it manually. To begin this demo, first stop Apache with this:

```
sudo systemctl stop httpd
```

Now, enable it by doing this:

```
[donnie@localhost ~]$ sudo systemctl enable httpd
Created symlink /etc/systemd/system/multi-user.target.wants/
httpd.service → /usr/lib/systemd/system/httpd.service.
[donnie@localhost ~]$
```

When we enable the Apache service, we create a symbolic link in the `/etc/systemd/system/multi-user.target.wants/` directory that points back to the `httpd.service` file. Now, I've been telling you all along that the unit files are in the `/lib/systemd/system/` directory. But the eagle-eyed among you will notice that the symbolic link points to the service file in the `/usr/lib/systemd/system/` directory. That's because the newer versions of many Linux distros have gotten rid of certain top-level directories and now just use the corresponding directories that have always been under the `/usr/` directory. But the Linux gurus in the sky have been nice enough to accommodate old codgers like me who are used to having those top-level directories. They did this by creating symbolic links in the root level of the filesystem, which you can see here:

```
[donnie@localhost /]$ pwd
/
[donnie@localhost /]$ ls -l lib*
lrwxrwxrwx. 1 root root 7 Aug 14  2020 lib -> usr/lib
lrwxrwxrwx. 1 root root 9 Aug 14  2020 lib64 -> usr/lib64
[donnie@localhost /]$
```

So, if you're like me and keep forgetting that those top-level directories are no longer there, it's okay. The symbolic links work just fine. But, I digress.

Go into the `/etc/systemd/system/multi-user.target.wants/` directory, and you'll see the symbolic link that got created with our `systemctl enable` command, as shown here:

```
[donnie@localhost ~]$ cd /etc/systemd/system/multi-user.target.
wants/
[donnie@localhost multi-user.target.wants]$ ls -l httpd.service
lrwxrwxrwx. 1 root root 37 Mar 30 19:22 httpd.service -> /usr/
lib/systemd/system/httpd.service
[donnie@localhost multi-user.target.wants]$
```

Okay, so you're now wondering what that `multi-user.target.wants` thing is all about. Well, I'll cover the `.target` concept in detail later. For now, just accept that the multi-user target is the *runlevel* in which the operating system is fully booted and is ready for normal operations. The `/etc/systemd/system/multi-user.target.wants/` directory contains the symbolic links for units that will automatically start whenever the operating system goes into multi-user mode. This directory mostly contains symbolic links to service units, but it can sometimes have links to other types of units. On this Alma Linux machine, there's also a link to the `cups.path` unit, as shown here:

```
[donnie@localhost multi-user.target.wants]$ ls -l cups*
lrwxrwxrwx. 1 root root 33 Feb 11 18:14 cups.path -> /usr/lib/systemd/system/cups.path
lrwxrwxrwx. 1 root root 36 Feb 11 18:14 cups.service -> /usr/lib/systemd/system/cups.service
[donnie@localhost multi-user.target.wants]$
```

To determine where a symbolic link should be created, the `systemctl enable` command pulls in the setting from the `[Install]` section of the service file. At the bottom of the `httpd.service` file on the Alma machine, you see this:

```
. . .
. . .
[Install]
WantedBy=multi-user.target
```

At the bottom of the `accounts-daemon.service` file, you'll see this:

```
. . .
. . .
[Install]
WantedBy=graphical.target
```

The symbolic link for this service, when it's enabled, is in the `/etc/systemd/system/graphical.target.wants/` directory.

Be aware that when you enable a service that isn't already running, the service doesn't automatically start until you reboot the machine. You can see that here:

```
[donnie@localhost multi-user.target.wants]$ systemctl is-enabled httpd
enabled
[donnie@localhost multi-user.target.wants]$ systemctl is-active
```

```
 httpd
inactive
[donnie@localhost multi-user.target.wants]$
```

You can issue a separate `start` command to start the service, or you can use the `enable --now` option to enable and start the service with just a single command, as shown here:

```
[donnie@localhost multi-user.target.wants]$ sudo systemctl
enable --now httpd
Created symlink /etc/systemd/system/multi-user.target.wants/
httpd.service → /usr/lib/systemd/system/httpd.service.
[donnie@localhost multi-user.target.wants]$
```

When you disable a unit, the symbolic link for it gets removed. We can see that here with the Apache service:

```
[donnie@localhost multi-user.target.wants]$ sudo systemctl
disable httpd
[sudo] password for donnie:
Removed /etc/systemd/system/multi-user.target.wants/httpd.
service.
[donnie@localhost multi-user.target.wants]$ ls -l httpd*
ls: cannot access 'httpd*': No such file or directory
[donnie@localhost multi-user.target.wants]$
```

If the service is running, it will remain running after you issue the `disable` command. You can issue a separate `stop` command or use the `disable --now` option to disable and stop the service at the same time.

Now, for you Ubuntu fans, here's the command to install Apache on your Ubuntu machine:

```
sudo apt install apache2
```

If you look at the official documentation on the Apache website, you'll see that the official way of doing business is to have `httpd` as the name of the Apache service. For some strange reason that I've never figured out, Debian developers have always marched to the beat of a different drummer in a few different ways. Ubuntu is derived from Debian, so Ubuntu developers generally carry on with Debian traditions. At any rate, you can try out the preceding commands on an Ubuntu machine and just replace `httpd` with `apache2`. The only real difference you'll see is that after you initially install Apache on Ubuntu, the service will already be enabled and running.

Another cool thing you can do is to disable the manual start, stop, and restart functions of a service. The best example of this is the `auditd` service on RHEL-type machines. In the `[Unit]` section of the `auditd.service` file on my Alma machine, we see the line that does that:

```
[Unit]
. . .
. . .
RefuseManualStop=yes
. . .
. . .
```

Trying to restart the service gives me the following error message:

```
[donnie@localhost ~]$ sudo systemctl restart auditd
Failed to restart auditd.service: Operation refused, unit
auditd.service may be requested by dependency only (it is
configured to refuse manual start/stop).
See system logs and 'systemctl status auditd.service' for
details.
[donnie@localhost ~]$
```

Curiously, though, I can manually stop or restart the `auditd` service just fine if I use the old-fashioned `service` command from the SysV days, as we see here:

```
[donnie@localhost ~]$ sudo service auditd restart
Stopping logging:                                          [
OK  ]
Redirecting start to /bin/systemctl start auditd.service
[donnie@localhost ~]$
```

I can understand why we'd want to restrict the ability to stop or restart `auditd`, since it is related to system security. But I've never understood why RHEL maintainers prevent users from doing it with `systemctl`, yet still allow us to do it with `service`. It's just one of those things that makes you go *Hmmmmm*. It's also interesting to note that when you install `auditd` on Ubuntu, you won't see the line that disables these functions. So, on Ubuntu, you can stop and restart `auditd` with `systemctl` in the normal manner.

Next, let's look at the proper way to kill a service.

Killing a service

It's sad, I know, but even on Linux things can sometimes crash. A great example is the Firefox web browser. Have you ever accidentally landed on a malicious web page that completely locked up your browser? I mean, you can't close the tab, there's an obnoxious noise blaring out of your computer speakers, and you can't close the browser in the normal way. You're just stuck. (Don't be embarrassed about it if you have, it's happened to all of us.) On a Linux machine, you'd get out of that by opening a terminal, using `ps aux | grep firefox` to find the PID for Firefox, and then issuing a `kill` command. For example, let's say that the PID for Firefox is `3901`. To kill it, just do:

```
kill 3901
```

By default, this will send a number `15`, or `SIGTERM`, signal to Firefox, which will give the process a chance to clean up after itself by shutting down any associated files or network connections. Sometimes, if a process is locked up really badly, the number `15` signal won't do the trick. For times like these, you'll need to pop the cork off a bottle of strong medicine and use the number `9`, or `SIGKILL`, signal, like so:

```
kill -9 3901
```

The number `9` signal is something you don't want to use unless you absolutely have to. It stops processes dead in their tracks, without giving them time to clean up after themselves.

> **Note**
>
> For more information about the various Linux signals, you'll want to look at the signal man page on your Ubuntu machine. (For some reason, the man page on the Alma Linux machine doesn't have nearly as much information.) The command is:
>
> `man signal`

Back in the SysV days, you would use the same method to kill troublesome services, except that you'd need sudo privileges to do it, because services don't run under your own user account. The problem with that is that some services spawn more than one active process, and a normal `kill` command might not shut them all down. Those services might linger on as *zombie* processes until the operating system finally reaps them and gets rid of them. (When I say *reaps*, think of the Grim Reaper who drives stakes into the hearts of zombies to finally kill them off. Oh, wait. The stake in the heart thing is for vampires, so never mind.) A good example of this would be the Apache service. We've already seen that the Apache service spawns multiple processes when it starts, and that's just on a machine that isn't yet running active websites. On an actual production web server, Apache might spawn multiple other processes for CGI scripts, PHP scripts, or whatever else. If you ever need to kill Apache, you'll want to make sure that those script processes also get killed, especially if they might be doing something malicious. On my Ubuntu machine with `systemd`, I'll do that with the `sudo systemctl kill apache2` command. The results should look like this:

```
donnie@ubuntu2004:~$ systemctl is-active apache2
active
donnie@ubuntu2004:~$ sudo systemctl kill apache2
donnie@ubuntu2004:~$ systemctl is-active apache2
inactive
donnie@ubuntu2004:~$
```

As with the normal `kill` command, this sends a number `15`, or `SIGTERM`, signal by default. If you need to send another signal, use the `-s` option along with the signal name. To see what happens with that, I'll start Apache back up on my Ubuntu machine, and send it the number `9`, or `SIGKILL` signal, like this:

```
donnie@ubuntu2004:~$ systemctl is-active apache2
active
donnie@ubuntu2004:~$ sudo systemctl kill -s SIGKILL apache2
donnie@ubuntu2004:~$ systemctl is-active apache2
active
donnie@ubuntu2004:~$
```

Oh, dear. That didn't do anything for us, did it? To see why, let's look in the `apache2.service` file. In the `[Service]` section, you'll find the answer:

```
[Service]
. . .
. . .
Restart=on-abort
```

The last line in the `[Service]` section, the `Restart=on-abort` line, causes Apache to automatically restart if it receives an unclean kill signal. It so happens that `SIGKILL` is considered unclean. You can see the explanation for this in the `systemd.service` man page. Open the page and scroll down to Table 2, and you'll find the different options for the `Restart=` parameter as follows:

Table 2. Exit causes and the effect of the Restart= settings on them

Restart settings/Exit causes	no	always	on-success	on-failure	on-abnormal	on-abort	on-watchdog
Clean exit code or signal		X	X				
Unclean exit code		X		X			
Unclean signal		X		X	X	X	
Timeout		X		X	X		
Watchdog		X		X	X		X

Figure 4.1 – Table 2 from the systemd.service man page

In the paragraphs just above and just below *Table 2*, you'll see explanations for the different options and how they affect using the various kill signals.

Back on the Alma Linux machine, things are a bit different. In its `httpd.service` file, there's no `Restart=` line. Instead, we see these lines:

```
[Service]
. . .
. . .
# Send SIGWINCH for graceful stop
KillSignal=SIGWINCH
KillMode=mixed
```

The KillSignal= line changes the default kill action from SIGTERM to SIGWINCH. This is curious, because SIGWINCH is supposed to kill a process only if the terminal window from which the process is running gets resized. Apache normally doesn't run from a terminal window. Still, somebody at Red Hat apparently decided that SIGWINCH would be the appropriate signal for killing Apache gracefully, so that's how it is. The KillMode=mixed line tells systemd to send a SIGTERM signal to the main Apache process but to send SIGKILL to the remaining processes in the Apache control group. The systemd.kill man page doesn't say what this line does when the preceding KillSignal= line is set to SIGWINCH, but I would assume that it will replace SIGTERM with SIGWINCH. Anyway, let's try to kill Apache on the Alma machine, just to see what happens:

```
[donnie@localhost ~]$ systemctl is-active httpd
active
[donnie@localhost ~]$ sudo systemctl kill httpd
[sudo] password for donnie:
[donnie@localhost ~]$ systemctl is-active httpd
inactive
[donnie@localhost ~]$
```

It looks just the same as it did on the Ubuntu machine. Send Apache a SIGKILL though, and you'll see something different as shown here:

```
[donnie@localhost ~]$ sudo systemctl kill -s SIGKILL httpd
[donnie@localhost ~]$ systemctl is-active httpd
failed
[donnie@localhost ~]$
```

Without the Restart=on-abort line that Ubuntu has in its apache2.service file, the Apache service on Alma won't automatically restart when it receives the SIGKILL signal. Note that the is-active output shows failed rather than inactive, as it does when you use SIGTERM or SIGWINCH. Either way, the service isn't running, so the end result is the same.

Okay, that's all good. But what if you want to prevent a service from ever running? Well, you'd mask it, which is what we'll look at next.

Masking a service

Now, let's say that you have a service that you never want to start, either manually or automatically. You can accomplish this by masking the service, like this:

```
[donnie@localhost ~]$ sudo systemctl mask httpd
Created symlink /etc/systemd/system/httpd.service → /dev/null.
[donnie@localhost ~]$
```

This time, instead of creating a symbolic link that points back to the service file, we've created one that points to the `/dev/null` device. Let's try to start our masked Apache service to see what happens:

```
[donnie@localhost ~]$ sudo systemctl start httpd
Failed to start httpd.service: Unit httpd.service is masked.
[donnie@localhost ~]$
```

If you change your mind, just use the `unmask` option.

Summary

We've covered a good bit of ground in this chapter, and even got to do some cool hands-on stuff. We looked at how to start, stop, restart, and reload services. We also looked at how to enable and disable services and looked at the symbolic links that get created when we enable a service. We wrapped things up by showing how to kill a service, and then how to mask a service. As a side benefit, we saw what some service parameters can do for us and how the maintainers of different Linux distros can set up services to behave differently on different distros.

But what if you don't like the way that a service is set up on the distro that you're using? No worries. We'll discuss that in the next chapter, when we talk about editing and creating service unit files. I'll see you there.

Questions

1. When you run the `sudo systemctl enable httpd` command, what will that do for you?

   a. It will start the `httpd` service.

   b. It will cause `httpd` to start when you boot the machine and will also do an immediate start.

   c. It will only cause `httpd` to start when you reboot the machine.

   d. It creates a symbolic link in the `/lib/systemd/system/` directory.

2. What is the effect of using the normal `kill` command on a service?

   a. It will shut down the service cleanly.

   b. It will shut down the main service process, but it might not shut down the spawned processes.

   c. It won't shut down a service.

   d. You can use `kill` without sudo privileges to shut down a service.

3. What is the `SIGTERM` signal?

   a. It kills a process dead in its tracks without giving it a chance to clean up after itself.

   b. It kills a process when it detects that a terminal window has been resized.

   c. It restarts a process.

   d. It kills a process gracefully, giving it time to clean up after itself.

4. How would you enable and start the `httpd` service with just one command?

   a. You can't

   b. `sudo systemctl enable httpd`

   c. `sudo systemctl start httpd`

   d. `sudo systemctl start --now httpd`

   e. `sudo systemctl enable --now httpd`

5. What does the `ExecRestart=` parameter do for us?

   a. It defines how to restart the service.

   b. It defines how to reload the service configuration.

   c. Nothing, because this parameter doesn't exist.

   d. It defines how to start a service.

Answers

1. c
2. b
3. d
4. e
5. c

Further reading

My *Managing Services* video: `https://youtu.be/IuDmg75n6FU`

How to manage `systemd` services: `https://www.howtogeek.com/216454/how-to-manage-systemd-services-on-a-linux-system/`

5
Creating and Editing Services

We've just seen what `systemd` services are and how to control them. Sometimes though, you might need to either alter the behavior of a service or create a completely new one. In this chapter, we'll look at the proper way to edit services. Then, we'll look at how to create a new one. The specific topics of this chapter are as follows:

- Editing an existing service
- Creating a new service
- Changing the default systemd editor
- Creating a new container service with podman

So, if you're ready, let's jump in.

Technical requirements

As before, I'll be using an Alma Linux 8 virtual machine and an Ubuntu Server 20.04 virtual machine. To perform the Secure Shell exercise, you'll need to go into the VirtualBox network settings for both virtual machines and choose **Bridged Adapter** from the **Attached to** drop-down list. Then, expand the **Advanced** menu and choose **Allow All** from the **Promiscuous Mode** drop-down list. When you boot up the virtual machine, obtain its IP address by opening a terminal and typing `ip a`. That way, you'll be able to remotely log into your virtual machines from the command line of your host machine.

Check out the following link to see the Code in Action video: `https://bit.ly/3xP0yOH`

Editing an existing service

We've seen that the unit files for our services live in the `/lib/systemd/system/` directory, so your first instinct might be to go there and edit files in your favorite text editor. You don't want to do that though, even though it would work. If you were to do a system update, it might overwrite the files that you edited, and you'd lose your changes.

The proper way to do this is to create edited versions of your service files in the `/etc/systemd/system/` directory. You can do that with your favorite text editor, the same as you would with any other configuration file. Indeed, that's the way that you *used to* have to do it. When Red Hat released RHEL 7.2, they added an `edit` function to the `systemctl` command, which makes life much easier. (Of course, that `edit` function is now available on all Linux distros that run `systemd`.)

> **Note**
>
> It has been brought to my attention that some people prefer to add their own custom unit files to the `/lib/systemd/system/` directory so that they'll be alongside the unit files that get installed by the operating system. If you're one of those people, please understand that this is *not* good practice. By doing this, you risk getting your custom unit files either deleted or overwritten when you do a system update. Also, keeping your custom unit files in the `/etc/systemd/system/` directory will make it much easier for you to keep track of which unit files you've added, and which ones were installed by the operating system.

Now, you might be wondering how you can know what changes you can make to a service file. The most simplistic answer is to read the man pages for the various unit types and look at all the parameters and options that you can add, delete, or modify. If you're like me though, you'll start reading these man pages and soon find that they're the perfect cure for insomnia. Don't get me wrong, the man pages are definitely useful. But if you want to really learn how to make services sing and dance the way you want them to, the most painless way to do it is to look at the service files that are already on your system and see how they're set up. Then, look at the parameters that are listed in those files, and look them up in the appropriate man pages to see what they're doing for you. As we go through this chapter, I'll give you plenty of examples of what I'm talking about.

When you use the `systemctl edit` function, you can either partially edit the file or edit the entire file. By default, you'll do a partial edit. Let's begin with the simplest example I can think of.

Creating a partial edit to the [Install] section

Let's fire up the Ubuntu server virtual machine and add an `Alias=` line to the `apache2.service` file. Start by doing this:

```
sudo systemctl edit apache2
```

What you'll get looks something like this:

Figure 5.1 – The systemd service editor on Ubuntu

Yeah, that doesn't look like much, does it? It's just an empty file opened in the nano text editor. Don't worry, though. All we're going to do here is to add one parameter, and we don't need to see the whole service file to do that. Since we're working with Ubuntu, the name of the Apache service is `apache2`. Let's say that you've just come over from the Red Hat world, and you're used to always using `httpd` as the Apache service name. Consequently, you get frustrated when you always instinctively type the wrong service name on the Ubuntu machine. It's kind of like if you've been used to driving with a standard transmission all your life, and then you start stomping around for a clutch when you get into a car with an automatic transmission. (Well, that's what I do, anyway.) We can easily fix that, but let's first look at an example that we already have.

In another window, look at the `[Install]` section of the `ssh.service` file on the Ubuntu machine, as shown here:

```
. . .
. . .
[Install]
WantedBy=multi-user.target
Alias=sshd.service
```

That `Alias=` line at the end is our example. Now, over in the nano window, type this:

```
[Install]
Alias=httpd.service
```

Save the file and exit the editor by doing a *Ctrl* + *X* sequence. When it asks if you want to save the modified buffer, hit the *y* key. Then, just hit the *Enter* key to accept the default filename. Next, look inside the `/etc/systemd/system/` directory. You'll see that we've just created a new `apache2.service.d` directory:

```
donnie@ubuntu20-04:/etc/systemd/system$ ls -l
total 104
drwxr-xr-x 2 root root 4096 Apr  5 16:55 apache2.service.d
. . .
. . .
```

Inside that directory, you'll see the following `override.conf` file:

```
donnie@ubuntu20-04:/etc/systemd/system/apache2.service.d$ ls -l
total 4
-rw-r--r-- 1 root root 30 Apr  5 16:55 override.conf
donnie@ubuntu20-04:/etc/systemd/system/apache2.service.d$
```

This file contains the parameter that we've just added, which looks like this:

```
[Install]
Alias=httpd.service
```

That's it – the entire file. When we start Apache, this parameter will get added to what's already in the original service file. The beauty of this is that if the original service file were to get replaced by a system update, you'd get the changes that were made by the update, and you'd still have this modification.

But, before you can use this modification, you'll need to load it into the system. Do that by doing:

```
donnie@ubuntu20-04:~$ sudo systemctl daemon-reload
[sudo] password for donnie:
donnie@ubuntu20-04:~$
```

Any time you modify or add a service file, you'll need to do a `daemon-reload`. When you add an `Alias=`, you'll also need to create a symbolic link for it in the `/etc/systemd/system/` directory. You can create it manually with an `ln -s` command, but you don't have to. When you add an `Alias=` line to the `[Install]` section of a service file, the link will get created automatically when you enable the service. On the Ubuntu machine, the Apache service is already enabled and running, so we'll just disable it and enable it again. (Note that there's no need to stop the service.) So, let's first disable Apache, like this:

```
donnie@ubuntu20-04:/etc/systemd/system$ sudo systemctl disable apache2
Synchronizing state of apache2.service with SysV service script with /lib/systemd/systemd-sysv-install.
Executing: /lib/systemd/systemd-sysv-install disable apache2
Removed /etc/systemd/system/multi-user.target.wants/apache2.service.
donnie@ubuntu20-04:/etc/systemd/system$
```

Now, we'll enable it again, like this:

```
donnie@ubuntu20-04:/etc/systemd/system$ sudo systemctl enable apache2
Synchronizing state of apache2.service with SysV service script with /lib/systemd/systemd-sysv-install.
Executing: /lib/systemd/systemd-sysv-install enable apache2
Created symlink /etc/systemd/system/httpd.service → /lib/systemd/system/apache2.service.
Created symlink /etc/systemd/system/multi-user.target.wants/apache2.service → /lib/systemd/system/apache2.service.
donnie@ubuntu20-04:/etc/systemd/system$
```

You can see in the output that the `enable` command reads in the `Alias=` line that we inserted into the `[Install]` section, and creates an `httpd.service` link that points back to the original `apache2.service` file. We can verify that with this `ls -l` command as follows:

```
donnie@ubuntu20-04:/etc/systemd/system$ ls -l httpd.service
lrwxrwxrwx 1 root root 35 Apr  5 17:39 httpd.service -> /lib/systemd/system/apache2.service
donnie@ubuntu20-04:/etc/systemd/system$
```

Now comes the moment of truth. Can we now control Apache on our Ubuntu machine by invoking the `httpd` service name? Let's see:

```
donnie@ubuntu20-04:~$ systemctl status httpd
● apache2.service - The Apache HTTP Server
     Loaded: loaded (/lib/systemd/system/apache2.service; enabled; vendor preset: enabled)
    Drop-In: /etc/systemd/system/apache2.service.d
             └─override.conf
     Active: active (running) since Mon 2021-04-05 17:19:08 UTC; 34min ago
. . .
. . .
```

Oh, yeah. It works like a champ. (Don't you just love it when a plan comes together?) To see the service file along with your new edit, use `systemctl cat`, like this:

```
donnie@ubuntu20-04:~$ systemctl cat apache2
# /lib/systemd/system/apache2.service
[Unit]
Description=The Apache HTTP Server
. . .
. . .
[Install]
WantedBy=multi-user.target

# /etc/systemd/system/apache2.service.d/override.conf
[Install]
Alias=httpd.service
donnie@ubuntu20-04:~$
```

The top part of the output shows the original service file, and the bottom part shows the `override.conf` file that you created.

Of course, you can also go the opposite way with this. If you're used to doing things the Ubuntu way and suddenly find yourself administering Apache on a RHEL-type machine, you can add an `Alias=apache2.service` line to the `httpd.service` file, and then disable and re-enable Apache in order to create the link. The only difference in the procedure is that on the Ubuntu machine, `systemctl edit` invokes the nano text editor, and on RHEL-type machines, it might invoke the vi text editor. (The RHEL-type distros just recently switched from vi to nano as the default systemd editor.)

> **Pro tip**
>
> Remember that whatever changes you make to the `[Install]` section of a service file affects what happens whenever you enable or disable that service.

Okay, now that we've added a cool option to the `[Install]` section, let's add a few to the `[Service]` section.

Creating a partial edit to the [Service] section

Let's continue on with our Ubuntu Server virtual machine, and just add to what we've already done. This time, we'll add a few options to the `[Service]` section that will beef up security a bit. Before we do that though, let's see how secure Apache really is. We'll do that with the `systemd-analyze` utility.

On the `systemd-analyze` man page, you'll see that there are quite a few uses for this utility. For now, we'll just cover the `security` option. Let's start by checking the overall security profile for the services on our Ubuntu VM by doing:

```
donnie@ubuntu20-04:~$ systemd-analyze security
UNIT                                 EXPOSURE PREDICATE HAPPY
accounts-daemon.service                   9.6 UNSAFE    😨
apache2.service                           9.2 UNSAFE    😨
apport.service                            9.6 UNSAFE    😨
. . .
. . .          🙂
systemd-udevd.service                     8.4 EXPOSED   🙁
thermald.service                          9.6 UNSAFE    😨
unattended-upgrades.service               9.6 UNSAFE    😨
user@1000.service                         9.4 UNSAFE    😨
uuidd.service                             4.5 OK        🙂
vgauth.service                            9.5 UNSAFE    😨
donnie@ubuntu20-04:~$
```

This command checks the security and sandboxing settings for each service and assigns an `EXPOSURE` score to each. The higher the score, the less safe the service is. So, this is like the game of golf, where you want to get the lowest score possible. The `HAPPY` column is supposed to show little face emoticons with varying degrees of happy or sad expressions, but the faces don't show when pasted into this book. That's okay though, because you can see them for yourself on your virtual machine.

Now, before you get too excited about seeing that a service is marked as `UNSAFE`, as we see here for the Apache service, you need to understand that this only examines the security settings in the service files. It doesn't account for any security settings that might be in the service's own configuration files, security options that are encoded into the service executable file, or any **Mandatory Access Control** (**MAC**) options that might be in effect. Still, though, this is a useful tool for suggesting ways to enhance your security settings.

Next, let's look at some suggestions for the Apache service:

```
donnie@ubuntu20-04:~$ systemd-analyze security apache2
  NAME
DESCRIPTION
EXPOSURE
✗ PrivateNetwork=
Service has access to the host's network
0.5
✗ User=/DynamicUser=
Service runs as root user
0.4
✗ CapabilityBoundingSet=~CAP_SET(UID|GID|PCAP)
Service may change UID/GID identities/capabilities
0.3
✗ CapabilityBoundingSet=~CAP_SYS_
ADMIN                            Service has administrator
privileges                                              0.3
✗ CapabilityBoundingSet=~CAP_SYS_
PTRACE                           Service has ptrace() debugging
abilities                                          0.3
. . .
. . .
```

There's too much output to show here in its entirety, but that's okay. Let's scroll down a bit and show some settings that are a bit more relevant to what we want to do:

```
. . .
. . .
✓ PrivateMounts=
Service cannot install system mounts
✓ PrivateTmp=
Service has no access to other software's temporary files
✗ PrivateUsers=
Service has access to other users
0.2
✗ ProtectClock=
Service may write to the hardware clock or system clock
0.2
```

```
X ProtectControlGroups=
Service may modify the control group file system
0.2
X ProtectHome=
Service has full access to home directories
0.2
. . .
. . .
X ProtectSystem=
Service has full access to the OS file hierarchy
0.2
. . .
. . .
```

When you see an `X` in front of an entry, it means that an unsafe setting is in effect. Having a checkmark in front of an entry means that that parameter is configured with a safe setting. But, if you go in all willy-nilly and change the unsafe settings to safe ones, you'll break the service so that it will no longer run. Some of these supposedly unsafe settings are necessary for the service to do its job. Take the `User=/DynamicUser=` setting, for example. We see here that not having that parameter allows the Apache service to run with root privileges. Is that bad? Not really, because the Apache service needs root privileges to do certain things that it has to do. If you set this option to a non-root user, Apache will fail to start. And besides, the Apache developers have already accounted for this. They set it up so that only the first Apache process runs with root privileges, and all other Apache processes—the ones to which web browsers connect—run without root privileges. We've already seen that on a RHEL-type distro, such as Alma Linux, the Apache processes run under the `apache` user account. On Ubuntu, we see here that they run under the `www-data` account:

```
donnie@ubuntu20-04:/etc/apache2$ ps aux | grep apache
root         2290  0.0  0.2   6520  4480 ?        Ss   18:40
0:00 /usr/sbin/apache2 -k start
www-data     2291  0.0  0.2 752656  4344 ?        Sl   18:40
0:00 /usr/sbin/apache2 -k start
www-data     2292  0.0  0.2 752656  4344 ?        Sl   18:40
0:00 /usr/sbin/apache2 -k start
donnie       2554  0.0  0.0   6432   724 pts/0    S+   19:55
0:00 grep --color=auto apache
donnie@ubuntu20-04:/etc/apache2$
```

This non-root user is defined in the Apache configuration files. Let's see if our good friend `grep` can help us find where this is set:

```
donnie@ubuntu20-04:/etc/apache2$ grep -r 'USER' *
apache2.conf:User ${APACHE_RUN_USER}
envvars:export APACHE_RUN_USER=www-data
donnie@ubuntu20-04:/etc/apache2$
```

So, on the Ubuntu machine, the non-root `www-data` user is defined in the `/etc/apache2/envvars` file and invoked in the `/etc/apache2/apache2.conf` file. (I'll leave it to you to find where this is set on the Alma Linux machine.) Anyway, that's enough about the settings that we can't change. Let's look at some settings that we *can* change.

> **Tip:**
> On RHEL-type machines, everything I'm about to show you is already covered by SELinux. But, you can still use these settings if you want double protection. Ubuntu and SUSE use AppArmor instead of SELinux. Unfortunately, AppArmor provides almost no protection at all for Apache unless you jump through the hoops of creating your own custom AppArmor profile. Setting up this protection in `systemd` is much easier.

Let's first look at protecting users' home directories. We'll once again use the `sudo systemctl edit apache2` command, which will open the `override.conf` file that we created previously. The `[Install]` section will still be there, so we'll just add a `[Service]` section, as follows:

```
[Service]
ProtectHome=yes
ProtectSystem=strict

[Install]
Alias=httpd.service
```

By default, the Apache service can read from or write to any place in the filesystem. The `ProtectHome=yes` setting prevents Apache from accessing the `/root/`, `/home/`, and the `/run/user/` directories, even if they're set up with world-readable permissions. We can also set this to `read-only` if users want to serve web content out of their own home directories while preventing Apache from writing to them.

The `ProtectSystem=strict` setting causes Apache to have read-only access to the entire filesystem, except for the `/dev/`, `/proc/`, and `/sys/` directories. Let's save the file and restart Apache to see what we've got:

```
donnie@ubuntu20-04:~$ sudo systemctl daemon-reload
donnie@ubuntu20-04:~$ sudo systemctl restart apache2
Job for apache2.service failed because the control process exited with error code.
See "systemctl status apache2.service" and "journalctl -xe" for details.
donnie@ubuntu20-04:~$
```

Oh, dear. This isn't good. Let's look at the status to see what the problem could be:

```
donnie@ubuntu20-04:~$ sudo systemctl status apache2
. . .
. . .
Apr 10 21:52:20 ubuntu20-04 apachectl[3848]: (30)Read-only file system: AH00091: apache2: could not open error log file /var/log/apache2/error.log.
Apr 10 21:52:20 ubuntu20-04 apachectl[3848]: AH00015: Unable to open logs
Apr 10 21:52:20 ubuntu20-04 apachectl[3836]: Action 'start' failed.
Apr 10 21:52:20 ubuntu20-04 apachectl[3836]: The Apache error log may have more information.
. . .
. . .
donnie@ubuntu20-04:~$
```

So, Apache wants to write to its log file in the /var/log/apache2/ directory, but it can't. Let's change the ProtectSystem setting to see if that helps:

```
[Service]
ProtectHome=yes
ProtectSystem=full

[Install]
Alias=httpd.service
```

Setting ProtectSystem= to full causes Apache to have read-only access to the /boot/, /usr/, and /etc/ directories. Apache normally doesn't need to write to any of those directories, so it should now work. Let's try it and see:

```
donnie@ubuntu20-04:~$ sudo systemctl daemon-reload
donnie@ubuntu20-04:~$ sudo systemctl restart apache2
donnie@ubuntu20-04:~$
```

There are no error messages, so that's good. Let's check the status:

```
donnie@ubuntu20-04:~$ sudo systemctl status apache2
● apache2.service - The Apache HTTP Server
     Loaded: loaded (/lib/systemd/system/apache2.service;
enabled; vendor preset: enabled)
    Drop-In: /etc/systemd/system/apache2.service.d
             └─override.conf
     Active: active (running) since Sat 2021-04-10 21:58:22
UTC; 4s ago
. . .
. . .
```

Yeah, that's good. So, yee-haw! We're golden, baby! But seriously, look in the systemd.exec man page, and you'll see a lot more security settings that you could possibly use.

> **Note**
>
> You can see here that I inadvertently used sudo to just look at a service status. Using sudo with systemctl is a force of habit with me, but fortunately, it doesn't hurt anything if I use it when it's not needed.

Just for fun, let's add in a few more security options, and then check the security status again. This time, we'll make our `[Service]` section look like this:

```
[Service]
ProtectHome=yes
ProtectSystem=full
PrivateDevices=yes
ProtectKernelTunables=yes
ProtectKernelModules=yes
ProtectControlGroups=yes
SystemCallFilter=@system-service
SystemCallErrorNumber=EPERM
NoNewPrivileges=yes
```

I'll leave it to you to read about these new parameters in the `systemd.exec` man page.

Once you've finished the edit, restart Apache to ensure that it will start properly. Then, run `systemd-analyze security apache2.service` again. You should see that the overall security score looks somewhat better than it did before.

There are a lot more security-related parameters that you can set in your service files. Remember though, that most services require that some settings be left in an `UNSAFE` mode for them to function correctly. Your best bet is to play around with these settings for various services on a virtual machine. That way, you can get a good idea of which settings work for the various services. And for goodness' sake, thoroughly test any service modifications you want to make before you put them into production.

Next, let's look at doing full edits for the Secure Shell service.

Creating a full edit

Doing partial edits works great when all you want to do is add a parameter that isn't already in the service file. But, it doesn't work if you need to delete a parameter, change the value of a parameter, or add a parameter that conflicts with some other existing parameter. To do any of these things, you'll need to do a full edit. The other reason for doing full edits is just that you might want to have the full file in front of you so that you can see what you're really doing. To do a full edit of the `ssh.service` file, for example, just use the `--full` option, like this:

```
donnie@ubuntu20-04:~$ sudo systemctl edit --full ssh.service
```

This time, you'll see the entire `ssh.service` file, as shown here:

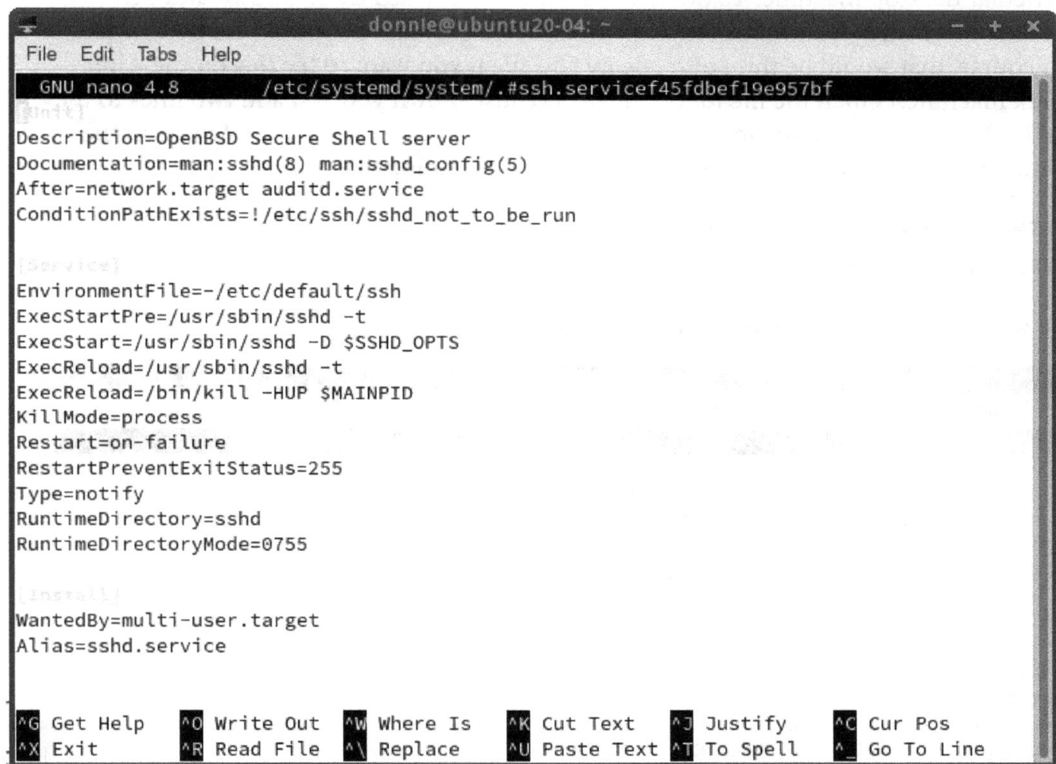

Figure 5.2 – Editing a service file with the --full option

For our demo this time, let's set up access control for our Secure Shell service.

> **Pro tip**
>
> If you've been on the Linux scene for a while, you might be familiar with the concept of `tcpwrappers`. It's a strange name, but the concept is simple. You would just configure the IP addresses that you'd want to allow to access a particular network service in the `/etc/hosts.allow` file, and then deny all other IP addresses in the `/etc/hosts.deny` file. This still works for Ubuntu, but the Red Hat folk have removed `tcpwrappers` from RHEL 8. So, if you want to configure access control on any RHEL 8-type distro, such as the Alma Linux 8 that we're using, you'll need to do it by configuring the service files. On Ubuntu, you can use either method.

So, let's say that you want to allow SSH logins to your server from only one particular desktop machine. To do that, we'll use the `IPAddressAllow=` and the `IPAddressDeny=` parameters in the `[Service]` section of the `ssh.service` file. (Of course, that would be the `sshd.service` file if you want to try this on the Alma Linux machine.) Open the file for editing as I've just shown you and add two lines to the end of the `[Service]` section, using the IP address of your own host machine in the `IPAddressAllow=` line. The lines should look something like this:

```
IPAddressAllow=192.168.0.222
IPAddressDeny=any
```

The whole file should now look something like this:

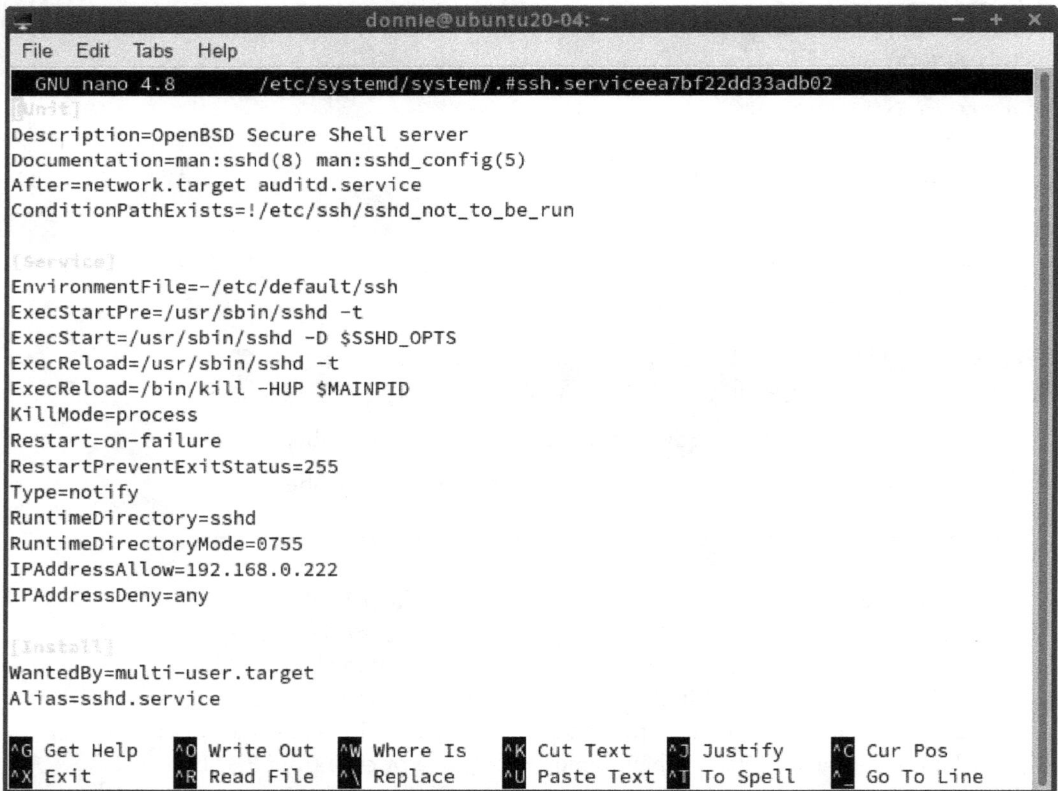

```
[Unit]
Description=OpenBSD Secure Shell server
Documentation=man:sshd(8) man:sshd_config(5)
After=network.target auditd.service
ConditionPathExists=!/etc/ssh/sshd_not_to_be_run

[Service]
EnvironmentFile=-/etc/default/ssh
ExecStartPre=/usr/sbin/sshd -t
ExecStart=/usr/sbin/sshd -D $SSHD_OPTS
ExecReload=/usr/sbin/sshd -t
ExecReload=/bin/kill -HUP $MAINPID
KillMode=process
Restart=on-failure
RestartPreventExitStatus=255
Type=notify
RuntimeDirectory=sshd
RuntimeDirectoryMode=0755
IPAddressAllow=192.168.0.222
IPAddressDeny=any

[Install]
WantedBy=multi-user.target
Alias=sshd.service
```


Figure 5.3 – The ssh.service file after editing

If you just insert the `IPAddressAllow=` line and don't insert the `IPAddressDeny=` line, you'll find that nothing gets blocked. So, any time you want to set up an access whitelist, you'll need to use both of these lines together.

Save the file and do `sudo systemctl daemon-reload`. Then, restart or reload the Secure Shell service. Assuming that you used the correct IP address for your host machine, you should be able to log in via SSH. To really test this feature out, edit the file again, and use an incorrect IP address for your host. This time, you should be blocked from doing an SSH login. Note though, that you won't have to do another `daemon-reload` command. This new setting will take effect immediately upon saving the file. So, if you're doing this remotely, you will get locked out if you've entered an incorrect IP address for your host. In real life, you'd have to fix it by entering the server room and configuring things correctly from the server's local terminal.

When you do a full edit, a complete new modified copy of the original service file will get saved in the `/etc/systemd/system/` directory, as we can see here:

```
donnie@ubuntu20-04:~$ cd /etc/systemd/system/
donnie@ubuntu20-04:/etc/systemd/system$ ls -l ssh.service
-rw-r--r-- 1 root root 586 Apr 11 20:07 ssh.service
donnie@ubuntu20-04:/etc/systemd/system$
```

As long as this file exists, it will always override the original file in the `/lib/systemd/system/` directory.

Next, let's look at creating a brand new service.

Creating a new service

To create a brand new service from scratch, use the `--force` and `--full` options together, like this:

```
donnie@ubuntu20-04:~$ sudo systemctl edit --force --full
timestamp.service
```

This will create a new service file in the `/etc/systemd/system/` directory, just as we saw previously.

For this demo, we'll create a service that will place a periodic timestamp into our system log file. Our `timestamp.service` file will look like this:

```
[Unit]
Description=Service Creation Demo
Wants=network.target
After=syslog.target network-online.target

```

```
[Service]
ExecStart=/usr/local/bin/timestamp.sh
Restart=on-failure
RestartSec=20
KillMode=process

[Install]
WantedBy=multi-user.target
```

Here, we see the `RestartSec=` parameter, which we haven't seen before. This works with the `Restart=` line and just says to wait for the designated number of seconds before restarting a crashed service. Here, we're saying to wait for 20 seconds. We don't see a `Type=` line here, because we don't need it. Without this line, `systemd` will just go with the default of `Type=simple`, which is what we want. (I'll leave it to you to read about the `simple` `Type` in the `systemd.service` man page.)

Next, we'll create the `timestamp.sh` script, which will place a timestamp into the system log file every 60 seconds. Let's make it look like this:

```
#!/bin/bash
echo "Starting the timestamp service" | systemd-cat -p info
while :
do
        echo "timestamp.service: The current time is $(date
'+%m-%d-%Y %H:%M:%S')" | systemd-cat -p info
        sleep 60
done
```

As you can see, it's just a simple `while` loop that pipes the current time into the `systemd-cat` utility every 60 seconds. In turn, `systemd-cat` sends the `timestamp` message to the system log file. The `-p info` option marks the message with an `info` level priority.

Next, make the script file executable, and copy it to the `/usr/local/bin/` directory. Then, start the service:

```
donnie@ubuntu20-04:~$ chmod u+x timestamp.sh
donnie@ubuntu20-04:~$ sudo cp timestamp.sh /usr/local/bin
donnie@ubuntu20-04:~$ sudo systemctl start timestamp
donnie@ubuntu20-04:~$
```

You can enable the service if you really want to, but for now, we don't need to.

The status should look like this:

```
donnie@ubuntu20-04:~$ systemctl status timestamp
● timestamp.service - Service Creation Demo
     Loaded: loaded (/etc/systemd/system/timestamp.service;
disabled; vendor preset: enabled)
     Active: active (running) since Sun 2021-04-11 21:57:26
UTC; 13min ago
   Main PID: 14293 (timestamp.sh)
      Tasks: 2 (limit: 2281)
     Memory: 820.0K
     CGroup: /system.slice/timestamp.service
             ├─14293 /bin/bash /usr/local/bin/timestamp.sh
             └─14411 sleep 60

Apr 11 22:00:26 ubuntu20-04 cat[14335]: timestamp.service: The
current time is 04-11-2021 22:00:26
. . .
. . .
```

To see the timestamps in the log file, do:

`donnie@ubuntu20-04:~$ journalctl -xe`

Or, you can see them getting added in real time by doing `sudo tail -f /var/log/syslog` on the Ubuntu machine, or `sudo tail -f /var/log/messages` on the Alma machine. When you've seen enough, just do *Ctrl* + *C* to quit.

Changing the default systemd editor

So far, I've been showing you how to do all of this in the nano text editor, which is the default `systemd` editor for most modern Linux distros. But, what if you don't like nano, and would prefer to use something else? Let's say that Vim is your favorite text editor, and you want to use it instead of nano.

One way to use an alternate text editor is to specify the alternate editor each time you run a `systemctl edit` command, like this:

```
[donnie@localhost ~]$ sudo EDITOR=vim systemctl edit --full
sshd
[donnie@localhost ~]$
```

That works, but doing it every time you want to run a `systemctl edit` command could get a bit tiresome. Fortunately, changing the default editor is easy, once you know how to do it.

First, edit the `.bashrc` file that's in your own home directory. At the very bottom of the file, add this line:

```
export SYSTEMD_EDITOR=vim
```

After saving the file, reload the new configuration:

```
[donnie@localhost ~]$ source .bashrc
[donnie@localhost ~]$
```

Next, open the `sudoers` file:

```
[donnie@localhost ~]$ sudo visudo
```

Scroll down to where you see the `Defaults` lines, and then add this line:

```
Defaults    env_keep += "SYSTEMD_EDITOR"
```

Save the file, and try running a `systemctl edit` command. You should now see vim instead of nano.

We've seen some cool stuff, but we're just getting started. For the ultimate in cool, let's look at using `podman` to automatically create container service files for us.

Creating a new container service with podman

Containers have been around for a long time, but they never became all that popular until Docker arrived on the scene with its new container management system. The original Docker system is cool, all right. But, it has some shortcomings, especially with security. For that reason, the good folk at Red Hat developed their own Docker replacement, which they call `podman`. `podman` comes with greatly enhanced security, and with cool features that aren't in Docker. The only problem is that `podman` is still only available on RHEL-type and Fedora distros, and everyone else still uses Docker. So, we'll perform these demos on the Alma Linux machine.

To install `podman` on your Alma machine, do:

```
[donnie@localhost ~]$ sudo dnf install podman-docker
```

This will install the podman package along with a shell script that invokes podman whenever you accidentally type docker. (Actually, that might not be by accident. You might have shell scripts that invoke docker commands, and installing the podman-docker package will prevent you from having to modify them to use podman commands.) To avoid confusion, I'll just be showing you podman commands in this demo.

The podman utility normally doesn't need root privileges, which is one of its advantages over Docker. But, in order to make this work, we'll need to create our Docker container under the root user account. We can do that either by going to the root user shell and doing everything there or by staying in the normal user shell and prefacing the podman commands with sudo. Since I normally like to avoid going to the root shell unless I absolutely have to, we'll do this with sudo.

Let's create a wordpress container, like this:

```
[donnie@localhost ~]$ sudo podman run -d -p 8080:80 --name
wordpress wordpress
```

WordPress is a free open source blogging platform. Here, we're running a wordpress container in detached, or background, mode with the -d switch. Instead of exposing the default port 80 to the network, we're exposing port 8080. (Note that if this fails to start, you might already have something listening on port 8080. If that's the case, try again with another port.) The --name switch sets the container name that we'll soon be using in the command to create the service file.

We'll verify that it's running with sudo podman ps:

```
[donnie@localhost ~]$ sudo podman ps
CONTAINER ID  IMAGE                                    COMMAND
CREATED        STATUS                 PORTS                  NAMES
cc06c35f21ce  docker.io/library/wordpress:latest  apache2-
foregroun...  2 minutes ago  Up 2 minutes ago  0.0.0.0:8080-
>80/tcp  wordpress
[donnie@localhost ~]$
```

You can also try to access WordPress from your host machine's web browser, but you'll first need to open port 8080/tcp on the Alma machine's firewall, like this:

```
[donnie@localhost ~]$ sudo firewall-cmd --permanent
--add-port=8080/tcp
success
[donnie@localhost ~]$ sudo firewall-cmd --reload
```

```
success
[donnie@localhost ~]$
```

Then, go to the web browser of your host machine and navigate to port `8080` of the IP address of your Alma machine. The URL should look something like this:

`http://192.168.0.9:8080/`

This should pull up the opening WordPress screen, which will lead you through the setup process.

Okay, that's great, except that when you reboot the machine, the container won't start back up automatically. To fix that, we'll use the `sudo podman generate systemd` command to create the service file, as follows:

```
[donnie@localhost ~]$ sudo podman generate systemd wordpress |
sudo tee /etc/systemd/system/wordpress-container.service
```

Note that using `sudo` to do a normal redirection with the > symbol doesn't work well in the `/etc/` directory, but piping the output into the `tee` utility does. As you'll see, the `tee` utility sends output to both the screen and to a specified file.

Doing `systemctl cat wordpress-container` will show you the generated service file:

```
# /etc/systemd/system/wordpress-container.service
# container-cc06c35f21cedd4d2384cf2c048f013748e84cabdc594b110a8c8529173f4c81.service
# autogenerated by Podman 2.2.1
# Wed Apr 14 15:22:43 EDT 2021

[Unit]
Description=Podman container-cc06c35f21cedd4d2384cf2c048f013748e84cabdc594b110a8c8529173f4c81.service
Documentation=man:podman-generate-systemd(1)
Wants=network.target
After=network-online.target

[Service]
Environment=PODMAN_SYSTEMD_UNIT=%n
Restart=on-failure
ExecStart=/usr/bin/podman start cc06c35f21cedd4d2384cf2c048f013748e84cabdc594b110a8c8529173f4c81
ExecStop=/usr/bin/podman stop -t 10 cc06c35f21cedd4d2384cf2c048f013748e84cabdc594b110a8c8529173f4c81
ExecStopPost=/usr/bin/podman stop -t 10 cc06c35f21cedd4d2384cf2c048f013748e84cabdc594b110a8c8529173f4c81
PIDFile=/var/run/containers/storage/overlay-containers/cc06c35f21cedd4d2384cf2c048f013748e84cabdc594b110a8c8529173f4c81/userdata/conmon.pid
KillMode=none
Type=forking

[Install]
WantedBy=multi-user.target default.target
~
lines 1-23/23 (END)
```

Figure 5.4 – The podman-generated service file

Now, if that isn't slick, I don't know what is. Let's enable the service and reboot, just to see what happens:

```
[donnie@localhost ~]$ sudo systemctl daemon-reload
```

```
[donnie@localhost ~]$ sudo systemctl enable wordpress-container
Created symlink /etc/systemd/system/multi-user.target.wants/
wordpress-container.service → /etc/systemd/system/wordpress-
container.service.
Created symlink /etc/systemd/system/default.target.wants/
wordpress-container.service → /etc/systemd/system/wordpress-
container.service.
[donnie@localhost ~]$ sudo shutdown -r now
```

When the reboot is complete, a `sudo podman ps` command should show you that the container is running:

```
[donnie@localhost ~]$ sudo podman ps
[sudo] password for donnie:
CONTAINER ID  IMAGE                                     COMMAND
CREATED          STATUS                     PORTS
NAMES
cc06c35f21ce  docker.io/library/wordpress:latest  apache2-
foregroun...  12 minutes ago  Up About a minute ago
0.0.0.0:8080->80/tcp  wordpress
[donnie@localhost ~]$
```

(You'll need to use `sudo` here only because the container is running under the root user's account.)

And of course, `systemctl status` should also show you that it's running:

```
[donnie@localhost ~]$ systemctl status wordpress-container
● wordpress-container.service - Podman container-cc06c35f21ced
d4d2384cf2c048f013748e84cabdc594b110a8c8529173f4c81.service
   Loaded: loaded (/etc/systemd/system/wordpress-container.
service; enabled; vendor preset: disabled)
   Active: active (running) since Wed 2021-04-14 15:27:37 EDT;
2min 38s ago
. . .
. . .
```

Okay, that's all good. But, what if you need to create a container service that you want to run from your own user account without root privileges? Well, we've got you covered there, too. Just create the service file in your own home directory, and run it from there.

We'll start as we did before, except with a different container name and from our normal user shell, like so:

```
[donnie@localhost ~]$ podman run -d -p 9080:80 --name
wordpress-noroot wordpress
```

We're using a different network port this time, so that it won't conflict with what we've already done. For now, let's stop the container:

```
[donnie@localhost ~]$ podman container stop wordpress-noroot
a6e2117dd4d5148d01a55d64ad8753c03436bfd9a573435e95d927f74
dc48f9e
[donnie@localhost ~]$
```

We'll next create a subdirectory within the user's own normal home directory:

```
[donnie@localhost ~]$ mkdir -p .config/systemd/user/
[donnie@localhost ~]$
```

We'll generate the service file, the same as we did before:

```
[donnie@localhost ~]$ podman generate systemd wordpress-noroot
> .config/systemd/user/wordpress-noroot.service
[donnie@localhost ~]$
```

I forgot to point out before that there's a slight difference in the `[Install]` section of these generated service files. Instead of seeing only one target listed, you'll see two, as shown here:

```
. . .
. . .
[Install]
WantedBy=multi-user.target default.target
```

`Default.target` is needed whenever you want to run a service from your own user account. From here on out, the management commands are mostly the same, except that you won't need `sudo` and you'll need to use the `--user` option to tell `systemd` that the service unit file is in your own home directory. Let's load the new service file, and check the status:

```
[donnie@localhost ~]$ systemctl --user daemon-reload
[donnie@localhost ~]$ systemctl --user status wordpress-noroot
● wordpress-noroot.service - Podman container-a6e2117dd4d5148d
01a55d64ad8753c03436bfd9a573435e95d927f74dc48f9e.service
```

```
   Loaded: loaded (/home/donnie/.config/systemd/user/wordpress-noroot.service; disabled; vendor preset: enabled)
   Active: inactive (dead)
. . .
. . .
```

Let's enable it and start it, and check the status again:

```
[donnie@localhost ~]$ systemctl --user enable --now wordpress-noroot
Created symlink /home/donnie/.config/systemd/user/multi-user.target.wants/wordpress-noroot.service → /home/donnie/.config/systemd/user/wordpress-noroot.service.
Created symlink /home/donnie/.config/systemd/user/default.target.wants/wordpress-noroot.service → /home/donnie/.config/systemd/user/wordpress-noroot.service.
[donnie@localhost ~]$ systemctl --user status wordpress-noroot
● wordpress-noroot.service - Podman container-a6e2117dd4d5148d01a55d64ad8753c03436bfd9a573435e95d927f74dc48f9e.service
   Loaded: loaded (/home/donnie/.config/systemd/user/wordpress-noroot.service; enabled; vendor preset: enabled)
   Active: active (running) since Wed 2021-04-14 15:44:26 EDT; 12s ago
. . .
. . .
```

If you have root privileges, you can open port `9080/tcp` on the firewall and access WordPress from an external machine, just as we did before.

As things stand now, our rootless WordPress service won't automatically start when you boot the machine. But, it will start when you log into the machine and will stop when you log out. Fix that by doing the following for your own user account:

```
[donnie@localhost ~]$ loginctl enable-linger donnie
[donnie@localhost ~]$
```

Now, the container service will remain running when I log out and will automatically start when I reboot the machine.

Summary

In this chapter, we looked at how to edit and create service unit files. Along the way, we looked at various parameters that we can set, including several security-related ones. We also saw the importance of testing any changes that we make to the service files before putting them into production. And of course, there's that one thing that I keep pointing out, about the importance of knowing how to use the `systemd` man pages.

In the next chapter, we'll look at `systemd` targets. I'll see you there.

Questions

1. How would you do a partial edit of the `ssh.service` file?

   a) `sudo systemctl edit --partial ssh.service`

   b) `sudo systemctl edit ssh.service`

   c) `sudo systemedit ssh.service`

   d) `sudo systemedit --partial ssh.service`
2. How would you create a brand-new service?

   a) `sudo systemctl edit --new newservice.service`

   b) `sudo systemctl edit --full newservice.service`

   c) `sudo systemctl edit --full --force newservice.service`

   d) `sudo systemctl edit newservice.service`
3. How would you create an access whitelist for a service?

   a) Just insert an `IPAddressAllow=` directive into the `[Service]` section.

   b) Insert both an `IPAddressAllow=` directive and an `IPAddressDeny=` directive in the `[Service]` section.

   c) Just insert an `IPAddressAllow=` directive into the `[Unit]` section.

   d) Insert both an `IPAddressAllow=` directive and an `IPAddressDeny=` directive in the `[Unit]` section.

Answers

b

c

b

Further reading

- How to create `systemd` service files: `https://linuxconfig.org/how-to-create-systemd-service-unit-in-linux`
- Securing and sandboxing applications and services: `https://www.redhat.com/sysadmin/mastering-systemd`
- Managing containers in `podman` with `systemd` unit files: `https://youtu.be/AGkM2jGT61Y`

6
Understanding systemd Targets

In this chapter, we'll look at what `systemd` targets are, and what they can do for us. Now, I have to tell you that there is a bit of confusion that surrounds this topic, and I hope to clear that up.

Specific topics covered in this chapter include the following:

- Understanding the purpose of `systemd` targets
- Understanding the structure of a target file
- Comparing `systemd` targets to SysVinit run levels
- Understanding target dependencies
- Changing the default target
- Temporarily changing the target

Understanding targets is important and can help you out either in the server room or in your own home. If you're ready, let's get started.

Technical requirements

For this chapter, you'll need a virtual machine that's running with a graphical desktop environment. I'll be using my *AlmaLinux virtual machine*, which is running with the *Gnome 3 desktop*.

Check out the following link to see the Code in Action video: `https://bit.ly/3Dgar9d`

As always, this is hands-on, so feel free to follow along.

Understanding the purpose of systemd targets

The legacy **SysVinit** system has *runlevels*, which define which services are to automatically start when the operating system enters a certain run state. For example, entering the graphical runlevel would bring up all of the services that allow the graphical mode to properly function. In `systemd`, we have *targets* instead of runlevels. Several of these targets perform the same function that runlevels used to. That part is easy to understand.

Where the confusion comes in is that targets are more than just runlevels. As we'll soon see, there are many different targets, all with their own specific purposes. In `systemd`, a target is a unit that groups together other `systemd` units for a particular purpose. The units that a target can group together include services, paths, mount points, sockets, and even other targets.

By doing a `systemctl list-units -t target` command, you can see all of the active targets on your system, which should look like this:

```
[donnie@localhost ~]$ systemctl list-units -t target
UNIT                    LOAD   ACTIVE SUB    DESCRIPTION
basic.target            loaded active active Basic System
cryptsetup.target       loaded active active Local Encrypted Volumes
getty.target            loaded active active Login Prompts
graphical.target        loaded active active Graphical Interface
local-fs-pre.target     loaded active active Local File Systems (Pre)
local-fs.target         loaded active active Local File Systems
multi-user.target       loaded active active Multi-User System
network-online.target   loaded active active Network is Online
network-pre.target      loaded active active Network (Pre)
network.target          loaded active active Network
nfs-client.target       loaded active active NFS client services
nss-user-lookup.target  loaded active active User and Group Name Lookups
paths.target            loaded active active Paths
remote-fs-pre.target    loaded active active Remote File Systems (Pre)
remote-fs.target        loaded active active Remote File Systems
rpc_pipefs.target       loaded active active rpc_pipefs.target
rpcbind.target          loaded active active RPC Port Mapper
slices.target           loaded active active Slices
sockets.target          loaded active active Sockets
sound.target            loaded active active Sound Card
sshd-keygen.target      loaded active active sshd-keygen.target
swap.target             loaded active active Swap
sysinit.target          loaded active active System Initialization
timers.target           loaded active active Timers

LOAD   = Reflects whether the unit definition was properly loaded.
ACTIVE = The high-level unit activation state, i.e. generalization of SUB.
SUB    = The low-level unit activation state, values depend on unit type.

24 loaded units listed. Pass --all to see loaded but inactive units, too.
To show all installed unit files use 'systemctl list-unit-files'.
[donnie@localhost ~]$
```

Figure 6.1 – Active targets on AlmaLinux

Add the `--inactive` option to see the inactive targets:

```
[donnie@localhost ~]$ systemctl list-units -t target --state inactive
  UNIT                        LOAD      ACTIVE   SUB  DESCRIPTION
  emergency.target            loaded    inactive dead Emergency Mode
  getty-pre.target            loaded    inactive dead Login Prompts (Pre)
  initrd-fs.target            loaded    inactive dead Initrd File Systems
  initrd-root-device.target   loaded    inactive dead Initrd Root Device
  initrd-root-fs.target       loaded    inactive dead Initrd Root File System
  initrd-switch-root.target   loaded    inactive dead Switch Root
  initrd.target               loaded    inactive dead Initrd Default Target
  nss-lookup.target           loaded    inactive dead Host and Network Name Lookups
  rescue.target               loaded    inactive dead Rescue Mode
  shutdown.target             loaded    inactive dead Shutdown
● syslog.target               not-found inactive dead syslog.target
  time-sync.target            loaded    inactive dead System Time Synchronized
  umount.target               loaded    inactive dead Unmount All Filesystems

LOAD   = Reflects whether the unit definition was properly loaded.
ACTIVE = The high-level unit activation state, i.e. generalization of SUB.
SUB    = The low-level unit activation state, values depend on unit type.

13 loaded units listed. Pass --all to see loaded but inactive units, too.
To show all installed unit files use 'systemctl list-unit-files'.
[donnie@localhost ~]$
```

Figure 6.2 – Inactive targets on AlmaLinux

You can probably figure out what a lot of these targets are doing just by looking at their names. For the ones that aren't so obvious, either just look in the `systemd.special` man page or search for a man page with a particular target name.

Next, let's peek inside a few of these target files to see what we can see.

Understanding the structure of a target file

As I've said before, the best way to learn `systemd` is to look at examples of the various unit files. In this section, we'll look at some `.target` files.

Understanding the sockets.target file

Let's start with the `sockets.target` file, which is one of the simplest targets we have:

```
[Unit]
Description=Sockets
Documentation=man:systemd.special(7)
```

Yeah, that's it, the entire file. The `[Unit]` section is the only section it has, and it only consists of the `Description=` line and the `Documentation=` line. At first glance, you would think that this can't possibly be doing anything for us. But that's where you'd be wrong. Look in the `/etc/systemd/system/sockets.target.wants` directory, and you'll see that this target is just a group of all the sockets that we need to have running:

```
[donnie@localhost sockets.target.wants]$ ls -l
total 0
lrwxrwxrwx. 1 root 43 May  1 17:27 avahi-daemon.socket -> /usr/
lib/systemd/system/avahi-daemon.socket
lrwxrwxrwx. 1 root 35 May  1 17:31 cups.socket -> /usr/lib/
systemd/system/cups.socket
. . .
. . .
lrwxrwxrwx. 1 root 39 May  1 17:34 sssd-kcm.socket -> /usr/lib/
systemd/system/sssd-kcm.socket
lrwxrwxrwx. 1 root 40 May  1 17:27 virtlockd.socket -> /usr/
lib/systemd/system/virtlockd.socket
lrwxrwxrwx. 1 root 39 May  1 17:27 virtlogd.socket -> /usr/lib/
systemd/system/virtlogd.socket
[donnie@localhost sockets.target.wants]$
```

To see how this works, let's look inside the `cups.socket` file:

```
[Unit]
Description=CUPS Scheduler
PartOf=cups.service

[Socket]
ListenStream=/var/run/cups/cups.sock

[Install]
WantedBy=sockets.target
```

You can see in the `[Install]` section that this socket is wanted by `sockets.target`. In other words, this socket for the **Common Unix Printing System** (**CUPS**) will be activated whenever `sockets.target` is activated. Of course, `sockets.target` is already active by default on pretty much any Linux system, so you normally won't have to worry about activating it yourself. `cups.socket` is also normally active by default, but you might not always need it. Let's say that you're running a text-mode server, and you know for a fact that you'll never need to print anything from it. You can disable `cups.socket` the same way that you'd disable a service:

```
[donnie@localhost ~]$ sudo systemctl disable --now cups.socket
[sudo] password for donnie:
Removed /etc/systemd/system/sockets.target.wants/cups.socket.
[donnie@localhost ~]$
```

When you do this, the associated `cups.service` is still running, so you'll also need to stop and disable it. If you change your mind, you can always re-enable the service and the socket.

Understanding dependencies in the sshd.service file

We've already looked at the `sshd.service` file, but it's worthwhile to look at it again. To save space, I'll just show the `[Unit]` and `[Install]` sections, which are the only two sections that we need to look at.

The [Unit] and [Install] sections

Here are the `[Unit]` and `[Install]` sections of the `sshd.service` file:

```
[Unit]
Description=OpenSSH server daemon
Documentation=man:sshd(8) man:sshd_config(5)
After=network.target sshd-keygen.target
Wants=sshd-keygen.target
. . .
. . .
[Install]
WantedBy=multi-user.target
```

We've already seen the `WantedBy=multi-user.target` line in the `[Install]` section, which means that the secure shell service will automatically start when the machine boots into multi-user mode.

In the `[Unit]` section of the `sshd.service` file, we see that `sshd.service` won't start until after `network.target` and `sshd-keygen.target` have started.

Now, let's see what's in the `network.target` file.

Understanding passive targets

The `network.target` file looks like this:

```
[Unit]
Description=Network
Documentation=man:systemd.special(7)
Documentation=https://www.freedesktop.org/wiki/Software/
systemd/NetworkTarget
After=network-pre.target
RefuseManualStart=yes
```

One interesting thing here is the `RefuseManualStart=yes` line that we see at the end. This just means that this target will start automatically and that we can't start it ourselves. This is why we consider `network.target` as a *passive* target. We also see that `network.target` will start after `network-pre.target`, which is also a passive target.

What's even more interesting, and a bit curious, is that this `network.target` doesn't appear to be doing anything for us. I mean, there's no code here that's really doing anything; it doesn't appear to be starting any services, and there's no `.wants` directory under the `/etc/systemd/system/` directory that would allow us to add services to it. We can see that here:

```
[donnie@localhost system]$ pwd
/etc/systemd/system
[donnie@localhost system]$ ls -l network.target.wants
ls: cannot access 'network.target.wants': No such file or
directory
[donnie@localhost system]$
```

So, what's going on here? Well, this is one of those things that takes a bit of detective work to find out, because the developers of `systemd` don't document it well. The answer is that several targets are *hardcoded* into the `systemd` executable file. `network.target` is one example. To get a bit of a clue about this, we can use the `strings` utility to view any text strings that might be in the `systemd` executable file. The command to use it is:

```
[donnie@localhost systemd]$ pwd
/lib/systemd
[donnie@localhost systemd]$ strings systemd | grep '\.target'
```

The output should look something like this:

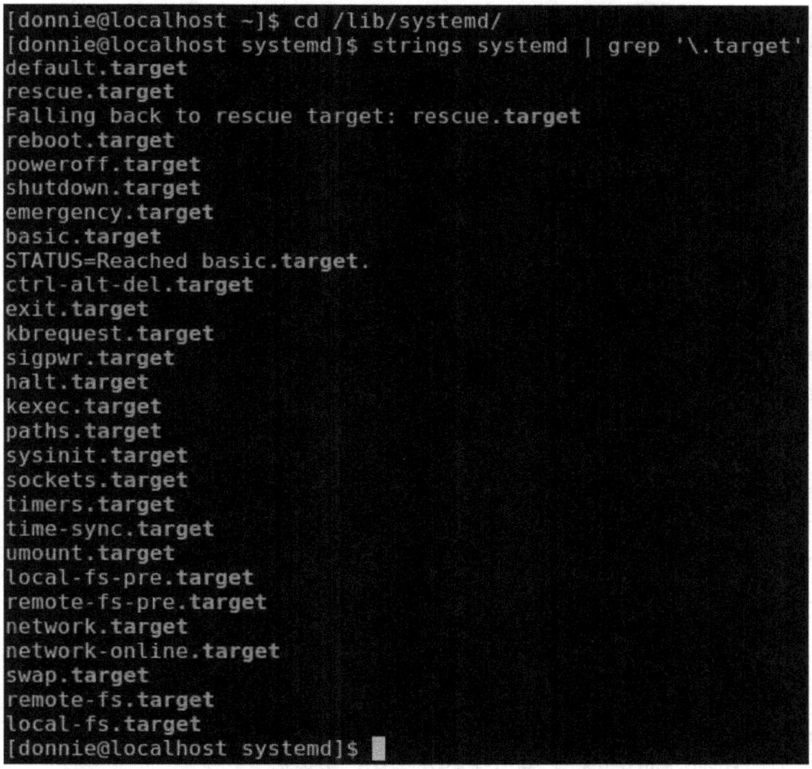

```
[donnie@localhost ~]$ cd /lib/systemd/
[donnie@localhost systemd]$ strings systemd | grep '\.target'
default.target
rescue.target
Falling back to rescue target: rescue.target
reboot.target
poweroff.target
shutdown.target
emergency.target
basic.target
STATUS=Reached basic.target.
ctrl-alt-del.target
exit.target
kbrequest.target
sigpwr.target
halt.target
kexec.target
paths.target
sysinit.target
sockets.target
timers.target
time-sync.target
umount.target
local-fs-pre.target
remote-fs-pre.target
network.target
network-online.target
swap.target
remote-fs.target
local-fs.target
[donnie@localhost systemd]$
```

Figure 6.3 – Targets that are hardcoded into the systemd executable

Understand that not all of these hardcoded targets are passive targets. For example, at the top of the list, you see several targets that have to do with powering down the machine, rebooting the machine, or rescuing the machine. (I'm talking about everything down to `emergency.target`.) These are targets that we can definitely invoke ourselves.

Passive targets are automatically started during the system initialization portion of the boot process. `network.target` gets activated when the machine is able to reach the network. By placing `After=network.target` in the `[Unit]` section of the `sshd.service` file, we ensure that the Secure Shell service won't start until after the network is activated and available.

Understanding service templates

To refresh our memories, let's take another look at the `[Unit]` section of our `sshd.service` file:

```
[Unit]
Description=OpenSSH server daemon
Documentation=man:sshd(8) man:sshd_config(5)
After=network.target sshd-keygen.target
Wants=sshd-keygen.target
```

We see that `sshd.service` wants `sshd-keygen.target`, and is not to start until after `sshd-keygen.target` has started. Let's peek inside the `sshd-keygen.target` file:

```
[Unit]
Wants=sshd-keygen@rsa.service
Wants=sshd-keygen@ecdsa.service
Wants=sshd-keygen@ed25519.service
PartOf=sshd.service
```

We see that `sshd.target` wants `sshd-keygen@.service` three different times. The @ symbol in the filename indicates that this is a service *template*. When we invoke a service template, we'll place the value of a variable after the @ symbol, which allows us to run a service multiple times with different parameters. To see what I'm talking about, let's look inside the `sshd-keygen@.service` file:

```
[Unit]
Description=OpenSSH %i Server Key Generation
ConditionFileNotEmpty=|!/etc/ssh/ssh_host_%i_key

[Service]
Type=oneshot
EnvironmentFile=-/etc/sysconfig/sshd
```

```
ExecStart=/usr/libexec/openssh/sshd-keygen %i

[Install]
WantedBy=sshd-keygen.target
```

The first thing to note is the `%i` variable. In the `sshd-keygen.target` file, we see that the three values for this variable are `rsa`, `ecdsa`, and `ed25519`. These values represent the three types of secure shell keys that we want on our system.

The `ConditionFileNotEmpty=|!/etc/ssh/ssh_host_%i_key` line verifies whether or not these three key files already exist. On my AlmaLinux system, the keys look like this:

```
[donnie@localhost ~]$ cd /etc/ssh
[donnie@localhost ssh]$ ls -l *key
-rw-r-----. 1 root ssh_keys  492 Feb 11 18:29 ssh_host_ecdsa_
key
-rw-r-----. 1 root ssh_keys  387 Feb 11 18:29 ssh_host_ed25519_
key
-rw-r-----. 1 root ssh_keys 2578 Feb 11 18:29 ssh_host_rsa_key
[donnie@localhost ssh]$
```

In this `ConditionFileNotEmpty=` line, the `!` means that we're looking for the *absence* of these three key files. The pipe symbol (|) that's before the `!` is the *trigger* symbol. When you put both of these symbols together, it means that nothing will happen if the three key files already exist. But if the key files *don't* exist, the | symbol will cause this service to run in order to create them.

In the `[Service]` section, we see the `ExecStart=/usr/libexec/openssh/sshd-keygen %i` line. This will cause the `sshd-keygen` command to run once for every value of the `%i` variable that's defined in `sshd-keygen.target`. Each time it runs, it will create one of the three key files that we need.

The last thing to look at here is the `Type=oneshot` line, which is also in the `[Service]` section. This causes the service to just run as a normal script that performs some specified one-time task, instead of as a continuously running daemon. After the specified commands have run, the service shuts down.

Okay, we've seen what targets are, and we've seen a few simple examples. Now, let's look at the targets that have replaced the old-fashioned runlevels.

Comparing systemd targets to SysVinit runlevels

The old SysV runlevels defined which services would run when the operating system reached a certain state. It was a simple concept, except that there were four different sets of runlevel definitions that a Linux user would have to know. There was the generic set, which was created by the big Linux gurus at the Linux Foundation as part of the *Linux Standard Base*. The Red Hat definitions were almost identical to the generic ones. The *Slackware* and *Debian* developers basically came out of left field and created their own definitions that didn't look anything like the generic ones. (Of course, Slackware and Debian are the two oldest surviving Linux distros, so it's possible that they might have created their own definitions before the Linux Foundation gurus created the generic definitions.) This made things a bit confusing for new Linux users, especially for those of us who had to study for the Linux Professional Institute certification exam. It also made things a bit difficult for developers who needed to create new services that would run on all the different families of Linux distros. Fortunately, all we need to consider for now is the generic definitions, and how they compare to the `systemd` targets. Let's look at the following table:

SysV runlevel	systemd target	What it does
`runlevel 0`	`poweroff.target`	It shuts down the operating system.
`runlevel 1`	`rescue.target`	It prevents all services from running and prevents all users except for the root user from logging in to the system. All filesystems are mounted normally. It's just a root shell for performing maintenance operations.

`runlevel 2`
`runlevel 3`
`runlevel 4`
	`multi-user.target`	The operating system is fully operational, without a graphical interface.

`runlevel 5`	`graphical.target`	The operating system is fully operational, with a graphical interface.
`runlevel 6`	`reboot.target`	This is for rebooting the system.

In `systemd`, there are some runlevel-type targets that have no SysV counterparts:

- `emergency.target` is like `rescue.target`, except that filesystems are mounted as read-only.
- `hibernate.target` saves the system state and then powers down the machine.
- `suspend.target` just puts the system to sleep without powering it down.

`hibernate.target` and `suspend.target`, which aren't needed on server implementations of Linux, are a big help to the growing numbers of people who use Linux on laptop and desktop computers. Prior to systemd, there was no good, standardized way of implementing these features.

Note that in the official generic definition set, `runlevel 2` and `runlevel 4` don't exactly correspond to the multi-user target. For some reason, every explanation of runlevels versus targets always places runlevels 2 and 4 here, and I'm not sure why.

A big difference between SysV and `systemd` is that on SysV, each runlevel is its own independent unit. So, if you had a machine set up to boot into `runlevel 5`, it would go directly to `runlevel 5`. On `systemd`, one target can depend upon another target, which in turn might depend upon yet another target. Take, for example, this `graphical.target` unit file:

```
[Unit]
Description=Graphical Interface
Documentation=man:systemd.special(7)
Requires=multi-user.target
Wants=display-manager.service
Conflicts=rescue.service rescue.target
After=multi-user.target rescue.service rescue.target display-manager.service
AllowIsolate=yes
```

The `Requires=multi-user.target` line means that `graphical.target` will fail to start unless `multi-user.target` is already running. All of the services that get started in multiuser mode will continue to run in graphical mode. The `Wants=display-manager.service` line means that it wants to start the display manager, but it won't fail if the display manager doesn't start.

The `Conflicts=rescue.service rescue.target` line tells `systemd` to shut down `graphical.target` if either `rescue.service` or `rescue.target` gets started, or to shut down `rescue.service` or `rescue.target` if `graphical.target` gets started. Of course, `shutdown.target` is also a conflict, but we don't need to list it. The `Conflicts=shutdown.target` parameter is already implied.

The `After=` line seems a bit strange, doesn't it? I mean, it does make sense that `graphical.target` can't run until after `multi-user.target` and `display-manager.service` have completed starting up. But what about `rescue.service` and `rescue.target`? Why would we need these rescue units to run before starting `graphical.target`? Well, we actually don't. It's just that the `After=` directive also affects what happens when you shut down a target. In this case, the directive says that if you decide to switch from `graphical.target` to `rescue.target`, `rescue.target` and `rescue.service` won't start until after `graphical.target` shuts down. So, by switching from graphical mode to rescue mode, the `After=` line operates in an inverse fashion.

The last line is `AllowIsolate=yes`. This just means that we can switch from this target to another, if we so desire. For example, if we need to drop out of graphical mode to a pure command-line mode, we can *isolate* to `multi-user.target`. (Yeah, the terminology is a bit strange, but that's just the way it is.) Before we move on to that, let's talk a bit more about *dependencies*.

Understanding target dependencies

In this `graphical.target` file, the `Requires=multi-user.target` line means that `multi-user.target` has to be running before `graphical.target` can start. So, `multi-user.target` is a dependency for `graphical.target`. Now, let's peek into the `multi-user.target` file:

```
[Unit]
Description=Multi-User System
Documentation=man:systemd.special(7)
Requires=basic.target
Conflicts=rescue.service rescue.target
After=basic.target rescue.service rescue.target
AllowIsolate=yes
```

Here, we see that `multi-user.target` requires `basic.target`. So, let's look at the `basic.target` file to see what it requires:

```
[Unit]
Description=Basic System
Documentation=man:systemd.special(7)
Requires=sysinit.target
Wants=sockets.target timers.target paths.target slices.target
```

```
After=sysinit.target sockets.target paths.target slices.target
tmp.mount
```

Okay, `basic.target` requires `sysinit.target`. So, let's see what `sysinit.target` requires:

```
[Unit]
Description=System Initialization
Documentation=man:systemd.special(7)
Conflicts=emergency.service emergency.target
Wants=local-fs.target swap.target
After=local-fs.target swap.target emergency.service emergency.
target
```

`sysinit.target` doesn't *require* anything, but it does *want* `local-fs.target` and `swap.target`. Some of these chained targets have their own `.wants` directories in the `/etc/systemd/system/` directory that contain symbolic links to the services that will start for those targets. Here, for example, is the contents of the `/etc/systemd/system/sysinit.target.wants/` directory:

```
[donnie@localhost sysinit.target.wants]$ ls -l
total 0
lrwxrwxrwx. 1 root 44 May  1 17:22 import-state.service -> /
usr/lib/systemd/system/import-state.service
lrwxrwxrwx. 1 root 44 May  1 17:27 iscsi-onboot.service -> /
usr/lib/systemd/system/iscsi-onboot.service
. . .
. . .
lrwxrwxrwx. 1 root 56 May  1 17:21 selinux-autorelabel-mark.
service -> /usr/lib/systemd/system/selinux-autorelabel-mark.
service
[donnie@localhost sysinit.target.wants]$
```

Trying to figure out all of a target's dependencies might seem like a complex operation, but it really isn't. To see the dependencies for `graphical.target`, we'll just do `systemctl list-dependencies graphical.target`, like this:

```
[donnie@localhost ~]$ systemctl list-dependencies graphical.
target
graphical.target
```

```
● ├─accounts-daemon.service
● ├─gdm.service
● ├─rtkit-daemon.service
● ├─systemd-update-utmp-runlevel.service
● ├─udisks2.service
● └─multi-user.target
●   ├─atd.service
●   ├─auditd.service
●   ├─avahi-daemon.service
. . .
. . .
```

The whole output is too long to list here, but you get the idea.

The `--after` and `--before` options show the dependencies that must start either *before* or *after* a target starts. (No, I didn't do that backward. The `--after` option indicates that the target must start after the listed dependencies, and the `--before` option indicates that the target must start before the listed dependencies.) For a simple example, let's see what must start before `network.target` can start:

```
[donnie@localhost ~]$ systemctl list-dependencies --after
network.target
network.target
● ├─NetworkManager.service
● ├─wpa_supplicant.service
● └─network-pre.target
●   ├─firewalld.service
●   └─nftables.service
[donnie@localhost ~]$
```

If you like, you can also create a graphical representation of a target's dependencies. To do that, you'll first need to install the `graphviz` package. The command to do that on the AlmaLinux machine is:

```
sudo dnf install graphviz
```

Next, let's use `systemd-analyze` to create the graphics file that shows the dependencies for `graphical.target`. The command looks like this:

```
[donnie@localhost ~]$ systemd-analyze dot graphical.target |
dot -Tsvg > graphical.svg
```

```
    Color legend: black      = Requires
                  dark blue = Requisite
                  dark grey = Wants
                  red       = Conflicts
                  green     = After
[donnie@localhost ~]$
```

Finally, open the resultant `graphical.svg` file in *Firefox*. Either resize the image to fit the screen or use the slider bar at the bottom to view different parts of the image:

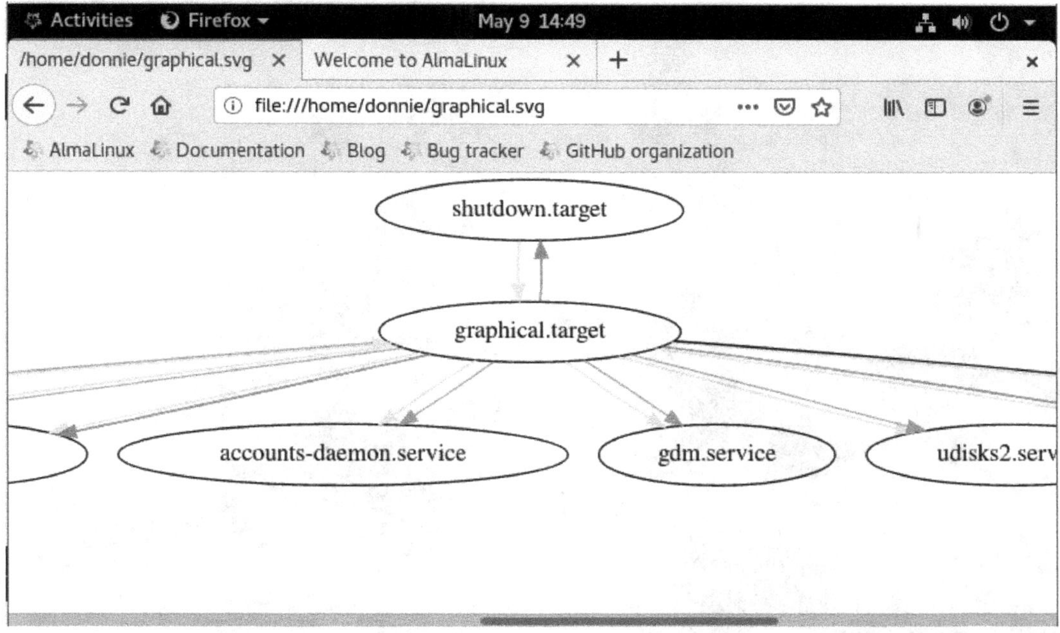

Figure 6.4 – The graphical.target dependencies

(Note that your graphic might not look exactly like mine. I don't know why, but that's how it is.)

The point I'm trying to make here is that targets can have an entire chain of dependencies. This allows us to have a more modular setup, so that we don't have to create each individual target file with its own complete list of dependencies. This is the opposite of how SysV works. With SysV, each runlevel has its own directory of symbolic links that point to all of the services that are to be started for the specified runlevel.

Now that we've seen what targets are and how they're constructed, let's see how to set the default target.

Changing the default target

When you install a Linux operating system, the installer will configure either `multi-user.target` or `graphical.target` as the default, depending upon whether or not you choose to install a graphical desktop environment. When you boot up a Linux machine, it can be quite obvious what the default target is. If a graphical desktop shows up, you can rest assured that `graphical.target` is set as the default:

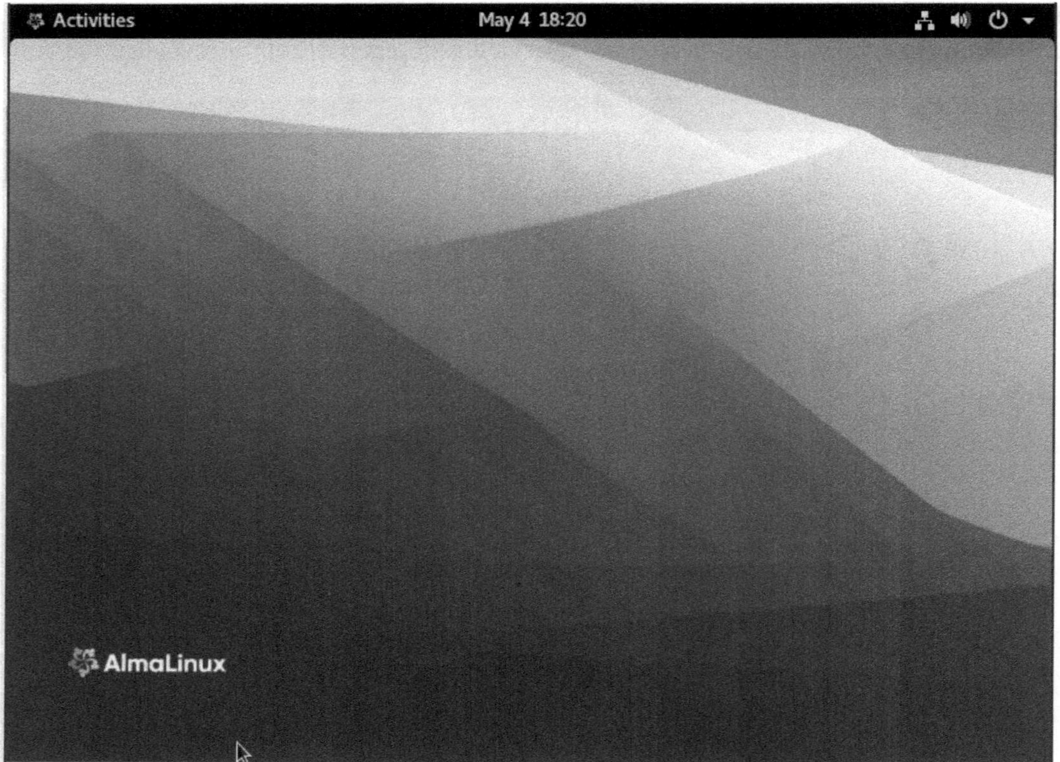

Figure 6.5 – AlmaLinux with the Gnome 3 desktop

However, if a graphical desktop doesn't show up, it doesn't necessarily mean that the machine is set up with `multi-user.target` as its default. It could be that `graphical.target` is the default, and that the graphical display manager has failed to start. (I've seen that happen a few times when a video card driver is configured incorrectly.)

To see which target is set as the default, use `systemctl get-default`:

```
[donnie@localhost system]$ systemctl get-default
graphical.target
[donnie@localhost system]$
```

You can also see the default setting by looking at the `/etc/systemd/system/default.target` symbolic link, which looks like this:

```
[donnie@localhost system]$ ls -l default.target
lrwxrwxrwx. 1 root 40 May  4 18:30 default.target -> /usr/lib/systemd/system/graphical.target
[donnie@localhost system]$
```

We see that the symbolic link points to the `graphical.target` file.

Now, let's say that you no longer want this machine to boot into graphical mode. Just set it to multiuser mode, like this:

```
[donnie@localhost system]$ sudo systemctl set-default multi-user
[sudo] password for donnie:
Removed /etc/systemd/system/default.target.
Created symlink /etc/systemd/system/default.target → /usr/lib/systemd/system/multi-user.target.
[donnie@localhost system]$
```

You can see that the `default.target` symbolic link now points to the `multi-user.target` file. When you reboot this machine now, the graphical desktop won't start up. After you've rebooted the machine to verify that this works, go ahead and change it back to graphical mode by doing:

```
[donnie@localhost ~]$ sudo systemctl set-default graphical
Removed /etc/systemd/system/default.target.
Created symlink /etc/systemd/system/default.target → /usr/lib/systemd/system/graphical.target.
[donnie@localhost ~]$
```

Then, reboot the machine to get back into graphical mode.

All right, this is all good. But there might be times when we'll just want to change to another target temporarily without changing the default. Let's look at that.

Temporarily changing the target

You can also change from one target to another without changing the default. This can come in handy for a few reasons. For example, let's say that you're setting up a gaming computer with an *Nvidia* graphics card. Now, if all you want to do with your Linux computer is just surf the web or do normal office work, the open source Nvidia drivers that come with your Linux distro work fine. For gaming though, the open source drivers might not give you the gaming performance that you really crave. To get around that, you'll go to the Nvidia website and download their proprietary driver. The first step in the installation procedure is to drop the machine out of graphical mode, into text mode. To do that with `systemd`, we'll use the `systemctl isolate` option, like this:

```
[donnie@localhost ~]$ sudo systemctl isolate multi-user
```

This will shut down the graphics server and bring you back to a text-mode login prompt:

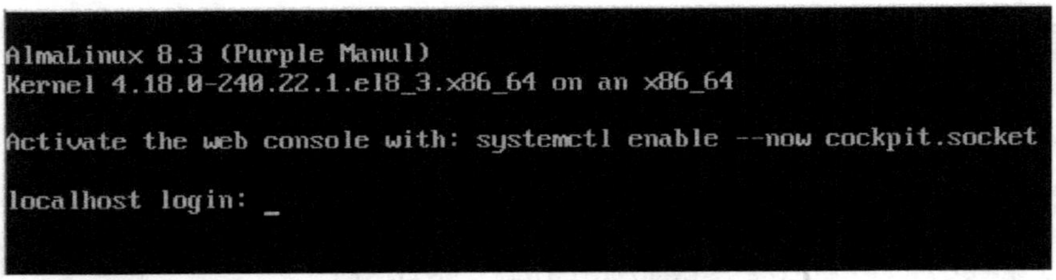

```
AlmaLinux 8.3 (Purple Manul)
Kernel 4.18.0-240.22.1.el8_3.x86_64 on an x86_64

Activate the web console with: systemctl enable --now cockpit.socket

localhost login: _
```

Figure 6.6 – Text-mode login on Alma Linux

To get back to graphical mode, you can reboot the machine, assuming that you still have `graphical.target` set as the default. Or, you can just run the `isolate` command again, like this:

```
[donnie@localhost ~]$ sudo systemctl isolate graphical
```

Be aware though that isolating back to graphical mode can sometimes be a bit quirky, so you might find it better to just reboot. Besides, if you're installing a video driver, you'll need to reboot in any case.

Now, if you're an old-as-dirt codger like me, you might be so used to the old way of doing things that you can't do things the new way. Well, I have good news. You can still use the old SysV commands to change targets if you really want to. To allow this to happen, the `systemd` developers created symbolic runlevel links that point to the corresponding targets. Here's what they look like:

```
[donnie@localhost ~]$ cd /lib/systemd/system
[donnie@localhost system]$ ls -l runlevel*.target
```

```
lrwxrwxrwx. 1 root 15 Apr  7 04:46 runlevel0.target ->
poweroff.target
lrwxrwxrwx. 1 root 13 Apr  7 04:46 runlevel1.target -> rescue.
target
lrwxrwxrwx. 1 root 17 Apr  7 04:46 runlevel2.target -> multi-
user.target
lrwxrwxrwx. 1 root 17 Apr  7 04:46 runlevel3.target -> multi-
user.target
lrwxrwxrwx. 1 root 17 Apr  7 04:46 runlevel4.target -> multi-
user.target
lrwxrwxrwx. 1 root 16 Apr  7 04:46 runlevel5.target ->
graphical.target
lrwxrwxrwx. 1 root 13 Apr  7 04:46 runlevel6.target -> reboot.
target
[donnie@localhost system]$
```

The legacy `init` and `telinit` commands are also still there, so you can still use either of them to change runlevels. For example, you can drop from graphical mode down to multiuser mode with either of these two commands:

```
sudo init 3
sudo telinit 3
```

To get back to graphical mode, just run either of these commands again, replacing the `3` with a `5`.

All jokes aside, it's great that they included the backward-compatibility stuff for those who really need it. Still though, you'll want to get used to the modern `systemctl isolate` way of doing things, because the `systemd` developers could pull this backward-compatibility stuff out at any time.

All righty, I think that about covers things. Let's wrap this chapter up and put a bow on it.

Summary

As we always do, we've covered a lot of ground and seen a lot of cool stuff. We looked at the purpose of `systemd` targets and how they're structured. Then, we looked at how `systemd` targets compare to the old SysVinit runlevels, and at how to view a target's dependencies. We finished by looking at how to set the default runlevel, and how to temporarily change the runlevel.

In the next chapter, we'll look at `systemd` timers. I'll see you there.

Questions

1. What is a target?

   a) It's just another name for the old-fashioned runlevels.

   b) It's a unit that groups together other units for a specific purpose.

   c) It's a unit that starts a service.

   d) It's a unit that listens for incoming network connections.

2. What is a passive target?

   a) It's a target that you can't start yourself.

   b) It's a placeholder target that doesn't do anything.

   c) A passive target is configured with the `TargetMode=passive` line.

   d) It's a target that just runs in the background.

3. How would you change from graphical mode to text mode?

   a) `sudo systemctl isolate text-mode`

   b) `sudo systemctl 3`

   c) `sudo systemctl isolate multi-user`

   d) `sudo runlevel multi-user`

4. What is a major difference between SysV runlevels and `systemd` targets?

   a) SysV runlevels depend upon each other. `systemd` targets are self-contained units.

   b) `systemd` targets depend upon each other. Each SysV runlevel has its own complete list of services to run.

   c) SysV runlevels run more efficiently than `systemd` targets.

   d) There is no real difference.

5. Which of the following commands shows you the default target?

   a) `systemctl show-target`

   b) `systemctl show-default`

   c) `systemctl default`

   d) `systemctl get-default`

Answers

1. b
2. a
3. c
4. b
5. d

Further reading

An explanation of `network.target`:

`https://www.freedesktop.org/wiki/Software/systemd/NetworkTarget/`

Booting CentOS into emergency or rescue mode:

`https://www.thegeekdiary.com/how-to-boot-into-rescue-mode-or-emergency-mode-through-systemd-in-centos-rhel-7-and-8/`

Booting Ubuntu into emergency or rescue mode:

`https://linuxconfig.org/how-to-boot-ubuntu-18-04-into-emergency-and-rescue-mode`

7
Understanding systemd Timers

Busy system administrators like to find ways to make their lives easier. One way to do that is to automate as many of their routine tasks as possible by setting them up to automatically run on a set schedule. In this chapter, we'll look at how to do this with `systemd` timers. The specific topics that we'll look at include the following:

- Comparing `systemd` timers with `cron`
- Understanding timer options
- Creating timers

If you're ready, let's get started.

Technical requirements

As always, we'll be using an Ubuntu Server 20.04 virtual machine and an Alma Linux 8 virtual machine for our demonstrations. It's all hands-on, so feel free to follow along with your own virtual machines.

Check out the following link to see the Code in Action video: `https://bit.ly/31pQdfS`

Comparing systemd timers with cron

The `cron` family of scheduling utilities has been a part of Unix and Unix-like operating systems since May 1975. In the 1980s, as part of Richard Stallman's new *free software* movement, several free-as-in-speech versions of `cron` were created. Paul Vixie, a member of the *Internet Hall of Fame*, created his own free version in 1987. Vixie's version became the most widely used version in the Linux world. (In fact, if you look at the `cron` man page, you'll still see Paul Vixie's name in the **Authors** section at the bottom.)

A big advantage of `cron` is its sheer simplicity. All it takes to create a `cron` job is one simple line of code, which would look something like this:

```
[donnie@centos6-vm ~]$ crontab -l
25,55 * * * *  /usr/bin/logger "This is a demo of the cron system."
[donnie@centos6-vm ~]$
```

Figure 7.1 – An example of a cron job

In this very simple example, which I took from one of my ancient CentOS 6 virtual machines, I'm running a simple task at 25 minutes and 55 minutes past every hour of every day. Twice every hour, this `cron` job inserts a message into the system log file. Any non-privileged user who needs to can create a `cron` job to perform some non-privileged task and anyone with the proper root-level privileges can create a system-level job. Jobs can be set up to run on a particular day of the week, a particular day of the month, at particular times of the day, or upon rebooting the machine. There's a lot of flexibility here, and it's all very simple to set up.

Another advantage of `cron` is that it's everywhere in the world of Unix and Unix-like operating systems, while `systemd` only exists in the world of Linux. If you're a system administrator in a large shop with a mix of both Unix and Linux servers, you might find it easier to stick with `cron`.

Setting up `systemd` timers isn't hard, but it does take a bit more time and effort. To begin with, you can't directly access a command or a script from a `systemd` timer. You first have to create a `systemd` service, then call that service from the timer. However, there are quite a few advantages of using `systemd` timers, so learning how to use them could be well worth the effort.

With `systemd` timers, you have a lot more flexibility and accuracy in the way you set up task schedules. The services that you create to go along with your timers can take advantage of resource management, security, and all of the other goodness that comes with using `systemd`. You can create timers that trigger upon some predefined event, or you can specify the calendar and clock time for when you want to trigger the timer. As an added bonus, `systemd` will log the completion of a timer event in the system log file. With `cron` jobs, you don't have any of that.

So, you're now wondering which of these two task-scheduling systems you should use. Well, `cron` does still come installed on modern Linux systems. If you just need to quickly create a simple job, there's certainly nothing wrong with using `cron`. But, if you need to set up something a bit fancier, then definitely go with a `systemd` timer. Even if you do just need something simple, it might still be worth your while to set up a timer in order to get familiar with the process.

Okay, that's probably enough for the introduction. Let's look at how to view information about the `systemd` timers on your system.

Viewing timer information

When you first install a Linux operating system, you'll see that there are already some active timers that take care of certain administrative tasks. You can see them by using the `systemctl list-unit-files -t timer` command. On your Alma Linux machine, the output should look something like this:

```
[donnie@localhost ~]$ systemctl list-unit-files -t timer
UNIT FILE                    STATE
chrony-dnssrv@.timer         disabled
dnf-makecache.timer          enabled
fstrim.timer                 disabled
fwupd-refresh.timer          disabled
mdadm-last-resort@.timer     static
mdcheck_continue.timer       disabled
mdcheck_start.timer          disabled
mdmonitor-oneshot.timer      disabled
mlocate-updatedb.timer       disabled
podman-auto-update.timer     disabled
systemd-tmpfiles-clean.timer static
unbound-anchor.timer         enabled

12 unit files listed.
[donnie@localhost ~]$
```

Figure 7.2 – Timers on Alma Linux

We see that 12 timers are installed, but only two are enabled. Two are static, which means that they can't be either enabled or disabled, and all the rest are disabled.

On the Ubuntu server machine, we see that quite a few more timers are enabled:

```
donnie@ubuntu2004:~$ systemctl list-unit-files -t timer
UNIT FILE                         STATE    VENDOR PRESET
apt-daily-upgrade.timer           enabled  enabled
apt-daily.timer                   enabled  enabled
e2scrub_all.timer                 enabled  enabled
fstrim.timer                      enabled  enabled
fwupd-refresh.timer               enabled  enabled
logrotate.timer                   enabled  enabled
man-db.timer                      enabled  enabled
mdadm-last-resort@.timer          static   enabled
mdcheck_continue.timer            enabled  enabled
mdcheck_start.timer               enabled  enabled
mdmonitor-oneshot.timer           enabled  enabled
motd-news.timer                   enabled  enabled
snapd.snap-repair.timer           enabled  enabled
systemd-tmpfiles-clean.timer      static   enabled
ua-messaging.timer                enabled  enabled
xfs_scrub_all.timer               disabled enabled

16 unit files listed.
donnie@ubuntu2004:~$
```

Figure 7.3 – Timers on Ubuntu server

The `systemctl list-timers` command shows you six fields of information, which look like this:

```
[donnie@localhost ~]$ systemctl list-timers
NEXT                         LEFT       LAST                         PASSED        UNIT                         ACTIVATES
Thu 2021-05-20 15:39:35 EDT  55min left Thu 2021-05-20 14:39:34 EDT  4min 45s ago  dnf-makecache.timer          dnf-makecache.service
Fri 2021-05-21 00:00:00 EDT  9h left    Thu 2021-05-20 12:29:35 EDT  2h 14min ago  unbound-anchor.timer         unbound-anchor.service
Fri 2021-05-21 12:44:16 EDT  21h left   Thu 2021-05-20 12:44:16 EDT  2h 0min ago   systemd-tmpfiles-clean.timer systemd-tmpfiles-clean.service

3 timers listed.
Pass --all to see loaded but inactive timers, too.
[donnie@localhost ~]$ systemctl list-timers
NEXT                         LEFT       LAST                         PASSED        UNIT                         ACTIVATES
Thu 2021-05-20 15:39:35 EDT  40min left Thu 2021-05-20 14:39:34 EDT  19min ago     dnf-makecache.timer          dnf-makecache.service
Fri 2021-05-21 00:00:00 EDT  9h left    Thu 2021-05-20 12:29:35 EDT  2h 29min ago  unbound-anchor.timer         unbound-anchor.service
Fri 2021-05-21 12:44:16 EDT  21h left   Thu 2021-05-20 12:44:16 EDT  2h 15min ago  systemd-tmpfiles-clean.timer systemd-tmpfiles-clean.service

3 timers listed.
Pass --all to see loaded but inactive timers, too.
[donnie@localhost ~]$
```

Figure 7.4 – systemctl list-timers

The six fields are as follows:

- **NEXT**: This shows the next time that the timer is scheduled to run.
- **LEFT**: This shows how much time is left before the timer runs again.
- **LAST**: This shows the time at which the timer last ran.
- **PASSED**: This shows how much time has elapsed since the timer last ran.

- **UNIT**: This is the name of the unit file for the timer.
- **ACTIVATES**: This is the name of the service that the timer runs. This will normally be the same name as the timer, but it doesn't have to be.

You can view some of this information with `systemctl status`, like this:

```
[donnie@localhost ~]$ systemctl status dnf-makecache.timer
● dnf-makecache.timer - dnf makecache --timer
   Loaded: loaded (/usr/lib/systemd/system/dnf-makecache.timer;
enabled; vendor preset: enabled)
   Active: active (waiting) since Thu 2021-05-20 12:29:35 EDT;
2h 55min ago
  Trigger: Thu 2021-05-20 15:39:35 EDT; 14min left

May 20 12:29:35 localhost.localdomain systemd[1]: Started dnf
makecache --timer.
[donnie@localhost ~]$
```

Just as you can do with services and targets, you can view the dependency tree for a timer, as follows:

```
[donnie@localhost ~]$ systemctl list-dependencies
dnf-makecache.timer
dnf-makecache.timer
● ├─network-online.target
● │ └─NetworkManager-wait-online.service
● └─sysinit.target
●   ├─dev-hugepages.mount
●   ├─dev-mqueue.mount
●   ├─dracut-shutdown.service
●   ├─import-state.service
●   ├─iscsi-onboot.service
●   ├─kmod-static-nodes.service
●   ├─ldconfig.service
. . .
. . .
```

We've seen several ways to view information about the timers on your system. Let's move on and look at some of the configuration options.

Understanding timer options

The best way to start explaining the timer options is to look at some examples of timers that are already on our systems. We'll begin by looking at a timer on the Alma Linux machine.

Understanding monotonic timers

There are two ways to specify the time at which you want a service to automatically run. In this section, we'll look at the *monotonic* method. This means that instead of configuring the job to run at a specific calendar and clock time, you'll instead configure the job to run after some sort of event that serves as a starting point. A starting point can be system bootup, timer activation, the time since a timer's associated service last ran, or any of several other things (you can see all of the monotonic starting points by looking at the `systemd.timer` man page). For an example of a monotonic timer, let's look at `dnf-makecache.timer` on the Alma Linux machine.

Red Hat-type operating systems, such as Alma Linux, use the `dnf` utility to perform update and package management. As with all Linux package management systems, `dnf` maintains a local cache of information about what is in the distro's package repositories. Periodically, the cache needs to be refreshed. We could do that manually with a `sudo dnf makecache` command, but Red Hat-type systems all come with a timer to do it automatically. Here's what the timer looks like:

```
[Unit]
Description=dnf makecache --timer
ConditionKernelCommandLine=!rd.live.image
# See comment in dnf-makecache.service
ConditionPathExists=!/run/ostree-booted
Wants=network-online.target

[Timer]
OnBootSec=10min
OnUnitInactiveSec=1h
Unit=dnf-makecache.service

[Install]
WantedBy=timers.target
```

In the `[Unit]` section, we see:

- `ConditionKernelCommandLine=!rd.live.image`: This prevents the timer from running if the machine is booted from some sort of live media, such as a live DVD.
- `ConditionPathExists=!/run/ostree-booted`: This looks for the `/run/ostree-booted` directory, and prevents the timer from running if this directory is found. (According to the `ostree` man page, you would use `ostree` to manage different versions of filesystem trees. These filesystem trees are mounted as read-only, so trying to update the cache on them wouldn't do much good.)
- `Wants=network-online.target`: This prevents the timer from running until after network services are available. (Already, you're seeing things you can do with `systemd` timers that you can't do with `cron`.)

Next, we see the `[Timer]` section, with two examples of monotonic timer settings. As I've already mentioned, monotonic timers are defined relative to a certain starting point, rather than by calendar and clock time:

- `OnBootSec=10min`: As we'll see in a moment, this timer activates the `dnf-makecache.service`. This line causes the service to run 10 minutes after the system has booted up.
- `OnUnitInactiveSec=1h`: This line says that the timer will run the `dnf-makecache.service` again one hour after the last time it ran. In other words, this line causes the service to run approximately every hour.
- `Unit=dnf-makecache.service`: In this case, it's not necessary to have this line. By default, a timer will activate a service that has the same name as the timer. The only time you really have to have this line is if the timer activates a service with a different name. Still though, some people like to use this parameter in any case, and there's nothing wrong with that.

> **Note**
>
> You can see the rest of the monotonic timer parameters on the `systemd.timer` man page.

The `[Install]` section is fairly standard stuff. All we see there is the `WantedBy=timers.target` line, which causes this timer to run when the `timers.target` starts.

While we're at it, we might as well look at the dnf-makecache.service that this timer activates:

```
[Unit]
Description=dnf makecache
ConditionPathExists=!/run/ostree-booted
After=network-online.target

[Service]
Type=oneshot
Nice=19
IOSchedulingClass=2
IOSchedulingPriority=7
Environment="ABRT_IGNORE_PYTHON=1"
ExecStart=/usr/bin/dnf makecache --timer
```

In the [Service] section, we see a few things that we haven't seen in service files before:

- Type=oneshot: Okay, we actually have seen this one before. I just want to show here that you need to use the oneshot type for services that are called by timers. (It really makes sense when you think about it.)
- Nice=19: This causes the service to run with a niceness value of 19, which means that the service will run with the lowest possible priority. (Niceness values range from -20 to positive 19. Although it seems counterintuitive, -20 denotes the highest priority that can be assigned to a process, and positive 19 denotes the lowest.) This setting helps prevent this service from bogging down other processes that might be more important.
- IOSchedulingClass=2: This sets the type of input/output scheduler scheme that we want to use. A value of 2 means that we want to use the best-effort type scheduling class. (You can see the other IOSchedulingClass types in the systemd.exec man page.)
- IOSchedulingPriority=7: IOSchedulingPriority values range from 0 through 7, with 0 as the highest priority and 7 as the lowest. This is just another way to keep this service from bogging down the rest of the system.

- `ExecStart=/usr/bin/dnf makecache --timer`: The `--timer` option here has nothing to do with `systemd` timers. Instead, this is an option that goes along with the `dnf` command. According to the `dnf` man page, `--timer` causes `dnf` to be more resource-aware, so that it won't run if the computer is running on battery power. It also causes the `dnf makecache` command to immediately abort if it has already been run recently.

The `[Install]` section of this service file is conspicuous by its absence. Not having the `[Install]` section makes this a *static* type of service that you can't enable. Instead, it will just run whenever the `dnf-makecache.timer` activates it.

Okay, that about does it for this example. Next, we'll look at the other ways to specify when to run a job.

Understanding real-time timers

You can use a *real-time* timer to run a job on whatever calendar day and at whatever clock time you want it to run. For our first simple example, let's look at the `fstrim.timer` on the Alma machine:

```
[Unit]
Description=Discard unused blocks once a week
Documentation=man:fstrim

[Timer]
OnCalendar=weekly
AccuracySec=1h
Persistent=true

[Install]
WantedBy=timers.target
```

Here's the breakdown:

- `OnCalendar=weekly`: You'll use the `OnCalendar` parameter to specify the time at which you want the job to run. Setting this job up to run weekly means that it will run every Monday morning at midnight. (We'll see in a bit where these parameters are defined.)

- `AccuracySec=1h`: This defines the amount of time by which the job is allowed to be delayed. A one-hour delay means that this job could run at any time from midnight to one o'clock on Monday morning. If you leave this line out, the default delay will be one minute. If you want the job to run exactly at midnight on Monday, you can change the `1h` to `1us`, which gives the greatest accuracy.
- `Persistent=true`: So, what happens if your machine is shut down at midnight on Monday morning? Without this line, this job will just be skipped. With this line, the job will run the next time you boot up the machine.

As you can see, there's no `Unit=` line in this timer, as there was in the previous example. So, by default, this `fstrim.timer` will activate the `fstrim.service`, which clears out unused blocks on your storage drives. Here's what the service looks like:

```
[Unit]
Description=Discard unused blocks

[Service]
Type=oneshot
ExecStart=/usr/sbin/fstrim -av
```

Okay, so there's nothing new here. It's just a standard static, `oneshot` type of service, as we saw in the previous example.

The `fstrim.timer` is disabled by default on the Alma machine, as we see here:

```
[donnie@localhost ~]$ systemctl is-enabled fstrim.timer
disabled
[donnie@localhost ~]$
```

The `fstrim.timer` comes in handy if you're running either a solid-state drive or thinly provisioned storage. If you need to enable the timer, just do it the same way that you'd enable a service, as shown here:

```
[donnie@localhost ~]$ sudo systemctl enable --now fstrim.timer
[sudo] password for donnie:
Created symlink /etc/systemd/system/timers.target.wants/fstrim.
timer → /usr/lib/systemd/system/fstrim.timer.
[donnie@localhost ~]$
```

On the Ubuntu machine, you'll see that the `fstrim.timer` is enabled by default:

```
donnie@ubuntu2004:~$ systemctl is-enabled fstrim.timer
enabled
donnie@ubuntu2004:~$
```

Next, let's take a closer look at how to define the `OnCalendar` times.

Understanding calendar events for real-time timers

Okay, here's where things can get a bit sticky. I mean, configuring times for `cron` jobs is easy and straightforward. Understanding how to set up times for a `systemd` timer takes a bit of getting used to. Your best bet is to open the `systemd.time` man page, and scroll down to the **CALENDAR EVENTS** section. The explanation there isn't as clear as it could be, but you can pretty much figure it out by looking at the examples. Let's see if we can make any sense of it.

In the `fstrim.timer` example that we just looked at, we saw the `OnCalendar=weekly` line, which causes the job to run at midnight every Monday morning. In the **CALENDAR EVENTS** section of the `systemd.time` man page, you'll see the complete list of predefined event times:

```
minutely → *-*-* *:*:00
hourly → *-*-* *:00:00
daily → *-*-* 00:00:00
monthly → *-*-01 00:00:00
weekly → Mon *-*-* 00:00:00
yearly → *-01-01 00:00:00
quarterly → *-01,04,07,10-01 00:00:00
semiannually → *-01,07-01 00:00:00
```

Most of these are easy to figure out. The only ones that might throw you a bit are `quarterly` and `semiannually`. A `quarterly` job will run at midnight on the first day of January, April, July, and October, as denoted by the `01,04,07,10` part. A `semiannually` job will run at midnight on the first day of January and July, as denoted by the `01,07` part.

Scroll down the `systemd.time` page a bit more and you'll see a whole big list of examples of how you can set up your job times. Rather than try to show you the whole list, I'll just show you one example, and then break it down for you. Here we go:

```
2003-03-05 → 2003-03-05 00:00:00
```

The left-hand side shows you the date and time as a human would normally write it. The right-hand side shows you the value that you'd use as an `OnCalendar=` parameter. I chose this example because it uses all of the fields. (And yes, I know that 2003 is in the past, but this is what's in the man page.) To create a job that would have run at midnight on March 3, 2003, the `OnCalendar=` line would look like this:

```
OnCalendar=2003-03-05 00:00:00
```

Since that's several years in the past, let's fix this so that it will run in the future:

```
OnCalendar=2525-03-05 00:00:00
```

Ah, yes. *In the year 2525, if man is still alive, and if woman can still survive. . .* (Who besides me is old enough to remember that silly song?)

Seriously though, this isn't near as hard as it first seems to be. We have `Year-Month-Date`, followed by `Hour:Minute:Second` in 24-hour format. So yeah, it's actually quite easy-peasy. Now, let's say that we want this to run every day at 6:15 in the evening. We'll just replace the `Year-Month-Date` fields with the standard wildcard symbol (`*`), and change the time:

```
OnCalendar=*-*-* 18:15:00
```

That's good, but I've changed my mind about running it every single day. I think I'll change it so that it will only run on the fifth day of every month, like so:

```
OnCalendar=*-*-05 18:15:00
```

Nah, that's not often enough. Let's make it run on the fifth, tenth, and fifteenth days of every month:

```
OnCalendar=*-*-05,10,15 18:15:00
```

The `Day-of-Week` field is optional. Let's make the job run on the fifth, tenth, and fifteenth days of the month, but only if they happen to fall on either a Monday or a Wednesday:

```
OnCalendar=Mon,Wed *-*-05,10,15 18:15:00
```

Better yet, let's just make it run every Monday and Wednesday:

```
OnCalendar=Mon,Wed *-*-* 18:15:00
```

You can use the tilde (~) symbol to count a specified number of days back from the end of a month. To have the job run on the third from last day of every February, just do this:

```
OnCalendar=*-02~03 18:15:00
```

Now, let's make the job run on the last Monday of every May:

```
OnCalendar=Mon *-05~07/1 18:15:00
```

Finally, let's get really crazy and make the job run every ten minutes:

```
OnCalendar=*:00/10
```

Okay, that should be enough to give you a clue. If you need to see any more examples, just look at the `systemd.time` man page.

Creating timers

Creating your own timer is a two-stage process. You'll first create the service that you want to run, and then you'll create and enable the timer.

Creating a system-level timer

Let's say that you're a security-conscious soul who suspects that someone might try to plant some rootkits on your machines. You want to set up Rootkit Hunter so that it will run every day after work hours.

> **Note**
>
> I wanted to do this with both Ubuntu and Alma Linux. Unfortunately, there's a bug in the Rootkit Hunter package for Ubuntu that prevents Rootkit Hunter from updating its signature database. That's not too surprising, because Ubuntu quality control has always been somewhat less than perfect. So, for this example, we'll just go with Alma.

Because there's a bug in the Rootkit Hunter package in Ubuntu, we'll just do this on the Alma machine. Rootkit Hunter isn't in the normal Alma repositories, so you'll first need to install the EPEL repository, like so:

```
sudo dnf install epel-release
sudo dnf update
sudo dnf install rkhunter
```

Create the `rkhunter.service` file by doing:

```
sudo systemctl edit --full --force rkhunter.service
```

Make the file look like this:

```
[Unit]
Description=Rootkit Hunter

[Service]
Type=oneshot
ExecStartPre=/usr/bin/rkhunter --propupd
ExecStartPre=/usr/bin/rkhunter --update
ExecStart=/usr/bin/rkhunter -c --cronjob --rwo
```

Before we do the actual scan, we want to create the `rkhunter.dat` file to store file properties and update the database of rootkit signatures. We'll do that with the two `ExecStartPre=` lines. In the `ExecStart=` line, we have three options, as follows:

- `-c`: This is the *check* option, which does the actual scan.
- `--cronjob`: Normally, Rootkit Hunter will pause several times during a scan and wait for user input. This option causes Rootkit Hunter to complete its run without pausing.
- `--rwo`: This option causes Rootkit Hunter to only report any problems that it finds.

Before creating the timer, it's a good idea to start the service manually to verify that it works. We'll do that with:

```
[donnie@localhost ~]$ sudo systemctl start rkhunter
```

When it's finished running, look at the `/var/log/rkhunter/rkhunter.log` file to verify that there aren't any problems. If everything looks good, we're ready to create the timer. Do that with:

```
[donnie@localhost ~]$ sudo systemctl edit --full --force
rkhunter.timer
```

For demonstration purposes, set the `OnCalendar=` time to just a few minutes into the future. That way, you won't have to wait long for it to run. When you're done, the file should look something like this:

```
[Unit]
Description=Rootkit Hunter

[Timer]
OnCalendar=*-*-* 17:50:00
Persistent=true

[Install]
WantedBy=timer.target
```

Do a `daemon-reload`, and then enable the timer:

```
[donnie@localhost ~]$ sudo systemctl daemon-reload
[donnie@localhost ~]$ sudo systemctl enable --now rkhunter.
timer
Created symlink /etc/systemd/system/timer.target.wants/
rkhunter.timer → /etc/systemd/system/rkhunter.timer.
[donnie@localhost ~]$
```

Now it's just a matter of waiting for the timer to run to see whether it works. After it has finished, you can view the results in the `/var/log/rkhunter/rkhunter.log` file.

Next, let's allow a normal, non-privileged user to create a timer.

Creating a user-level timer

You can try this demonstration on either the Ubuntu or the Alma virtual machine. I haven't shown much love to the Ubuntu machine for a while, so I'll go with that one.

Now, let's say that you're just a normal user who wants to back up your home directory to one of those handy-dandy portable drives. You'll plug it into the USB port of your computer, and the system will automatically mount it under the `/media/backup/` directory.

> **Note**
>
> If you don't have a portable backup drive, you can simulate this by manually creating a backup directory, and setting the permissions so that normal users can write to it, like this:
>
> **sudo mkdir /media/backup**
>
> **sudo chmod 777 /media/backup**

Now it's just a matter of creating the service and the timer. Any non-privileged user can do that by using the `--user` option switch.

As before, we'll start by creating the service, like this:

```
donnie@ubuntu2004:~$ systemctl edit --user --full --force
backup.service
```

This will automatically create the necessary files and directories under the `/home/donnie/.config/` directory. I'll use `rsync` to do the backup, so my `backup.service` file will look like this:

```
[Unit]
Description=Backup my home directory

[Service]
Type=oneshot
ExecStart=/usr/bin/rsync -a /home/donnie /media/backup
```

I want to make sure that this works, so I'll do a `daemon-reload` and then try running the service manually before I create the timer:

```
donnie@ubuntu2004:~$ systemctl daemon-reload --user
donnie@ubuntu2004:~$ systemctl start --user backup.service
donnie@ubuntu2004:~$
```

If it runs successfully, I should see a `donnie/` directory under `/media/backup/`:

```
donnie@ubuntu2004:~$ ls -l /media/backup/
total 20
drwxr-xr-x 6 donnie donnie  4096 May 21 15:58 donnie
drwx------ 2 root   root   16384 May 22 15:34 lost+found
donnie@ubuntu2004:~$
```

So far, so good. Let's see what's in that `donnie/` directory:

```
donnie@ubuntu2004:~$ ls -la /media/backup/donnie/
total 44
drwxr-xr-x 6 donnie donnie 4096 May 21 15:58 .
drwxrwxrwx 4 root   root   4096 May 22 15:49 ..
-rw------- 1 donnie donnie 3242 May 21 22:07 .bash_history
-rw-r--r-- 1 donnie donnie  220 Feb 25  2020 .bash_logout
-rw-r--r-- 1 donnie donnie 3771 Feb 25  2020 .bashrc
drwx------ 2 donnie donnie 4096 Jan  6 01:47 .cache
drwxr-xr-x 4 donnie donnie 4096 May 21 20:30 .config
-rw------- 1 donnie donnie  263 Apr  3 19:00 .lesshst
drwxrwxr-x 3 donnie donnie 4096 May 21 15:58 .local
-rw-r--r-- 1 donnie donnie  807 Feb 25  2020 .profile
-rw-r--r-- 1 donnie donnie    0 Jan  6 01:47 .sudo_as_admin_
successful
drwxr-xr-x 3 donnie donnie 4096 Jan  6 01:56 snap
donnie@ubuntu2004:~$
```

Nice. The backup service works, and I have achieved coolness. Now, it's time to create the timer:

```
donnie@ubuntu2004:~$ systemctl edit --user --full --force
backup.timer
```

I'll just have it run daily at midnight, so I'll make it look like this:

```
[Unit]
Description=Back up my home directory

[Timer]
OnCalendar=daily
Persistent=true

[Install]
WantedBy=timer.target default.target
```

Of course, if you don't want to wait around until midnight to see whether this works, just set the `OnCalendar=` time to whatever you want.

Note that when we use the `--user` option, we need to have the `default.target` in the `WantedBy=` line.

Next, I'll do a `daemon-reload` and enable the timer:

```
donnie@ubuntu2004:~$ systemctl daemon-reload --user
donnie@ubuntu2004:~$ systemctl enable --user --now backup.timer
Created symlink /home/donnie/.config/systemd/user/timer.target.wants/backup.timer → /home/donnie/.config/systemd/user/backup.timer.
Created symlink /home/donnie/.config/systemd/user/default.target.wants/backup.timer → /home/donnie/.config/systemd/user/backup.timer.
donnie@ubuntu2004:~$
```

I can also use the `--user` switch to view information about this timer:

```
donnie@ubuntu2004:~$ systemctl list-timers --user
NEXT                            LEFT    LAST
PASSED     UNIT            ACTIVATES
Sun 2021-05-23 00:00:00 UTC 7h left Sat 2021-05-22 15:47:05 UTC
41min ago backup.timer backup.service

1 timers listed.
Pass --all to see loaded but inactive timers, too.
donnie@ubuntu2004:~$
```

As things stand now, this timer will only run while I'm actually logged in to the system. To ensure that it runs even when I'm not logged in, I'll enable the `linger` function for myself:

```
donnie@ubuntu2004:~$ loginctl enable-linger donnie
donnie@ubuntu2004:~$
```

Okay, I think that does it for this chapter. Let's go ahead and wrap it up.

Summary

In this chapter, we've looked at `systemd` timers, and compared them to the legacy `cron` system. We looked at different timer options, and at different ways to specify when a timer should run. Finally, we looked at how to create timers for both system-level and user-level jobs.

In the next chapter, we'll take a brief look at the bootup process under `systemd`. I'll see you there.

Questions

1. How do `cron` and `systemd` timers differ?

   a. It's much easier to set up `systemd` timers.

   b. Non-privileged users can set up their own `cron` jobs, but they can't set up their own timers.

   c. A `cron` job can run a command or script directly, but a `systemd` timer can only run an associated service.

   d. Non-privileged users can set up their own `systemd` timers, but they can't set up their own `cron` jobs.

2. What are the two ways of specifying when a job will run? (Choose two.)

   a. monotonic

   b. wallclock

   c. calendartime

   d. realtime

3. Which of the following man pages would tell you how to format times for the `OnCalendar=` parameter?

   a. `systemd.time`

   b. `systemd.timer`

   c. `systemd.unit`

   d. `systemd.exec`

4. Which of the following time configurations equates to the monthly setting?

   a. `*-01-01 00:00:00`

   b. `*-*-* 00:00:00`

   c. `*-*-01 00:00:00`

   d. `*-01-01 00:00:00`

Answers

1. c
2. a, d
3. a
4. c

Further reading

- Comparing `systemd` timers with `cron`:

  `https://trstringer.com/systemd-timer-vs-cronjob/`

  `https://medium.com/horrible-hacks/using-systemd-as-a-better-cron-a4023eea996d`

- Using `systemd` timers with Docker:

  `https://matthiasadler.info/blog/running-scheduled-tasks-in-docker-containers-with-systemd/`

- Using `systemd` timers as a `cron` replacement:

  `https://www.maketecheasier.com/use-systemd-timers-as-cron-replacement/`

8
Understanding the systemd Boot Process

In this chapter, we'll take a brief look at the `systemd` boot process. Now, you might think that this would be a bit dull, but I can assure you that it won't be. Rather than lead you through a dull slog about all that happens during bootup, my aim is to give you practical information that can make bootups run more efficiently. After that, I'll show you some ways in which `systemd` has been made somewhat backward-compatible with the legacy **System V** (**SysV**) stuff. Specific topics in this chapter include the following:

- Comparing SysV bootup and `systemd` bootup
- Analyzing bootup performance
- Some differences on Ubuntu Server 20.04
- Understanding `systemd` generators

Note that we won't be talking about bootloaders in this chapter because we're saving that for later.

All right—if you're ready, let's get started.

Technical requirements

The technical requirements are the same as always—just have an Ubuntu and an Alma **virtual machine** (**VM**) fired up so that you can follow along.

Check out the following link to see the Code in Action video: `https://bit.ly/3phdZ6o`

Comparing SysV bootup and systemd bootup

Computer bootups all start pretty much the same way, regardless of which operating system is running. You turn on the power switch, then the machine's **Basic Input/Output System** (**BIOS**) or **Unified Extensible Firmware Interface** (**UEFI**) initializes the hardware and then pulls the operating system boot information from the **master boot record** (**MBR**) of the machine's drive. After that, things are different for the various operating systems. Let's first look at what's common for the SysV and `systemd` bootup sequence.

Understanding SysV and systemd bootup similarities

Once the machine can access the MBR of the machine's drive, the operating system begins to load. In the `/boot/` directory, you'll see a compressed Linux kernel file that generally has `vmlinuz` in its filename. You'll also see an **initial RAM (random-access memory) disk image** that will normally have either `initramfs` or `initrd` in its filename. The first step of this process is for the Linux kernel image to get uncompressed and loaded into the system memory. At this stage, the kernel still can't access the root filesystem because it can't access the proper drivers for it. These drivers are in the initial RAM disk image. So, the next step is to load this initial RAM disk image, which will establish a temporary root filesystem that the kernel can access. Once the kernel has loaded the proper drivers, the image will unload. The boot process will then continue by accessing whatever it needs to access on the machine's root filesystem.

After this, things get different. To show how, let's take a whirlwind tour of the SysV bootup process.

Understanding the SysV bootup process

I'm not going to go deep into the details of the SysV bootup process because there's no need to. All I want to do is to show you enough information so that you can understand how it differs from the `systemd` bootup.

The `init` process, which is always **process identifier 1** (`PID 1`), is the first process to start. This `init` process will control the rest of the boot sequence with a series of complex, convoluted bash shell scripts in the `/etc/` directory. At some point, the `init` process will obtain information about the default run level from the `/etc/inittab` file. Once the basic system initialization has been completed, system services will get started from bash shell scripts in the `/etc/init.d/` directory, as determined by what's enabled for the default runlevel.

Bootups on a SysV machine can be rather slow because everything gets started in a serial mode—in other words, SysV can only start one service at a time during bootup. Of course, I may have made SysV sound worse than it really is. Although it's outdated by today's standards, it did work well for the hardware of its time. I mean, when you're talking about a server that's running with a pair of single-core 750 **megahertz** (**MHz**) Pentium III processors and 512 **megabytes** (**MB**) of memory, there's not much you can do to speed it up in any case. (I still have a few of those old machines in my collection, but I haven't booted them up in ages.)

As I said, this is a whirlwind tour. For our present purposes, this is all you need to know about SysV bootup. So, let's leave this topic and look at how the `systemd` bootup process works.

Understanding the systemd bootup process

With `systemd`, the `systemd` process is the first process to start. It also runs as `PID 1`, as you can see here on the Alma machine:

```
[donnie@localhost ~]$ ps aux
USER         PID %CPU %MEM    VSZ   RSS TTY      STAT START
TIME COMMAND
root           1  1.9  0.8 186956 15088 ?        Ss   14:18
0:07 /usr/lib/systemd/systemd --switched-root --system
--deserialize 17
. . .
. . .
```

Curiously, `PID 1` still shows up as the `init` process on the Ubuntu machine, as we see here:

```
donnie@ubuntu20-04:~$ ps aux
USER         PID %CPU %MEM    VSZ   RSS TTY      STAT START
TIME COMMAND
```

```
root                 1  1.2  0.5 101924 11308 ?        Ss   18:26
0:04 /sbin/init maybe-ubiquity
. . .
. . .
```

This is because the Ubuntu developers, for some bizarre reason, created an `init` symbolic link that points to the `systemd` executable, as we see here:

```
donnie@ubuntu20-04:~$ cd /sbin
donnie@ubuntu20-04:/sbin$ ls -l init
lrwxrwxrwx 1 root root 20 Mar 17 21:36 init -> /lib/systemd/
systemd
donnie@ubuntu20-04:/sbin$
```

I have no idea why the Ubuntu developers thought they needed to do that. It works though, so it's all good.

Instead of running complex bash shell scripts to initialize the system, `systemd` runs targets. It starts by looking at the `default.target` file to see if it's set to `graphical` or `multi-user`. As I pointed out in *Chapter 6, Understanding systemd Targets*, there's a chain of dependencies that begins with whatever the default target is and stretches backward. Let's say that our machine has the graphical target set as its default. In the `graphical.target` file, we see the following line:

```
Requires=multi-user.target
```

This means that the graphical target can't start until after the multi-user target has started. In the `multi-user.target` file, we see this line:

```
Requires=basic.target
```

Now, if we keep tracing this chain back to its origin, we'll see that the basic target *Requires* the `sysinit.target` file, which in turn *Wants* the `local-fs.target` file, which in turn starts `after` the `local-fs-pre.target` file.

So, what does all this mean? Well, it's just that once the `systemd` process has determined what the default target is, it starts loading the bootup targets in the following order:

1. `local-fs-pre.target`
2. `local-fs.target`
3. `sysinit.target`

4. `basic.target`
5. `multi-user.target`
6. `graphical.target` (if enabled)

Okay—I know. You're now yelling: *But Donnie. You said that systemd starts its processes in parallel, not in sequence.* Indeed, `systemd` does start its bootup processes in parallel. Remember what I told you before. A target is a *collection* of other `systemd` units that are grouped together for a particular purpose. Within each target, processes start up in parallel.

> **Note**
> You can see a graphical representation of this bootup chain on the `bootup` man page.

I've also pointed out before that some of these targets are hardcoded into the `systemd` executable file. This means that some of these targets don't have their own `.target` files, and others have `.target` files that seem to not do anything. There are a few ways to see what's going on with these hardcoded targets. The first way is to look at a target with `systemctl list-dependencies`. Here's what we see when we look at the `local-fs.target` file:

```
[donnie@localhost ~]$ systemctl list-dependencies local-fs.
target
local-fs.target
  ├─-.mount
  ├─boot.mount
  ├─ostree-remount.service
  └─systemd-remount-fs.service
[donnie@localhost ~]$
```

This target starts the services that mount the filesystems. We see that it mounts the `boot` partition, which is represented by `boot.mount`. It then mounts the `root` filesystem, which is represented by `-.mount`.

I showed you before how to look at a list of targets that are hardcoded into the `systemd` executable file. We can also look for information that's specific to just one target. Here's how that looks for the `local-fs.target` file:

```
[donnie@localhost systemd]$ strings /lib/systemd/systemd | grep
-A 100 'local-fs.target'
local-fs.target
options
fstype
Failed to parse /proc/self/mountinfo: %m
Failed to get next entry from /proc/self/mountinfo: %m
. . .
. . .
mount_process_proc_self_mountinfo
mount_dispatch_io
mount_enumerate
mount_enumerate
mount_shutdown
[donnie@localhost systemd]$
```

By default, `grep` only shows the line in which it finds the search term that you specify. The `-A` option makes it show a specified number of lines that come after the line in which the search term is found. The `-A 100` option that I'm using here tells `grep` to show me the next 100 lines that follow the line that contains `local-fs.target`. We don't see the exact program code like this, but the embedded text strings do give us some sense of what's going on. My choice of 100 lines was completely arbitrary, but you can keep increasing that if you like, until you start seeing lines that have nothing to do with mounting filesystems.

A third way to get information about these hardcoded targets is to look at the `bootup` and the `systemd.special` man pages. Neither of these man pages gives much detail, but you still might learn a little something from them.

Now, with this out of the way, let's look at how to analyze bootup problems.

Analyzing bootup performance

Let's say that your server is taking longer than you think it should to boot up, and you want to know why. Fortunately, `systemd` comes with the built-in `systemd-analyze` tool that can help.

Let's start by looking here at how long it took to boot up my AlmaLinux machine with its GNOME 3 desktop:

```
[donnie@localhost ~]$ systemd-analyze
Startup finished in 2.397s (kernel) + 19.023s (initrd) + 1min 26.269s (userspace) = 1min 47.690s
graphical.target reached after 1min 25.920s in userspace
[donnie@localhost ~]$
```

If you don't specify an option, `systemd-analyze` just uses the `time` option. (You can type in `systemd-analyze time` if you really want to, but you'll get the same results that you see here.) The first line of output shows how long it took for the kernel, the initial RAM disk image, and the user space to load. The second line shows how long it took for the graphical target to come up. In reality, the total bootup time doesn't look too bad, especially when you consider the age of the host machine that I'm using to run this VM. (This host machine is a 2009-or-so vintage Dell, running with an old-fashioned Core 2 Quad **central processing unit** (**CPU**).) If I were either running this VM on a newer model host or running Alma on bare metal, the bootup time could possibly be a bit quicker. There's also the fact that this VM is running with the GNOME 3 desktop environment, which is somewhat resource-intensive. I personally prefer lighter-weight desktops, which could possibly cut the bootup time down a bit. Unfortunately, **Red Hat Enterprise Linux 8** (**RHEL 8**) and all of its free-of-charge offspring only come with GNOME 3. (It is possible to install the lightweight **XForms Common Environment** (**XFCE**) desktop if you have the third-party **Extra Packages for Enterprise Linux** (**EPEL**) repository installed, but that's beyond the scope of this book.)

Now, let's say that the bootup process on this machine really is too slow, and you want to speed it up if possible. First, let's use the `blame` option to see who we want to *blame*:

```
[donnie@localhost ~]$ systemd-analyze blame
     1min 4.543s plymouth-quit-wait.service
         58.883s kdump.service
         32.153s wordpress-container.service
         32.102s wordpress2-container.service
         18.200s systemd-udev-settle.service
         14.690s dracut-initqueue.service
         13.748s sssd.service
         12.638s lvm2-monitor.service
```

```
          10.781s NetworkManager-wait-online.service
          10.156s tuned.service
           9.504s firewalld.service
. . .
. . .
```

This `blame` option shows you all of the services that got started during the bootup, along with the time it took to start each service. The services are listed in descending order of how long it took each one to start. Look through the whole list, and see if there are any services that you can safely disable. For example, further down the list, you'll see that the `wpa_supplicant.service` is running, as I show you here:

```
[donnie@localhost ~]$ systemd-analyze blame | grep 'wpa_
supplicant'
            710ms wpa_supplicant.service
[donnie@localhost ~]$
```

That's great if you're working with either a desktop machine or a laptop where you might need to use a wireless adapter, but it's not necessary on a server that doesn't have wireless. So, you might consider disabling this service. (Of course, this service only took 710 **milliseconds** (**ms**) to start, but that's still something.)

> **Note**
> Disabling unnecessary services is good for both performance and security. A basic tenet of security that's been around forever is that you should always minimize the number of running services on your system. This provides potential attackers with fewer attack vectors.

If you want to see how long it took for each target to start during bootup, use the `critical-chain` option, like this:

```
[donnie@localhost ~]$ systemd-analyze critical-chain
The time after the unit is active or started is printed after
the "@" character.
The time the unit takes to start is printed after the "+"
character.
graphical.target @2min 1.450s
. . .
. . .
```

```
                  └─local-fs-pre.target @26.988s
                    └─lvm2-monitor.service @4.022s +12.638s
                                              └─dm-event.socket
@3.973s
                                                └─-.mount
                                                  └─system.
slice
                                                    └─-.slice
[donnie@localhost ~]$
```

For formatting reasons, I can only show you a small portion of the output, so try it for yourself to see how the whole thing looks.

These commands work the same on an Ubuntu machine as they do here on the Alma machine, but there are a few differences with how the default target is set up on Ubuntu Server 20.04. So, let's look at that.

Some differences on Ubuntu Server 20.04

My Ubuntu Server 20.04 machine, which runs purely in text mode, boots considerably faster, as you can see here:

```
donnie@ubuntu20-04:~$ systemd-analyze
Startup finished in 8.588s (kernel) + 44.944s (userspace) =
53.532s
graphical.target reached after 38.913s in userspace
donnie@ubuntu20-04:~$
```

I must confess that I haven't worked that much with Ubuntu Server 20.04 since it's been out, and I still encounter some new things about it that surprise me. Before I set up the VMs for this chapter, I had never before noticed that Ubuntu Server 20.04 comes with `graphical.target` as the default, even though no graphical interface is installed. The explanation for that is that the `accounts-daemon.service` file gets started by the graphical target, not by the multi-user target, as we can see here:

```
donnie@ubuntu20-04:/etc/systemd/system/graphical.target.wants$
ls -l
total 0
lrwxrwxrwx 1 root 43 Feb  1 17:27 accounts-daemon.service -> /
lib/systemd/system/accounts-daemon.service
donnie@ubuntu20-04:/etc/systemd/system/graphical.target.wants$
```

If you look in the `graphical.target` file, you'll see that it only *Wants* the `display-manager.service` file and doesn't *Require* it, as evidenced by this line:

```
Wants=display-manager.service
```

So, even though the display manager doesn't exist on this VM, it still goes into the `graphical.target` just fine. But, let's get back to that `accounts-daemon.service` file. What is it, exactly? Well, according to the official documentation at `https://www.freedesktop.org/wiki/Software/AccountsService/`, "*AccountsService is a D-Bus service for accessing the list of user accounts and information attached to those accounts.*" Yeah, I know—that isn't much of an explanation. A better explanation is that it's a service that allows you to manage users and user accounts from **graphical user interface** (**GUI**)-type utilities. So, why do we have it enabled on Ubuntu Server when there's no graphical interface? That's a good question, to which I don't have a good answer. It's not something that we need running on a text-mode server. That's okay, though. We'll take care of that in just a bit.

So now, what's D-Bus?

D-Bus, which is short for **Desktop Bus**, is a messaging protocol that allows applications to communicate with each other. It also allows the system to launch daemons and applications *on demand*, whenever they're needed. Once the D-Bus protocol starts a service, the service continues to run until you either stop it manually or shut down the machine. The `accounts-daemon.service` file is one service that's meant to be started by D-Bus messages. We can see that here in the `Type=dbus` line of the `[Service]` section of the `accounts-daemon.service` file:

```
[Service]
Type=dbus
BusName=org.freedesktop.Accounts
ExecStart=/usr/lib/accountsservice/accounts-daemon
Environment=GVFS_DISABLE_FUSE=1
Environment=GIO_USE_VFS=local
Environment=GVFS_REMOTE_VOLUME_MONITOR_IGNORE=1
```

However, we see here in the `[Install]` section that we're still going to start this service during the bootup process for performance reasons:

```
[Install]
# We pull this in by graphical.target instead of waiting for
the bus
```

```
# activation, to speed things up a little: gdm uses this anyway
so it is nice
# if it is already around when gdm wants to use it and doesn't
have to wait for
# it.
WantedBy=graphical.target
```

(The `gdm` that's mentioned here stands for **GNOME Display Manager**, which handles user login operation for systems with the GNOME 3 desktop.)

As I said before, we don't need this `accounts-daemon.service` file to run on a text-mode server. So, let's set the `default.target` file to `multi-user` for this Ubuntu machine, which will prevent the `accounts-daemon.service` file from automatically starting when we boot up the machine. As you might remember, this is the command to do that:

```
donnie@ubuntu20-04:~$ sudo systemctl set-default multi-user
```

When you reboot the machine now, you should see it boot a bit faster. On the off-chance that the `accounts-daemon.service` ever is needed, a D-Bus message would start it.

Out of curiosity, I created a new AlmaLinux VM without the GNOME desktop, to see if it would also default to `graphical.target`. It turned out that that Alma without GNOME defaults to `multi-user.target` and doesn't even install the `AccountsService` package. (So, without GUI-type user management utilities, the `accounts-daemon.service` file isn't even needed.)

Next, let's *generate* some real excitement with `systemd` generators.

Understanding systemd generators

`systemd` generators can make life somewhat easier for a busy administrator and also provide some backward compatibility with legacy SysV stuff. Let's first look at how generators make disk and partition configuration easier.

Understanding mount units

Look in the /lib/systemd/system/ directory of either VM, and you'll see several mount unit files that got created when you installed the operating system, as shown here on this Alma machine:

```
[donnie@localhost system]$ ls -l *.mount
-rw-r--r--. 1 root 750 Jun 22  2018 dev-hugepages.mount
-rw-r--r--. 1 root 665 Jun 22  2018 dev-mqueue.mount
-rw-r--r--. 1 root 655 Jun 22  2018 proc-sys-fs-binfmt_misc.
mount
-rw-r--r--. 1 root root 795 Jun 22  2018 sys-fs-fuse-
connections.mount
-rw-r--r--. 1 root root 767 Jun 22  2018 sys-kernel-config.
mount
-rw-r--r--. 1 root root 710 Jun 22  2018 sys-kernel-debug.mount
-rw-r--r--. 1 root root 782 May 20 08:24 tmp.mount
[donnie@localhost system]$
```

All of these mount units, except for the tmp.mount file, are for kernel functions and have nothing to do with the drives and partitions that we want to mount. Unlike Ubuntu, Alma mounts the /tmp/ directory on its own partition, which is why you don't see the tmp.mount file on the Ubuntu machine. Let's peek inside the tmp.mount file to see what's there. Here's the [Unit] section:

```
[Unit]
Description=Temporary Directory (/tmp)
Documentation=man:hier(7)
Documentation=https://www.freedesktop.org/wiki/Software/
systemd/APIFileSystems
ConditionPathIsSymbolicLink=!/tmp
DefaultDependencies=no
Conflicts=umount.target
Before=local-fs.target umount.target
After=swap.target
```

The ConditionPathIsSymbolicLink=!/tmp line prevents the system from mounting /tmp/ if /tmp is found to be a symbolic link instead of the actual mount point directory. (Remember that the ! sign negates an operation.) We then see that this mount unit Conflicts with the umount.target file, which means that a umount operation will *unmount* /tmp/.

Next, let's see what's in the `[Mount]` section:

```
[Mount]
What=tmpfs
Where=/tmp
Type=tmpfs
Options=mode=1777,strictatime,nosuid,nodev
```

The `What=` and `Type=` lines denote this as a *temporary filesystem*. The `Where=` line defines the mountpoint directory. Finally, there's the `Options=` line, with the following options:

- `mode=1777`: This sets the permissions value for the mountpoint directory. The `777` part sets full read, write, and execute permissions for everybody. The `1` part sets the *sticky bit*, which prevents users from deleting each others' files.
- `strictatime`: This causes the kernel to maintain full access-time (`atime`) updates on all files on this partition.
- `nosuid`: If any files on this partition have the **Set User ID** (**SUID**) bit set, this option prevents SUID from doing anything. (The SUID bit is a way to escalate privileges for non-privileged users and can be a security problem if it's set on files that shouldn't have it.)
- `nodev`: This security feature prevents the system from recognizing any character device or block device files that might be on this partition. (You should only see device files in the `/dev/` directory.)

Finally, we have the `[Install]` section, which looks like this:

```
[Install]
WantedBy=local-fs.target
```

So, this partition gets mounted by the `local-fs.target` file, right at the beginning of the bootup process.

Okay—you now have a basic understanding of what a mount unit file looks like. You're now wondering: *Where are the mount unit files for our normal disk partitions?* Ah, I'm glad you asked.

It is possible to manually create mount unit files for your normal disk partitions, but it isn't necessary. In fact, the `systemd.mount` man page recommends against this. Under the `FSTAB` section of this man page, you'll see that it's both possible and *recommended* to configure partitions in the `/etc/fstab` file, just like you've always done. A `systemd` generator will dynamically create the appropriate mount unit files, based on the information that's in the `fstab` file. For example, here's the `fstab` file from the Alma machine:

```
/dev/mapper/almalinux-root /       xfs     defaults        0 0
UUID=42b88c40-693d-4a4b-ac60-ae042c742562 /boot   xfs
defaults        0 0
/dev/mapper/almalinux-swap none    swap    defaults        0 0
```

The two `/dev/mapper` lines indicate that the root filesystem partition and the swap partition are mounted as logical volumes. We also see that the root partition is formatted as an `xfs` partition. The `UUID=` line indicates that the `/boot/` partition is mounted as a normal partition that's designated by its **universally unique identifier** (**UUID**) number. (That makes sense because Linux systems can't boot from a logical volume.)

Okay—the SysV system would just take the information from the `fstab` file and use it directly. As I've already indicated, `systemd` will take this information and use it to dynamically generate the mount unit files under the `/run/systemd/generator/` directory, as we see here:

```
[donnie@localhost ~]$ cd /run/systemd/generator/
[donnie@localhost generator]$ ls -l
total 12
-rw-r--r--. 1 root root 254 Jun 15 14:16  boot.mount
-rw-r--r--. 1 root root 235 Jun 15 14:16 'dev-mapper-almalinux\
x2dswap.swap'
drwxr-xr-x. 2 root root  80 Jun 15 14:16  local-fs.target.
requires
-rw-r--r--. 1 root root 222 Jun 15 14:16  -.mount
drwxr-xr-x. 2 root root  60 Jun 15 14:16  swap.target.requires
[donnie@localhost generator]$
```

It's fairly obvious which of these files correspond to the `/boot/` and `swap` partitions. What isn't so obvious is that the `-.mount` file corresponds to the root filesystem partition. Let's peek into the `boot.mount` file to see what's there:

```
# Automatically generated by systemd-fstab-generator
[Unit]
```

```
SourcePath=/etc/fstab
Documentation=man:fstab(5) man:systemd-fstab-generator(8)
Before=local-fs.target

[Mount]
Where=/boot
What=/dev/disk/by-uuid/42b88c40-693d-4a4b-ac60-ae042c742562
Type=xfs
```

From what you've already seen in the previous example and in the `fstab` file, you should be able to figure out what's going on here.

You might want to see what's in the `-.mount` file, but you can't do that the normal way. If you try it, you'll get this:

```
[donnie@localhost generator]$ cat -.mount
cat: invalid option -- '.'
Try 'cat --help' for more information.
[donnie@localhost generator]$
```

This will happen regardless of which command-line utility you try. That's because the - sign that's in the prefix of the filename makes the Bash shell think that we're dealing with an option switch. To make this work, just precede the filename with `./` so that you'll be working with an absolute path. The command will look like this:

```
[donnie@localhost generator]$ cat ./-.mount
# Automatically generated by systemd-fstab-generator

[Unit]
SourcePath=/etc/fstab
Documentation=man:fstab(5) man:systemd-fstab-generator(8)
Before=local-fs.target

[Mount]
Where=/
What=/dev/mapper/almalinux-root
Type=xfs
[donnie@localhost generator]$
```

Okay—I think that covers it for the mount units. Let's shift over to the Ubuntu Server 20.04 machine and check out one of the backward-compatibility features of `systemd`.

Understanding backward compatibility

You can also use `systemd` generators to control services from old-fashioned SysV `init` scripts. You won't see much of that with Red Hat-type systems, but you will with Debian and Ubuntu systems. (For some strange reason, the Debian and Ubuntu maintainers still haven't converted all of their services over to native `systemd` services.) To demonstrate, disable and stop the normal `ssh` service on the Ubuntu machine by doing:

```
donnie@ubuntu20-04:~$ sudo systemctl disable --now ssh
```

Next, install `Dropbear`, which is a lightweight replacement for the normal OpenSSH package. Do that with the following two commands:

```
sudo apt update
sudo apt install dropbear
```

When the installation completes, you should see that the Dropbear service is already enabled and running:

```
donnie@ubuntu20-04:~$ systemctl status dropbear
  dropbear.service - LSB: Lightweight SSH server
     Loaded: loaded (/etc/init.d/dropbear; generated)
     Active: active (running) since Tue 2021-06-15 16:15:40
UTC; 3h 40min ago
. . .
. . .
```

So far, everything looks normal, except for the part about how it loaded the service from the `/etc/init.d/dropbear init` script. If you look for a `dropbear.service` file in the `/lib/systemd/system/` directory, you won't find it. Instead, you'll see the `dropbear init` script in the `/etc/init.d/` directory:

```
donnie@ubuntu20-04:~$ cd /etc/init.d
donnie@ubuntu20-04:/etc/init.d$ ls -l dropbear
-rwxr-xr-x 1 root root 2588 Jul 27  2019 dropbear
donnie@ubuntu20-04:/etc/init.d$
```

When the Dropbear service starts, `systemd` will generate a `dropbear.service` file in the `/run/systemd/generator.late/` directory, as you see here:

```
donnie@ubuntu20-04:/run/systemd/generator.late$ ls -l dropbear.service
-rw-r--r-- 1 root root 513 Jun 15 16:16 dropbear.service
donnie@ubuntu20-04:/run/systemd/generator.late$
```

This file isn't permanently saved to disk and only lasts as long as the system is running. Look inside, and you'll see that it's just a normal service unit file:

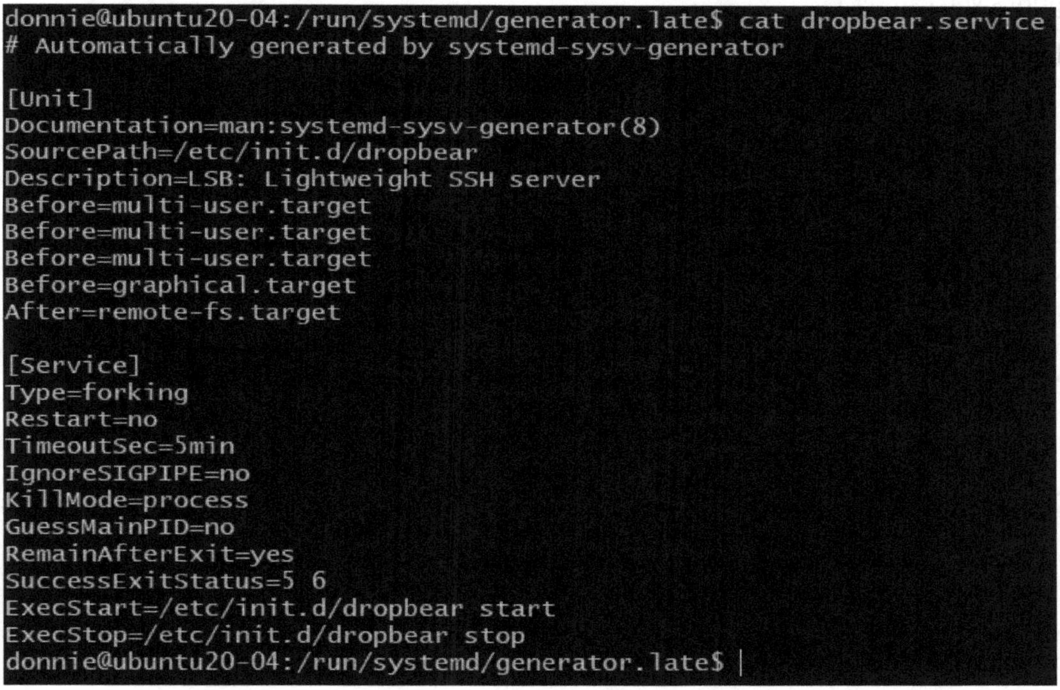

```
donnie@ubuntu20-04:/run/systemd/generator.late$ cat dropbear.service
# Automatically generated by systemd-sysv-generator

[Unit]
Documentation=man:systemd-sysv-generator(8)
SourcePath=/etc/init.d/dropbear
Description=LSB: Lightweight SSH server
Before=multi-user.target
Before=multi-user.target
Before=multi-user.target
Before=graphical.target
After=remote-fs.target

[Service]
Type=forking
Restart=no
TimeoutSec=5min
IgnoreSIGPIPE=no
KillMode=process
GuessMainPID=no
RemainAfterExit=yes
SuccessExitStatus=5 6
ExecStart=/etc/init.d/dropbear start
ExecStop=/etc/init.d/dropbear stop
donnie@ubuntu20-04:/run/systemd/generator.late$ |
```

Figure 8.1 – A generated service file for the Dropbear service

Okay—maybe it's not *completely* normal. (I have no idea why it lists the `Before=multi-user.target` line three different times.) Also, it's missing the `[Install]` section because this is actually meant to be a static service.

If you really want to, you can trick the system into creating a normal `dropbear.service` file in the `/etc/systemd/system/` directory, just by doing a normal `sudo systemctl edit --full dropbear` command. Delete the `SourcePath=/etc/init.d/dropbear` line from the `[Unit]` section because you no longer need it. Next, insert the following line into the `[Service]` section:

```
EnvironmentFile=-/etc/default/dropbear
```

This will allow you to set certain Dropbear parameters in the `/etc/default/dropbear` file, which is already there. (Look at the `Dropbear` man page to see which options you can set.)

Then, add the `[Install]` section, which will look like this:

```
[Install]
WantedBy=multi-user.target
```

Save the file and do a `sudo systemctl daemon-reload` command. Then, enable Dropbear and reboot the VM to verify that it works. Finally, look in the `/run/systemd/generator.late/` directory. You'll see that the `dropbear.service` file is no longer there because `systemd` is no longer using the `dropbear init` script. Instead, it's using the `dropbear.service` file that you just created in the `/etc/systemd/system/` directory. If you need to, you can now edit this service file the same way that you'd edit any other service file.

Summary

Yes indeed, ladies and gents, we've once again covered a lot of ground and looked at some cool stuff. We started with an overview of the SysV and `systemd` boot processes, and then looked at some ways to analyze bootup performance. We then looked at an oddity about the Ubuntu Server bootup configuration. Finally, we wrapped things up by looking at two uses for `systemd` generators.

In the next chapter, we'll use some `systemd` utilities to set certain system parameters. I'll see you there.

Questions

1. How does `systemd` handle a service that still uses an old-fashioned `init` script?

   a. It just uses the `init` scripts directly.

   b. It creates and saves a service unit file in the `/etc/systemd/system/` directory.

   c. It dynamically generates a service unit file in the `/run/systemd/generator.late/` directory.

   d. It won't run a service that only has an `init` script.

2. What is the recommended way of configuring disk partitions on a `systemd` machine?

   a. Manually create a mount unit file for each partition.

   b. Edit the `/etc/fstab` file as you normally would.

   c. Manually create partition device files in the `/dev/` directory.

   d. Use the `mount` utility.

3. Which of the following files represents the root filesystem?

   a. `root.mount`

   b. `-.mount`

   c. `/.mount`

   d. `rootfs.mount`

4. Which of the following commands would show you how long each service takes to start during bootup?

   a. `systemctl blame`

   b. `systemctl time`

   c. `systemd-analyze`

   d. `systemd-analyze time`

   e. `systemd-analyze blame`

Answers

1. c
2. b
3. b
4. e

Further reading

D-Bus documentation:

`https://www.freedesktop.org/wiki/Software/dbus/`

`AccountsService` documentation:

`https://www.freedesktop.org/wiki/Software/AccountsService/`

Cleaning up the Linux startup process:

`https://www.linux.com/topic/desktop/cleaning-your-linux-startup-process/`

9
Setting System Parameters

In this chapter, we'll look at how to use `systemd` utilities to set certain parameters that you used to have to set by either editing configuration files or creating symbolic links. We'll also look at the services that get involved when you use these utilities.

In this chapter, we will cover the following topics:

- Setting the locale parameter
- Setting time and time zone parameters
- Setting the hostname and machine information

If you're ready, let's jump in!

Technical requirements

The technical requirements are the same as in the previous chapters. So, fire up your Ubuntu server and AlmaLinux virtual machines and follow along.

Check out the following link to see the Code in Action video: `https://bit.ly/3xKA7K0`

Setting the locale parameter

Computers are used all over the world, by people of many different cultures and languages. (I know that you already knew that, but I'm telling you anyway.) Fortunately, all major operating systems have ways to accommodate users of almost all languages on Earth. On Unix and Linux systems, the `locale` set of parameters helps us out with that. Let's start by taking a closer look at it.

Understanding the locale

`locale` is a set of parameters that define lots of things that could be important to a user. There are parameters for the user's preferred language, character encoding, currency formats, and several other things.

Normally, `locale` is set when you install the operating system, and you won't have to mess around with it afterward. Linux installers don't have a screen that specifically says *Choose your locale*, but they do have a screen for you to choose a keyboard layout and another for you to choose your time zone. In my case, I would choose the US English keyboard layout and the US Eastern time zone. From that, the installer can figure out that I want to use a locale with settings for the United States.

There are a few differences in how `locale` is implemented on Debian/Ubuntu and Red Hat systems. One difference is in where `locale` is defined. On Red Hat-type systems, such as my Alma virtual machine, and on the openSUSE host machine that I'm using to write this, it's set in the `/etc/locale.conf` file, as we see here:

```
[donnie@localhost ~]$ cd /etc
[donnie@localhost etc]$ ls -l locale.conf
-rw-r--r--. 1 root root 19 May  6 19:06 locale.conf
[donnie@localhost etc]$
```

Inside the `locale.conf` file, we only see this one line:

```
LANG="en_US.UTF-8"
```

So, `locale` is set by the `LANG=` parameter, which consists of two parts. The first part (`en_US`) defines the language and region that I want to use, while the second part (`UTF-8`) defines the character set that I want to use.

Okay, the language and region part are self-explanatory. But what's a character set? Well, it's just the set of characters that the operating system can display. A character set consists of alphanumeric characters, punctuation characters, and other miscellaneous special characters. Just like everything else on a computer, a character – also known as a *code point* – consists of a combination of ones and zeros. A character set defines the combinations of ones and zeros that make up each character. Early characters sets, such as the old EBCDIC and ASCII sets, were limited in the number of characters that they could display. Making things worse is that the design of the EBCDIC set contains flaws that make it hard for programmers to use. UTF-8 was designed to address these shortcomings.

On Ubuntu Server, `locale` is set in the `/etc/default/locale` file. *If* the Ubuntu installer worked correctly – I'll comment more about that in a few moments – the file should look something like this:

```
donnie@ubuntu2:~$ cat /etc/default/locale
LANG=en_US.UTF-8
donnie@ubuntu2:~$
```

The only difference is that in the Ubuntu file, the `locale` specification isn't surrounded by double quotes as it is on the Alma machine.

Next, let's take a look at what's in the `locale` setting. We'll do that with the `locale` utility, like this:

```
[donnie@localhost ~]$ locale
LANG=en_US.UTF-8
LC_CTYPE="en_US.UTF-8"
LC_NUMERIC=en_US.UTF-8
LC_TIME="en_US.UTF-8"
LC_COLLATE="en_US.UTF-8"
LC_MONETARY="en_US.UTF-8"
. . .
. . .
LC_ADDRESS="en_US.UTF-8"
LC_TELEPHONE="en_US.UTF-8"
LC_MEASUREMENT="en_US.UTF-8"
LC_IDENTIFICATION="en_US.UTF-8"
LC_ALL=
[donnie@localhost ~]$
```

To see what these settings are all about, you'll need to consult a `locale` man page. The only catch is that there are several `locale` man pages, as you can see here:

```
[donnie@localhost ~]$ whatis locale
locale (7)           - description of multilanguage support
locale (1)           - get locale-specific information
locale (5)           - describes a locale definition file
locale (1p)          - get locale-specific information
locale (3pm)         - Perl pragma to use or avoid POSIX
locales for built-in operations
[donnie@localhost ~]
```

We want the number `5` man page in this case. Open it by doing:

```
[donnie@localhost ~]$ man 5 locale
```

Only because I can read your mind, I already know what your next question is. *Exactly what do these locale settings affect?* Ah, I'm glad you asked. (And I hope it doesn't seem too creepy that I can read your mind.)

The various `locale` settings affect how utilities such as `awk`, `grep`, and `sort` display their output. On desktop machines, they might be used by the display manager for login purposes. Finally, as I'm about to demonstrate, they're also used by certain shell programming functions. I'll demonstrate this on the Alma machine since it already has several different locales available for use. The Bash shell's `printf` function provides us with the perfect demo. (Note that you might have to modify this demo a bit for your particular locale.)

On the command line of the Alma machine, let's see how `printf` works with the default `en_US.UTF-8` locale set by trying to print out a decimal number:

```
[donnie@localhost ~]$ printf "%.2f\n" 3.14
3.14
[donnie@localhost ~]$
```

This works because in the US, the period (`.`) is the decimal point symbol. In most of Europe, though, the comma (`,`) is the decimal point symbol. We can change just one individual `locale` setting, so let's temporarily change the `LC_NUMERIC` setting to a European one, just to see what happens:

```
[donnie@localhost ~]$ export LC_NUMERIC="en_DK.utf8"
[donnie@localhost ~]$ printf "%.2f\n" 3.14
```

```
-bash: printf: 3.14: invalid number
0,00
[donnie@localhost ~]$
```

This time, `printf` gives us an invalid number error. That's because it's now expecting to see a European number format. If we try this again with a comma, it should work. Let's see if it does:

```
[donnie@localhost ~]$ printf "%.2f\n" 3,14
3,14
[donnie@localhost ~]$
```

Yeah, it works like a champ. And don't worry about that `LC_NUMERIC` setting – it will go away as soon as you log out of the terminal window.

So far, we've only used the legacy `locale` utility, which has been around forever. To bring this back to the `systemd` topic, let's use `localectl` to see what the default `locale` setting is:

```
[donnie@localhost ~]$ localectl
   System Locale: LANG=en_US.UTF-8
       VC Keymap: us
      X11 Layout: us
[donnie@localhost ~]$
```

It works, but it doesn't give us as much information as the legacy `locale` tool.

Next, let's learn how to change the default locale.

Changing the default locale on the Alma machine

We'll continue using the Alma machine for this since it already has several locales installed.

Before you change the default locale, you need to see whether the locale you want is installed on your system. You can do that with either the `locale -a` command or with the `localectl list-locales` command. Either way, you'll get the same output, which will look something like this:

```
[donnie@localhost ~]$ localectl list-locales
C.utf8
en_AG
en_AU
```

```
en_AU.utf8
. . .
. . .
en_ZA.utf8
en_ZM
en_ZW
en_ZW.utf8
[donnie@localhost ~]$
```

There are two ways to change the `locale` setting. You could just open the `/etc/locale.conf` file in your text editor and change the setting, but where's the fun in that? Instead, let's use our handy-dandy `localectl` tool to do this, like so:

```
[donnie@localhost ~]$ sudo localectl set-locale en_CA.utf8
[sudo] password for donnie:
[donnie@localhost ~]$ cat /etc/locale.conf
LANG=en_CA.utf8
[donnie@localhost ~]$
```

So, I've set the machine to Canadian English.

Curiously, the double quotes that were there are now gone. So, I'm guessing that they aren't really needed. Also, note that this setting won't take effect until we log out of the machine and then log back in. Once we do, we'll see that the locale setting has changed, but that the keymap setting hasn't:

```
[donnie@localhost ~]$ localectl
   System Locale: LANG=en_CA.utf8
       VC Keymap: us
      X11 Layout: us
[donnie@localhost ~]$
```

The `localectl list-keymaps` command shows us what keymap settings are available. Let's say that I want to change the keymap to Canadian, to match my locale. I'll do it like this:

```
[donnie@localhost ~]$ sudo localectl set-keymap ca
[donnie@localhost ~]$ sudo localectl set-x11-keymap ca
[donnie@localhost ~]$
```

After logging out and logging back in again, the `localectl` status will look something like this:

```
[donnie@localhost ~]$ localectl
   System Locale: LANG=en_CA.utf8
       VC Keymap: ca
      X11 Layout: ca
[donnie@localhost ~]$
```

Whenever you use `localectl` to change any settings, it's `systemd-localed.service` that does the work. I can't show you the entire `systemd-localed.service` file due to formatting reasons, so I'll just show you the relevant part:

```
[Unit]
Description=Locale Service
Documentation=man:systemd-localed.service(8) man:locale.conf(5)
man:vconsole.conf(5)
Documentation=https://www.freedesktop.org/wiki/Software/
systemd/localed

[Service]
ExecStart=/usr/lib/systemd/systemd-localed
BusName=org.freedesktop.locale1
. . .
. . .
SystemCallArchitectures=native
LockPersonality=yes
ReadWritePaths=/etc
```

I'd like for you to note two things here. First, in the `[Service]` section, note the `BusName=org.freedesktop.locale1` line. There's no `Type=dbus` line, but that's okay. Just having a `BusName=` line automatically makes this a `dbus` type of service. Also, note that there's no `[Install]` section, which makes this a static type of service that we can't enable. Instead, any time that you use `localectl` to change a setting, `localectl` will start the service by sending it a `dbus` message.

Once you've seen what you want to see, feel free to go back to your normal settings.

Next, let's look at how the process is different on Ubuntu.

Changing the default locale on Ubuntu

Ubuntu comes with a variety of `locale` definitions, but you have to build them before you can use them. In the `/etc/locale.gen` file, you'll see a list of locales that you can build. Here's what the top part of the file looks like:

```
donnie@ubuntu20-04:/etc$ cat locale.gen
# This file lists locales that you wish to have built. You can
find a list
# of valid supported locales at /usr/share/i18n/SUPPORTED, and
you can add
# user defined locales to /usr/local/share/i18n/SUPPORTED. If
you change
# this file, you need to rerun locale-gen.

# aa_DJ ISO-8859-1
# aa_DJ.UTF-8 UTF-8
# aa_ER UTF-8
# aa_ER@saaho UTF-8
# aa_ET UTF-8
# af_ZA ISO-8859-1
. . .
. . .
```

If the Ubuntu installer worked correctly, you should see that all but one of the `locale` listings in the file have been commented out. The one that isn't commented out is the one that was built on your system. On the Ubuntu machine that I showed you previously, the `en_US.UTF-8` locale is the only one that isn't commented out, as we see here:

```
. . .
. . .
# en_US ISO-8859-1
# en_US.ISO-8859-15 ISO-8859-15
en_US.UTF-8 UTF-8
# en_ZA ISO-8859-1
# en_ZA.UTF-8 UTF-8
# en_ZM UTF-8
. . .
. . .
```

So, this locale is the only one that was built.

Now, remember, I said that this would be the case *if* the Ubuntu installer worked properly. This virtual machine is the second Ubuntu machine that I set up for this chapter, and the installer did work properly in this instance. When I set up the first Ubuntu virtual machine, the installer did *not* work properly, and no locales were built. When I look at the `/etc/default/locale` file on it, I see this:

```
donnie@ubuntu20-04:~$ cat /etc/default/locale
LANG=C.UTF-8
donnie@ubuntu20-04:~$
```

In this `/etc/locale.gen` file, all the locale listings are commented out, which tells me that no locales were built. So, this Ubuntu machine defaults to the generic `C` locale, which may or may not work in all situations. To change that, I'll open the `/etc/locale.gen` file in my text editor and remove the comment symbol at the front of the `en_US.UTF-8 UTF-8` line. Next, I'll generate the locale, like this:

```
donnie@ubuntu20-04:~$ sudo locale-gen
Generating locales (this might take a while)...
  en_US.UTF-8... done
Generation complete.
donnie@ubuntu20-04:~$
```

Finally, I'll set the default locale and keymap settings the same way that I did on the Alma machine:

```
donnie@ubuntu20-04:~$ sudo localectl set-locale en_US.UTF-8
donnie@ubuntu20-04:~$ sudo localectl set-keymap us
donnie@ubuntu20-04:~$ sudo localectl set-x11-keymap us
donnie@ubuntu20-04:~$
```

After I logged out and logged back in, everything was as it should be, as we see here:

```
donnie@ubuntu20-04:~$ localectl
   System Locale: LANG=en_US.UTF-8
       VC Keymap: us
      X11 Layout: us
donnie@ubuntu20-04:~$
```

Now, I have to say that I have no idea why the Ubuntu installer didn't set the locale correctly for this machine. All I know is that with Ubuntu, I've come to expect an occasional bit of weirdness.

Okay, I think that that about covers it for `locale`. Now, let's talk about setting time and timezone information.

Setting time and timezone parameters

Back in the Stone Age of computing, maintaining accurate time on a computer wasn't all that important. To set the time on my old 8088-powered Sanyo PC clone, I just typed in whatever my watch said. That wasn't the most accurate way of doing things, but it didn't matter. The only real reason to set the computer time at all was to have somewhat accurate timestamps on the files that I created.

Nowadays, accurate timekeeping on computers is vitally important for a lot of reasons. Fortunately, we now have the **Network Time Protocol** (**NTP**), which is a lot more accurate than what my old-fashioned wind-up wristwatch was. The `systemd` suite comes with the `timedatectl` utility and `systemd-timedated.service` to help us out. In this chapter, we'll talk about `timedatectl`, but we'll save discussing `systemd-timedated.service` until *Chapter 17, Understanding systemd and Bootloaders.*

To see the status of your machine's timekeeping, just use `timedatectl`, as I show you here:

```
[donnie@localhost ~]$ timedatectl
               Local time: Sun 2021-06-20 17:34:08 EDT
           Universal time: Sun 2021-06-20 21:34:08 UTC
                 RTC time: Sun 2021-06-20 21:33:06
                Time zone: America/New_York (EDT, -0400)
System clock synchronized: yes
              NTP service: active
          RTC in local TZ: no
[donnie@localhost ~]$
```

`Local time` is the time for my timezone, which is **Eastern Daylight Time** (**EDT**). This is the time that's set in the operating system.

`Universal time` (**UTC**) is the time in Greenwich, England, which is the timezone that's used as a worldwide reference. (UTC used to be known as **Greenwich Mean Time**, or **GMT**.)

`RTC`, which stands for Real-Time Clock, is the time that's set in the computer's hardware clock. You can see that the RTC time nearly matches the UTC time. Of the two, UTC will normally be more accurate, because it periodically fetches the current time from time servers that are either on the Internet or the local network. Somewhat less periodically, the operating system updates the RTC time from UTC. It is possible to configure the RTC time to update from local time, but that will cause problems with setting timezones and knowing when to switch to and from Daylight Savings Time.

We can also see that the system clock is synchronized, that the **NTP service** is active, and that RTC has *not* been set to local time.

In the `timedatectl` man page, you'll find directions on how to manually change the system's time. Years ago, when I first got into Linux, I used to have to do this all the time, because the older NTP services wouldn't automatically set the time if the machine's clock was more than a few minutes off. The modern NTP services work much better. Now, as long as an NTP server is available when you boot the machine, the NTP service will set the time properly, regardless of how far off the machine's clock is. So, there's a good chance that you'll never need to set the time manually.

You also might not ever need to set the timezone manually, because that's normally set up when you install the operating system. However, there might be times when you will, such as if you ever have to move a server from one timezone to another. To do this, you'll have to look at the list of available timezones, like this:

```
[donnie@localhost ~]$ timedatectl list-timezones
Africa/Abidjan
Africa/Accra
Africa/Addis_Ababa
Africa/Algiers
Africa/Asmara
. . .
. . .
```

That's a very long list, so let's use our good friend `grep` to narrow it down. Let's say that I'm only interested in US timezones. My `grep` filter will look like this:

```
[donnie@localhost ~]$ timedatectl list-timezones | grep
'America'
America/Adak
America/Anchorage
America/Anguilla
```

```
America/Antigua
America/Araguaina
America/Argentina/Buenos_Aires
America/Argentina/Catamarca
America/Argentina/Cordoba
America/Argentina/Jujuy
. . .
. . .
```

Okay; that doesn't narrow things down as much as I'd like since `America` covers timezones in both North and South America. Also, instead of choosing the actual name of a timezone, we have to choose a city that's in the desired timezone. In my case, even though I'm down in the southeast corner of Georgia, USA, I have to choose `America/New_York` for my zone because New York just happens to be here in the Eastern timezone. Let's say that for some crazy reason, I've decided to move to the west coast. To change the timezone on my computer, I would do:

```
[donnie@localhost ~]$ sudo timedatectl set-timezone America/
Los_Angeles
[sudo] password for donnie:
[donnie@localhost ~]$
```

The status would now look like this:

```
[donnie@localhost ~]$ timedatectl
               Local time: Sun 2021-06-20 15:13:41 PDT
           Universal time: Sun 2021-06-20 22:13:41 UTC
                 RTC time: Sun 2021-06-20 22:12:40
                Time zone: America/Los_Angeles (PDT, -0700)
System clock synchronized: yes
              NTP service: active
          RTC in local TZ: no
[donnie@localhost ~]$
```

So, I'm now set up for Pacific Daylight Savings Time.

In the `timedatectl` man page, you'll see a couple of commands that work on Ubuntu but don't work on Alma. That's because Ubuntu is configured to use `systemd-timesyncd.service` as its timekeeping service, and Alma is configured to use `chronyd`. On an Ubuntu machine, you can view the status of the timekeeping service like this:

```
donnie@ubuntu20-04:~$ timedatectl timesync-status
       Server: 91.189.94.4 (ntp.ubuntu.com)
Poll interval: 34min 8s (min: 32s; max 34min 8s)
         Leap: normal
      Version: 4
      Stratum: 2
    Reference: 83BC03DC
    Precision: 1us (-23)
Root distance: 52.680ms (max: 5s)
       Offset: -417us
        Delay: 116.531ms
       Jitter: 5.671ms
 Packet count: 14
    Frequency: -5.210ppm
donnie@ubuntu20-04:~$
```

That pretty much covers it for timekeeping. Let's move on to setting `hostname` and machine information.

Setting the hostname and machine information

Setting a proper hostname on a computer is very useful in the business world. It allows the computer to be registered in a **Domain Name Service** (**DNS**) zone, which allows users and administrators to reach the computer via its hostname. After all, it's a lot easier to remember a computer's hostname than to remember its IP address, especially if it's an IPv6 address. (Has anyone in history ever memorized an `IPv6` address?) Before we look at how to set this information, let's learn how to view it. (Note that this hostname can be automatically registered either by using **Dynamic Domain Name Service** (**DDNS**) or by using orchestration tools such as Puppet, Chef, or Ansible.)

Viewing the information

A computer's hostname is set in the `/etc/hostname` file, as we see here on my Alma machine:

```
[donnie@localhost ~]$ cd /etc
[donnie@localhost etc]$ cat hostname
localhost.localdomain
[donnie@localhost etc]$
```

The installers for most Linux operating systems allow you to set your own custom hostname during system installation. I didn't do that for this virtual machine, so it just uses the default `localhost.localdomain`. In this case, we're using a **Fully Qualified Domain Name** (**FQDN**), which consists of two parts. The `localhost` part is the actual hostname, while the `localdomain` part is the network domain to which the computer belongs. On a for-real network, the domain part would be the same for every computer on the network, and the `hostname` part would be unique for each computer. On a home network, or any other time that a whole FQDN isn't required, you could just have a hostname without a domain name.

On an old SysV machine, all you have is just the hostname or FQDN that's been set in the `/etc/hostname` file. With `systemd`, there's a whole lot more. On the Alma machine, let's look at the extra information that the `hostnamectl` command gives us:

```
[donnie@localhost ~]$ hostnamectl
   Static hostname: localhost.localdomain
         Icon name: computer-vm
           Chassis: vm
        Machine ID: 3a17f34dc2694acda37caa478a339408
           Boot ID: 37c1204df0ea439388727dce764f322f
    Virtualization: oracle
  Operating System: ]8;;https://almalinux.org/AlmaLinux 8.3
(Purple Manul)]8;;
       CPE OS Name: cpe:/o:almalinux:almalinux:8.3:GA
            Kernel: Linux 4.18.0-240.22.1.el8_3.x86_64
      Architecture: x86-64
[donnie@localhost ~]$
```

Here's the breakdown:

- `Static hostname`: This is the hostname or FQDN that's set in the `/etc/hostname` file.
- `Icon name`: Certain graphical applications will represent a computer as an icon. `Icon name` is the name that will show up with the icon for this computer. I haven't set `Icon name` on this virtual machine, so it just defaults to `computer-vm`. (The system automatically detected that this is a virtual machine, which explains the `vm` part.)
- `Chassis`: This denotes the type of computing device that we're using. I didn't set this one either, so it just defaults to `vm`, for *virtual machine*. (Most of the time, `systemd` can automatically detect the correct `Chassis` type.)
- `Machine ID`: This hexadecimal number is a unique number that gets assigned to the computer either during system installation or the first bootup. According to the `machine-id` man page, this ID number should be treated as confidential information, and should never be exposed to an untrusted network. This ID number is stored in the `/etc/machine-id` file.
- `Boot ID`: This number changes every time you boot the machine. The `hostnamectl` command pulls this number from the `/proc/sys/kernel/random/boot_id` file.
- `Virtualization`: This line only shows up for virtual machines. I'm running this virtual machine under Oracle VirtualBox, so the parameter shows up here as `oracle`.
- `Operating System`: Information about the operating system comes from the `/etc/os-release` file.
- `CPE OS Name`: This is the name of the operating system in **Common Platform Enumeration** (**CPE**) format. (I won't go into the details about CPE here, but you can read about it by following the link in the *Further reading* section, at the end of this chapter.)
- `Kernel`: This is the version of the running Linux kernel. You can see the same information by using the `uname -r` command.
- `Architecture`: This shows the type of CPU that's in the computer. You can see the same information by using the `uname -m` command.

Just for fun, let's look at the `hostnamectl` output from my host machine, which is running openSUSE 15.2:

```
donnie@localhost:~> hostnamectl
   Static hostname: n/a
Transient hostname: localhost.localdomain
         Icon name: computer-desktop
           Chassis: desktop
        Machine ID: 3d824afd08e94e34afeefca4f6fe0c95
           Boot ID: 32a49640e4fb4bc293b7cf312b80a2d7
  Operating System: openSUSE Leap 15.2
       CPE OS Name: cpe:/o:opensuse:leap:15.2
            Kernel: Linux 5.3.18-lp152.78-default
      Architecture: x86-64
donnie@localhost:~>
```

There are a few differences here that I want you to note. First, there's no `Static hostname` value. Unlike the AlmaLinux installer, the openSUSE installer doesn't put anything into the `/etc/hostname` file if you don't assign a hostname during installation. The file is there, but there's nothing in it, as you can see here:

```
donnie@localhost:~> cat /etc/hostname
donnie@localhost:~>
```

Instead of a `Static hostname` value, we have a `Transient hostname` value. This `Transient hostname` value is a dynamic hostname that's maintained by the Linux kernel. It's normally pulled in from the `Static hostname` property that's set in the `/etc/hostname` file. If nothing is in the `hostname` file, `Transient hostname` will default to `localhost.localdomain`, unless a hostname is assigned by either a DHCP or mDNS server.

Finally, `Icon name` and `Chassis` reflect the fact that this is a desktop machine, running on bare metal. (Today, that bare metal is a 2009 vintage Hewlett-Packard workstation, running with a pair of AMD Opteron quad-core processors. It's old, but it still gets the job done.) Again, the system automatically detected the correct `Chassis` value, just as it did with the virtual machine.

> **Note**
>
> To see the other available `Chassis` types, look at the `machine-info` man page.

Now that we've *viewed* how to view the hostname and machine information, let's learn how to set it.

Setting the information

There are three types of hostnames on `systemd` machines, and you've already seen two of them. In addition to `Static hostname` and `Transient hostname`, there's also `Pretty hostname`. To explain the *pretty* concept, let's look at the criteria for `Static hostname` and `Transient hostname`.

In the man page for the `hostname` file, which you can access with the `man 5 hostname` command, you'll see the criteria for creating hostnames. Here's a breakdown of what it says:

- **Requirement**: The hostname cannot be more than 64 characters in length.
- **Recommendations**:

  A. Only use characters from the old 7-bit ASCII character set. (See the link in the *Further reading* section to see which characters belong to this set.)

  B. All letters should be in lowercase.

  C. Do not have spaces or dots in the hostname. (The only dots should be between the name of the host and the domain name, and between the two parts of the domain name.)

  D. Use a format that's compatible with DNS domain name labels.

So, you're somewhat limited with how you create traditional hostnames. Now, with `Pretty hostname`, you can create a hostname that's more human-friendly, such as `Donnie's Computer`. (Okay, I didn't use a lot of imagination with that one, but you get the point.)

When you use `hostnamectl` to set a hostname, the default is to set all three `hostname` types at once. For example, let's say that I want my computer to be `Donnie's Computer`. Here's the command that I would use:

```
[donnie@localhost ~]$ sudo hostnamectl set-hostname "Donnie's Computer"
[sudo] password for donnie:
[donnie@localhost ~]$
```

Now, let's view the `hostnamectl` information:

```
[donnie@localhost ~]$ hostnamectl
   Static hostname: DonniesComputer
   Pretty hostname: Donnie's Computer
         Icon name: computer-vm
           Chassis: vm
        Machine ID: 3a17f34dc2694acda37caa478a339408
           Boot ID: 7dae067e901a489580025ebdbec19211
    Virtualization: oracle
  Operating System: ]8;;https://almalinux.org/AlmaLinux 8.3
(Purple Manul)]8;;
       CPE OS Name: cpe:/o:almalinux:almalinux:8.3:GA
            Kernel: Linux 4.18.0-240.22.1.el8_3.x86_64
      Architecture: x86-64
[donnie@localhost ~]$
```

Here, you can see that `hostnamectl` automatically converted `Pretty hostname` into the proper format for `Static hostname`, except that it still allows uppercase letters. After I log out and log back in, the new `Static hostname` value will show up in the command prompt, which will look like this:

```
[donnie@localhost ~]$ exit
logout
Connection to 192.168.0.9 closed.
donnie@localhost:~> ssh donnie@192.168.0.9
donnie@192.168.0.9's password:
Last login: Wed Jun 23 13:31:57 2021 from 192.168.0.222
[donnie@DonniesComputer ~]$
```

Okay, that's great for a home computer, but it's not so good for a business network. This time, let's create an FQDN that's suitable for use with DNS. Let's say that my local network has been set up as the `tevault.com` domain and that I want to name this computer `development-1`. My command to create the FQDN would look like this:

```
[donnie@DonniesComputer ~]$ sudo hostnamectl set-hostname
development-1.tevault.com
[sudo] password for donnie:
[donnie@DonniesComputer ~]$
```

Use `hostnamectl` again, and you'll see that `Pretty hostname` is now gone:

```
[donnie@DonniesComputer ~]$ hostnamectl
   Static hostname: development-1.tevault.com
         Icon name: computer-vm
           Chassis: vm
        Machine ID: 3a17f34dc2694acda37caa478a339408
           Boot ID: 7dae067e901a489580025ebdbec19211
    Virtualization: oracle
  Operating System: ]8;;https://almalinux.org/AlmaLinux 8.3
(Purple Manul)]8;;
       CPE OS Name: cpe:/o:almalinux:almalinux:8.3:GA
            Kernel: Linux 4.18.0-240.22.1.el8_3.x86_64
      Architecture: x86-64
[donnie@DonniesComputer ~]$
```

After I log out and log back in again, I'll see the proper DNS-friendly hostname in the command prompt:

```
[donnie@DonniesComputer ~]$ exit
logout
Connection to 192.168.0.9 closed.
donnie@localhost:~> ssh donnie@192.168.0.9
donnie@192.168.0.9's password:
Last login: Wed Jun 23 14:34:24 2021 from 192.168.0.222
[donnie@development-1 ~]$
```

If I just want to set a `Pretty hostname` value, I can do it like this:

```
[donnie@development-1 ~]$ sudo hostnamectl set-hostname
--pretty "Development 1"
[sudo] password for donnie:
[donnie@development-1 ~]$
```

There are several other things that you can set with `hostnamectl`, which you can see on the `machine-info` man page. The `hostnamectl` man page shows you the commands for setting these extra parameters. For example, let's set the location of this virtual machine to my current location, which is the teeming metropolis of Saint Marys, Georgia:

```
[donnie@development-1 ~]$ sudo hostnamectl set-location "Saint
Marys GA"
[donnie@development-1 ~]$
```

The location will now show up in the output of `hostnamectl`. Also, the first time you use `hostnamectl` to add any of these additional parameters, it will create the `/etc/machine-info` file, which wasn't there previously. Here's what mine looks like now that I've added a `Pretty hostname` value and location:

```
[donnie@development-1 ~]$ cat /etc/machine-info
PRETTY_HOSTNAME="Development 1"
LOCATION="Saint Marys GA"
[donnie@development-1 ~]$
```

Cool. Saint Marys, Georgia, is now world-famous.

As we've already seen with `localectl`, using `hostnamectl` to change a parameter invokes a dbus-type service. In this case, it's `systemd-hostnamed.service`. Here's what it looks like:

```
[Unit]
Description=Hostname Service
Documentation=man:systemd-hostnamed.service(8) man:hostname(5) man:machine-info(5)
Documentation=https://www.freedesktop.org/wiki/Software/systemd/hostnamed

[Service]
ExecStart=/usr/lib/systemd/systemd-hostnamed
BusName=org.freedesktop.hostname1
WatchdogSec=3min
CapabilityBoundingSet=CAP_SYS_ADMIN
PrivateTmp=yes
PrivateDevices=yes
PrivateNetwork=yes
ProtectSystem=strict
ProtectHome=yes
ProtectControlGroups=yes
ProtectKernelTunables=yes
ProtectKernelModules=yes
MemoryDenyWriteExecute=yes
RestrictRealtime=yes
RestrictNamespaces=yes
RestrictAddressFamilies=AF_UNIX
RestrictSUIDSGID=yes
SystemCallFilter=@system-service sethostname
SystemCallErrorNumber=EPERM
SystemCallArchitectures=native
LockPersonality=yes
ReadWritePaths=/etc
```

Figure 9.1 – The systemd-hostnamed.service file

Note that a lot of security-related parameters have been set, which gives this service pretty much the same protection as a good mandatory access control system such as SELinux. The `ProtectHome=yes` line and the `ProtectSystem=strict` line make most of this machine's filesystem inaccessible to this service, but the `ReadWritePaths=/etc` line at the bottom provides an exception. The `ReadWritePaths=/etc` line allows the service to read from or write to files in the `/etc/` directory. (`systemd-localed.service`, which we looked at in the *Changing the default locale on the Alma machine* section, is set up the same way, but I neglected to point that out at the time.)

Okay, I think that pretty much wraps it up for this chapter. Let's summarize and then move on.

Summary

As always, we've seen some cool stuff in this chapter. We started by looking at what locales are and how to set the default locale on a `systemd` system. Then, we saw how to set the time and timezones, and finished up by setting hostnames and machine information. In the next chapter, we'll give your brain a bit of a rest by looking at something a bit easier – that is, we'll look at the various ways to shut down or reboot your system. I'll see you there!

Questions

1. Which of the following commands shows you what locales are installed on your system?

   A. `systemctl list-locales`

   B. `locale list-locales`

   C. `localectl list-locales`

   D. `localectl -a`

2. What type of service gets invoked when you use either `localectl` or `hostnamectl` to set a parameter?

   A. `dbus`

   B. `oneshot`

   C. `notify`

   D. `forking`

3. What happens if your computer has nothing in its `hostname` file?

   A. It sets the default `Static hostname` value to `localhost.localdomain` or to whatever it might get from a local DHCP or mDNS server.

   B. The computer will have no hostname.

   C. It sets `Pretty hostname` to `localhost.localdomain`.

   D. It sets the default `Transient hostname` value to `localhost.localdomain` or to whatever it might get from a local DHCP or mDNS server.

4. What time does the computer's hardware clock normally show?

   A. Local time

   B. UTC time

Answers

1. C
2. A
3. D
4. B

Further reading

To learn more about the topics that were covered in this chapter, take a look at the following resources:

- Setting the locale:

  `https://www.tecmint.com/set-system-locales-in-linux/`

- Defining the locale and language settings:

  `https://www.shellhacks.com/linux-define-locale-language-settings/`

- Eric S. Raymond's Jargon File entry for EBCDIC:

  `http://www.catb.org/jargon/html/E/EBCDIC.html`

- The ASCII character set:

  `http://www.asciitable.com/`

- **Common Platform Enumeration** (CPE):

  `https://csrc.nist.gov/projects/security-content-automation-protocol/specifications/cpe`

- Configuring hostnames:

  `https://access.redhat.com/documentation/en-us/red_hat_enterprise_linux/7/html/networking_guide/ch-configure_host_names#sec-Recommended_Naming_Practices`

10 Understanding Shutdown and Reboot Commands

By this point in your career, you most likely know the basic commands for shutting down or rebooting a text-mode Linux server. In this chapter, we'll look at some things that are more specific to the systemd method. So, bear with me. There's a chance that you might learn something that you didn't know before.

Specific topics in this chapter include the following:

- Shutting down with `systemctl`
- Halting with `systemctl`
- Rebooting with `systemctl`
- Using `shutdown` instead of `systemctl`

If you're ready, let's go.

Technical requirements

Although either of your virtual machines will work equally well for this, all you need is a text-mode virtual machine, so there's no need to fire up the Alma desktop virtual machine if you don't want to. Toward the end of the chapter, we'll be working with some shell scripts. If you don't want to type them in yourself, simply download them from our Git repository.

Check out the following link to see the Code in Action video: `https://bit.ly/3G6nbkD`

> **Note**
>
> Throughout this book, I've been using AlmaLinux 8 as a replacement for the soon-to-be discontinued CentOS 8. (Of course, depending upon when you're reading this, CentOS 8 may have already been discontinued.)
>
> A few days before I started writing this chapter, the stable release of Rocky Linux 8 finally became available. Using it is the same as using AlmaLinux, or any other RHEL 8 clone for that matter. However, if security is your thing, Rocky does have one huge advantage. Unlike the other RHEL 8 clones, Rocky comes with a set of OpenSCAP profiles that you can apply either during or after the installation of the operating system. As things stand now, Rocky Linux is the only RHEL 8 clone that fully supports OpenSCAP. (If you want to learn more about OpenSCAP, be sure to check out my other book, *Mastering Linux Security and Hardening*, also from Packt Publishing.)

All right, if you're ready, let's get cracking.

Shutting down with systemctl

Shutting down a systemd system is really easy, but there are a few options that you might not know about. Let's start with the basic command to shut down and power off a machine, which looks like this:

```
donnie@ubuntu20-04:~$ sudo systemctl poweroff
```

So, what exactly is happening here? If you open the `systemctl` man page and scroll down to the `poweroff` item, you'll see that this command starts `poweroff.target`, which looks like this:

```
[Unit]
Description=Power-Off
Documentation=man:systemd.special(7)
DefaultDependencies=no
```

```
Requires=systemd-poweroff.service
After=systemd-poweroff.service
AllowIsolate=yes
JobTimeoutSec=30min
JobTimeoutAction=poweroff-force

[Install]
Alias=ctrl-alt-del.target
```

In the `[Unit]` section, you see that this *requires* `systemd-poweroff.service`, which means that this service will now get started. At the bottom of the `[Unit]` section, you will see two new parameters. The `JobTimeoutSec=30min` line gives systemd plenty of time to gracefully shut down all running services before it turns off the power. The `JobTimeoutAction=poweroff-force` line means that if all of the services haven't gracefully shut down within that 30-minute window, then systemd will turn off the power regardless. In the `[Install]` section, we see the `Alias=ctrl-alt-del.target` line. That seems a bit odd because the *Ctrl* + *Alt* + *Del* key sequence is for rebooting a machine, not for shutting it down. It's not just an Ubuntu oddity this time – it's the same way on the Alma machine. However, this is easy to explain. It's just that if the system hangs hard during a shutdown, doing the *Ctrl* + *Alt* + *Del* key sequence 7 times within 2 seconds will force the machine to do a reboot. You can then just boot to the GRUB command prompt, and shut the machine down from there. (You can read more about *Ctrl* + *Alt* + *Del* under the **SIGINT** section of the `systemd` man page.)

Remember, using *Ctrl* + *Alt* + *Del* to reboot a machine doesn't require root privileges. That's not normally a problem, because mission-critical servers should be locked away in a secure room where only authorized personnel can get to them. Even so, you might want to place restrictions on the ability to reboot servers. If this is the case, disable the *Ctrl* + *Alt* + *Del* reboot feature by masking `ctrl-alt-del.target`. The command to do that is:

```
donnie@ubuntu20-04:~$ sudo systemctl mask ctrl-alt-del.target
```

Now, you can do *Ctrl* + *Alt* + *Del* key sequences until the end of time, and nothing will happen.

On a desktop machine with a graphical interface, the *Ctrl* + *Alt* + *Del* key sequence is controlled by the desktop configuration, which might be different across various desktop environments. On the Alma machine with its Gnome 3 environment, doing *Ctrl* + *Alt* + *Del* brings up the normal shutdown menu, which looks like this:

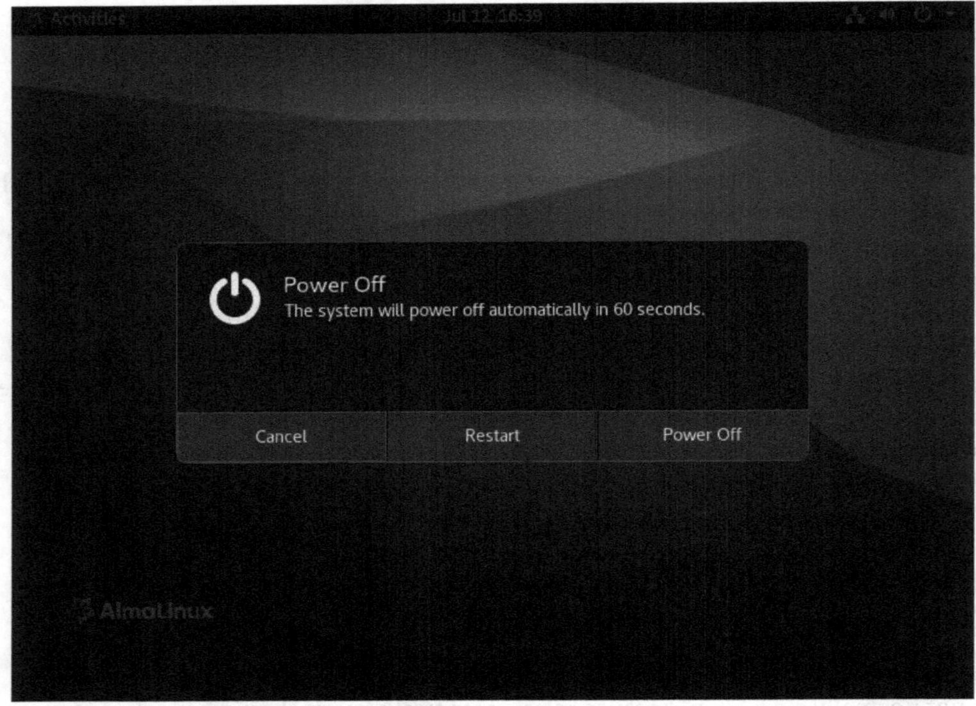

Figure 10.1 – The Gnome 3 Power Off menu on the Alma machine

Masking `ctrl-alt-del.target` on a desktop machine does not affect this behavior.

`systemd-poweroff.service` only has a `[Unit]` section, which we see here:

```
[Unit]
Description=Power-Off
Documentation=man:systemd-halt.service(8)
DefaultDependencies=no
Requires=shutdown.target umount.target final.target
After=shutdown.target umount.target final.target
SuccessAction=poweroff-force
```

This service requires `shutdown.target`, `umount.target`, and `final.target`. If we look in the unit files for these targets, we can see that they don't appear to do anything. For example, here's what the `shutdown.target` file looks like:

```
[Unit]
Description=Shutdown
Documentation=man:systemd.special(7)
DefaultDependencies=no
RefuseManualStart=yes
```

Our good friend `strings` shows us that `shutdown.target` is defined in the `systemd` executable file, as we see here:

```
donnie@ubuntu20-04:/lib/systemd$ strings systemd | grep
'shutdown.target'
shutdown.target
donnie@ubuntu20-04:/lib/systemd$
```

The same thing is true of `umount.target`, as we see here:

```
donnie@ubuntu20-04:/lib/systemd$ strings systemd | grep
'umount.target'
umount.target
donnie@ubuntu20-04:/lib/systemd$
```

Finally, we have `final.target`, as we see here:

```
[Unit]
Description=Final Step
Documentation=man:systemd.special(7)
DefaultDependencies=no
RefuseManualStart=yes
After=shutdown.target umount.target
```

Although it also doesn't appear to be doing anything, it's not defined in the `systemd` executable file, as we see here:

```
donnie@ubuntu20-04:/lib/systemd$ strings systemd | grep 'final.
target'
donnie@ubuntu20-04:/lib/systemd$
```

So, I don't know where `final.target` is defined, but that's okay. For our current topic, it's not important. I also couldn't find any information about what `final.target` actually does, other than this short blurb in the `systemd.special` man page:

"A special target unit that is used during the shutdown logic and may be used to pull in late services after all normal services are already terminated and all mounts unmounted."

I don't know what those *late services* are supposed to be, but again, that's okay. For our present discussion, it doesn't matter.

According to the `systemctl` man page, a `systemctl poweroff` command is supposed to send a `wall` message to all users who are logged into the system. However, that is incorrect. No message gets sent out, and there's no option switch to make it happen.

Normally, a `systemctl poweroff` command would shut down running services and unmount all mounted filesystems in an orderly manner. Using the `--force` option would shut down the system without taking time to shut down the services first. This could be handy if you have a service that's hung up and refuses to stop normally. Using the `--force` option *twice* would shut down the system without taking time to either shut down services normally or to unmount any mounted filesystems. Of course, this isn't recommended unless it's an absolute emergency, because it could corrupt your filesystem and cause data loss. On the other hand, using `--force --force` could be handy if the `systemd` process has crashed. This is because `--force --force` allows the `systemctl` executable to shut down the system without having to contact the `systemd` process.

Okay, let's *power off* the discussion about `poweroff`. Let's now talk briefly about halting a system.

Halting with systemctl

Using a `sudo systemctl halt` command halts the operating system, but it doesn't power down the computer. Because I can read your mind, I know that you're saying, *But Donnie. Why would I want to halt the operating system but leave the computer running?* Well, I don't know. That's something that I've never figured out in my entire Linux career.

But seriously, `halt.target` works pretty much the same as `poweroff.target`. So, I'll leave it to you to look at the associated unit files, if you really want to.

All right, let's *reboot* this discussion by talking about rebooting.

Rebooting with systemctl

You'll never guess what the command is to reboot a system. Okay, if you said `sudo systemctl reboot`, then you win today's grand prize. (Sadly, the grand prize consists of absolutely nothing, except for the good feeling that comes with giving a correct answer.)

Again, I'll leave it to you to look at the associated `reboot.target` files, because this also works pretty much the same as `poweroff.target`. One difference to note is that this time, the `Alias=ctrl-alt-del.target` line in the `[Install]` section actually does something for us. On a text mode machine, doing a *Ctrl* + *Alt* + *Del* sequence at the local terminal will reboot the machine. So yes, that old three-finger salute is still with us. (You don't even need to enter an admin password to make this work. So, fortunately, doing *Ctrl* + *Alt* + *Del* from a remote terminal doesn't work.) If you want to try this on your VirtualBox virtual machine, you'll need to click on the virtual machine's **Input** menu, click on **Keyboard**, and then click on **Insert Ctrl-Alt-Del**.

Once again, I'm reading your mind. I know that you're saying, *But Donnie. These systemctl commands don't give us the cool options that we used to have with the old shutdown commands.* Yeah, you're right, which is why I still use the old `shutdown` commands. So, let's talk about them next, shall we?

Using shutdown instead of systemctl

The old `shutdown` commands that we used on SysV systems came with some cool options. We could schedule a shutdown or reboot for some time in the future, cancel a scheduled shutdown, and broadcast a message about an impending shutdown or reboot to all users who were logged into the system. With the `systemctl` commands, you can't do any of that. Fortunately, the old `shutdown` options are still with us, in the form of a symbolic link that points to the `systemctl` executable, as we see here:

```
donnie@ubuntu20-04:~$ cd /usr/sbin/
donnie@ubuntu20-04:/usr/sbin$ ls -l shutdown
lrwxrwxrwx 1 root root 14 May 27 11:16 shutdown -> /bin/
systemctl
donnie@ubuntu20-04:/usr/sbin$
```

Even though you can't use the old `shutdown` options with `systemctl`, you can use them with the `shutdown` link that points to `systemctl`. (Strange, but true.) Now, I realize that you old-timers might know these `shutdown` commands already, and that's okay. You won't hurt my feelings if you're tempted to just skim over this. On the other hand, if you bear with me until the end, you'll see some cool stuff that you might not currently know about. If you're a Linux newbie, you're almost sure to find some useful information here. So, let's go.

Whenever you do a `shutdown` command, you can specify the time at which you want the shutdown to occur. For example, to perform an immediate shutdown, just do:

```
donnie@ubuntu20-04:~$ sudo shutdown now
```

On an old SysV system, this command would have just halted the operating system. To power down the machine, you would have had to use the `-h` option. On a systemd machine, this command powers off the machine, so the `-h` option switch is no longer necessary. (Curiously, the `-h` switch is still mentioned in the `shutdown` man page, even though it no longer does anything.)

You can also specify the time at which you want the shutdown to occur, using the 24-hour time format. For example, to shut down the machine at 6:00 P.M., do:

```
donnie@ubuntu20-04:~$ sudo shutdown 18:00
Shutdown scheduled for Sun 2021-06-27 18:00:00 EDT, use
'shutdown -c' to cancel.
donnie@ubuntu20-04:~$
```

At about 25 minutes before the scheduled shutdown time, the system will start sending broadcast messages to all logged-in users, as we see here for Goldie:

```
goldie@ubuntu20-04:~$
Broadcast message from root@ubuntu20-04 on pts/0 (Sun 2021-06-
27 17:50:00 EDT):

The system is going down for poweroff at Sun 2021-06-27
18:00:00 EDT!


Broadcast message from root@ubuntu20-04 on pts/0 (Sun 2021-06-
27 17:51:00 EDT):

The system is going down for poweroff at Sun 2021-06-27
18:00:00 EDT!
```

The system will continue sending out this broadcast message until the shutdown actually occurs. The frequency with which the message gets sent out depends upon how soon the shutdown is scheduled to occur. Within the last ten minutes, the message will get sent out every minute. Fortunately, Goldie can regain use of the command prompt by just hitting the *Enter* key, which will allow her to finish what she's doing. (In case you're wondering, *Goldie* is the name of my youngest kitty. You'll never guess what color she is.)

If you change your mind and want to cancel the shutdown, use the `-c` option switch, as shown here:

```
donnie@ubuntu20-04:~$ sudo shutdown -c
donnie@ubuntu20-04:~$
```

You can also send out your own customized broadcast message by simply placing it after the `shutdown` command:

```
donnie@ubuntu20-04:~$ sudo shutdown 18:45 "At 6:45 PM, this
server will go down for maintenance. So, get your work done and
log off."
Shutdown scheduled for Sun 2021-06-27 18:45:00 EDT, use
'shutdown -c' to cancel.
donnie@ubuntu20-04:~$
```

At five minutes before the scheduled shutdown time, a `nologin` file will get created in the `/run/` directory, as we see here:

```
donnie@ubuntu20-04:/run$ ls -l no*
-rw-r--r-- 1 root root 121 Jun 27 18:40 nologin
donnie@ubuntu20-04:/run$
```

This will prevent any other users from logging in. The next time you boot up this system, this `nologin` file will get deleted.

Any time you schedule a future shutdown job, a `scheduled` file gets created in the `/run/systemd/shutdown/` directory. Look inside the file, and you'll see something like this:

```
donnie@ubuntu20-04:/run/systemd/shutdown$ cat scheduled
USEC=1624917600000000
WARN_WALL=1
MODE=poweroff
donnie@ubuntu20-04:/run/systemd/shutdown$
```

The `USEC=` line specifies the time for the scheduled shutdown, in Unix epoch format. If you don't know when the system is scheduled to shut down and you want to find out, you can use a shell script to translate this to human-readable format. The first example of this type of script uses a `perl` command to do the actual translation. Here's what it looks like:

```
#!/usr/bin/bash

if [ -f /run/systemd/shutdown/scheduled ]; then
        perl -wne 'm/^USEC=(\d+)\d{6}$/ and printf("Shutting down at: %s\n", scalar localtime $1)' < /run/systemd/shutdown/scheduled
else
        echo "No shutdown is scheduled."
fi
exit
```

Save the file as `scheduled_shutdown_1.sh`, and set the executable permission, like this:

```
donnie@ubuntu20-04:~$ chmod u+x scheduled_shutdown_1.sh
donnie@ubuntu20-04:~$
```

Schedule a shutdown for whatever time you want, and then run the script. The output should look something like this:

```
donnie@ubuntu20-04:~$ ./scheduled_shutdown_1.sh
Shutting down at: Tue Jun 29 19:05:00 2021
donnie@ubuntu20-04:~$
```

If `perl` isn't installed on your system or if you'd prefer to not use `perl`, then you can use `awk` to perform the translation. The script with `awk` looks like this:

```
#/bin/bash
if [ -f /run/systemd/shutdown/scheduled ]; then
        date -d "@$( awk -F '=' '/USEC/{ $2=substr($2,1,10); print $2 }' /run/systemd/shutdown/scheduled )"
else
        echo "No shutdown is scheduled."
fi
exit
```

Both of these scripts are set up to search for the `scheduled` file, and to only run the translation command if the `scheduled` file exists. If the file doesn't exist, the script will inform you of that, and then exit gracefully.

To reboot a machine, just use `shutdown` with the `-r` option, like this:

```
donnie@ubuntu20-04:~$ sudo shutdown -r now
```

You can schedule a reboot and send custom broadcast messages the same way that you would do for a shutdown operation.

> **Note**
>
> You old-timers might remember that on SysV systems, there was also an `f` option that you could use with the `-r` option. Doing a `sudo shutdown -rf now` command would reboot the machine, and would cause an `fsck` operation to be performed on the machine's filesystems before mounting them. That `f` option is now gone, because systemd systems are set up to always do an `fsck` operation on all supported filesystems every time you boot the machine. This happens because `systemd-fsckd.service` runs as part of the boot-up process if any supported filesystems are detected. (By *supported* filesystems, I mean that `fsck` works on the `ext4` filesystem that's the default for Ubuntu, but it doesn't work on the `xfs` filesystem, which is the default for RHEL and RHEL clones. So, don't be too disappointed if you see that `systemd-fsckd.service` doesn't run on your Alma machine.)

In *Chapter 7, Understanding systemd Timers*, we learned how to set up a job to automatically run when you boot up your machine. Now, let's see how to set up a job to run when you shut down the machine.

Running a job before shutting down

Let's say that you want to have a job automatically run every time you shut down your computer. (I'll let you use your imagination about what kind of job that could be.) To set that up, just create your own custom service that's `WantedBy the shutdown.target`. Let's check out how.

We'll demonstrate this by creating a dummy shell script that goes along with our new service. In the /usr/local/bin/ directory, create the script.sh file with the following contents:

```
#!/bin/bash
# Run script with systemd only at shutdown, and not for reboot.
systemctl list-jobs | egrep -q 'reboot.target.*start' && echo
"Testing myscript.service for reboot" > /root/reboot_test.txt
systemctl list-jobs | egrep -q 'shutdown.target.*start' && echo
"Testing myscript.service for shutdown" > /root/shutdown_test.
txt
```

The first systemctl list-jobs command will search through the list of running jobs, looking for the reboot.target.*start* text string. If the text string is found, the && operator will cause the echo command to run. The echo output will go to the reboot_test.txt file in the /root/ directory. However, this will never actually happen, because this service will only get activated by shutdown.target, and not by reboot.target. The next line is the same, except it's looking for the shutdown.target.*start* text string. If that text string is found, the echo command will send its output to the /root/shutdown_test.txt file. After you've saved the file, set the executable permission by doing:

```
donnie@ubuntu20-04:/usr/local/bin$ sudo chmod u+x script.sh
```

Next, use sudo systemctl edit --full --force myscript.service to create the service. Add the following contents:

```
[Unit]
Description=Run this service only when shutting down
DefaultDependencies=no
Conflicts=reboot.target
Before=poweroff.target halt.target shutdown.target
Requires=poweroff.target

[Service]
Type=oneshot
ExecStart=/usr/local/bin/script.sh
RemainAfterExit=yes

[Install]
WantedBy=shutdown.target
```

The `ExecStart=` line activates our shell script. In the `[Install]` section, we see that this service is `WantedBy` the `shutdown.target`.

Once you've saved this file, do the normal `sudo systemctl daemon-reload` and `sudo systemctl enable myscript.service` operations. To test things out, first shut the machine down and then start it back up. You should now see the `shutdown_test.txt` file in the `/root/` directory:

```
donnie@ubuntu20-04:~$ sudo ls -l /root/
[sudo] password for donnie:
total 8
-rw-r--r-- 1 root root   38 Jun 29 18:19 shutdown_test.txt
drwxr-xr-x 3 root root 4096 Jun  3 20:20 snap
donnie@ubuntu20-04:~$ sudo cat /root/shutdown_test.txt
Testing myscript.service for shutdown
donnie@ubuntu20-04:~$
```

Next, reboot the machine. This time, you'll see that no file gets created, proving that this service will run only for a shutdown, and not for a reboot.

Okay, I think that's about it. Let's wrap this baby up.

Summary

As usual, we've seen some cool stuff in this chapter. We started out by looking at the `systemctl` commands for shutting down, halting, or rebooting a machine. We then saw that the old-style `shutdown` commands still work, and will allow you to use the scheduling and messaging features that you've always been used to using. We ended by creating a service that would run a job whenever you shut down the machine.

I realize that a lot of you might already have been familiar with a lot of what I presented in this chapter, but I did present some cool things at the end, and I hope that you enjoyed it.

This concludes part 1 of *Mastering systemd*. In part 2, we'll delve into the mysteries of *cgroups*. I'll see you there.

Questions

1. What is the command for rebooting a Linux machine?

   a) `sudo shutdown now`

   b) `sudo systemctl -r now`

   c) `sudo systemctl reboot now`

   d) `sudo systemctl reboot`

   e) `sudo shutdown --reboot`

2. What happens 5 minutes before a scheduled shutdown time?

   a) The `scheduled` file gets created in the `/run/systemd/shutdown/` directory.

   b) The `scheduled` file gets created in the `/run/` directory.

   c) The `nologin` file gets created in the `/run/systemd/shutdown/` directory.

   d) The `nologin` file gets created in the `/run/` directory.

3. When you schedule a future shutdown, which of the following happens?

   a) A `nologin` file gets created in the `/run/systemd/shutdown/` directory.

   b) A `scheduled` file gets created in the `/run/systemd/shutdown/` directory.

   c) A `nologin` file gets created in the `/run/systemd/` directory.

   d) A `scheduled` file gets created in the `/run/` directory.

4. What could happen if you do a `sudo systemctl poweroff --force --force` command?

   a) Using the `--force` option twice would result in an error message.

   b) The system will ignore the second `--force` option.

   c) You could damage your filesystem, which could result in data loss.

   d) If the first `--force` doesn't ensure that the `power off` command works, the second one surely will.

Answers

1. d
2. d
3. b
4. c

Further reading

Run a script on a systemd system at shutdown: Note that the script doesn't work as it's shown in this article. This is because it has you create the script and save the output files in the `/tmp/` directory, which gets cleaned out every time you shut down the machine:

`https://www.golinuxcloud.com/run-script-with-systemd-at-shutdown-only-rhel/`

How to check the time for a delayed shutdown: You can find the answers to lots of your Linux admin questions with simple DuckDuckGo searches, as I did with this. Learn how to use DuckDuckGo. It can be a Linux administrator's best friend:

`https://unix.stackexchange.com/questions/229745/systemd-how-to-check-scheduled-time-of-a-delayed-shutdown`

Section 2: Understanding cgroups

In this part, you will learn what cgroups are and how they can help control resource usage and enhance security.

This part of the book comprises the following chapters:

11
Understanding cgroups Version 1

In this chapter, we'll introduce you to **Control Groups**, more commonly called `cgroups`. (More specifically, we'll be looking at cgroups Version 1.) You'll learn what cgroups are, how they're constructed, and how you can benefit by taking advantage of them. We'll also briefly look at the history of cgroups.

Now, I have to tell you that discussing cgroups can become quite complex and convoluted. You might have already seen some online cgroups tutorials that do nothing but make your head hurt. My goal is to strip away as much complexity as possible and provide you with just enough information to help you manage resources on a systemd machine.

Specific topics include:

- Understanding the history of cgroups
- Understanding the purpose of cgroups
- Understanding the structure of cgroups Version 1
- Understanding the cgroup Version 1 filesystem

All right – if you're ready, let's get started!

Technical requirements

To make things more interesting, we'll use the same Alma virtual machine that we set up in *Chapter 5, Creating and Editing Services*. You might remember that on that virtual machine, we set up one WordPress container service that's running in system mode, and another WordPress container service that running in user mode. If you don't have that virtual machine, go back to *Chapter 5, Creating and Editing Services*, and follow the steps for creating the WordPress container services. As always, this chapter will be hands-on. So fire up that virtual machine, and let's dig in.

Check out the following link to see the Code in Action video: `https://bit.ly/3ltmKsO`

Understanding the history of cgroups

This might shock you, but the cgroups technology didn't start as a part of systemd, and it wasn't invented by Red Hat. It's actually a component in the Linux kernel that can run on non-systemd Linux distros. A pair of Google engineers started cgroups development back in 2006, four years before Red Hat engineers started developing systemd. The first enterprise-grade Linux distro to include cgroups technology was *Red Hat Enterprise Linux 6*, which ran a hybrid upstart/SysV setup instead of systemd. Using cgroups on RHEL 6 was optional, and you had to jump through some hoops to set them up.

Nowadays, cgroups are enabled by default on all of the major enterprise-type Linux distros and are tightly integrated with systemd. RHEL 7 was the first enterprise distro to use systemd and was also the first enterprise distro to always have cgroups enabled.

There are currently two versions of the cgroups technology. Version 1 works well for the most part, but it does have some flaws, which I won't get into here. Version 2 was developed in 2013, primarily by an engineer at Facebook. In this chapter, I'll confine the discussion to Version 1. Even though Version 2 might be much better, it still hasn't been widely adopted, and many container technologies still depend upon Version 1. The current versions of all enterprise-grade Linux distros run with Version 1 by default.

> **Note**
>
> Fedora, Arch, and Debian 11 are the only Linux distros of which I'm aware that run cgroups Version 2 by default. I've also seen some speculation that the next non-LTS version of Ubuntu, Ubuntu 21.10, is supposed to come with Version 2. (Of course, you'll likely know that for sure by the time you read this.) So, which one should you learn about? Well, if you're an administrator working with any of the major enterprise-grade Linux distros, you'll want to concentrate on learning Version 1. If you're a developer, you'll probably want to start learning Version 2, because Version 2 is the future.

Now that we've covered the history of cgroups, I suppose that I should now make some history by explaining what they are and why we need them. So, allow me to do just that.

Understanding the purpose of cgroups

Back in the days of single-core CPUs, resource management wasn't such a big deal. Servers generally came with anywhere from one to four single-core CPUs installed, so they were already limited in the number of services that could run simultaneously. All we needed for resource management back then were simple tools such as `nice`, `renice`, and `ulimit`.

Nowadays, it's an entirely different story. Servers now come with one or more multi-core CPUs and gobs of memory. (The current king-of-the-hill server CPU is the AMD Epyc, which now comes in a 64-core variety that can run 128 simultaneous threads. Yeah, that's enough to make us hard-core geeks salivate.) Although it might seem counter-intuitive, resource management on these beasts is more important than it was on the old systems. That's because one server can now run multiple services, multiple virtual machines, multiple containers, and multiple user accounts all at the same time. A whole roomful of the old physical servers that could only run one or two services can now be replaced by just one physical server. Those simple resource management tools that we used to use still have their uses, but we also now need something a lot more powerful to ensure that all processes and users play nice with each other. Enter cgroups.

With cgroups, an administrator can:

- Manage resource usage by either processes or users.
- Keep track of resource usage by users on multi-tenant systems to provide accurate billing.
- More easily isolate running processes from each other. This not only makes for better security but also allows us to have better containerization technologies than we had previously.
- Run servers that are densely packed with virtual machines and containers due to better resource management and process isolation.
- Enhance performance by ensuring that processes always run on the same CPU core or set of CPU cores, instead of allowing the Linux kernel to move them around to different cores.
- Whitelist or blacklist hardware devices.
- Set up network traffic shaping.

Now that we've seen the purpose of cgroups, my own purpose now is to show you the structure of cgroups.

Understanding the structure of cgroups Version 1

To understand the structure of cgroups, you'll need to understand some of the cgroups terminology. Let's start with just a few terms that you need to know:

- **cgroups**: The term *cgroup* has two different meanings. What concerns us most is that a cgroup is a collection of processes. The processes within each cgroup are bound to limits and parameters that are defined within the *cgroup filesystem*. (We'll talk more about the cgroup filesystem in a bit.) The term *cgroup* can also refer to the Linux kernel code that implements cgroups technology.
- **services**: These are groups of processes that are started by systemd, and that are configured by the different unit configuration files. The individual processes in a service are started and stopped as one set. An example of a service would be the Apache web server service, which would be called `httpd.service` or `apache2.service`. (Okay, you already knew this, but I told you again anyway.)
- **scopes**: A scope is a group of processes that are started by some external means. Virtual machines, containers, and user sessions are examples of scopes.
- **slices**: A slice does not contain any processes. Rather, it's a group of hierarchically organized units. A slice manages processes that are running in either scopes or services. The four default slices are as follows:
    - `-.slice`: This is the *root* slice, which is the root of the whole slice hierarchy. Normally, it won't directly contain any other units. However, you can use it to create default settings for the entire slice tree.
    - `system.slice`: By default, system services that have been started by systemd would go here.
    - `user.slice`: By default, user-mode services would go here. An implicit slice is assigned to each logged-in user.
    - `machine-slice`: If you're running containers or virtual machines, their services will show up here.

In addition, the system administrator can define custom slices, and assign scopes and services to them.

To see a more graphical representation of all this, use the `systemd-cgls` command as a normal user. Just for fun, let's look at the Alma 8 virtual machine that we used to create the WordPress containers back in *Chapter 5, Creating and Editing Services*. The output of `systemd-cgls` should look something like this:

```
Control group /:
-.slice
├─user.slice
│ └─user-1000.slice
│   ├─user@1000.service
│   │ ├─wordpress-noroot.service
│   │ │ ├─ 918 /usr/bin/podman
│   │ │ ├─1013 /usr/bin/slirp4netns --disable-host-loopback
--mtu 65520 --enabl>
│   │ │ ├─1019 containers-rootlessport
. . .
. . .
```

I don't have a desktop environment installed on this virtual machine, so we can't see any of the Gnome stuff that you would see on a machine that does have a desktop. However, we do see the user-mode WordPress container service that we created in *Chapter 5, Creating and Editing Services*. (If you have Gnome on your virtual machine, that's fine. It just means that you'll have to scroll down a bit more to see your WordPress container service.)

The `systemd-cgls` tool shows us a hierarchical listing of the cgroups that are running on the system. The first one listed is the / cgroup, which is how the root cgroup is designated. The second line begins the listing for the root slice (`-.slice`), and directly under it is `user.slice`. Next, we can see `user-1000.slice`, which is a child of `user.slice`. In this case, I'm the only user who's logged into the system, so this slice belongs to me. The `user-1000.slice` designation corresponds to my User ID number, which is `1000`. Following that, we can see the services that are running in my slice, which we'll get to in just a bit.

> **Note**
>
> If you want to see user slices, you'll need to run the `systemd-cgls` command from *outside* of the cgroup filesystem. If you `cd` into the `/sys/fs/cgroup/` directory, you won't see the user slices. The further down you go into the cgroup filesystem, the less you'll see with `systemd-cgls`.

The `user.slice` is defined by the `/lib/systemd/system/user.slice` unit file, which looks like this:

```
[Unit]
Description=User and Session Slice
Documentation=man:systemd.special(7)
Before=slices.target
```

Here, we can see that this slice has to finish starting before the `slices.target` can start. The `slices.target` file looks like this:

```
[Unit]
Description=Slices
Documentation=man:systemd.special(7)
Wants=-.slice system.slice
After=-.slice system.slice
```

According to the `systemd.special` man page, `slices.target` is responsible for setting up the slices that are to run when you boot up your machine. By default, it starts up `system.slice` and the root slice (`-.slice`), as we see here in the `Wants=` line, and the `After=` line. We can also add more slices to that list, as we've just seen in the `user.slice` file. We'll look at `-.slice` and `system.slice` in a moment. For now, let's get back to `user.slice`.

In my `user-1000.slice`, the first listed service is `user@1000.service`. This service is responsible for all the other services that run within my slice. It's set up by the `user@.service` template. The `[Unit]` section of the `user@.service` file looks like this:

```
[Unit]
Description=User Manager for UID %i
After=systemd-user-sessions.service
After=user-runtime-dir@%i.service
Requires=user-runtime-dir@%i.service
```

When this service runs, the `%i` variable will be replaced with a User ID number. The `[Service]` section of the file looks like this:

```
[Service]
User=%i
PAMName=systemd-user
Type=notify
```

```
ExecStart=-/usr/lib/systemd/systemd --user
Slice=user-%i.slice
KillMode=mixed
Delegate=pids memory
TasksMax=infinity
TimeoutStopSec=120s
```

Here's the breakdown:

- `ExecStart=`: This line causes systemd to start a new systemd session for each user who logs in.
- `Slice=`: This line creates a separate slice for each user.
- `TasksMax=`: This line is set to infinity, which means that there's no limit to the number of processes that a user can run.
- `Delegate=`: We'll discuss this directive in *Chapter 12, Controlling Resource Usage with cgroups Version 1*.

The next thing we see in the output of `systemd-cgls` is that all of the services that are running in my user slice are children of the `user@1000.service`. When I scroll down, I'll eventually get past the list of services, and will see the *scope* for my login session. In this case, my login session at the local terminal is designated as `session-2.scope`, and my remote login session is designated as `session-3.scope`. Here's what this looks like:

```
. . .
. . .
├─session-2.scope
│   │ ├─ 794 login -- donnie
│   │ └─1573 -bash
│   └─session-3.scope
│     ├─ 1644 sshd: donnie [priv]
│     ├─ 1648 sshd: donnie@pts/0
│     ├─ 1649 -bash
│     ├─11493 systemd-cgls -l
│     └─11494 systemd-cgls -l
. . .
. . .
```

According to the `systemd.scope` man page, scopes can't be created by creating unit files. Instead, they're created programmatically at runtime. So, don't expect to see any `.scope` files in the `/lib/systemd/system/` directory.

Further down in the `systemd-cgls` output, we finally get past my user slice. The next thing we can see after my user slice is the `init.scope` and the `system.slice`, as we see here:

```
. . .
├─init.scope
│ └─1 /usr/lib/systemd/systemd --switched-root --system
--deserialize 18
├─system.slice
│ ├─rngd.service
│ │ └─732 /sbin/rngd -f --fill-watermark=0
│ ├─systemd-udevd.service
│ │ └─620 /usr/lib/systemd/systemd-udevd
│ ├─wordpress-container.service
│ │ └─1429 /usr/bin/conmon --api-version 1 -c
cc06c35f21cedd4d2384cf2c048f01374>
│ ├─polkit.service
│. . .
```

Here, we can see system services that have nothing to do with my user session. One service that we see here is the WordPress container service that's running in system mode.

The fact that I have a system-mode container service running means that there's something in `machine.slice`, as we see here:

```
. . .
. . .
└─machine.slice
  └─libpod-cc06c35f21cedd4d2384cf2c048f013748e84cabdc594b110a8c
8529173f4c81.sco>
    ├─1438 apache2 -DFOREGROUND
    ├─1560 apache2 -DFOREGROUND
    ├─1561 apache2 -DFOREGROUND
    ├─1562 apache2 -DFOREGROUND
    ├─1563 apache2 -DFOREGROUND
    └─1564 apache2 -DFOREGROUND
```

The `libpod` branch of this `machine.slice` tree represents our `podman-docker` container. (Note that the user-mode container service only shows up directly under the user slice, and doesn't show up here under the machine slice.)

Okay, let's shift back to an Alma machine that's running with the Gnome desktop. As we see here, there's a lot more going on with the output of `systemd-cgls`:

```
Control group /:
-.slice
├─user.slice
│ └─user-1000.slice
│   ├─user@1000.service
│   │ ├─gvfs-goa-volume-monitor.service
│   │ │ └─2682 /usr/libexec/gvfs-goa-volume-monitor
│   │ ├─xdg-permission-store.service
│   │ │ └─2563 /usr/libexec/xdg-permission-store
│   │ ├─tracker-store.service
│   │ │ └─3041 /usr/libexec/tracker-store
│   │ ├─evolution-calendar-factory.service
│   │ │ ├─2725 /usr/libexec/evolution-calendar-factory
. . .
. . .
```

On any desktop machine, you'll always have a lot more running services than you'd have on a strictly text-mode machine.

Next, create a new user account for Frank. Then, have Frank log in to this machine via a remote SSH session. The top part of the output of `systemd-cgls` now looks like this:

```
Control group /:
-.slice
├─user.slice
│ ├─user-1001.slice
│ │ ├─session-10.scope
│ │ │ ├─8215 sshd: frank [priv]
│ │ │ ├─8250 sshd: frank@pts/1
│ │ │ └─8253 -bash
│ │ └─user@1001.service
│ │   ├─pulseaudio.service
```

```
| |   | └─8248 /usr/bin/pulseaudio --daemonize=no
--log-target=journal
| |   ├─gvfs-daemon.service
. . .
. . .
```

Frank now has his own user slice, which is `user-1001.slice`. We see that he's logged in remotely, as well as the name of the virtual terminal that he used to log in. (In case you're wondering, *Frank* is the name of my formerly feral Flame Point Siamese kitty, who has been with me for many years. Until just a moment ago, he was sleeping on the computer table where my keyboard should be, which was making it quite awkward for me to type.)

If you don't want to see the entire cgroups tree, you can use `systemctl status` to see just one part of it. For example, to just see the `user.slice`, I'd do `systemctl status user.slice`. The output would look something like this:

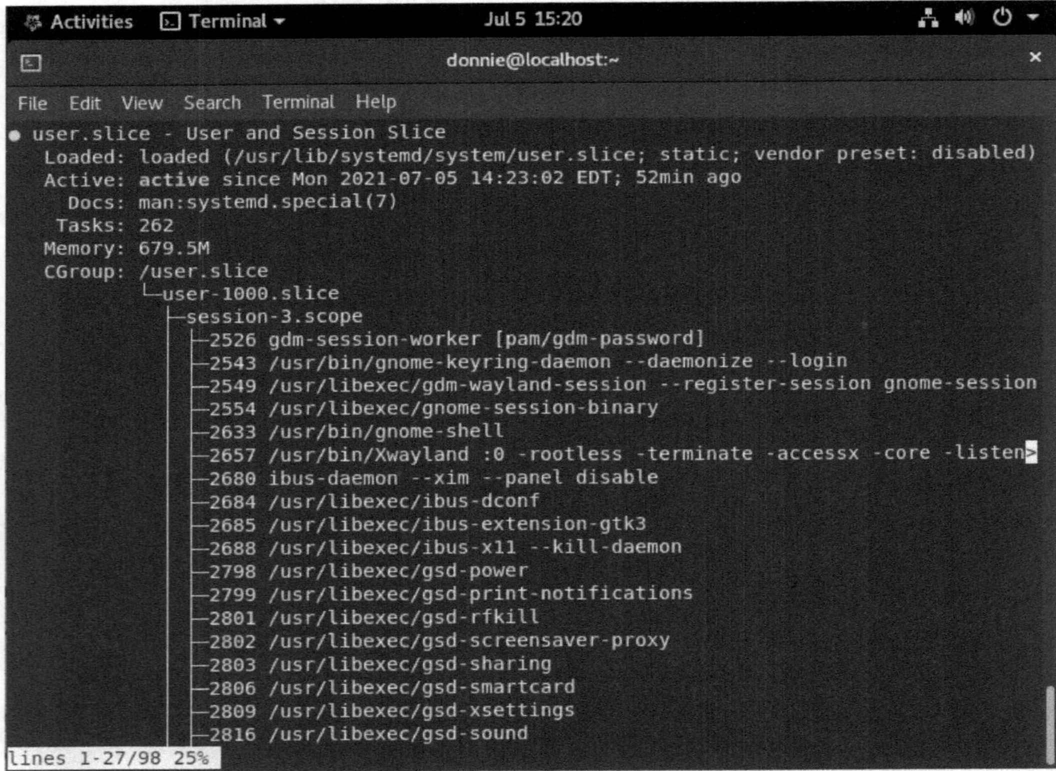

Figure 11.1 – user.slice on Alma Linux with the Gnome desktop

Here, we see that Frank has logged out and that I'm now the only user who is logged in. (After all, Frank is a cat, which means that he spends most of his time sleeping.) We can also view information about the other slices, as well as about scopes. For example, doing `systemctl status session-3.scope` shows me information about the session scope that's running under my user slice, which would look like this:

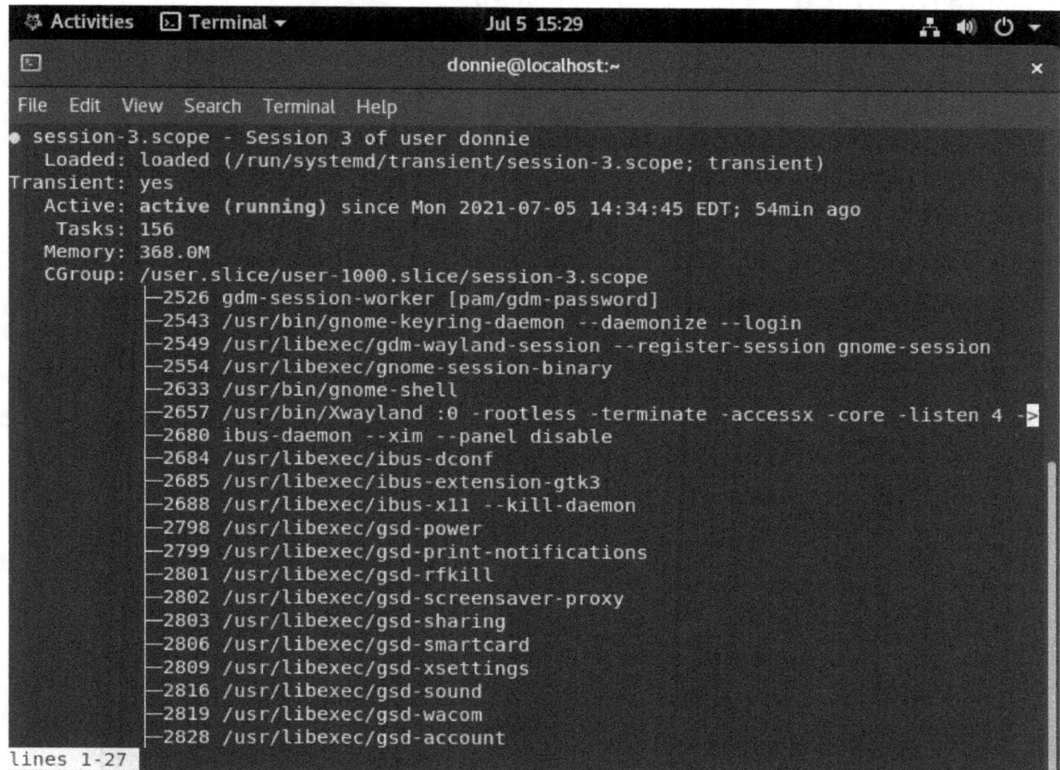

Figure 11.2 – Session scope on Alma Linux

All right, that pretty much covers it for the basic structure of cgroups. Now, let's move on and look at the cgroup filesystem.

Understanding the cgroup filesystem

On any system that runs cgroups, you'll see a `cgroup` directory under the `/sys/fs/` virtual filesystem, as shown here:

```
[donnie@localhost ~]$ cd /sys/fs
[donnie@localhost fs]$ ls -ld cgroup/
drwxr-xr-x. 14 root root 360 Jul  3 15:52 cgroup/
[donnie@localhost fs]$
```

As with all virtual filesystems, the cgroup filesystem only exists in memory at runtime and disappears when you shut down the machine. There's no permanent copy of it on the machine's drive.

When you look inside the `/sys/fs/cgroup/` directory, you'll see something like this:

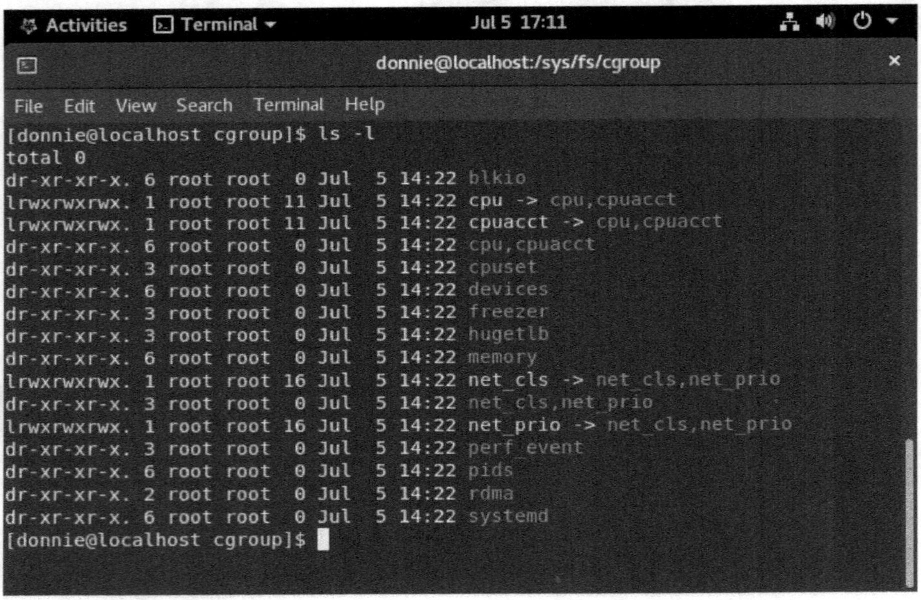
Activities
Terminal
Jul 5 17:11
donnie@localhost:/sys/fs/cgroup
File Edit View Search Terminal Help
[donnie@localhost cgroup]$ ls -l
total 0
dr-xr-xr-x. 6 root root 0 Jul 5 14:22 blkio
lrwxrwxrwx. 1 root root 11 Jul 5 14:22 cpu -> cpu,cpuacct
lrwxrwxrwx. 1 root root 11 Jul 5 14:22 cpuacct -> cpu,cpuacct
dr-xr-xr-x. 6 root root 0 Jul 5 14:22 cpu,cpuacct
dr-xr-xr-x. 3 root root 0 Jul 5 14:22 cpuset
dr-xr-xr-x. 6 root root 0 Jul 5 14:22 devices
dr-xr-xr-x. 3 root root 0 Jul 5 14:22 freezer
dr-xr-xr-x. 3 root root 0 Jul 5 14:22 hugetlb
dr-xr-xr-x. 6 root root 0 Jul 5 14:22 memory
lrwxrwxrwx. 1 root root 16 Jul 5 14:22 net_cls -> net_cls,net_prio
dr-xr-xr-x. 3 root root 0 Jul 5 14:22 net_cls,net_prio
lrwxrwxrwx. 1 root root 16 Jul 5 14:22 net_prio -> net_cls,net_prio
dr-xr-xr-x. 3 root root 0 Jul 5 14:22 perf_event
dr-xr-xr-x. 6 root root 0 Jul 5 14:22 pids
dr-xr-xr-x. 2 root root 0 Jul 5 14:22 rdma
dr-xr-xr-x. 6 root root 0 Jul 5 14:22 systemd
[donnie@localhost cgroup]$

Figure 11.3 – cgroupfs on Alma Linux

Each of these directories represents a cgroup *susbsystem*. (You'll also see them referred to as either *controllers* or *resource controllers*.) Inside each of these directories is a set of files that represent the cgroup's *tunables*. These files hold information about any resource control or tuning parameters that you would set. (We'll talk more about that in *Chapter 12, Controlling Resource Usage with cgroups Version 1*.) For example, here's what we have in the `blkio` directory:

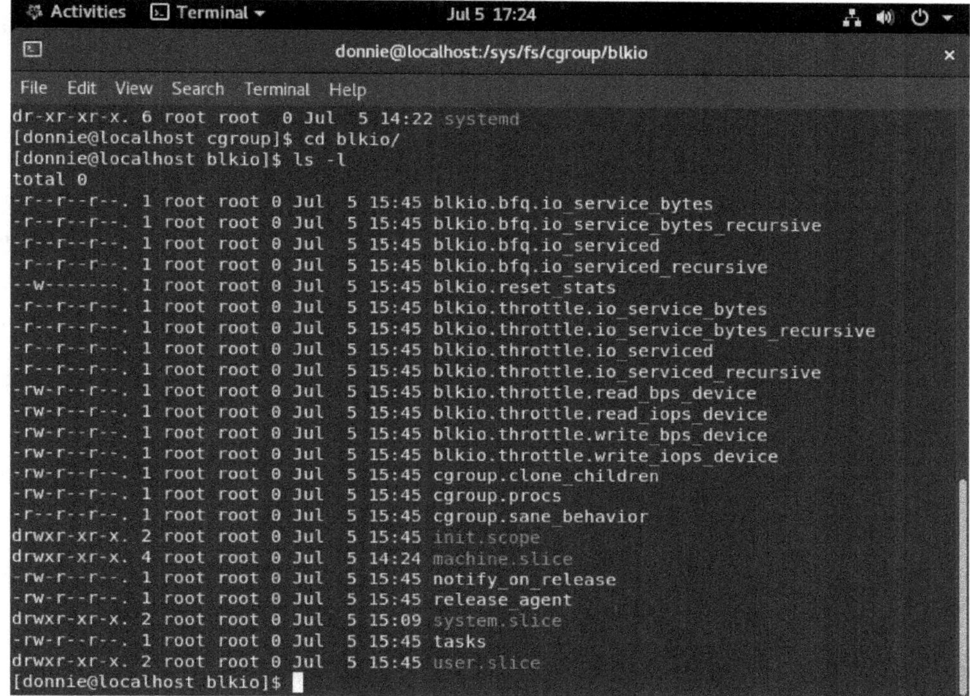

Figure 11.4 – The blkio filesystem

Each of these files represents a parameter that can be custom-tuned for the best performance. Toward the bottom, we also see directories for `init.scope`, `machine.slice`, `system.slice`, and `user.slice`. Each also has its own set of tunable parameters.

When we use the `mount` command and pipe it through `grep`, we'll see that each of these resource controllers is mounted on its own virtual partition. Here's what that looks like:

```
[donnie@localhost ~]$ mount | grep 'cgroup'
tmpfs on /sys/fs/cgroup type tmpfs
(ro,nosuid,nodev,noexec,seclabel,mode=755)
cgroup on /sys/fs/cgroup/systemd type cgroup
(rw,nosuid,nodev,noexec,relatime,seclabel,xattr,release_agent=/
usr/lib/systemd/systemd-cgroups-agent,name=systemd)
. . .
. . .
cgroup on /sys/fs/cgroup/freezer type cgroup
(rw,nosuid,nodev,noexec,relatime,seclabel,freezer)
[donnie@localhost ~]$
```

Okay, I think that that should do it for our basic introduction to cgroups Version 1. So, let's wrap up this chapter and move on!

Summary

In this chapter, we looked at the history of the cgroups technology, what cgroups are, and why we need them. We then looked at the structure of cgroups and the cgroup filesystem.

A major challenge that comes with learning about cgroup technology is that there isn't much available documentation about it. I mean, you'll see a lot of blog posts and YouTube videos about it, but much of it either isn't very comprehensive or is woefully out of date. Hopefully, I've been able to give you a better understanding of cgroup technology and how it works together with systemd.

In the next chapter, we'll look at controlling resource usage with cgroups Version 1. I'll see you there.

Questions

1. What is the default location of the cgroup filesystem?

   a. `/proc/fs/cgroup/`

   b. `/sys/cgroup/`

   c. `/sys/fs/cgroup/`

   d. `/proc/cgroup/`

2. What must you do to see user slices with `systemd-cgls`?

   a. Run the command only from the local terminal.

   b. Run the command only from outside the cgroup filesystem.

   c. Run the command with root privileges.

   d. You can't. User slices never show up.

3. How can you create your own cgroup scope?

   a. Use `systemctl edit --full --force`, just as you would with other systemd units.

   b. Manually create a unit file in the `/etc/systemd/system/` directory.

   c. You can't. Scopes are created programmatically, and there are no `.scope` unit files.

   d. Manually create a unit file in the `/lib/systemd/system/` directory.

4. What does a slice do?

   a. It directly manages user mode processes.

   b. It directly manages system mode processes.

   c. It manages processes that are in either scopes or services.

   d. It manages user login sessions.

Answers

1. c
2. b
3. c
4. c

Further reading

Take a look at the following links for more information about cgroups:

- A Linux sysadmin's introduction to cgroups:

  `https://www.redhat.com/sysadmin/cgroups-part-one`

- cgroups documentation at kernel.org:

  `https://www.kernel.org/doc/Documentation/cgroup-v1/cgroups.txt`

12
Controlling Resource Usage with cgroups Version 1

Now that we've seen what `cgroups` are and how they're structured, it's time to look at how to actually use them. In this chapter, we'll cover these specific topics:

- Understanding resource controllers
- Controlling CPU usage
- Controlling memory usage
- Controlling `blkio` usage
- Understanding `pam_limits` and `ulimit`

Learning how to control resource usage with `cgroups` can help you make your data center run more securely and efficiently. So, buckle your seat belts and let's get going.

Technical requirements

To get the most out of this chapter, you'll want to use a somewhat new host computer with a multi-core CPU and plenty of memory. In my case, I'm using a fairly late-model Dell workstation with a hexacore Xeon CPU and 32 GB of RAM. Hyperthreading is enabled, which gives me a total of 12 CPU cores to play with.

Set your virtual machines to run with at least two CPU cores and a decent amount of RAM. I'm setting mine to use four cores, as you see here:

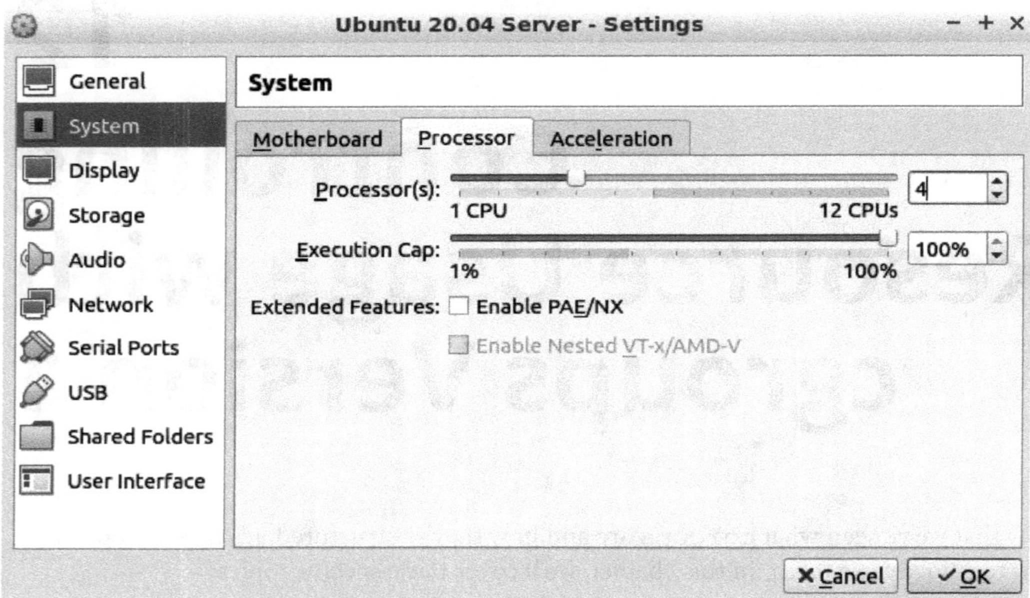

Figure 12.1 – Setting the CPU cores in VirtualBox

I'm also setting my virtual machines to run with eight GB of RAM, as you see here:

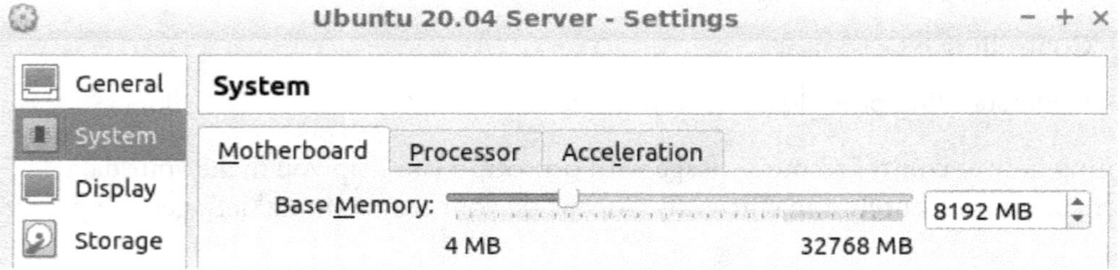

Figure 12.2 – Setting the RAM in VirtualBox

As usual, I'll be using my Ubuntu Server 20.04 and AlmaLinux 8 virtual machines for the demos.

Check out the following link to see the Code in Action video: `https://bit.ly/3xJ61qi`

Now that we have everything set up, let's dig in.

Understanding resource controllers

There are a few different names for this cgroups feature. I prefer to use the term *resource controllers*. In other documentation, you may see these resource controllers referred to as either *subsystems* or just as *controllers*. All of these terms refer to the same thing, which is the cgroups technology that allows us to control the resource usage of the various running processes. Before we start getting our hands too dirty, let's see what resource controllers we have.

Examining the resource controllers

The best way to see what resource controllers we have is to install some cgroup tools. On the Ubuntu machine, do:

```
donnie@ubuntu2004:~$ sudo apt install cgroup-tools
```

On the Alma machine, do:

```
[donnie@localhost ~]$ sudo dnf install libcgroup-tools
```

On either machine, we can now use `lssubsys` to view our active resource controllers, like this:

```
donnie@ubuntu2004:~$ lssubsys
cpuset
cpu,cpuacct
blkio
memory
devices
freezer
net_cls,net_prio
perf_event
hugetlb
pids
rdma
donnie@ubuntu2004:~$
```

Here's a brief description of each of them:

- `cpuset`: If you're running a system with multiple CPU cores, this allows you to assign a process to one specific CPU core or a set of CPU cores. This enhances performance by forcing a process to use a portion of the CPU cache that's already been filled with the data and the instructions that the process needs. By default, the Linux kernel scheduler can move processes around from one CPU core to another, or from one set of CPU cores to another. Every time this happens, the running process must access the main system memory to refill the CPU cache. This costs extra CPU cycles, which can hurt performance.
- `cpu,cpuacct`: There used to be two separate controllers for `cpu` and `cpuacct`. Now, they've been combined into one single controller. This controller lets you control CPU usage for either processes or users. On a multi-tenant system, it allows you to monitor users' CPU usage, which is handy for billing purposes.
- `blkio`: This is short for **Block Input/Output**. This controller allows you to set limits on how fast processes and users can read from or write to block devices. (A block device is something such as a hard drive or a hard drive partition.)
- `memory`: As you might have guessed, this one allows you to set limits on the amount of system memory that a process or user can use.
- `devices`: This allows you to control access to system devices.
- `freezer`: This one has a strange name, but its purpose is simple. It allows you to suspend running processes in a cgroup. This can be handy for when you need to move processes from one cgroup to another. When you're ready, just resume the processes.
- `net_cls,net_prio`: This allows you to place class identifier (`classid`) tags on network packets. The Linux traffic controller and the Linux firewall can use these tags to control and prioritize network traffic for the various cgroups.
- `perf_event`: This allows you to monitor cgroups with the `perf` tool.
- `hugetlb`: This one allows your cgroups to use huge virtual memory pages, and to place limits upon their use. (This is a bit beyond the scope of this book, so we won't say anything more about it.)
- `pids`: This allows you to place a limit on the number of processes that can run in a cgroup.
- `rdma`: **Remote direct memory access** allows one computer to directly access the memory of another computer without having to involve either computer's operating system. This is mainly used for parallel computing clusters, which is also beyond the scope of this book.

On the `cgroups` man page, you'll see a brief mention of these controllers under the *Cgroups version 1 controllers* section. To see a detailed description of them, you'll need to look at the documentation that comes packaged with the Linux kernel source code. On the Alma machine, you can install that documentation as a separate package by doing:

```
[donnie@localhost ~]$ sudo dnf install kernel-doc
```

In the `/usr/share/doc/kernel-doc-4.18.0/Documentation/cgroup-v1/` directory, you'll now find text files that contain more detailed explanations about the resource controllers. (I also looked for that documentation package on the Ubuntu machine, but couldn't find it.) Of course, it's only fair to warn you that these documentation pages are mainly written for Linux kernel programmers, so you might not get much out of them. But then, who knows? Go ahead and give them a quick glance to see whether there's anything there that can help you. (You might also find that they're a great sleeping aid, for those nights when you have a severe case of insomnia.)

When you look in the `/sys/fs/cgroup/` directory, you'll see that each of these resource controllers has its own directory. Here's what that looks like on the Ubuntu machine:

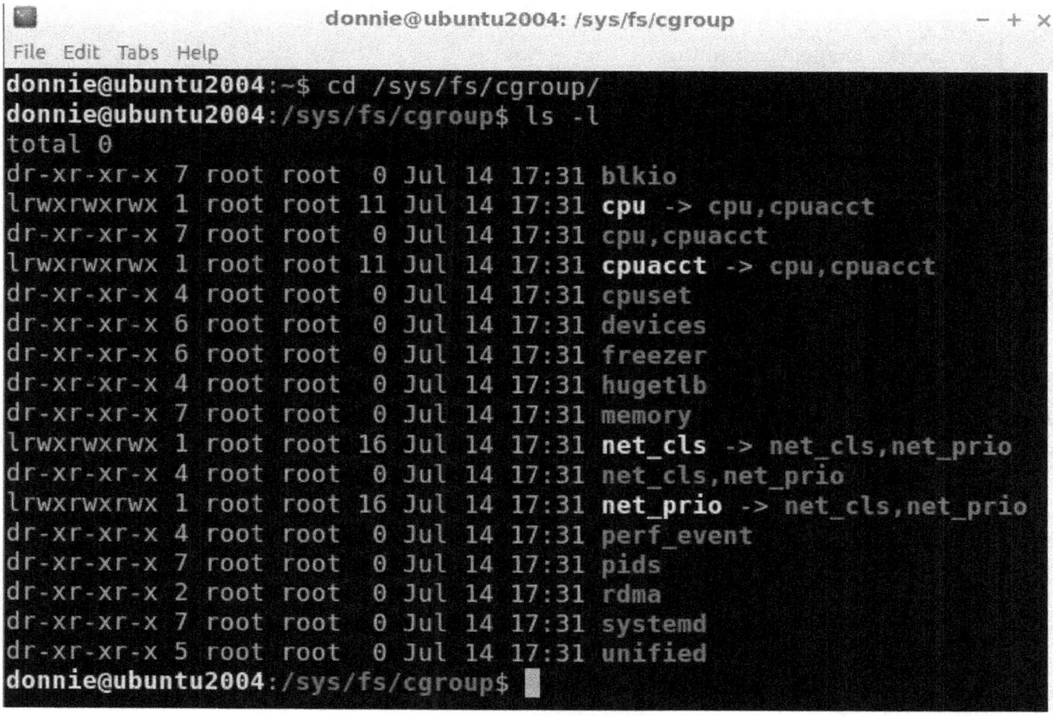
donnie@ubuntu2004: /sys/fs/cgroup
File Edit Tabs Help
donnie@ubuntu2004:~$ cd /sys/fs/cgroup/
donnie@ubuntu2004:/sys/fs/cgroup$ ls -l
total 0
dr-xr-xr-x 7 root root 0 Jul 14 17:31 blkio
lrwxrwxrwx 1 root root 11 Jul 14 17:31 cpu -> cpu,cpuacct
dr-xr-xr-x 7 root root 0 Jul 14 17:31 cpu,cpuacct
lrwxrwxrwx 1 root root 11 Jul 14 17:31 cpuacct -> cpu,cpuacct
dr-xr-xr-x 4 root root 0 Jul 14 17:31 cpuset
dr-xr-xr-x 6 root root 0 Jul 14 17:31 devices
dr-xr-xr-x 6 root root 0 Jul 14 17:31 freezer
dr-xr-xr-x 4 root root 0 Jul 14 17:31 hugetlb
dr-xr-xr-x 7 root root 0 Jul 14 17:31 memory
lrwxrwxrwx 1 root root 16 Jul 14 17:31 net_cls -> net_cls,net_prio
dr-xr-xr-x 4 root root 0 Jul 14 17:31 net_cls,net_prio
lrwxrwxrwx 1 root root 16 Jul 14 17:31 net_prio -> net_cls,net_prio
dr-xr-xr-x 4 root root 0 Jul 14 17:31 perf_event
dr-xr-xr-x 7 root root 0 Jul 14 17:31 pids
dr-xr-xr-x 2 root root 0 Jul 14 17:31 rdma
dr-xr-xr-x 7 root root 0 Jul 14 17:31 systemd
dr-xr-xr-x 5 root root 0 Jul 14 17:31 unified
donnie@ubuntu2004:/sys/fs/cgroup$

Figure 12.3 – Resource controllers on Ubuntu

For now, we'll ignore the two directories at the bottom of the screen. (The `systemd` directory is for the root cgroup, and the `unified` directory is for Version 2 controllers.) Even though we're running cgroups Version 1 here, it's still possible to use Version 2 controllers. (You won't see the `unified` directory on the Alma machine, because the RHEL 8-type distros don't have Version 2 controllers enabled by default.) Note that we'll only talk about Version 1 controllers in this chapter.

Also, note that we have four symbolic links that point to two different directories. That's because the `cpu` and `cpuacct` controllers used to be two separate controllers, but they're now combined into just one controller. The same is true of the `net_cls` and `net_prio` controllers. The symbolic links provide us with some backward compatibility.

> **Note**
> Space doesn't permit me to cover all of these resource controllers in detail. So, we'll just focus on the *big three* that you'll be most likely to use. These are the `cpu`, `memory`, and `blkio` controllers. That's just as well, because with cgroups Version 1, these are the only three resource controllers that you can directly configure via `systemd`. (To use any of the other Version 1 resource controllers, you'll have to jump through some hoops and use some non-systemd management utilities.)

All right, enough theory for now. Let's start getting our hands dirty.

Preparing for the demos

For the first few demos, we'll use the `stress-ng` tool to simulate some real-world problems. On the Ubuntu machine, install it by doing:

```
donnie@ubuntu2004:~$ sudo apt install stress-ng
```

To install it on the Alma machine, you'll first need to have the EPEL repository installed. If you haven't already, install it by doing:

```
[donnie@localhost ~]$ sudo dnf install epel-release
```

Then, install the `stress-ng` package by doing:

```
[donnie@localhost ~]$ sudo dnf install stress-ng
```

Next, create a new, non-privileged user account. (I've created an account for Vicky, who is my teenage solid gray kitty.)

Then, open a terminal on your host machine and have your new user log in to a remote session on the virtual machine. Open a second terminal on the host machine, and log in to your own account on the virtual machine. Keep the virtual machine's local terminal off to the side, because you'll be using it, too.

Now that we're all set up, let's talk about the `cpu` resource controller.

Controlling CPU usage

You can control resource usage either by using the `systemctl set-property` command or by editing systemd unit files. For the first demo, we'll have Vicky put some stress on the virtual machine's CPUs. We'll deal with it by using `systemctl set-property` to configure the `cpu` resource controller.

Controlling Vicky's CPU usage

By default, all users on a Linux system have unlimited use of the system resources. That could be problematic on a system with multiple users. Any user could decide to hog all the resources, which could effectively cause a Denial-of-Service situation for all the other users. In real life, a user could cause trouble by doing something completely innocent, such as rendering a large video file. An authorized user could also cause a Denial-of-Service by doing something they aren't supposed to do, such as using server resources to do some cryptocurrency mining. In any case, we want to limit the resources that a user can use. We'll do that by assigning limits to the user's slice.

So, let's say that Vicky is logged in remotely and is hogging all the CPU time from the other users. Simulate that by having Vicky do:

```
vicky@ubuntu2004:~$ stress-ng -c 4
```

The `-c 4` option in this command indicates that Vicky is doing a stress test on four cores of the CPU. Change that number to however many cores you've assigned to your own virtual machine.

In the remote terminal where you're logged in to your own account, open the `top` utility. It should look something like this:

```
top - 19:46:54 up  1:08,  3 users,  load average: 4.73, 2.52, 1.61
Tasks: 184 total,   5 running, 179 sleeping,   0 stopped,   0 zombie
%Cpu(s): 94.5 us,  3.7 sy,  0.0 ni,  0.0 id,  0.0 wa,  0.0 hi,  1.8 si,  0.0 st
MiB Mem :   7961.7 total,   4841.4 free,   1152.4 used,   1967.9 buff/cache
MiB Swap:   3936.0 total,   3936.0 free,      0.0 used.   6578.8 avail Mem

    PID USER      PR  NI    VIRT    RES    SHR S  %CPU  %MEM     TIME+ COMMAND
  82755 vicky     20   0   50196   7040   3596 R  99.0   0.1   2:14.87 stress-+
  82754 vicky     20   0   50196   7032   3600 R  98.0   0.1   2:14.62 stress-+
  82757 vicky     20   0   50196   7056   3628 R  98.0   0.1   2:15.09 stress-+
  82756 vicky     20   0   50196   7052   3624 R  97.0   0.1   2:14.09 stress-+
   3565 root      20   0 2421896 621780  75944 S   3.0   7.6   8:20.46 kube-ap+
   4832 root      20   0 1340948  45096  32048 S   1.0   0.6   2:26.06 calico-+
    908 root      20   0  816844 108488  65532 S   0.7   1.3   1:51.88 kube-co+
   3682 root      20   0 1779232 102204  66216 S   0.7   1.3   1:54.07 kubelet
      1 root      20   0  102304  11880   8408 S   0.3   0.1   0:21.04 systemd
    915 root      20   0  748544  52512  35528 S   0.3   0.6   0:15.47 kube-sc+
  85386 donnie    20   0    8032   3808   3160 R   0.3   0.0   0:00.02 top
      2 root      20   0       0      0      0 S   0.0   0.0   0:00.00 kthreadd
      3 root       0 -20       0      0      0 I   0.0   0.0   0:00.00 rcu_gp
      4 root       0 -20       0      0      0 I   0.0   0.0   0:00.00 rcu_par+
      6 root       0 -20       0      0      0 I   0.0   0.0   0:00.00 kworker+
      8 root       0 -20       0      0      0 I   0.0   0.0   0:00.00 mm_perc+
      9 root      20   0       0      0      0 S   0.0   0.0   0:00.28 ksoftir+
```

Figure 12.4 – The top display with Vicky's stress test

At the top of the `top` display, we see that Vicky is hogging nearly 100% of all four CPU cores. Do I have to tell you that that isn't good?

Keep `top` going on your own remote terminal, and go to the virtual machine's local terminal. To get proper results, make sure that you're not anywhere within the `/sys/fs/cgroup/` filesystem. Use `systemd-cgls` to find Vicky's user slice, which should look like this:

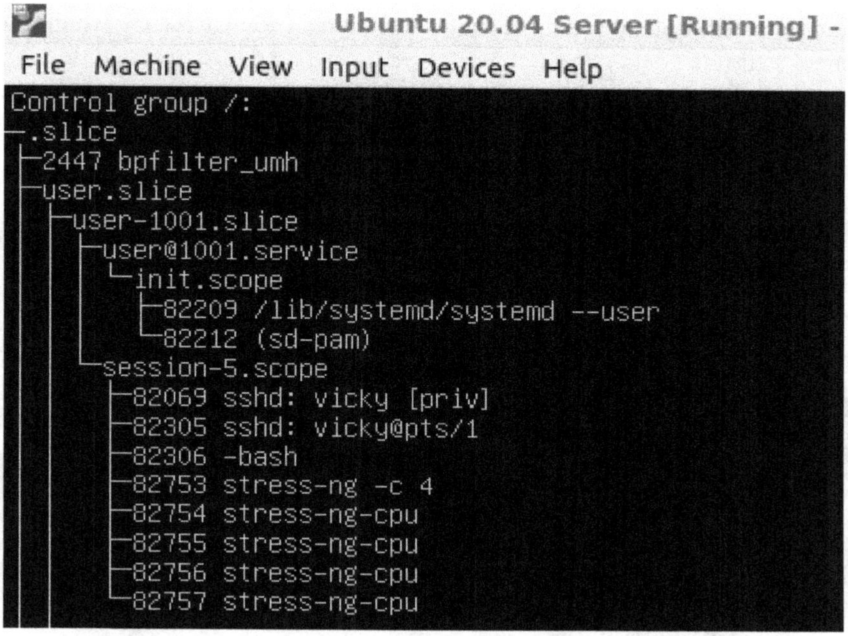

Ubuntu 20.04 Server [Running] -

File Machine View Input Devices Help

```
Control group /:
-.slice
├─2447 bpfilter_umh
├─user.slice
│ ├─user-1001.slice
│ │ ├─user@1001.service
│ │ │ └─init.scope
│ │ │   ├─82209 /lib/systemd/systemd --user
│ │ │   └─82212 (sd-pam)
│ │ └─session-5.scope
│ │   ├─82069 sshd: vicky [priv]
│ │   ├─82305 sshd: vicky@pts/1
│ │   ├─82306 -bash
│ │   ├─82753 stress-ng -c 4
│ │   ├─82754 stress-ng-cpu
│ │   ├─82755 stress-ng-cpu
│ │   ├─82756 stress-ng-cpu
│ │   └─82757 stress-ng-cpu
```

Figure 12.5 – Vicky's user slice

We see that she's user number `1001`, and we want to show her who's the boss around here. We're just not going to let her get away with hogging the CPU like this. So, on the local terminal, reduce her `CPUQuota` to `10%` by doing:

```
donnie@ubuntu2004:~$ sudo systemctl set-property user-1001.
slice CPUQuota=10%
```

This command creates some new files in the `/etc/systemd/` directory, which means that you'll need to do `sudo systemctl daemon-reload`, just as you'd do when creating a new unit file. You should now see Vicky's CPU usage go down to practically nothing, as we see here:

```
donnie@ubuntu2004: ~
File Edit Tabs Help
top - 20:03:46 up  1:25,  4 users,  load average: 1.21, 3.69, 3.59
Tasks: 190 total,   5 running, 185 sleeping,   0 stopped,   0 zombie
%Cpu(s):  6.9 us,  2.5 sy,  0.0 ni, 88.8 id,  1.5 wa,  0.0 hi,  0.3 si,  0.0 st
MiB Mem :   7961.7 total,   4768.1 free,   1183.4 used,   2010.2 buff/cache
MiB Swap:   3936.0 total,   3936.0 free,      0.0 used.   6546.1 avail Mem

    PID USER      PR  NI    VIRT    RES    SHR S  %CPU  %MEM     TIME+ COMMAND
   3565 root      20   0 2421896 622400  75916 S  11.6   7.6   9:28.58 kube-ap+
 105375 root      20   0  745112  41148  26248 S   5.0   0.5   0:00.15 kubectl
   4832 root      20   0 1340948  45312  32048 S   2.7   0.6   2:41.58 calico-+
  82754 vicky     20   0   50196   7032   3600 R   2.7   0.1  16:18.12 stress-+
  82757 vicky     20   0   50196   7056   3628 R   2.7   0.1  16:19.32 stress-+
    908 root      20   0  816844 108672  65532 S   2.3   1.3   2:04.04 kube-co+
   3682 root      20   0 1779232 102204  66216 S   2.3   1.3   2:08.24 kubelet
  82755 vicky     20   0   50196   7040   3596 R   2.3   0.1  16:19.29 stress-+
  82756 vicky     20   0   50196   7052   3624 R   2.3   0.1  16:17.60 stress-+
   3304 root      20   0 1269192  57432  27260 S   0.7   0.7   0:53.19 contain+
   4742 root      20   0  712284  11248   5808 S   0.7   0.1   0:18.75 contain+
      1 root      20   0  103612  13344   8408 S   0.3   0.2   0:25.32 systemd
    325 root      20   0       0      0      0 S   0.3   0.0   0:03.57 jbd2/dm+
    639 root      rt   0  280200  17992   8200 S   0.3   0.2   0:00.75 multipa+
    859 message+  20   0    7624   4712   4044 S   0.3   0.1   0:05.70 dbus-da+
    884 root      20   0 1271120  86016  47400 S   0.3   1.1   0:18.59 dockerd
    915 root      20   0  748544  52512  35528 S   0.3   0.6   0:17.27 kube-sc+
```

Figure 12.6 – After reducing Vicky's CPUQuota

Okay, maybe reducing Vicky's `CPUQuota` down to only `10%` is a bit too radical. In real life, you could adjust `CPUQuota` to whatever you need it to be. On a machine with multiple cores, there's a trick to this that you should know about. It's that whatever quota you give to Vicky is spread across all available CPU cores. So, in this case, we're not giving Vicky 10% of each core. Instead, we're spreading that 10% across four cores, which allows her to consume only about 2.5% of the CPU cycles from each core, as you can see in *Figure 12.6*. Also, setting Vicky's `CPUQuota` to `100%` doesn't give her 100% usage of each core. Instead, she would have only about 25% usage of each core. To allow her to have 50% usage of each core, set `CPUQuota` to `200%`. The maximum setting that we can have on this machine with four cores is `400%`, which would give her 100% usage of each core.

> **Note**
>
> Keep in mind that the figures I've just given you are based on having four cores assigned to the virtual machine. These figures will differ if you've assigned a different number of cores to your own virtual machine.

The first time you execute a `systemctl set-property` command, you'll create the `system.control/` directory under the `/etc/systemd/` directory, which looks like this:

```
donnie@ubuntu2004:/etc/systemd$ ls -ld system.control/
drwxr-xr-x 3 root root 4096 Jul 14 19:59 system.control/
donnie@ubuntu2004:/etc/systemd$
```

Under that directory, you'll see a directory for Vicky's user slice. Under her user slice directory, you'll see the configuration file for Vicky's `CPUQuota`, as you see here:

```
donnie@ubuntu2004:/etc/systemd/system.control$ ls -l
total 4
drwxr-xr-x 2 root root 4096 Jul 14 20:25 user-1001.slice.d
donnie@ubuntu2004:/etc/systemd/system.control$ cd user-1001.
slice.d/
donnie@ubuntu2004:/etc/systemd/system.control/user-1001.slice.
d$ ls -l
total 4
-rw-r--r-- 1 root root 143 Jul 14 20:25 50-CPUQuota.conf
donnie@ubuntu2004:/etc/systemd/system.control/user-1001.slice.
d$
```

Here you see that I've just set Vicky's quota up to `200%`:

```
donnie@ubuntu2004:/etc/systemd/system.control/user-1001.slice.
d$ cat 50-CPUQuota.conf
# This is a drop-in unit file extension, created via "systemctl
set-property"
# or an equivalent operation. Do not edit.
[Slice]
CPUQuota=200%
donnie@ubuntu2004:/etc/systemd/system.control/user-1001.slice.
d$
```

Now, be aware that you'll only need to do a `daemon-reload` when you first create this file. Any subsequent changes you make to this file with the `systemctl set-property` command will take effect immediately.

In the cgroup filesystem, under Vicky's user slice directory, you'll see her current `CPUQuota` setting in the `cpu.cfs_quota_us` file. Here's what it looks like when set to `200%`:

```
donnie@ubuntu2004:/sys/fs/cgroup/cpu/user.slice/user-1001.
slice$ cat cpu.cfs_quota_us
200000
donnie@ubuntu2004:/sys/fs/cgroup/cpu/user.slice/user-1001.
slice$
```

To get the actual 200% figure, just chop the last three zeros off from the `200000` that you see.

Okay, we're through with this demo. In Vicky's window, do a *Ctrl* + *C* to stop the stress test.

Next, let's see how to limit CPU usage for a service.

Controlling CPU usage for a service

For this demo, perform the commands at the virtual machine's local terminal, and keep `top` going on your own remote terminal.

The first step of this demo is to create `cputest.service` at the virtual machine's local terminal, like this:

```
donnie@ubuntu2004:~$ sudo systemctl edit --full --force
cputest.service
```

The contents of the file will look like this:

```
[Unit]
Description=CPU stress test service
[Service]
ExecStart=/usr/bin/stress-ng -c 4
```

You see that there's nothing fancy here. It's just enough to get the job done. As you did before, change the `-c` option to reflect the number of cores that you've assigned to your own virtual machine. Next, do a `daemon-reload` and then start the service:

```
donnie@ubuntu2004:~$ sudo systemctl daemon-reload
donnie@ubuntu2004:~$ sudo systemctl start cputest.service
donnie@ubuntu2004:~$
```

In the top display, you should see `cputest.service` hogging 100% of the CPU:

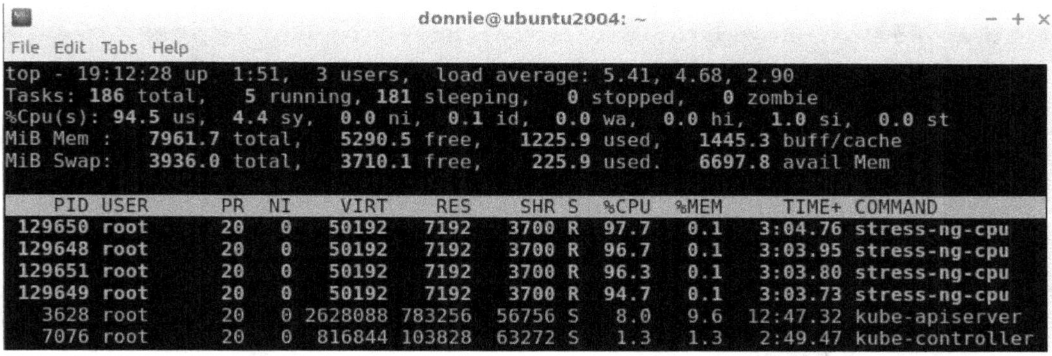

```
donnie@ubuntu2004: ~
File  Edit  Tabs  Help
top - 19:12:28 up  1:51,  3 users,  load average: 5.41, 4.68, 2.90
Tasks: 186 total,   5 running, 181 sleeping,   0 stopped,   0 zombie
%Cpu(s): 94.5 us,  4.4 sy,  0.0 ni,  0.1 id,  0.0 wa,  0.0 hi,  1.0 si,  0.0 st
MiB Mem :   7961.7 total,   5290.5 free,   1225.9 used,   1445.3 buff/cache
MiB Swap:   3936.0 total,   3710.1 free,    225.9 used.   6697.8 avail Mem

    PID USER      PR  NI    VIRT    RES    SHR S  %CPU  %MEM     TIME+ COMMAND
 129650 root      20   0   50192   7192   3700 R  97.7   0.1   3:04.76 stress-ng-cpu
 129648 root      20   0   50192   7192   3700 R  96.7   0.1   3:03.95 stress-ng-cpu
 129651 root      20   0   50192   7192   3700 R  96.3   0.1   3:03.80 stress-ng-cpu
 129649 root      20   0   50192   7192   3700 R  94.7   0.1   3:03.73 stress-ng-cpu
   3628 root      20   0 2628088 783256  56756 S   8.0   9.6  12:47.32 kube-apiserver
   7076 root      20   0  816844 103828  63272 S   1.3   1.3   2:49.47 kube-controller
```

Figure 12.7 – cputest.service with no limits

Next, let's set the `CPUQuota` for this service from the command line.

Setting CPUQuota from the command line

Setting the `CPUQuota` for a service is no different from setting it for a user. Let's say that we only want to allow a 90% `CPUQuota` for this service. Let's set that from the command line, just as we did when we set this for Vicky:

```
donnie@ubuntu2004:~$ sudo systemctl set-property cputest.
service CPUQuota=90%
[sudo] password for donnie:
donnie@ubuntu2004:~$
```

Doing this creates another directory in the `/etc/systemd/system.control/` directory:

```
donnie@ubuntu2004:/etc/systemd/system.control$ ls -l
total 8
drwxr-xr-x 2 root root 4096 Jul 15 19:15 cputest.service.d
```

```
drwxr-xr-x 2 root root 4096 Jul 15 17:53 user-1001.slice.d
donnie@ubuntu2004:/etc/systemd/system.control$
```

Inside the `/etc/systemd/system.control/cputest.service.d/` directory, you'll see the `50-CPUQuota.conf` file, which is set up the same as the one that we created for Vicky:

```
donnie@ubuntu2004:/etc/systemd/system.control/cputest.service.
d$ cat 50-CPUQuota.conf
# This is a drop-in unit file extension, created via "systemctl
set-property"
# or an equivalent operation. Do not edit.
[Service]
CPUQuota=90%
donnie@ubuntu2004:/etc/systemd/system.control/cputest.service.
d$
```

This allows `cputest.service` to use only about 22.5% of each CPU core, as we see here:

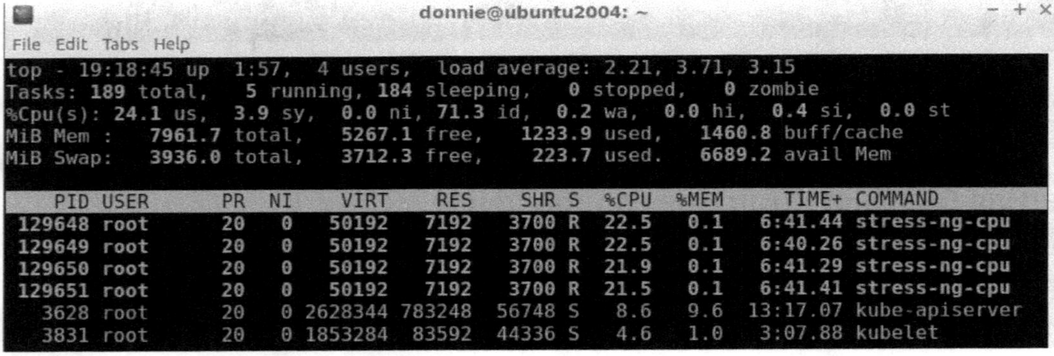

```
donnie@ubuntu2004: ~
File Edit Tabs Help
top - 19:18:45 up  1:57,  4 users,  load average: 2.21, 3.71, 3.15
Tasks: 189 total,   5 running, 184 sleeping,   0 stopped,   0 zombie
%Cpu(s): 24.1 us,  3.9 sy,  0.0 ni, 71.3 id,  0.2 wa,  0.0 hi,  0.4 si,  0.0 st
MiB Mem :   7961.7 total,   5267.1 free,   1233.9 used,   1460.8 buff/cache
MiB Swap:   3936.0 total,   3712.3 free,    223.7 used.   6689.2 avail Mem

    PID USER      PR  NI    VIRT    RES    SHR S  %CPU  %MEM     TIME+ COMMAND
 129648 root      20   0   50192   7192   3700 R  22.5   0.1   6:41.44 stress-ng-cpu
 129649 root      20   0   50192   7192   3700 R  22.5   0.1   6:40.26 stress-ng-cpu
 129650 root      20   0   50192   7192   3700 R  21.9   0.1   6:41.29 stress-ng-cpu
 129651 root      20   0   50192   7192   3700 R  21.5   0.1   6:41.41 stress-ng-cpu
   3628 root      20   0 2628344 783248  56748 S   8.6   9.6  13:17.07 kube-apiserver
   3831 root      20   0 1853284  83592  44336 S   4.6   1.0   3:07.88 kubelet
```

Figure 12.8 – cputest with 90% CPUQuota

Here, in the cgroup filesystem, we see that `CPUQuota` is indeed set to `90%`:

```
donnie@ubuntu2004:/sys/fs/cgroup/cpu/system.slice/cputest.
service$ cat cpu.cfs_quota_us
90000
donnie@ubuntu2004:/sys/fs/cgroup/cpu/system.slice/cputest.
service$
```

Note that this limit is only placed on the *service*, and not on the root user who owns the service. The root user can still run other programs and services without any limits.

Next, let's set `CPUQuota` in the `cputest.service` file.

Setting CPUQuota in the service file

First, stop `cputest.service`, like this:

```
donnie@ubuntu2004:~$ sudo systemctl stop cputest.service
donnie@ubuntu2004:~$
```

Next, delete the `cputest.service.d/` directory that you created with the `systemctl set-property` command:

```
donnie@ubuntu2004:/etc/systemd/system.control$ sudo rm -rf cputest.service.d/
donnie@ubuntu2004:/etc/systemd/system.control$
```

Do `systemctl daemon-reload` and then start `cputest.service`. You should see that the service now hogs the CPU, as it did at first. Stop the service, and then edit the unit file by doing:

```
donnie@ubuntu2004:~$ sudo systemctl edit --full cputest.service
```

Add the `CPUQuota=90%` line, so that the file now looks like this:

```
[Unit]
Description=CPU stress test service

[Service]
ExecStart=/usr/bin/stress-ng -c 4
CPUQuota=90%
```

Save the file and start the service. You should see in the `top` display that the new setting has taken effect.

That's all there is to it. Easy, right?

> **Note**
>
> The `systemd.resource-control` man page explains the various directives you can use to control resource usage. When you read through it, take note of which ones are for cgroups Version 1 and which ones are for cgroups Version 2. Also, take note of the directives that are marked as *deprecated*. For example, many cgroups tutorials that you'll find on the web tell you to use the `CPUShares` directive, which is listed on this man page as deprecated. (In Linux-speak, something that has been deprecated still works for now, but it will quit working at some point in the future. In this case, these deprecated directives work for Version 1, but they won't work for Version 2.)

We won't need `cputest.service` anymore, so go ahead and stop it. Let's move on to see how to control Vicky's memory usage.

Controlling memory usage

Let's start by having Vicky do something that will hog all of the system memory. As before, we'll use the `stress-ng` utility to simulate that, like this:

```
vicky@ubuntu2004:~$ stress-ng --brk 4
```

Wait a few moments, and you'll see some fairly ugly things in the `top` display:

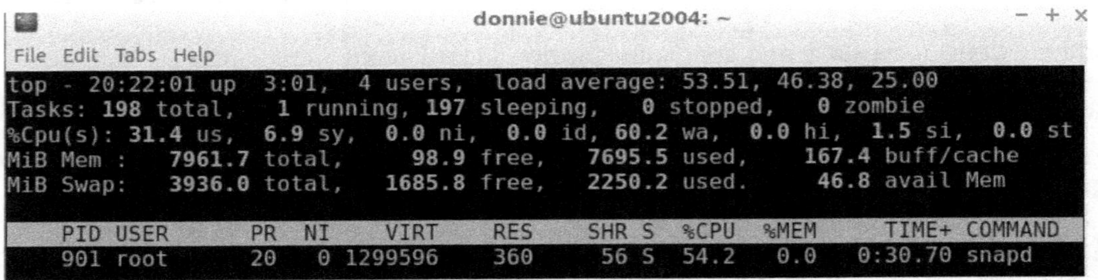

Figure 12.9 – The top display for Vicky's memory usage

Yeah, only 98.9 bytes of free memory, and super-high load averages. In fact, after about 2 minutes or so, this virtual machine is completely unresponsive to any commands. Ouch!

Now, understand that I still have the 200% `CPUQuota` set for Vicky. So, CPU usage isn't the problem here. The load average is a representation of how many tasks are waiting to be serviced by the CPU. In the top part of the `top` display, as shown in *Figure 12.9*, the `53.51` that you see is the 1-minute average, `46.38` is the 5-minute average, and `25.00` is the 15-minute average. These load averages are spread across all available CPU cores. This means that the more cores you have, the higher the load averages can go without hurting system performance. With only four cores, my virtual machine can't even begin to handle load averages like these. By hogging all of the system memory, Vicky is preventing the CPU from servicing tasks in a timely manner.

In order to shut down Vicky's program on this unresponsive virtual machine, I had to close down her remote terminal window by clicking on the **x** button in the top corner, which in turn closed down her `stress-ng` session. I mean, there was just no other way to do it. If this were to happen in real life on the local terminal of a physical server, you'd likely have to take the drastic step of either hitting the power switch or pulling the power cord. Even doing a `kill` command on this `stress-ng` process won't work, because the system won't be able to execute it.

To prevent this from happening again, let's set a 1GB memory limit for Vicky, like this:

```
donnie@ubuntu2004:~$ sudo systemctl set-property --runtime
user-1001.slice MemoryMax=1G
[sudo] password for donnie:
donnie@ubuntu2004:~$
```

`MemoryMax`, eh? That could be the name of a memory-enhancing nutritional supplement for us senior citizens.

Seriously though, you see that I'm using the `--runtime` option, which I didn't use before. This option makes the setting temporary, so that it will disappear when I reboot this machine. Instead of creating a permanent configuration file in the `/etc/systemd/system.control/user-1001.slice.d/` directory, this handy-dandy `--runtime` option created a temporary configuration file in the `/run/systemd/system.control/user-1001.slice.d/` directory, which looks like this:

```
donnie@ubuntu2004:/run/systemd/system.control/user-1001.slice.
d$ cat 50-MemoryMax.conf
# This is a drop-in unit file extension, created via "systemctl
set-property"
# or an equivalent operation. Do not edit.
[Slice]
```

```
MemoryMax=1073741824
donnie@ubuntu2004:/run/systemd/system.control/user-1001.slice.
d$
```

To make the setting permanent, just run the command again without the `--runtime` option, and then do `daemon-reload`.

Now, when Vicky runs her evil memory-hogging program, she won't be able to lock up the system.

Controlling blkio usage

In this scenario, Vicky is once again trying to hog system resources for herself. This time, she's reading so much from the system hard drive that nobody else can use it. Before we get to that, you'll need to install `iotop` on your virtual machines, so that you can measure the amount of bandwidth that Vicky is using. On the Ubuntu machine, do:

```
sudo apt install iotop
```

On the Alma machine, do:

```
sudo dnf install iotop
```

In the remote login window where you're running `top`, quit `top` and then do:

```
sudo iotop -o
```

Now that we have things set up, let's see about setting a `blkio` limit for Vicky.

Setting a blkio limit for Vicky

In Vicky's remote login window, have her use our good friend `dd` to create a dummy file, like this:

```
vicky@ubuntu2004:~$ dd if=/dev/zero of=afile bs=1M count=10000
10000+0 records in
10000+0 records out
10485760000 bytes (10 GB, 9.8 GiB) copied, 17.4288 s, 602 MB/s
vicky@ubuntu2004:~$
```

Cool. Vicky has created a 10 GB file full of nothing but zeros. Next, let's have Vicky use `dd` to copy the contents of the file over to the `/dev/null` device, while watching the `iotop -o` display in our own remote login window. The command looks like this:

```
vicky@ubuntu2004:~$ dd if=afile of=/dev/null
20480000+0 records in
20480000+0 records out
10485760000 bytes (10 GB, 9.8 GiB) copied, 69.2341 s, 151 MB/s
vicky@ubuntu2004:~$
```

So, it appears that she read this file at an average rate of 151 MB per second. The `iotop` display looks like this:

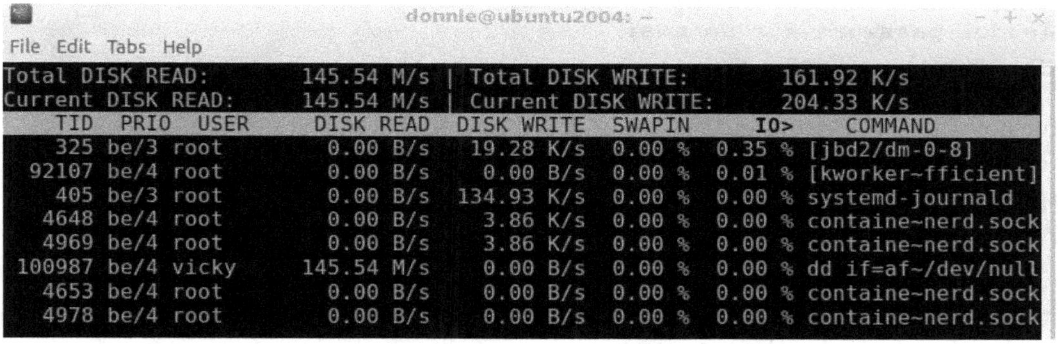

```
donnie@ubuntu2004: ~
File Edit Tabs Help
Total DISK READ:       145.54 M/s | Total DISK WRITE:        161.92 K/s
Current DISK READ:     145.54 M/s | Current DISK WRITE:      204.33 K/s
    TID  PRIO  USER     DISK READ  DISK WRITE  SWAPIN     IO>    COMMAND
    325 be/3 root       0.00 B/s   19.28 K/s  0.00 %  0.35 % [jbd2/dm-0-8]
  92107 be/4 root       0.00 B/s    0.00 B/s  0.00 %  0.01 % [kworker~fficient]
    405 be/3 root       0.00 B/s  134.93 K/s  0.00 %  0.00 % systemd-journald
   4648 be/4 root       0.00 B/s    3.86 K/s  0.00 %  0.00 % containe~nerd.sock
   4969 be/4 root       0.00 B/s    3.86 K/s  0.00 %  0.00 % containe~nerd.sock
 100987 be/4 vicky    145.54 M/s    0.00 B/s  0.00 %  0.00 % dd if=af~/dev/null
   4653 be/4 root       0.00 B/s    0.00 B/s  0.00 %  0.00 % containe~nerd.sock
   4978 be/4 root       0.00 B/s    0.00 B/s  0.00 %  0.00 % containe~nerd.sock
```

Figure 12.10 – Vicky's read bandwidth with no restrictions

To limit her read bandwidth, we first need to know where she is reading the file from. We can use the `lsblk` utility to get a clue, like this:

```
donnie@ubuntu2004:~$ lsblk
NAME                          MAJ:MIN RM   SIZE RO TYPE MOUNTPOINT
loop0                           7:0    0  99.4M  1 loop /snap/
core/11316
. . .
. . .
sda                             8:0    0     1T  0 disk
├─sda1                          8:1    0     1M  0 part
├─sda2                          8:2    0     1G  0 part /boot
└─sda3                          8:3    0     1T  0 part
  └─ubuntu--vg-ubuntu--lv 253:0    0   200G  0 lvm  /
```

```
sdb                                 8:16    0     10G  0 disk
└─sdb1                              8:17    0     10G  0 part /media/
backup
sr0                                11:0     1   1024M  0 rom
donnie@ubuntu2004:~$
```

We know that Vicky's file is in her own home directory. We see here that the /home/ directory isn't mounted separately. So, it must be in the root partition, which is mounted as a logical volume on the /dev/sda drive. Let's now say that we want to limit Vicky's read bandwidth to only one MB per second for this logical volume. The command would look like this:

```
donnie@ubuntu2004:~$ sudo systemctl set-property user-1001.
slice BlockIOReadBandwidth="/dev/sda 1M"
[sudo] password for donnie:
donnie@ubuntu2004:~$
```

Note how the device name and the rate limit setting both have to be surrounded by a pair of double quotes. Also, note that we set bandwidth limits for the entire drive, not just for a specific partition or logical volume. Of course, we've created a new set file in the /etc/systemd/system.control/ directory, so be sure to do a daemon-reload.

Next, have Vicky repeat her dd if=afile of=/dev/null command. Be aware that with her reduced bandwidth, this will take a while to complete. While it's running, note Vicky's reduced speed in the iotop window:

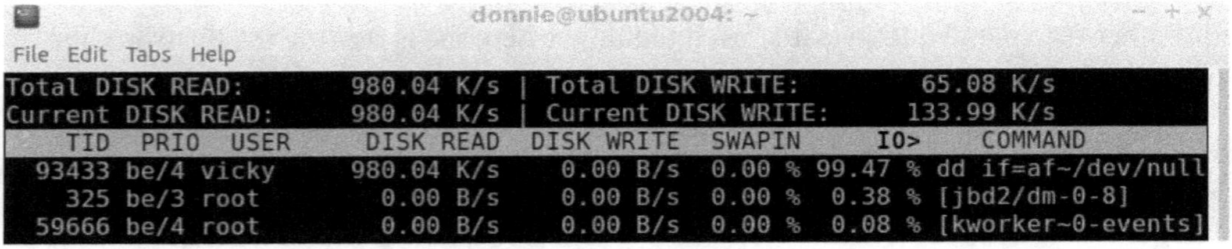

```
donnie@ubuntu2004: ~
File  Edit  Tabs  Help
Total DISK READ:        980.04 K/s | Total DISK WRITE:         65.08 K/s
Current DISK READ:      980.04 K/s | Current DISK WRITE:      133.99 K/s
    TID  PRIO  USER     DISK READ  DISK WRITE  SWAPIN     IO>    COMMAND
  93433 be/4 vicky     980.04 K/s    0.00 B/s  0.00 % 99.47 % dd if=af~/dev/null
    325 be/3 root        0.00 B/s    0.00 B/s  0.00 %  0.38 % [jbd2/dm-0-8]
  59666 be/4 root        0.00 B/s    0.00 B/s  0.00 %  0.08 % [kworker~0-events]
```

Figure 12.11 – Vicky's reduced bandwidth

Yeah, she's just under one MB per second, just where we want her to be. By the way, don't feel bad if you want to abort this operation before it finishes. At this one MB per second rate, it will be a long time before it finishes on its own.

Finally, while Vicky is still logged in, look at the attribute file that this command modified in the cgroup filesystem:

```
donnie@ubuntu2004:/sys/fs/cgroup/blkio/user.slice/user-1001.
slice$ cat blkio.throttle.read_bps_device
```

```
8:0 1000000
donnie@ubuntu2004:/sys/fs/cgroup/blkio/user.slice/user-1001.
slice$
```

In this `blkio.throttle.read_bps_device` file, the `8:0` represents the major and minor numbers of the `/dev/sda` device, as you can see here:

```
donnie@ubuntu2004:/dev$ ls -l sda
brw-rw---- 1 root disk 8, 0 Aug 19 14:01 sda
donnie@ubuntu2004:/dev$
```

Setting a blkio limit for a service

Of course, you can also set the `BlockIOReadBandwidth` parameter for a service. For example, let's use the `set-property` option to set it for the Apache web server. On the Ubuntu machine, the command is:

```
donnie@ubuntu2004:~$ sudo systemctl set-property apache2.
service BlockIOReadBandwidth="/dev/sda 1M"
```

On the AlmaLinux machine, the command is:

```
[donnie@localhost ~]$ sudo systemctl set-property httpd.service
BlockIOReadBandwidth="/dev/sda 1M"
```

If you want to set this `BlockIOReadBandwidth` parameter in a service file, there's a bit of a trick that you need to know about. When you set this on the command line, you had to surround the `/dev/sda 1M` part with a pair of double quotes. When you set this in a service file, you do *not* surround the `/dev/sda 1M` within double quotes. To demonstrate, let's set up an FTP server and set a `blkio` limit on it. On the Ubuntu machine, install the FTP server by doing:

```
donnie@ubuntu2004:~$ sudo apt install vsftpd
```

On the AlmaLinux machine, do:

```
[donnie@localhost ~]$ sudo dnf install vsftpd
```

On either machine, edit the service file by doing:

```
donnie@ubuntu2004:~$ sudo systemctl edit --full vsftpd
```

In the `[Service]` section, add the new parameter, but without the double quotes:

```
[Service]
. . .
.. .
BlockIOReadBandwidth=/dev/sda 1M
```

Do a `daemon-reload` and restart the `vsftpd` service. You should see the new setting show up in the cgroup filesystem:

```
donnie@ubuntu2004:/sys/fs/cgroup/blkio/system.slice/vsftpd.
service$ cat blkio.throttle.read_bps_device
8:0 1000000
donnie@ubuntu2004:/sys/fs/cgroup/blkio/system.slice/vsftpd.
service$
```

There are a lot more resource management directives than what we can cover here. To see more, just consult the `systemd.resource-management` man page.

Before we close this chapter, let's commit a bit of sacrilege by talking about `pam_limits` and `ulimit`, which have nothing at all to do with either systemd or cgroups.

Understanding pam_limits and ulimit

Before the cgroup and systemd technologies were invented, we had other methods for controlling resource usage. These methods are still with us, and we can do some things with them that we can't do with cgroups. To demonstrate, let's briefly look at two of these older methods.

The ulimit command

The `ulimit` command allows us to dynamically control resource usage for a shell session and for any processes that get started by the shell session. Let's use the `-a` option to see what the default settings are for my current shell session:

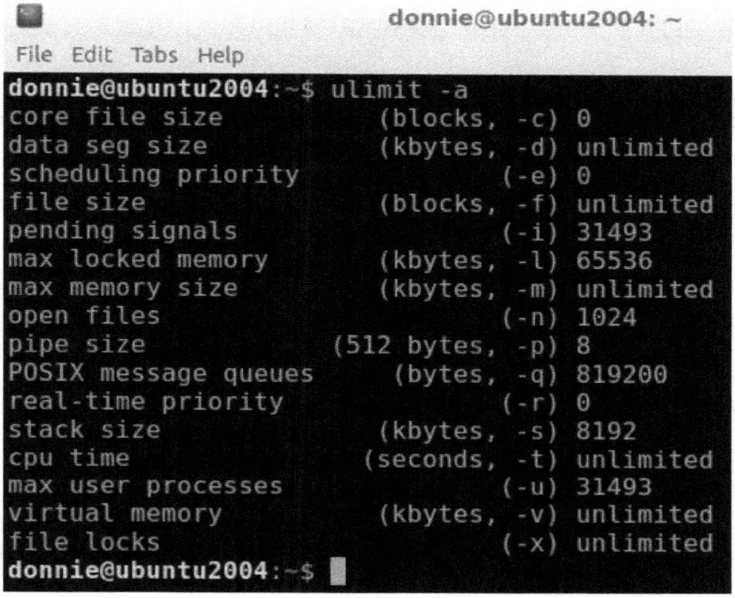

```
donnie@ubuntu2004: ~
File Edit Tabs Help
donnie@ubuntu2004:~$ ulimit -a
core file size          (blocks, -c) 0
data seg size           (kbytes, -d) unlimited
scheduling priority             (-e) 0
file size               (blocks, -f) unlimited
pending signals                 (-i) 31493
max locked memory       (kbytes, -l) 65536
max memory size         (kbytes, -m) unlimited
open files                      (-n) 1024
pipe size            (512 bytes, -p) 8
POSIX message queues     (bytes, -q) 819200
real-time priority              (-r) 0
stack size              (kbytes, -s) 8192
cpu time               (seconds, -t) unlimited
max user processes              (-u) 31493
virtual memory          (kbytes, -v) unlimited
file locks                      (-x) unlimited
donnie@ubuntu2004:~$
```

Figure 12.12 – The default ulimit settings

As you can see, doing `ulimit -a` also shows us the option switches that we'd use to set the various limits. The trick is that you can either set or lower limits as a normal user, but you need `sudo` privileges to increase any limits. For example, let's say that we want to limit the size of any new files to only ten MB. We'll use the `-f` option, and specify the file size in terms of the number of 1,024-byte blocks. Ten MB works out to be 10,240 blocks, so our command looks like this:

```
donnie@ubuntu2004:~$ ulimit -f 10240
donnie@ubuntu2004:~$
```

The new limit shows up in the `ulimit -a` output:

```
donnie@ubuntu2004:~$ ulimit -a
. . .
. . .
file size               (blocks, -f) 10240
. . .
. . .
```

Now, watch what happens when I try to increase this limit:

```
donnie@ubuntu2004:~$ ulimit -f 20000
-bash: ulimit: file size: cannot modify limit: Operation not permitted
donnie@ubuntu2004:~$
```

So, a normal user can set a limit that hasn't been set before, but sudo privileges are needed to increase an existing limit. But you can reset everything back to the default settings by either closing the terminal window and opening a new one or by logging out and logging back in. Then, just set a new limit to whatever you want it to be.

Now, when I try to create a ten MB size file, things work fine:

```
donnie@ubuntu2004:~$ dd if=/dev/zero of=afile bs=1M count=10
10+0 records in
10+0 records out
10485760 bytes (10 MB, 10 MiB) copied, 0.0440278 s, 238 MB/s
donnie@ubuntu2004:~$
```

But things don't work so fine when I try to create an eleven MB file:

```
donnie@ubuntu2004:~$ dd if=/dev/zero of=afile bs=1M count=11
File size limit exceeded (core dumped)
donnie@ubuntu2004:~$
```

The `ulimit` command can come in handy for developers who need to test new software, or for anyone who needs to set resource limits from within a shell script. To read more about `ulimit`, open the `bash-builtins` man page and search for `ulimit`.

Next, let's talk about using a configuration file to set limits.

The pam_limits module

The `pam_limits` module is part of the **Pluggable Authentication Modules** system, which most people just know as **PAM**. It allows you to set non-volatile limits on either users or groups. You'll do this by either editing the `/etc/security/limits.conf` file or by creating new drop-in files in the `/etc/security/limits.d/` directory. To get an idea of how this works, open the `/etc/security/limits.conf` file and look at the commented-out examples. For a more detailed explanation of things, look at the `limits.conf` man page.

Let's say that we want to prevent Pogo from creating any files that are larger than 20 MB. We'll do that by adding a line to the bottom of the `/etc/security/limits.conf` file, which will look like this:

```
. . .
. . .
#<domain>       <type>  <item>          <value>
#
. . .
. . .
pogo             hard    fsize           20480
# End of file
```

Log in as Pogo, and let him try to create a file:

```
pogo@ubuntu2004:~$ dd if=/dev/zero of=afile bs=1M count=19
19+0 records in
19+0 records out
19922944 bytes (20 MB, 19 MiB) copied, 0.0989717 s, 201 MB/s
pogo@ubuntu2004:~$
```

Keep repeating this command with a larger `count=` number until you get an error.

All right, I think that this about covers things for this chapter. Let's wrap this baby up.

Summary

In this chapter, we looked at the basics of using cgroups Version 1 to control resources. A lot of information you've likely seen in your web searches is out of date and somewhat confusing. My goal for this chapter has been to bring you up-to-date information and present it in an understandable manner.

We started by looking at the cgroups Version 1 controllers and giving a brief explanation of each one. After that, we saw how to control CPU usage, memory usage, and block device bandwidth usage for both users and services. We wrapped up by showing you the old, non-cgroup way of setting limits, which is still useful.

In the next chapter, we'll look at cgroups Version 2. I'll see you there.

Questions

1. Your computer has six CPU cores. What would Vicky's `CPUQuota` setting be if you want to limit her to only 16.66% for each CPU core?

   A. 16.66%

   B. 33.00%

   C. 100%

   D. 200%

2. According to the `systemd.resource-control` man page, which of the following directives represents the most modern way of limiting someone's memory usage?

   A. `MemoryLimit`

   B. `MemoryMax`

   C. `LimitMemory`

   D. `MaxMemory`

3. What does the `--runtime` option for `systemctl set-property` do?

   A. It makes the new setting permanent.

   B. Nothing, because it's already the default behavior.

   C. It makes the new setting temporary.

   D. It makes the command run faster.

4. Which of the following is true about CPU load averages?

   A. Machines with more CPU cores can handle higher CPU load averages.

   B. CPU load averages have nothing to do with how many CPU cores a machine has.

   C. Excessive memory usage won't cause CPU load averages to go too high.

   D. High CPU load averages have no effect on any machine.

Answers

1. C
2. B
3. C
4. A

Further reading

- Using control groups Version 1 with `systemd`:

  `https://access.redhat.com/documentation/en-us/red_hat_enterprise_linux/8/html/managing_monitoring_and_updating_the_kernel/using-control-groups-version-1-with-systemd_managing-monitoring-and-updating-the-kernel`

- The Linux kernel Completely Fair Scheduler:

  `https://www.kernel.org/doc/html/latest/scheduler/sched-design-CFS.html`

- For anyone who still needs to work with RHEL 7 or RHEL 7 clones on machines with multiple CPUs, here's a procedure for using the `cpuset` controller:

  `https://www.redhat.com/en/blog/world-domination-cgroups-part-6-cpuset`

- How to set a `ulimit` value permanently:

  `https://linuxhint.com/permanently_set_ulimit_value/`

13
Understanding cgroup Version 2

In this chapter, we'll look at **cgroup Version 2**. We'll see how it's different from **cgroups Version 1**, and how it improves upon Version 1. After that, we'll take a brief look at how to work with it. We'll wrap up by converting the **AlmaLinux** machine to use cgroup Version 2. Learning how to use cgroup Version 2 will be very helpful to developers of new software, as well as to **Linux** administrators who want to be prepared for the future.

By the way, that's not a typo that you see in the chapter title. One of the Version 2 changes is in the official name of the technology. So, we have *cgroups* Version 1, and *cgroup* Version 2. Strange, but true. (I didn't explain this before, because I didn't want to create more confusion).

Specific topics in this chapter include:

- Understanding the need for Version 2
- Understanding the improvements in Version 2
- Setting resource limits on rootless containers
- Understanding **cpuset**
- Converting RHEL 8-type distros to cgroup version 2

With the introduction out of the way, let's get started.

Technical requirements

This time, we'll use a **Fedora virtual machine** that's set to use as many CPU cores and as much memory as you can spare. (I'll still have mine set to use four CPU cores and eight GB of memory.) So, download your favorite spin of Fedora, and create a virtual machine from it.

For the *Understanding cpuset* section, it would be helpful to have a host computer with at least two physical CPUs. I realize that not many people will have access to a machine like that, and that's okay. I do have such a machine, so I can show you what you need to see.

We'll also use the AlmaLinux machine for a couple of brief demos.

All right, let's get with it.

Check out the following link to see the Code in Action video: `https://bit.ly/3xJNcDx`

Understanding the need for Version 2

As good as cgroups Version 1 is, it does have a few rather serious flaws. Let's take a quick look.

Version 1 complexity

To begin with, Version 1 has too many resource controllers and too many attributes per controller. Very few people use more than just the *Big Three* controllers that we covered in *Chapter 12*, Controlling Resource Usage with cgroups Version 1. Some unnecessary controllers have been removed from Version 2.

There's also too much complexity with the Version 1 hierarchy, which makes it a bit confusing to use and can hurt performance. To see what I mean, think back about what we saw in the Version 1 `cgroup` filesystem. You saw that each resource controller has its own subdirectory, as we see here:

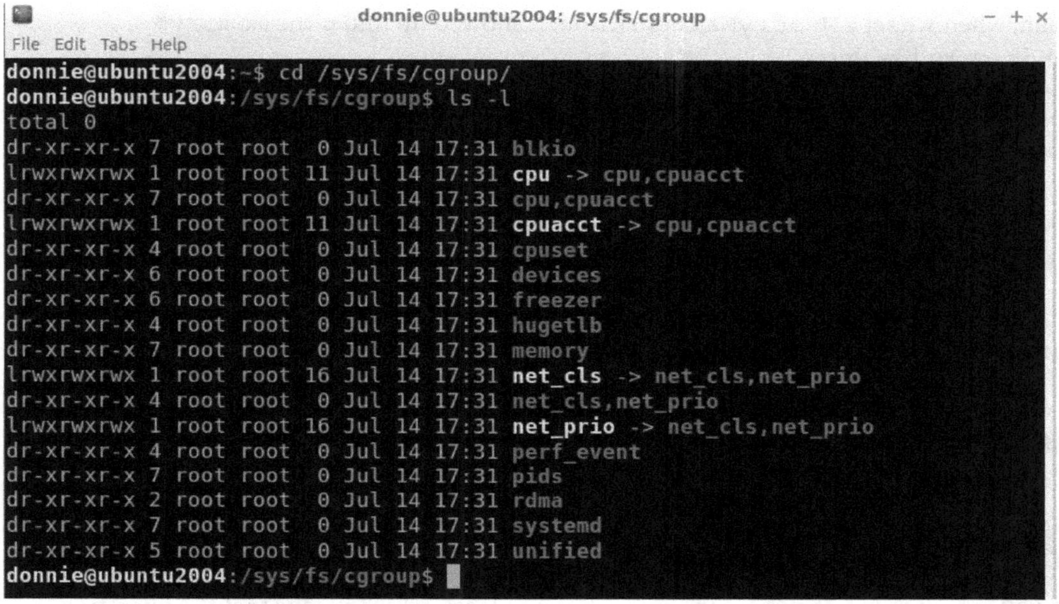

```
donnie@ubuntu2004: /sys/fs/cgroup
File Edit Tabs Help
donnie@ubuntu2004:~$ cd /sys/fs/cgroup/
donnie@ubuntu2004:/sys/fs/cgroup$ ls -l
total 0
dr-xr-xr-x 7 root root  0 Jul 14 17:31 blkio
lrwxrwxrwx 1 root root 11 Jul 14 17:31 cpu -> cpu,cpuacct
dr-xr-xr-x 7 root root  0 Jul 14 17:31 cpu,cpuacct
lrwxrwxrwx 1 root root 11 Jul 14 17:31 cpuacct -> cpu,cpuacct
dr-xr-xr-x 4 root root  0 Jul 14 17:31 cpuset
dr-xr-xr-x 6 root root  0 Jul 14 17:31 devices
dr-xr-xr-x 6 root root  0 Jul 14 17:31 freezer
dr-xr-xr-x 4 root root  0 Jul 14 17:31 hugetlb
dr-xr-xr-x 7 root root  0 Jul 14 17:31 memory
lrwxrwxrwx 1 root root 16 Jul 14 17:31 net_cls -> net_cls,net_prio
dr-xr-xr-x 4 root root  0 Jul 14 17:31 net_cls,net_prio
lrwxrwxrwx 1 root root 16 Jul 14 17:31 net_prio -> net_cls,net_prio
dr-xr-xr-x 4 root root  0 Jul 14 17:31 perf_event
dr-xr-xr-x 7 root root  0 Jul 14 17:31 pids
dr-xr-xr-x 2 root root  0 Jul 14 17:31 rdma
dr-xr-xr-x 7 root root  0 Jul 14 17:31 systemd
dr-xr-xr-x 5 root root  0 Jul 14 17:31 unified
donnie@ubuntu2004:/sys/fs/cgroup$
```

Figure 13.1 – The resource controllers for version 1 on Ubuntu

In *Chapter 12*, *Controlling Resource Usage with cgroups Version 1*, we also saw that when we set a `CPUQuota` for Vicky, it appeared in her `user-1001.slice` subdirectory that's under the `cpu/user.slice` subdirectory, like this:

```
vicky@ubuntu2004:/sys/fs/cgroup/cpu/user.slice/user-1001.slice$ cat cpu.cfs_quota_us
200000
vicky@ubuntu2004:/sys/fs/cgroup/cpu/user.slice/user-1001.slice$
```

Then, when we set a `MemoryMax` restriction, it showed up under the `memory` subdirectory, like this:

```
vicky@ubuntu2004:/sys/fs/cgroup/memory/user.slice/user-1001.
slice$ cat memory.max_usage_in_bytes
30994432
vicky@ubuntu2004:/sys/fs/cgroup/memory/user.slice/user-1001.
slice$
```

Okay, you'll never guess what happened when we set Vicky's `BlockIOReadBandwidth` parameter. That's right, it shows up under the `blkio` subdirectory, like this:

```
vicky@ubuntu2004:/sys/fs/cgroup/blkio/user.slice/user-1001.
slice$ cat blkio.throttle.read_bps_device
8:0 1000000
vicky@ubuntu2004:/sys/fs/cgroup/blkio/user.slice/user-1001.
slice$
```

So you see, Vicky's settings are in three different places, which means that the operating system has to look in all three places to get them all.

> **Note**
>
> I accidentally used Vicky's login window instead of my own for these screenshots, but that's okay. It shows you that Vicky can see the settings in her own cgroup files. Of course, she can't change the settings, because she doesn't have the correct root privileges.

Version 1 attribute filenames

Another problem with Version 1 is that there's no consistent naming convention for the attribute files of the different resource controllers. For example, setting `MemoryMax` on Version 1 places a value in the `memory.max_usage_in_bytes` file, as we see here for Vicky:

```
donnie@ubuntu2004:/sys/fs/cgroup/memory/user.slice/user-1001.
slice$ cat memory.max_usage_in_bytes
30789632
donnie@ubuntu2004:/sys/fs/cgroup/memory/user.slice/user-1001.
slice$
```

However, Vicky's `CPUQuota` setting shows up in the `cpu.cfs_quota_us` file, as we see here:

```
donnie@ubuntu2004:/sys/fs/cgroup/cpu/user.slice/user-1001.
slice$ cat cpu.cfs_quota_us
200000
donnie@ubuntu2004:/sys/fs/cgroup/cpu/user.slice/user-1001.
slice$
```

As we'll see in a few moments, naming conventions are a lot more consistent with Version 2.

Okay, let's get to the real root of the problem by talking about *rootless containers.*

No support for rootless containers

As you saw in *Chapter 5, Creating and Editing Services*, we can use **Red Hat**'s new `podman` to create and run **Docker** containers without either root privileges or membership in the docker group. However, with cgroups Version 1, it's not possible for a non-privileged user to set runtime resource limits when creating a container. For example, let's go to the AlmaLinux machine and create a new user account for my buddy, Pogo, by doing:

```
[donnie@localhost ~]$ sudo useradd pogo
[donnie@localhost ~]$ sudo passwd pogo
```

Look at what happens to the poor guy when he tries to create a container with a 50% `CPUQuota`:

```
[pogo@localhost ~]$ podman run -it --cpu-period=100000
--cpu-quota=50000 ubuntu /bin/bash
Error: OCI runtime error: container_linux.go:367: starting
container process caused: process_linux.go:495: container
init caused: process_linux.go:458: setting cgroup config for
procHooks process caused: cannot set cpu limit: container could
not join or create cgroup
[pogo@localhost ~]$
```

Alas, poor Pogo doesn't have root privileges. So, he can create and run `podman` containers, but he can't set any resource limits for them.

> **Note**
> Actually, with cgroups Version 1, it *is* possible for a non-privileged user to set runtime resource limits on rootless `podman` containers. But, it requires that you delegate this ability to non-root users. With cgroups Version 1, that constitutes a security hazard because it could allow someone to create a container that could freeze your system. So, we're not going to do it (We'll talk more about delegation in just a bit).

Now, let's contrast that with what we see on the Fedora machine, which is running a pure cgroup Version 2 environment.

Understanding the improvements in cgroup Version 2

Version 2 is a bit more streamlined and simpler to understand. At the time of writing, Fedora, **Arch**, and **Debian 11** are the only three Linux distros of which I know that run cgroup Version 2 by default (that will likely change by the time you read this).

> **Note**
> It is possible to convert RHEL 8-type distros, such as **Alma** and **Rocky**, over to a pure Version 2 setup. Unfortunately, the RHEL-type distros use an older implementation of Version 2 that still doesn't have all of the resource controllers that we need enabled. So, to see everything that we need to see, we'll use Fedora.

To begin, let's log in to the Fedora machine and create a user account for my buddy Pogo (Pogo is the awesome opossum who comes in through my cat door at night to chow down on the cat food – Yes,seriously.) Then,Then, have Pogo log in from a remote terminal (Note that on Fedora, you might have to start and enable the `sshd` service first.) On your own local terminal, look at the cgroup filesystem, which looks like this:

```
[donnie@fedora ~]$ cd /sys/fs/cgroup/
[donnie@fedora cgroup]$ ls -l
total 0
-r--r--r--.  1 root root 0 Jul 30 16:55 cgroup.controllers
-rw-r--r--.  1 root root 0 Jul 30 16:56 cgroup.max.depth
-rw-r--r--.  1 root root 0 Jul 30 16:56 cgroup.max.descendants
-rw-r--r--.  1 root root 0 Jul 30 16:55 cgroup.procs
-r--r--r--.  1 root root 0 Jul 30 16:56 cgroup.stat
-rw-r--r--.  1 root root 0 Jul 30 17:42 cgroup.subtree_control
-rw-r--r--.  1 root root 0 Jul 30 16:56 cgroup.threads
-rw-r--r--.  1 root root 0 Jul 30 16:56 cpu.pressure
-r--r--r--.  1 root root 0 Jul 30 16:56 cpuset.cpus.effective
-r--r--r--.  1 root root 0 Jul 30 16:56 cpuset.mems.effective
-r--r--r--.  1 root root 0 Jul 30 16:56 cpu.stat
drwxr-xr-x.  2 root root 0 Jul 30 17:39 dev-hugepages.mount
drwxr-xr-x.  2 root root 0 Jul 30 17:39 dev-mqueue.mount
drwxr-xr-x.  2 root root 0 Jul 30 16:55 init.scope
-rw-r--r--.  1 root root 0 Jul 30 16:56 io.cost.model
-rw-r--r--.  1 root root 0 Jul 30 16:56 io.cost.qos
-rw-r--r--.  1 root root 0 Jul 30 16:56 io.pressure
-r--r--r--.  1 root root 0 Jul 30 16:56 io.stat
-r--r--r--.  1 root root 0 Jul 30 16:56 memory.numa_stat
-rw-r--r--.  1 root root 0 Jul 30 16:55 memory.pressure
-r--r--r--.  1 root root 0 Jul 30 16:56 memory.stat
-r--r--r--.  1 root root 0 Jul 30 16:56 misc.capacity
drwxr-xr-x.  2 root root 0 Jul 30 17:39 sys-fs-fuse-connections.mount
drwxr-xr-x.  2 root root 0 Jul 30 17:39 sys-kernel-config.mount
drwxr-xr-x.  2 root root 0 Jul 30 17:39 sys-kernel-debug.mount
drwxr-xr-x.  2 root root 0 Jul 30 17:39 sys-kernel-tracing.mount
drwxr-xr-x. 47 root root 0 Jul 30 17:41 system.slice
drwxr-xr-x.  4 root root 0 Jul 30 17:39 user.slice
[donnie@fedora cgroup]$
```

Figure 13.2 – The cgroup filesystem on Fedora

The attribute files that we see here are for the global settings, which we don't really care about for now. What I really want you to see is under the `system.slice` and `user.slice` subdirectories. Let's look at the `user.slice` subdirectory first.

Under the `user.slice` subdirectory, you'll see lots of files for things that can be set at the user slice level. At the bottom, we see the subdirectories for both Pogo and me, as we see here:

```
[donnie@fedora user.slice]$ ls -l
total 0
-r--r--r--. 1 root root 0 Jul 30 16:55 cgroup.controllers
. . .
. . .
```

```
-rw-r--r--. 1 root root 0 Jul 30 16:55 pids.max
drwxr-xr-x. 5 root root 0 Jul 30 17:24 user-1000.slice
drwxr-xr-x. 4 root root 0 Jul 30 17:09 user-1001.slice
[donnie@fedora user.slice]$
```

Each of these user slice subdirectories contains attribute files for all of the resource controllers, as we see here:

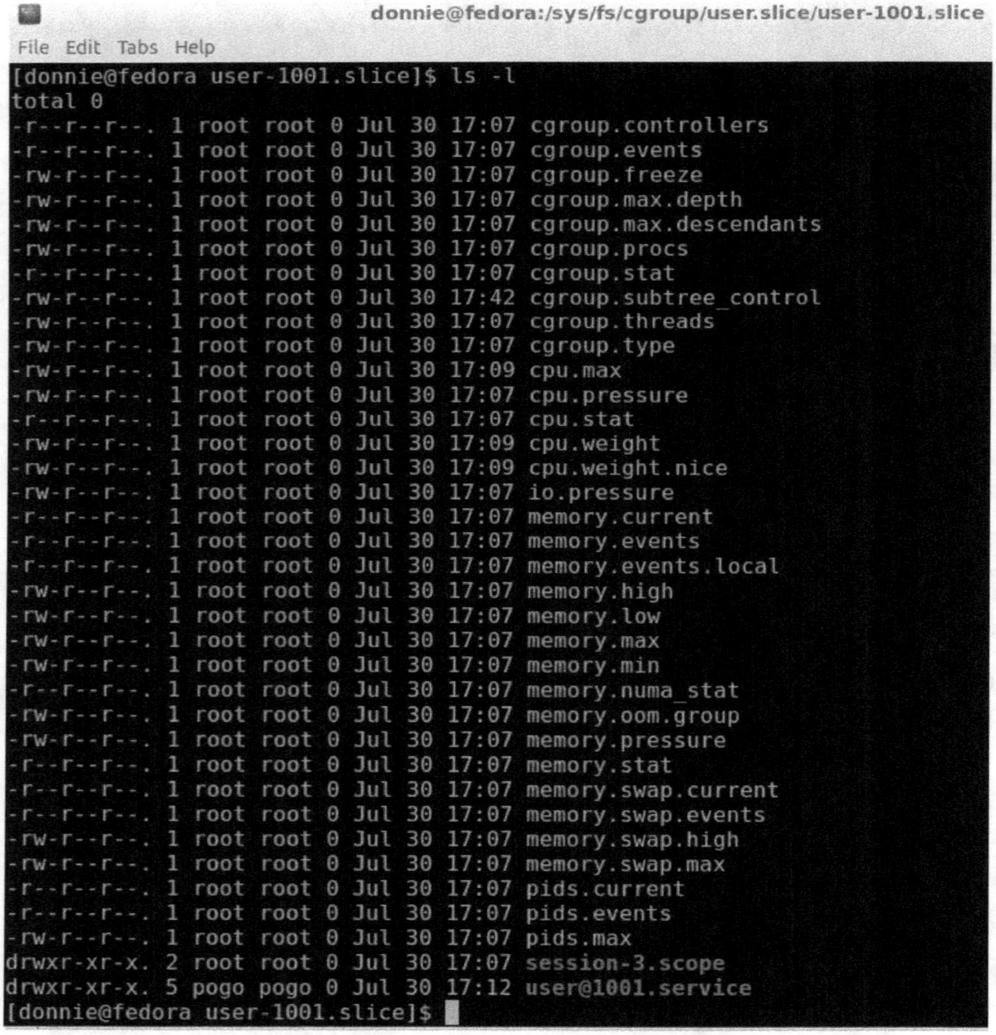

```
donnie@fedora:/sys/fs/cgroup/user.slice/user-1001.slice
File Edit Tabs Help
[donnie@fedora user-1001.slice]$ ls -l
total 0
-r--r--r--. 1 root root 0 Jul 30 17:07 cgroup.controllers
-r--r--r--. 1 root root 0 Jul 30 17:07 cgroup.events
-rw-r--r--. 1 root root 0 Jul 30 17:07 cgroup.freeze
-rw-r--r--. 1 root root 0 Jul 30 17:07 cgroup.max.depth
-rw-r--r--. 1 root root 0 Jul 30 17:07 cgroup.max.descendants
-rw-r--r--. 1 root root 0 Jul 30 17:07 cgroup.procs
-r--r--r--. 1 root root 0 Jul 30 17:07 cgroup.stat
-rw-r--r--. 1 root root 0 Jul 30 17:42 cgroup.subtree_control
-rw-r--r--. 1 root root 0 Jul 30 17:07 cgroup.threads
-rw-r--r--. 1 root root 0 Jul 30 17:07 cgroup.type
-rw-r--r--. 1 root root 0 Jul 30 17:09 cpu.max
-rw-r--r--. 1 root root 0 Jul 30 17:07 cpu.pressure
-r--r--r--. 1 root root 0 Jul 30 17:07 cpu.stat
-rw-r--r--. 1 root root 0 Jul 30 17:09 cpu.weight
-rw-r--r--. 1 root root 0 Jul 30 17:09 cpu.weight.nice
-rw-r--r--. 1 root root 0 Jul 30 17:07 io.pressure
-r--r--r--. 1 root root 0 Jul 30 17:07 memory.current
-r--r--r--. 1 root root 0 Jul 30 17:07 memory.events
-r--r--r--. 1 root root 0 Jul 30 17:07 memory.events.local
-rw-r--r--. 1 root root 0 Jul 30 17:07 memory.high
-rw-r--r--. 1 root root 0 Jul 30 17:07 memory.low
-rw-r--r--. 1 root root 0 Jul 30 17:07 memory.max
-rw-r--r--. 1 root root 0 Jul 30 17:07 memory.min
-r--r--r--. 1 root root 0 Jul 30 17:07 memory.numa_stat
-rw-r--r--. 1 root root 0 Jul 30 17:07 memory.oom.group
-rw-r--r--. 1 root root 0 Jul 30 17:07 memory.pressure
-r--r--r--. 1 root root 0 Jul 30 17:07 memory.stat
-r--r--r--. 1 root root 0 Jul 30 17:07 memory.swap.current
-r--r--r--. 1 root root 0 Jul 30 17:07 memory.swap.events
-rw-r--r--. 1 root root 0 Jul 30 17:07 memory.swap.high
-rw-r--r--. 1 root root 0 Jul 30 17:07 memory.swap.max
-r--r--r--. 1 root root 0 Jul 30 17:07 pids.current
-r--r--r--. 1 root root 0 Jul 30 17:07 pids.events
-rw-r--r--. 1 root root 0 Jul 30 17:07 pids.max
drwxr-xr-x. 2 root root 0 Jul 30 17:07 session-3.scope
drwxr-xr-x. 5 pogo pogo 0 Jul 30 17:12 user@1001.service
[donnie@fedora user-1001.slice]$
```

Figure 13.3 – Resource controllers for user-1001.slice

So now, all of the applicable settings for a particular user would be contained in the `user slice` directory for that user. The operating system now only has to look in one place to get all of the settings for a user.

Next, have Pogo log in from a remote terminal. Then, in your own terminal window, set `CPUQuota` for Pogo. The good news is that the command to do that is exactly the same as it was in Version 1. If you don't remember, the command is:

```
[donnie@fedora ~]$ sudo systemctl set-property user-1001.slice
CPUQuota=40%
[sudo] password for donnie:
[donnie@fedora ~]$
```

Then, do a `daemon-reload`. Once that's done, look at the `cpu.max` file in Pogo's user slice directory, which should look like this:

```
[donnie@fedora ~]$ cd /sys/fs/cgroup/user.slice/user-1001.
slice/
[donnie@fedora user-1001.slice]$ cat cpu.max
40000 100000
[donnie@fedora user-1001.slice]$
```

The `40000` figure represents the 40% `CPUShare`, and `100000` represents the time interval over which `CPUShare` is measured. The default time setting, which you see here, is 100 milliseconds (you can change that time interval, but you'll likely never need to).

You would also set Pogo's memory limit the same you did with Version 1, as we see here:

```
[donnie@fedora user-1001.slice]$ sudo systemctl set-property
user-1001.slice MemoryMax=1G
[sudo] password for donnie:
[donnie@fedora user-1001.slice]$
```

This time, the setting shows up in Pogo's `memory.max` file, as we see here:

```
[donnie@fedora user-1001.slice]$ cat memory.max
1073741824
[donnie@fedora user-1001.slice]$
```

Now, understand that this `MemoryMax` setting is a hard limit. In other words, Pogo absolutely cannot use more memory than what `MemoryMax` allocates. If you look in the `systemd.resource-control` man page, you'll see other options that are available for Version 2 and that aren't available for Version 1. (Note that this man page always refers to cgroup Version 2 as the *unified control group hierarchy*.) One such parameter is `MemoryHigh`, which is more of a soft limit. `MemoryHigh` would allow Pogo to exceed his memory allocation if it's unavoidable, but his processes would be throttled until his memory usage goes back down to within his allocation. This makes it easier for a system to deal with temporary spikes in memory usage for any given process or user.

Version 2 also has the `MemoryLow` and `MemoryMin` parameters, which cause a process to reclaim memory from unprotected processes if the amount of free memory for the protected process drops to the specified threshold. If you want to control swap memory usage, Version 2 lets you do that with the `MemorySwapMax` parameter.

Setting limits on `block I/O` usage is a bit different, because the parameter names have changed. To limit Pogo's read bandwidth, we'll first use `df` to see what drive devices we have, as we see here:

```
[donnie@fedora ~]$ df -h | grep -v tmpfs
Filesystem      Size  Used Avail Use% Mounted on
/dev/sda2        21G  2.6G   18G  13% /
/dev/sda2        21G  2.6G   18G  13% /home
/dev/sda1       976M  256M  654M  29% /boot
[donnie@fedora ~]$
```

The desktop versions of Fedora now use the `btrfs` filesystem by default, which is why we just see regular drive partitions instead of logical volumes. (There's no need to use logical volumes with `btrfs` because it has its own built-in drive pooling mechanism.) If you're using **Fedora Server** though, you'll still see `ext4` and logical volumes. Anyway, we see that the `/home/` directory is mounted on the `/dev/sda` drive, which of course is where Pogo's home directory is. (As we saw with version 1, you can set a rate limit on an entire drive, but not on a specific partition of that drive.)

We'll now use the `IOReadBandwidthMax` parameter to limit the rate at which Pogo can transfer files, like this:

```
[donnie@fedora ~]$ sudo systemctl set-property user-1001.slice
IOReadBandwidthMax="/dev/sda 1M"
[sudo] password for donnie:
[donnie@fedora ~]$
```

Note that because there's a blank space in the `/dev/sda 1M` parameter, you have to surround it with a pair of double-quotes (`" "`) when you set this from the command line.

Next, look at the `io.max` file in Pogo's user slice directory, which should look like this:

```
[donnie@fedora user-1001.slice]$ cat io.max
8:0 rbps=1000000 wbps=max riops=max wiops=max
[donnie@fedora user-1001.slice]$
```

Here, we see another benefit of using Version 2. Instead of having four separate attribute files for the four available parameter settings, as we had with Version 1, Version 2 places the `IOReadBandwidthMax`, `IOWriteBandwidthMax`, `IOReadIOPSMax`, and `IOWriteIOPSMax` settings all in one file.

Also, note that the `8:0` we see at the beginning of the line in this `io.max` file represents the major and minor numbers of the entire `sda` drive, as we see here:

```
[donnie@fedora dev]$ pwd
/dev
[donnie@fedora dev]$ ls -l sd*
brw-rw----. 1 root disk 8, 0 Jul 31 14:30 sda
brw-rw----. 1 root disk 8, 1 Jul 31 14:30 sda1
brw-rw----. 1 root disk 8, 2 Jul 31 14:30 sda2
[donnie@fedora dev]$
```

Okay, if you really want to, you can play around with `stress-ng` for Pogo as you did for Vicky in *Chapter 12, Controlling Resource Usage with cgroups Version 1*, but I'm not going to repeat the directions for that here.

The main thing to know about setting limits on services is that each system service has its own subdirectory under the `/sys/fs/cgroup/system.slice/` directory, as we see here:

```
[donnie@fedora system.slice]$ pwd
/sys/fs/cgroup/system.slice
[donnie@fedora system.slice]$ ls -l
total 0
drwxr-xr-x. 2 root root 0 Jul 31 14:30  abrtd.service
drwxr-xr-x. 2 root root 0 Jul 31 14:30  abrt-journal-core.
service
drwxr-xr-x. 2 root root 0 Jul 31 14:30  abrt-oops.service
```

```
drwxr-xr-x. 2 root root 0 Jul 31 14:30  abrt-xorg.service
drwxr-xr-x. 2 root root 0 Jul 31 14:30  alsa-state.service
drwxr-xr-x. 2 root root 0 Jul 31 14:31  atd.service
drwxr-xr-x. 2 root root 0 Jul 31 14:30  auditd.service
. . .
. . .
```

Within each of these subdirectories, you'll see the same attribute files that you saw for Pogo. Also, the procedure for setting limits on services is the same as it was for Version 1, so I also won't repeat any of that.

> **Note**
> Be aware that certain parameters that you may be used to using under cgroups Version 1 have been renamed for cgroup Version 2. Specifically, the `CPUShares`, `StartupCPUShares`, and `MemoryLimit` parameters in Version 1 have been replaced by `CPUWeight`, `StartupCPUWeight`, and `MemoryMax`, respectively. Also, all Version 1 parameter names that have the `BlockIO` prefix have been replaced with parameter names that have the `IO` prefix.

All righty, now that we know about the cgroup Version 2 filesystem, let's see if we can let Pogo set some resource limits on a rootless container.

Setting resource limits on rootless containers

A few moments ago, I told you about the concept of *delegation*. Normally, you need root privileges in order to set any resource limits. However, you can delegate this chore to non-privileged users. The best news is that unlike delegation under cgroups Version 1, delegation under cgroup Version 2 is perfectly safe.

To see the default setting, open the `/lib/systemd/system/user@.service` file, and look for the `Delegate=` line in the `[Service]` section. The applicable lines should look like this:

```
[Service]
. . .
. . .
Delegate=pids memory
. . .
. . .
```

By default, Fedora only allows non-privileged users to set resource limits for memory and for the maximum number of running processes. We need to edit that to include the cpu, cpuset, and io resource controllers, like this:

```
[donnie@fedora ~]$ sudo systemctl edit --full user@.service
```

Edit the Delegate= line so that it will look like this:

```
Delegate=pids memory io cpu cpuset
```

Save the file and do a daemon-reload. Note that if any users are logged in, they might have to log out and log back in again for this to take effect.

Keep Pogo's original login window open, and then open a second one for him. He'll create a container in one window, and look at the container information in the second window. Have Pogo create an **Ubuntu** container, like this:

```
[pogo@fedora ~]$ podman run -it --cpu-period=100000
--cpu-quota=50000 ubuntu /bin/bash
root@207a59e45e9b:/#
```

Pogo is setting a CPUQuota of 50% over a 100-millisecond time interval. In Pogo's other login window, have him view the information about his container. He'll first do a podman ps, like this:

```
[pogo@fedora ~]$ podman ps
CONTAINER ID  IMAGE                                COMMAND
CREATED         STATUS                   PORTS      NAMES
207a59e45e9b  docker.io/library/ubuntu:latest  /bin/bash   55
minutes ago  Up 55 minutes ago                   funny_zhukovsky
[pogo@fedora ~]$
```

Pogo didn't assign a name to this container, so podman randomly assigned the name funny_zhukovsky. (Remember that Pogo is a opossum, so don't be too hard on him for forgetting to assign a name.) Now, have Pogo inspect the inner workings of this container, using whatever container name that came up for you:

```
[pogo@fedora ~]$ podman inspect funny_zhukovsky
```

There's a lot of output here, but you only need to look at two lines. Keep scrolling down, and you should find them. They should look like this:

```
"CpuPeriod": 100000,
"CpuQuota": 50000,
```

So far, so good. But, here's where things get a bit tricky. It's just that the attribute file for this container is buried deep within the cgroup filesystem where it's hard to find. Fortunately, Pogo is a more clever opossum than I thought he was, so he found a way to cheat. He knew that the `50000` text string would only show up in one of the attribute files under his user slice directory, so he used `grep` to find it, like this:

```
[pogo@fedora ~]$ cd /sys/fs/cgroup/user.slice/user-1001.slice/
[pogo@fedora user-1001.slice]$ grep -r '50000' *
user@1001.service/user.slice/libpod-207a59e45e9b14c3397d9904
b41ba601dc959d85962e6ede45a1b54463ae731b.scope/container/cpu.
max:50000 100000
[pogo@fedora user-1001.slice]$
```

At last, Pogo found the attribute file:

```
[pogo@fedora container]$ pwd
/sys/fs/cgroup/user.slice/user-1001.slice/user@1001.service/
user.slice/libpod-207a59e45e9b14c3397d9904b41ba601dc959d85962e6
ede45a1b54463ae731b.scope/container
[pogo@fedora container]$ cat cpu.max
50000 100000
[pogo@fedora container]$
```

That wraps it up for rootless containers. So now, let's get set to talk about `cpuset`.

Understanding cpuset

When you're dealing with a server that's running lots of containers and processes, it's sometimes beneficial to assign a container or a process to a certain CPU core or set of CPU cores. On a machine with more than one physical CPU, it might also be beneficial to assign a memory node, as well. To see what I'm talking about, install `numactl` on your Fedora machine, like this:

```
[donnie@fedora ~]$ sudo dnf install numactl
```

Use the -H option to look at the hardware list, like this:

```
[donnie@fedora ~]$ numactl -H
available: 1 nodes (0)
node 0 cpus: 0 1 2 3
node 0 size: 7939 MB
node 0 free: 6613 MB
node distances:
node   0
  0:  10
[donnie@fedora ~]$
```

There's one NUMA node, which is `node 0`, and which is associated with four CPUs. Well, in reality, there's only *one CPU* that has *four CPU cores*. We also see the amount of memory that is assigned to this node.

So, now you're saying, *But Donnie, what is this NUMA business, and why should I care?*. Okay, **NUMA** stands for **non-uniform memory access**. It has to do with how the operating system deals with memory on machines with more than one physical CPU. On systems with only a single CPU, such as your Fedora virtual machine, NUMA doesn't do anything for us, because there's only one memory node. On machines with more than one CPU, each CPU has its own associated memory node. For example, check out this photo of one of my junk motherboards:

Figure 13.4 – A dual-CPU motherboard

There are two CPU sockets, each with its own bank of memory sockets. Each bank of memory constitutes a NUMA node. Now, let's look at one of my running multi-CPU systems, which is an old **Hewlett-Packard** workstation that's running with two quad-core **AMD Opterons** and **Fedora 34**:

```
[donnie@fedora-teaching ~]$ numactl -H
available: 2 nodes (0-1)
node 0 cpus: 0 2 4 6
node 0 size: 7959 MB
node 0 free: 6982 MB
node 1 cpus: 1 3 5 7
node 1 size: 8053 MB
node 1 free: 7088 MB
node distances:
node   0   1
  0:  10  20
  1:  20  10
[donnie@fedora-teaching ~]$
```

So, we see two NUMA nodes this time. The even-number CPU cores are assigned to `node 0`, and the odd-number CPU cores are assigned to `node 1`.

By default, most processes run under a randomly chosen CPU core or set of CPU cores upon startup. Sometimes, the operating system might move a running process from one core or set of cores to another. On a normal workstation like I'm running here, that doesn't matter. But, it might matter on a server that's running lots of processes. You could possibly improve efficiency and performance by assigning certain processes to their own dedicated CPU cores and NUMA nodes. If you're dealing with cgroups Version 1, you'll need to jump through hoops and perform unnatural acts to make this work, because the Version 1 `cpuset` controller doesn't directly work with `systemd`. With cgroup Version 2, it's a breeze. It's just a matter of either using `systemctl set-property` to set the `AllowedCPUs=` and `AllowedMemoryNodes=` parameters, or setting them in the `[Service]` section of the service file.

Now, even though you only have one CPU for your Fedora virtual machine, you can still try this to see what it looks like. First, install the **Apache** web server by doing:

```
[donnie@fedora ~]$ sudo dnf install httpd
[donnie@fedora ~]$ sudo systemctl enable --now httpd
```

Next, assign the Apache service to CPU cores `0` and `2`, like this:

```
sudo systemctl set-property httpd.service AllowedCPUs="0 2"
```

> **Reminder**
>
> As before, remember to surround any set of parameters that contains a blank space with a pair of double-quotes.

Now, pretend that this virtual machine has more than one NUMA node, and assign the Apache service to NUMA node `0`, like this:

```
sudo systemctl set-property httpd.service AllowedMemoryNodes=0
```

These two commands will affect the `cpuset.cpus` and `cpuset.mems` attribute files, as you see here:

```
[donnie@fedora httpd.service]$ pwd
/sys/fs/cgroup/system.slice/httpd.service
[donnie@fedora httpd.service]$ cat cpuset.cpus
0,2
[donnie@fedora httpd.service]$ cat cpuset.mems
0
[donnie@fedora httpd.service]$
```

On my trusty dual-CPU Hewlett-Packard, I instead modified the `httpd.service` file to add these two parameters. The two new lines look like this:

```
. . .
. . .
[Service]
. . .
. . .
AllowedCPUs=0 2
AllowedMemoryNodes=0
. . .
. . .
```

So, in both examples, I'm allowing Apache to use CPU cores 0 and 2, which are both associated with NUMA `node 0`.

> **Pro Tip**
>
> You can separate the core numbers in your list with either a comma or a blank space, or use a dash (-) to list a range of CPU cores. Also, note that you do not surround the 0 2 in double-quotes when you add this AllowedCPUs= parameter to the unit file.)

After a `daemon-reload` and restart of the Apache service, we should see the appropriate attribute files show up in the `/sys/fs/cgroup/system.slice/httpd.service/` directory. Again, here's what the `cpuset.cpus` file looks like:

```
[donnie@fedora-teaching httpd.service]$ cat cpuset.cpus
0,2
[donnie@fedora-teaching httpd.service]$
```

Cool. Apache is running on CPU cores `0` and `2`, just like we want. Now, let's look in the `cpuset.mems` file:

```
[donnie@fedora-teaching httpd.service]$ cat cpuset.mems
0
[donnie@fedora-teaching httpd.service]$
```

Again, it's just what we want to see. Apache can now only use NUMA `node 0`. So, thanks to cgroup Version 2, we have achieved coolness with the bare minimum of effort.

> **Note**
>
> NUMA doesn't mean that a process that's running on one CPU can't access memory that's in the NUMA node for another CPU. By default, any process can access all system memory on all NUMA nodes. You would use the `AllowedMemoryNodes` parameter to change that.

So, now you're wondering, "*Can I use cgroup Version 2 on my RHEL 8-type machine?*". Well, let's take a look.

Converting RHEL 8-type distros to cgroup version 2

It's an easy matter to convert a Red Hat Enterprise Linux 8-type distro to cgroup Version 2. Step 1 is to edit the `/etc/default/grub` file on your AlmaLinux machine. Find the line that starts with `GRUB_CMDLINE_LINUX=`. At the end of that line, add `systemd.unified_cgroup_hierarchy=1`. The whole line should now look like this:

```
GRUB_CMDLINE_LINUX="crashkernel=auto resume=/dev/mapper/vl-swap rd.lvm.lv=vl/root rd.lvm.lv=vl/swap rhgb quiet systemd.unified_cgroup_hierarchy=1"
```

Next, rebuild the `GRUB` configuration, like this:

```
[donnie@localhost ~]$ sudo grub2-mkconfig -o /boot/grub2/grub.cfg
```

Reboot the machine, and then look in the `/sys/fs/cgroup/` directory. You should now see the same filesystem that you see on the Fedora machine. However, don't be too disappointed if you can't get all of the previous labs to work. It's just that the RHEL 8-type distros all use an older version of the Linux kernel, which doesn't yet have all of the cgroup resource controllers enabled. Will they ever be enabled in the RHEL 8 distros? Well, maybe. Red Hat's policy is to stick with one certain kernel version for the whole ten-year lifespan of each major release of RHEL. So, all of the RHEL 8-type distros will be stuck on the old kernel version *4.18* until they reach end-of-life in 2029. Sometimes, Red Hat will backport features from newer kernels into their older RHEL kernel, but there's no guarantee that they'll do this with any newer cgroup Version 2 code. At any rate, once you've seen what you need to see on your AlmaLinux machine, feel free to delete the edit that you made to the `grub` file, and rebuild the GRUB configuration. This will convert the machine back to using cgroups Version 1.

So, have you seen enough about cgroups? Hopefully not, because it's something that's worthwhile learning in depth. But, there's lots more that we need to cover, so let's go do that.

Summary

In this chapter, we've learned a lot about cgroup Version 2. We started with a discussion about the deficiencies in cgroups Version 1, and how cgroup Version 2 is better. Then, we looked at how to allow non-privileged users to set resource limits on their containers, and how to use the `cpuset` resource controller. Finally, we took a brief look at how to convert a RHEL 8-type machine to use cgroup Version 2.

Once again, I'm reading your mind, and you're wondering why cgroup Version 2 hasn't yet been universally adopted if it's so good. Well, it's just that certain critical programs and services, especially containerization services, are still hardcoded to use Version 1. Fortunately, the situation is improving, and it's a safe bet that Version 2 will become the standard within our lifetimes.

All right, this concludes Part 2 of this tome. Let's start Part 3 with a discussion of `journald`. I'll see you there.

Questions

1. Which of the following statements is true?

   A. You can safely use `podman` under cgroups Version 1 to set resource limits on rootless containers.

   B. You can safely use `podman` under cgroup Version 2 to set resource limits on rootless containers.

   C. You can't set resource limits on `podman` containers.

   D. No special privileges are required to set resource limits on rootless `podman` containers.

2. What is the difference between `MemoryMax` and `MemoryHigh`?

   A. `MemoryMax` is a hard limit, and `MemoryHigh` is a soft limit.

   B. `MemoryHigh` is a hard limit, and `MemoryMax` is a soft limit.

   C. They both do the same thing.

   D. Neither one does anything.

3. Which of the following statements is true about delegation?

   A. It's perfectly safe for both cgroups Version 1 and cgroup Version 2.

   B. It's only safe for cgroups Version 1.

   C. It's never safe to use delegation.

   D. It's only safe for cgroup Version 2.

4. What is the first step for converting a RHEL 8-type system to cgroup Version 2?

   A. Edit the `/etc/grub.cfg` file.

   B. Edit the `/etc/default/grub` file.

   C. Edit the `/boot/grub2/grub.cfg` file.

   D. Edit the `/boot/grub` file.

Answers

1. B
2. A
3. D
4. B

Further reading

A Red Hat blog post about cgroup Version 2:

`https://www.redhat.com/en/blog/world-domination-cgroups-rhel-8-welcome-cgroups-v2`

An **Oracle** blog post about why Version 2 is better than Version 1:

`https://blogs.oracle.com/linux/post/cgroup-v2-checkpoint`

Comparing Version 1 and Version 2:

`https://chrisdown.name/talks/cgroupv2/cgroupv2-fosdem.pdf`

Using cgroup Version 2 for rootless Docker containers:

`https://rootlesscontaine.rs/getting-started/common/cgroup2/`

The current adoption status of cgroup v2 in containers:

`https://medium.com/nttlabs/cgroup-v2-596d035be4d7`

Section 3: Logging, Timekeeping, Networking, and Booting

In this section, we'll look at the logkeeping, timekeeping, and networking components of the systemd ecosystem, and compare them to their non-systemd counterparts. We'll then look at using the GRUB2 and systemd-boot bootloaders, and wrap up by looking at how to use systemd-logind and polkit to help manage users.

This part of the book comprises the following chapters:

- *Chapter 14, Using journald*
- *Chapter 15, Using systemd-networkd and systemd-resolved*
- *Chapter 16, Understanding Timekeeping with systemd*
- *Chapter 17, Understanding systemd and Bootloaders*
- *Chapter 18, Understanding systemd-logind*

14
Using journald

In this chapter, we will turn our attention to a new way of logging. Although the `journald` logging system isn't part of systemd's `init` system, it is part of the `systemd` ecosystem. The `journald` system has its advantages over the old `rsyslog` system. However, there are also a couple of big reasons why we still haven't completed the transition to `journald`. Still, `journald` is an important tool that can help a busy Linux administrator easily see what's going on.

Specific topics in this chapter include:

- Understanding the pros and cons of `rsyslog`
- Understanding the pros and cons of `journald`
- Understanding `journald` on Ubuntu
- Using `journalctl`
- Sealing `journald` log files for security
- Setting up remote logging with `journald`

Technical requirements

All you need for this chapter is your normal Ubuntu Server 20.04 and Alma Linux 8 virtual machines. (You'll need both because `journald` is implemented differently on each.) Now, let's start by looking at the old `rsyslog`.

Check out the following link to see the Code in Action video: `https://bit.ly/3dbJmJR`

Understanding the pros and cons of rsyslog

Fedora was the first Linux distro to come with `rsyslog` as its default logging system, way back in 2007. It has quite a few improvements over the old syslog, and it eventually replaced syslog as the standard logging system on Linux, Unix, and Unix-like operating systems. Despite now having `journald`, `rsyslog` is still with us, as we'll see in just a bit.

One of the best features of `rsyslog` is also its biggest weakness. That is, it stores log files in plaintext format. That's great in a way because you can use your normal text search and viewing utilities to view the log files and find whatever information that you need to find. The less, head, tail, awk, and grep utilities are your friends when it comes to working with these plaintext log files. This also makes it very easy to write shell scripts to extract and parse information automatically.

But there are a few problems with using plaintext log files. The first one is that plaintext files can become quite large and eventually consume a lot of disk space. To deal with this, Linux distros all come with the `logrotate` system, which automatically deletes all the log files except the ones for the previous four weeks. If you need to keep log files for longer than that, you'll need to either edit the `/etc/logrotate.conf` file or transfer the older log files to another location before `logrotate` automatically deletes them. This can also make it a bit awkward to find things. If you search through the current log file soon after a log rotation has taken place, you'll see that the file is mostly empty. Then, you'll have to search through the archive files to find what you need.

The second problem, according to the `journald` developers at least, is that there's no built-in way to structure the view of `rsyslog` log files, as shown in the following snippet from the AlmaLinux messages file:

```
Jul 30 16:31:02 localhost rsyslogd[1286]: [origin
software="rsyslogd" swVersion=
"8.1911.0-7.el8_4.2" x-pid="1286" x-info="https://www.rsyslog.
com"] rsyslogd was
 HUPed
```

```
Jul 30 17:10:55 localhost journal[3086]: Could not delete
runtime/persistent state file: Error removing file /run/
user/1000/gnome-shell/runtime-state-LE.:0/screenShield.locked:
No such file or directory
Jul 30 17:10:56 localhost NetworkManager[1056]: <info>
[1627679456.0025] agent-manager: agent[24ffba3d1b1cfac7,:1.270/
org.gnome.Shell.NetworkAgent/1000]: agent registered
Jul 30 17:26:17 localhost systemd[1]: Starting dnf makecache...
Jul 30 17:26:17 localhost dnf[4951]: Metadata cache refreshed
recently.
Jul 30 17:26:17 localhost systemd[1]: dnf-makecache.service:
Succeeded.
```

You see here that every entry begins with the **date**, **timestamp**, **hostname/IPaddress**, and **subsystem[PID]** fields. The last field is unstructured free-form text, so you'd need to use external programs to create any kind of structured view. These external programs include the text manipulation utilities that are already installed on your Linux distro, as well as various third-party utilities. By default, `journald` displays log data in `rsyslog`-compatible format. However, `journald` also includes an API that allows developers to define custom fields for log messages, and the `journalctl` utility allows you to view log data in many different ways.

Another argument against `rsyslog` is its security. Any hacker who breaks into your system and gains root privileges could easily alter plaintext log files to delete any record of his or her malicious deeds. The theory is that the binary log files that `journald` creates are harder for an attacker to alter. Is it impossible, though? Well, perhaps not, because a bit later we'll see how to verify if `journald` log files have been altered. Also, the `lastlog`, `utmp`, `wtmp`, and `btmp` binary log files have been in Linux for many years, and it is possible to alter them. It might be a bit harder, but not impossible.

The final problem with `rsyslog` is that there are no built-in search capabilities. Yeah, it's good that we can use tools such as awk, grep, and the built-in search function of less to search for text strings or text string patterns. But, wouldn't it be nice to have a built-in function that could make those searches a bit easier? As we'll soon see, we have that capability with `journald`.

> **Note**
>
> I must mention that not everyone agrees that not having searching and formatting capabilities built into `rsyslog` is a problem. The `journald` developers *do* see it as a problem, of course. But, a lot of text manipulation and search utilities come installed on pretty much every Linux distro, and it's not hard to use them. Even a shell-scripting beginner could easily whip up a script that would automate the process of finding and formatting pertinent information from plaintext log files. For example, several years ago, I wrote such a shell script to help out one of my buddies. (It was for Apache log files, but the principle still applies.) Anyway, you can check out the article that I wrote about it here:
>
> `http://beginlinux.com/blog/2009/08/detect-cross-site-scripting-attacks-with-a-bash-shell-script/`.
>
> (It says at the top that the article was posted by *Mike*, but if you scroll to the bottom, you'll see that I wrote it.)
>
> Having said all this, I should also mention that some things are still a bit difficult to do with plaintext files, such as converting them into JSON format. As we'll see shortly, `journald` is much better for that.

Another advantage of `rsyslog` is that it's extremely easy to set up a central `rsyslog` server that can receive log files from other machines on the network. Of course, configuring the server to separate the files from different machines into their own sets of log files is a bit awkward, but it isn't that complex once you know how to do it.

Understanding the pros and cons of journald

In contrast to `rsyslog`, `journald` stores its log files in binary format. This allows us to store more data in a smaller amount of disk space, which reduces the need to constantly rotate the log files. Reducing the need for rotation allows us to keep log files for the long term, without having to worry about moving them elsewhere.

Using binary files also gives us an extra bit of security. It's harder for an attacker to alter binary files, and there's also a way to see if the files have been altered.

The `journalctl` utility comes with built-in filtering and viewing functions. We can even view the log information in JSON format, which makes it easier to export log data into other log-parsing programs.

Yet another cool thing about `journald` is that it stores system log files and user log files separately. Each user has his or her own set of log files. A user with administrative privileges can view files for the system and all users, and a non-privileged user can just view his or her log files. With `rsyslog`, only users with administrator privileges can view any of these log files.

Unfortunately, this cloud's silver lining does have a bit of tarnish. It is possible to set up a central log server that can receive `journald` logs from other machines, but this feature is still in development and isn't considered production-ready. So, because of that and the fact that most third-party log aggregation tools still expect to see plaintext `rsyslog` files, `rsyslog` is still with us, and likely will be with us for quite some time to come. At the time of this writing, I don't know of any Linux distros that have completely transitioned to `journald`. Every Linux distro that I know of runs both `journald` and `rsyslog` together.

> **Note**
>
> It's just been pointed out to me that the Fedora team initially had Fedora 21 running with nothing but `journald`. However, they received so many complaints about it that they had to do an update that brought back `rsyslog`. I didn't know this, because I had abandoned Fedora quite a few years ago due to its instability issues. I didn't start working with it again until Fedora 23, after the instability issues had gotten worked out. Anyway, you can read a bit more about this drama here:
>
> `https://www.linuxquestions.org/questions/linux-newbie-8/where-are-var-log-dmesg-and-var-log-messages-4175533513/`.

However, there are differences between how the various distros do this. In the next section, we'll look at how Ubuntu does it.

Understanding journald on Ubuntu

On Ubuntu systems, the `journald` and `rsyslog` services are both enabled by default, and they both run as completely independent entities. The `journald` logs are persistent, which means that they are permanently stored on disk, instead of getting deleted every time you shut down the machine. The `rsyslog` log files are also present, and they get rotated every week.

Two things make the `journald` log files persistent. First, is the very first configuration option in the `/etc/systemd/journald.conf` file, which looks like this:

```
[Journal]
#Storage=auto
. . .
. . .
```

When you look at this whole file, you'll see that every line in it is commented out. This just means that all of these options have been set to their default values. To change something, just uncomment the line and change the value. However, we don't need to do anything with this `#Storage=auto` line. The `auto` here means that if the `/var/log/journal/` directory exists, then `journald` will permanently store its log files there. If the `/var/log/journal/` directory doesn't exist, a transient set of log files will be created in the `/run/log/journal/` directory every time you boot the machine. When you shut the machine down, these transient log files will be deleted. On Ubuntu machines, the `/var/log/journal/` directory is already there for you, which means that the log files are persistent. To show you how persistent the `journald` log files are, let's take a quick look at what I have on the host machine that I'm using to write this. This machine is running `Lubuntu 18.04`, which is just Ubuntu with an alternate desktop environment. I'll use the `journalctl` command without any options, like this:

```
donnie@siftworkstation: ~
$ journalctl
-- Logs begin at Wed 2018-11-21 17:38:02 EST, end at Mon 2021-08-09 16:42:10 EDT. --
Nov 21 17:38:02 lubuntula kernel: microcode: microcode updated early to revision 0x713, date = 2018-01-26
. . .
. . .
```

Here, we can see that the logs begin in November 2018, which is almost three years ago. (I'm writing this in August 2021.) Surely, three years of logs would take up lots of disk space, right? Well, let's use the `journalctl --disk-usage` command to find out:

```
donnie@siftworkstation: ~
$ journalctl --disk-usage
Archived and active journals take up 904.1M in the file system.
donnie@siftworkstation: ~
$
```

So, three years' worth of `journald` log files doesn't even take up a whole GB of disk space. That's a lot less space than what three years' worth of `rsyslog` text files would require. To see the actual `journald` log files, go into the `/var/log/journal/` directory. There, you'll see a directory with a rather long hexadecimal number as its directory name, like this:

```
donnie@siftworkstation: ~
$ cd /var/log/journal/
donnie@siftworkstation: /var/log/journal
$ ls
92fe2206f513462da1869220d8191c1e
donnie@siftworkstation: /var/log/journal
$
```

Within that directory, you'll see the log files:

```
donnie@siftworkstation: /var/log/journal
$ cd 92fe2206f513462da1869220d8191c1e/
donnie@siftworkstation: /var/log/
journal/92fe2206f513462da1869220d8191c1e
$ ls -l
total 925888
-rw-r-----+ 1 root systemd-journal 16777216 Nov 28  2018
system@00057bbf27f5178e-5ed563c9fd14588f.journal~
. . .
. . .
-rw-r-----+ 1 root systemd-journal  8388608 Aug  9 13:12 user-
1000.journal
donnie@siftworkstation: /var/log/
journal/92fe2206f513462da1869220d8191c1e
```

We can use `wc -l` to easily count how many files there are, like this:

```
donnie@siftworkstation: /var/log/
journal/92fe2206f513462da1869220d8191c1e
$ ls -l | wc -l
75
donnie@siftworkstation: /var/log/
journal/92fe2206f513462da1869220d8191c1e
$
```

So, there are 75 `journald` log files on this machine. That's because `journald` is configured to store information in lots of smaller files instead of storing everything in one big honkin' monolithic file.

> **Note**
>
> When those of us in the southern United States say that something is *big honkin'*, we mean that it's *really big.*

The coolest part is that when you use `journalctl` to view the files, it will automatically open all of these files as necessary, instead of making you open each file with a separate command. (This is another huge advantage that `journald` has over `rsyslog`.)

If you ever do need to limit the amount of disk space that `journald` uses for log file storage, you can set the proper parameters in the `/etc/systemd/journald.conf` file. (See the `journald.conf` man page for details.) Also, the `journalctl` man page shows you how to rotate log files and then delete old archived log files with the `--vacuum-size=`, `--vacuum-time=`, and `--vacuum-files=` options. Let's look at an example of how to do that.

First, shut down the virtual machine and take a snapshot of it. (You'll need to have plenty of log files for the upcoming demos.) Then, restart the virtual machine and ensure that the persistent logs are up-to-date with the transient logs, like this:

```
donnie@ubuntu2004:~$ sudo journalctl --flush
donnie@ubuntu2004:~$
```

Next, combine the `--rotate` and `--vacuum-time` options to archive the current log files, create new empty log files, and delete all the archived log files that are older than five days, like this:

```
donnie@ubuntu2004:~$ sudo journalctl --rotate --vacuum-time=5d
Deleted archived journal /var/log/
journal/55520bc0900c428ab8a27f5c7d8c3927/system@
a2d77617383f477da0a4d539e137b488-0000000000000001-
0005b8317f856d88.journal (8.0M).
Deleted archived journal /var/log/
journal/55520bc0900c428ab8a27f5c7d8c3927/user-1000@
d713d47989e84072bc1445c9829a0c1f-0000000000000415-
0005b8318153a5b1.journal (8.0M)
. . .
. . .
```

```
Vacuuming done, freed 2.1G of archived journals from /var/log/journal/55520bc0900c428ab8a27f5c7d8c3927.
Vacuuming done, freed 0B of archived journals from /var/log/journal.
Vacuuming done, freed 0B of archived journals from /run/log/journal.
donnie@ubuntu2004:~$
```

Finally, shut down the virtual machine, restore from the snapshot, and restart the virtual machine.

> **Note**
>
> If you don't want your Ubuntu machine to persistently store `journald` log files, either delete the `/var/log/journal/` directory or go into the `/etc/systemd/journald.conf` file and change the `#Storage=auto` line to `Storage=volatile`.

The final thing I want to mention about Ubuntu is that when you install the operating system, the user that gets created by the installer is a member of both the `sudo` and `adm` groups. Members of the `sudo` group have full `sudo` privileges, as you probably already know. On most other distros, you'd need to use `sudo` to view system log files. On Ubuntu machines, members of the `adm` group can view all `rsyslog` or `journald` logs without `sudo` privileges.

Okay, that does it for `journald` on Ubuntu. Now, let's move on and look at `journald` on RHEL-type systems.

Understanding journald on RHEL-type systems

There are a few big differences in how things are done in the Red Hat world. First, on your AlmaLinux machine, you'll see that there is no `/var/log/journal/` directory, which means that `journald` log files will only be created in the `/run/log/journal/` directory and will disappear every time you shut down or reboot the machine. If you want to change that, all you have to do is create that journal subdirectory, like this:

```
[donnie@localhost ~]$ sudo mkdir /var/log/journal
```

You'll immediately see that the `journald` log files are now persistent.

> **Note**
>
> Before you make the `journald` log files persistent on a production machine, evaluate whether or not you need to.

The other big difference is that on RHEL-type systems, `journald` and `rsyslog` work together, instead of independently. Instead of having both `journald` and `rsyslog` gather information from the rest of the operating system, only `journald` does. Then, `rsyslog` obtains the information from `journald` and stores it in the normal `rsyslog` text files. We can see how that's enabled in the top portion of the `/etc/rsyslog.conf` file:

```
#### MODULES ####

. . .
. . .
module(load="imjournal"             # provides access to the
systemd journal
       StateFile="imjournal.state") # File to store the
position in the journal
. . .
. . .
```

Unlike the old `syslog` service that `rsyslog` replaced, you can extend the capabilities of `rsyslog` by adding new modules to it. Here, we can see the `imjournal` module, that allows `rsyslog` to receive data from the `journald` service. So, on RHEL 8-type machines, `journald` gathers the data from the rest of the system and passes it to `rsyslog`.

The final big difference is that on RHEL-type systems, you'll need the proper `sudo` privileges to view all of the log files. The `adm` group is there, but adding yourself to it doesn't do anything for you.

Now that we've seen the differences between how `journald` is set up on Ubuntu and RHEL, let's look at how to use `journalctl`, which works the same across all distros.

Using journalctl

The `journalctl` utility is cool because it has so much flexibility. Let's start by looking at the various ways to search for and display log data. We'll do this on the Ubuntu machine because Ubuntu's persistent `journald` logs will give us more to look at.

Searching for and viewing log data with journalctl

The simplest command for viewing log files is just `journalctl`. As we see here, this will show you pretty much the same information that you'd see when you open a normal `rsyslog` file in `less`. You'll also see that the `journalctl` output is automatically piped into `less`:

```
donnie@ubuntu2004:~$ journalctl
-- Logs begin at Tue 2021-01-05 20:46:55 EST, end at Tue 2021-08-10 14:23:17 ED>
Jan 05 20:46:55 ubuntu2004 kernel: Linux version 5.4.0-59-generic (buildd@lcy01>
Jan 05 20:46:55 ubuntu2004 kernel: Command line: BOOT_IMAGE=/vmlinuz-5.4.0-59-g>
Jan 05 20:46:55 ubuntu2004 kernel: KERNEL supported cpus:
Jan 05 20:46:55 ubuntu2004 kernel:   Intel GenuineIntel
Jan 05 20:46:55 ubuntu2004 kernel:   AMD AuthenticAMD
Jan 05 20:46:55 ubuntu2004 kernel:   Hygon HygonGenuine
. . .
. . .
Jan 05 20:46:55 ubuntu2004 kernel: BIOS-e820: [mem 0x00000000fffc0000-0x0000000>
Jan 05 20:46:55 ubuntu2004 kernel: BIOS-e820: [mem 0x0000000100000000-0x0000000>
Jan 05 20:46:55 ubuntu2004 kernel: NX (Execute Disable) protection: active
Jan 05 20:46:55 ubuntu2004 kernel: SMBIOS 2.5 present.
lines 1-26
```

A big difference from what you're used to with `rsyslog` is that long lines don't wrap around. Instead, they extend beyond the right-hand side of the visible window. To see the rest of these lines, you'll need to use the right cursor key. Other than that, you can use the same search and navigation commands that you'd normally use with the `less` utility. For example, to go directly to the bottom of the `journalctl` output, just use the *Shift* + *G* key combination. (Be patient, though, because `journalctl` has to read through all of those files that I showed you earlier, which takes a while.) To go to a specific line, just enter the line number followed by the lowercase `g`. To search for a text string, hit the / key and enter the search term. When you're done, just hit the *Q* key to quit.

> **Note**
> I should point out that since I'm using the Ubuntu virtual machine for this, where I'm a member of the `adm` group, I don't need `sudo` privileges to view all system logs. If you decide to try this on the AlmaLinux machine, you'll need to use `sudo`. Otherwise, you'll only see your user logs.

If you look at the `journalctl` man page, you'll see a wide selection of display and search options. I can't demonstrate all of them to you, but we can look at a few examples.

On a machine with persistent `journald` log files, you might just want to see the log entries from the current boot-up session. Now, to make this work, reboot your machine a few times so that you'll have more to see. Then, use `journalctl -b`, like this:

```
donnie@ubuntu2004:~$ journalctl -b
-- Logs begin at Tue 2021-01-05 20:46:55 EST, end at Tue 2021-08-10 15:03:43 ED>
Aug 10 14:20:38 ubuntu2004 kernel: Linux version 5.4.0-80-generic (buildd@lcy01>
Aug 10 14:20:38 ubuntu2004 kernel: Command line: BOOT_IMAGE=/vmlinuz-5.4.0-80-g>
. . .
. . .
```

Here, you can see that the logs began in January 2021, but the first entry it shows here is for the current date of August 10 at 2:20 P.M., which is when I last booted this virtual machine. To see the log entries from the previous boot-up session, just add a `-1`, like this:

```
donnie@ubuntu2004:~$ journalctl -b -1
-- Logs begin at Tue 2021-01-05 20:46:55 EST, end at Tue 2021-08-10 15:07:27 ED>
Aug 10 13:36:44 ubuntu2004 kernel: Linux version 5.4.0-80-generic (buildd@lcy01>
Aug 10 13:36:44 ubuntu2004 kernel: Command line: BOOT_IMAGE=/vmlinuz-5.4.0-80-g>
. . .
. . .
```

So, it looks like I had booted this machine earlier today, at 1:36 P.M. You can also view files from earlier boot-up sessions by specifying a different number. For example, you can use `-2` to display files from two boot-up sessions ago, `-10` to show files from 10 boot-up sessions ago, and so on.

To see a list of all bootups, use the `--list-boots` option:

```
donnie@ubuntu2004:~$ journalctl --list-boots
-46 7c611db8974b4cdb897853c4367048cf Tue 2021-01-05 20:46:55
EST—Tue 2021-01-05 20:57:29 EST
-45 643f70296ebf4b5c8e798f8f878c0ac5 Thu 2021-02-11 16:16:06
EST—Thu 2021-02-11 20:03:42 EST
-44 139f7be3bc3d43c69421c68e2a5c76b8 Mon 2021-03-15 15:36:01
EDT—Mon 2021-03-15 16:42:32 EDT
. . .
. . .
-1 9a4781c6b0414e6e924cc391b6129185 Wed 2021-08-25 17:24:56
EDT—Wed 2021-08-25 21:48:06 EDT
  0 354575e3e3d747039f047094ffaaa0d2 Mon 2021-08-30 16:28:29
EDT—Mon 2021-08-30 16:39:49 EDT
donnie@ubuntu2004:~$
```

It looks like I've booted this virtual machine 47 times since I've created it. The long hexadecimal number you can see in the second field is the ID number of the boot-up session.

The `-g` option allows you to grep for either specific text strings or Perl-compatible regular expressions. If your search term consists only of lowercase letters, then the search will be case-insensitive. If the search term includes any uppercase letters, then the search is case-sensitive. For example, using `journalctl -g fail` shows you all the entries that contain some form of *fail*, regardless of whether *fail* contains lowercase, uppercase, or both upper and lowercase letters. But if you use `journalctl -g Fail`, you'll only see entries that contain the specific specific string, `Fail`. If your search term consists of only lowercase letters and you want to make the search case-sensitive, just use the `--case-sensitive=` option, like this:

```
donnie@ubuntu2004:~$ journalctl -g fail --case-sensitive=true
```

The priority levels for `journald` log messages are the same as for the `ryslog` log messages. The only difference is that you can now use either the name or the number of the priority level in your searches. In order of descending importance, the priority levels are:

- `0` or `emerg`: This is the emergency level, for things such as kernel panics. (Hopefully, you'll rarely ever see these.)
- `1` or `alert`: These aren't quite an emergency, but they're still bad news.

- `2` or `crit`: Don't be too surprised if you see some critical messages. These can be caused by something as simple as a user fumble-fingering his or her password. They could also be caused by someone trying to brute-force a password, so it's worth your while to pay attention to these.
- `3` or `err`: These could be caused by a service that fails to start, a program that runs out of memory, problems with accessing a hardware device, and so forth.
- `4` or `warning`: You'll see lots of these, but most are nothing to worry about. Normally, most of them will be kernel messages from when you boot up the machine.
- `5` or `notice`: These don't constitute an emergency, but you still want to take *notice* of them. (See what I did there?)
- `6` or `info`: Most log messages you see should be of the `info` level.
- `7` or `debug`: This is is the lowest priority. It's not enabled by default on `rsyslog`, but it is on `journald`.

Now, let's say that you want to only see the `emerg` (emergency) messages. Use the `-p` option with either the number or the name of the priority level, like this:

```
donnie@ubuntu2004:~$ journalctl -p 0
-- Logs begin at Tue 2021-01-05 20:46:55 EST, end at Tue 2021-08-31 14:50:38 EDT. --
-- No entries --
donnie@ubuntu2004:~$ journalctl -p emerg
-- Logs begin at Tue 2021-01-05 20:46:55 EST, end at Tue 2021-08-31 14:50:39 EDT. --
-- No entries --
donnie@ubuntu2004:~$
```

So, there are no emergency messages, which is a good thing. What about `alert` messages? Let's see:

```
donnie@ubuntu2004:~$ journalctl -p 1
-- Logs begin at Tue 2021-01-05 20:46:55 EST, end at Tue 2021-08-31 14:51:35 EDT. --
-- No entries --
donnie@ubuntu2004:~$
```

Cool. There are none of them, either. But from priority level 2 (`crit`) on down, it's a different story, as we see here:

```
donnie@ubuntu2004:~$ journalctl -p 2
-- Logs begin at Tue 2021-01-05 20:46:55 EST, end at Tue 2021-08-31 14:51:38 EDT. --
Apr 03 17:09:22 ubuntu2004 sudo[185694]: pam_unix(sudo:auth): auth could not identify password for [donnie]
-- Reboot --
Jul 23 15:16:14 ubuntu2004 sudo[48285]: pam_unix(sudo:auth): auth could not identify password for [donnie]
-- Reboot --
Jul 27 15:27:54 ubuntu2004 sudo[156593]: pam_unix(sudo:auth): auth could not identify password for [donnie]
-- Reboot --
Aug 17 17:10:51 ubuntu2004 sudo[222044]: pam_unix(sudo:auth): auth could not identify password for [donnie]
donnie@ubuntu2004:~$
```

So, there are a few `critical` messages. Now, things get a bit trickier. It's just that when you specify a priority level, you'll see messages from that priority up through all of the upper priorities that also have messages. So, if I were to specify level 3 (`err`) right now, I'd also see the level 2 (`crit`) messages. To see nothing but level 3 messages, specify a range with level 3 as both the starting point and the ending point, like this:

```
donnie@ubuntu2004:~$ journalctl -p 3..3
```

Curiously, the `journalctl` man page tells you that you can specify ranges, but it doesn't tell you that you have to use two dots for it. I had to do a DuckDuckGo search to find out.

Another carryover from `rsyslog` is the concept of *facilities*. Different Linux subsystems create different types, or facilities, of messages. The standard facilities are:

- `auth`: Messages generated by the authorization system, login, `su`, and so on.
- `authpriv`: Messages generated by the authorization system but only readable by selected users.
- `cron`: Messages generated by the cron service.
- `daemon`: Messages generated by all system daemons (`sshd`, `ftpd`, and so on),
- `ftp`: Messages generated by a **File Transfer Protocol** (**FTP**) service.

- `kern`: Messages generated by the Linux kernel.
- `lpr`: Messages generated by the line printer spooling.
- `mail`: Messages generated by the operating system's internal mail system.
- `mark`: These are periodic timestamps that can be inserted into the logs.
- `news`: This facility deals with messages from Usenet newsgroup services, which have pretty much died off. So, you'll likely never see any of these messages.
- `syslog`: Messages that are generated by rsyslog.
- `user`: Messages generated by users.
- `uucp`: Messages from the Unix-to-Unix copy system. This system also has pretty much died off, so you'll likely never see any of these messages, either.
- `local0` through `local7`: You can use these to define custom facilities.

To see messages from one specific facility, use the `--facility` option, like this:

```
donnie@ubuntu2004:~$ journalctl --facility uucp
-- Logs begin at Tue 2021-01-05 20:46:55 EST, end at Tue 2021-08-31 15:46:58 EDT. --
-- No entries --
donnie@ubuntu2004:~$
```

Okay, I did tell you that there would likely be no `uucp` messages. For a more realistic example, let's look at `auth` and `authpriv` messages, and compare the difference between them:

```
donnie@ubuntu2004:~$ journalctl --facility authpriv
. . .
. . .
donnie@ubuntu2004:~$ journalctl --facility auth
```

For our final example, let's get fancy. Let's look at priority `4` `daemon` messages that have come up since yesterday:

```
donnie@ubuntu2004:~$ journalctl --facility daemon -p 4..4 -S yesterday
```

All right, that about covers it for priorities and facilities.

> **Note**
> To see a list of all of the available facilities, just do:
> **`journalctl --facility=help`**

You can also view log entries for a certain user. To do that, you must obtain the user's UID, like this:

```
donnie@ubuntu2004:~$ id frank
uid=1002(frank) gid=1002(frank) groups=1002(frank)
donnie@ubuntu2004:~$
```

So, Frank's UID is `1002`. Now, let's view his log entries:

```
donnie@ubuntu2004:~$ journalctl _UID=1002
-- Logs begin at Tue 2021-01-05 20:46:55 EST, end at Tue 2021-08-10 15:47:17 ED>
Jul 23 15:10:01 ubuntu2004 systemd[40881]: Reached target Paths.
Jul 23 15:10:01 ubuntu2004 systemd[40881]: Reached target Timers.
. . .
. . .
```

Okay, that's good. But all I want to see is his log entries for today. I can use either the `-S` or `--since` option for this:

```
donnie@ubuntu2004:~$ journalctl _UID=1002 -S today
-- Logs begin at Tue 2021-01-05 20:46:55 EST, end at Tue 2021-08-10 15:49:27 ED>
-- No entries --
lines 1-2/2 (END)
```

Okay, Frank hasn't logged in today, which isn't surprising. Remember that Frank is a cat, which means that he spends most of his time sleeping.

Now, let's say that you want to view information about the Apache web server service, but you want to see it in JSON format. All right, let's do this:

```
donnie@ubuntu2004:~$ journalctl -u apache2 -o json
{"_EXE":"/usr/lib/systemd/systemd","SYSLOG_IDENTIFIER":
"systemd","_CMDLINE":"/s>
{"__CURSOR":"s=a2d77617383f477da0a4d539e137b488;i=37181;
b=88df3ae40cb9468a8d13a>
{"_HOSTNAME":"ubuntu2004","JOB_ID":"3311","__CURSOR":
"s=a2d77617383f477da0a4d53>
. . .
. . .
```

Is this output not pretty enough for you? No problem; we can make it pretty:

```
donnie@ubuntu2004:~$ journalctl -u apache2 -o json-pretty
{
        "_UID" : "0",
        "_CMDLINE" : "/sbin/init maybe-ubiquity",
        "_CAP_EFFECTIVE" : "3fffffffff",
        "JOB_TYPE" : "start",
        "_PID" : "1",
        "_GID" : "0",
        "CODE_FILE" : "src/core/job.c",
        "__CURSOR" : "s=a2d77617383f477da0a4d539e137b488;i=
3717c;b=88df3ae40cb9>
. . .
. . .
```

Note that more data fields show up in JSON format than in the standard default format. That's because the default output format for `journalctl` is meant to emulate the standard `rsyslog` format.

Now, let's say that you just want to see Apache information from yesterday, and you want to save it to a JSON file and view the output on the screen at the same time. The `--no-pager` option allows you to pipe the `journalctl` output into another utility, as we're doing here with the tee utility:

```
donnie@ubuntu2004:~$ journalctl -u apache2 -S yesterday -U
today -o json --no-pager | tee apache2.json
```

You can also use `--no-pager` to pipe output into the standard Linux text filtering and manipulation utilities, such as grep or awk. This can be handy if you need to write shell scripts for use in Nagios or Icinga plugins, for example.

I could give you a lot more examples, but you get the idea. Besides, this is one of those rare instances in the world of free-as-in-speech software where the documentation that other people have written is so good that I can't improve upon their efforts. So, if you want to see more, I'll direct your attention to the `journalctl` man page and the resources in the *Further reading* section.

Sealing journald log files for security

I've already told you how easy it is for a malicious person to tamper with the text-mode `rsyslog` files to delete his or her nefarious activities. The `journald` log files are already harder to tamper with because they're in binary format. We can make it even harder to tamper with them by *sealing* them. (Of course, this only works if you have persistent `journald` logs.)

The first step is to create a set of **Forward Secure Sealing** (**FSS**) keys, like this:

```
donnie@ubuntu2004:~$ sudo journalctl --setup-keys
```

This command creates two keys. The *sealing key* is named `fss` and is stored in the same directory as the `journald` log files, as we see here:

```
donnie@ubuntu2004:~$ cd /var/log/
journal/55520bc0900c428ab8a27f5c7d8c3927/
donnie@ubuntu2004:/var/log/
journal/55520bc0900c428ab8a27f5c7d8c3927$ ls -l fss
-rw-------+ 1 root systemd-journal 482 Aug 10 16:50 fss
donnie@ubuntu2004:/var/log/
journal/55520bc0900c428ab8a27f5c7d8c3927$
```

The verification key only appears as a text string on your screen, as we see here:

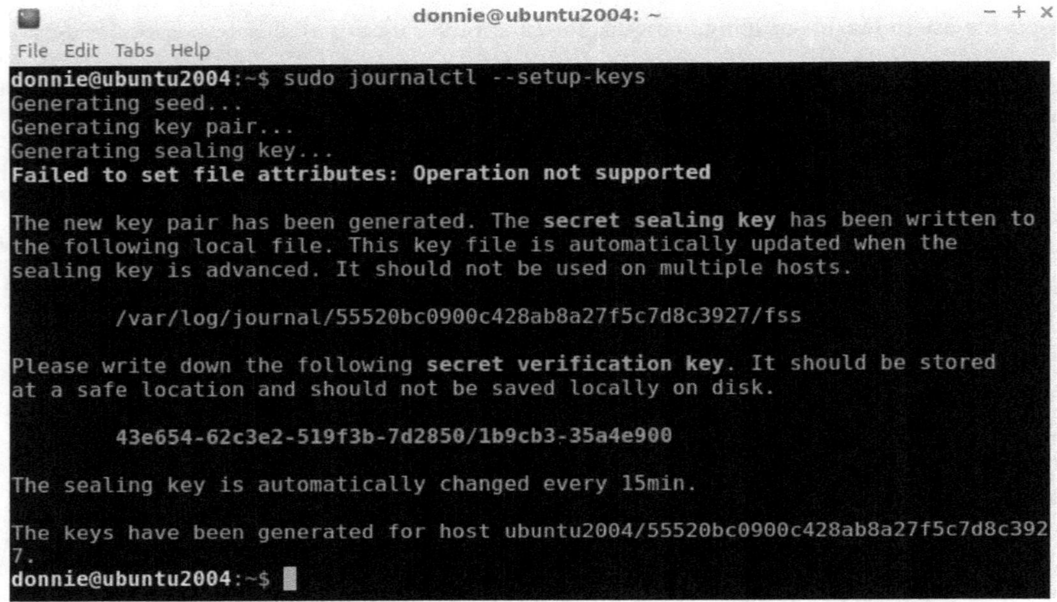

Figure 14.1 – Creating the Forward Secure Sealing (FSS) keys

It says to write this key down, but I'd rather cheat by copying and pasting it into a text file that I can store in a secure location. (For this demo, you can just store the text file in your home directory.)

Now, you can periodically run a `verify` operation to ensure that nobody has tampered with your log files. Just copy and paste the verification key into the command, like this:

```
donnie@ubuntu2004:~$ sudo journalctl --verify --verify-key=43e654-62c3e2-519f3b-7d2850/1b9cb3-35a4e900
PASS: /var/log/journal/55520bc0900c428ab8a27f5c7d8c3927/user-1000@3ebae2fd52f7403bac3983eb8a90d2ef-0000000000052181-0005beefb66cbef3.journal
PASS: /var/log/journal/55520bc0900c428ab8a27f5c7d8c3927/user-1000@53aedefe543040f48dd89ba98d7f9aae-00000000000a33c1-0005c704cacbdd12.journal
. . .
. . .
```

That's about it for sealing your log files. Now, let's talk very briefly about setting up remote logging with `journald`.

Setting up remote logging with journald

Sometimes, it's handy to set up a central log collection server and have all the other machines on the network send their log files to it.

As I've already said, `journald` remote logging is still in a proof-of-concept phase and isn't considered ready for production use. Also, most third-party log-aggregation utilities are still set up to use plaintext `rsyslog` files. So, if you have remote logging on your site or if you need to set up remote logging, you'll most likely use `rsyslog`.

However, I do realize that some of you might be interested in playing around with a remote `journald` logging setup. If that's the case, I'd like to direct your attention to the procedure that's linked in the *Further reading* section. However, be aware that you'll need to install security certificates on the `journald` log server and all of the clients. This procedure has you install certificates from *Let's Encrypt*, which requires you to have your machines in a domain that's registered on the public **Domain Name Service** (**DNS**) servers. If the Let's Encrypt installer can't find your machines on a public DNS server, the install operation will abort.

Fortunately, if you just want to set up centralized `journald` logging for an internal LAN, you can modify the procedure so that it uses certificates that you create locally from a local Certificate Authority server. (Showing you how to set up a local Certificate Authority is beyond the scope of this book, but you can read about it in my other book, *Mastering Linux Security and Hardening.*)

Well, I think that that should do it for `journald`. Let's wrap things up and move on.

Summary

In this chapter, we covered the `journald` logging system and compared it to the tried-and-true `rsyslog`. First, we looked at the pros and cons of both `rsyslog` and `journald`. Then, we saw how the two logging systems are implemented in both Ubuntu and RHEL distros. After that, we saw the various viewing, searching, and formatting options that we can use with the `journalctl` utility. We wrapped up by learned how to make our `journald` log files more tamper-resistant and briefly discussed setting up a centralized `journald` log server.

In the next chapter, we'll look at using systemd's own network services. I'll see you there!

Questions

Answer the following questions to test your knowledge of this chapter:

1. What is the major difference between `journald` and `rsyslog`?

   A. `journald` stores files in plaintext format, while `rsyslog` stores files in binary format.

   B. There is no difference.

   C. `rsyslog` stores files in plaintext format, while `journald` stores files in binary format.

2. Which of the following statements is true?

   A. Modern systemd-based Linux distros come with either `rsyslog` or `journald`, but not both.

   B. `journald` and `rsyslog` always work independently of each other.

   C. Modern systemd-based Linux distros come with both `rsyslog` and `journald`.

   D. `journald` and `rsyslog` can never work independently of each other.

3. What are two major differences in how `journald` is implemented on Ubuntu and RHEL? (Choose 2.)

   A. `journald` logs are persistent on RHEL, but not on Ubuntu.

   B. On RHEL, `journald` works completely independently of `rsyslog`. On Ubuntu, they work together.

   C. On RHEL, `journald` and `rsyslog` work together. On Ubuntu, they work independently.

   D. On Ubuntu, `journald` logs are persistent. On RHEL, they are not.

   E. There is no difference.

4. Which of the following commands would delete all but the most recent one GB worth of `journald` log files?

   A. `sudo journalctl --vacuum-size=1G`

   B. `sudo journalctl --rotate`

   C. `sudo journalctl --size=1G`

   D. `sudo journalctl --clean=1G`

Answers

1. C
2. C
3. C, D
4. A

Further reading

The rocket-fast syslog server (the `rsyslog` project page):

- `https://www.rsyslog.com/`
- Why `journald`?
- `https://www.loggly.com/blog/why-journald/`
- Understanding `journald`:
- `https://linuxconcept.com/tutorial/understanding-journald/`
- How to use `journalctl` to view and manipulate `systemd` logs:
- `https://www.digitalocean.com/community/tutorials/how-to-use-journalctl-to-view-and-manipulate-systemd-logs`
- Did you know that `journald` can give JSON output?
- `https://ailogs.design.blog/2020/02/01/linux-logs-did-you-know-systemd-journald-can-give-json-output/`
- Logging with `journald`:
- `https://sematext.com/blog/journald-logging-tutorial/`
- How to centralize logs with `journald` on Ubuntu 20.04:
- `https://www.digitalocean.com/community/tutorials/how-to-centralize-logs-with-journald-on-ubuntu-20-04`

15
Using systemd-networkd and systemd-resolved

The systemd ecosystem has its own networking components. Using these components is purely optional, and you might even find that you'll never need to use them. However, there are times when using systemd's networking components might help you do things that you can't do with the traditional Linux NetworkManager.

In this chapter, we will cover the following topics:

- Understanding `networkd` and `resolved`
- Understanding Netplan on Ubuntu
- Understanding networkd and resolved on RHEL-type machines
- Using `networkctl` and `resolvectl`
- Viewing the networkd and resolved unit files

All right, let's jump in!

Technical requirements

We'll start with the Ubuntu Server virtual machine. (Note that you need to use Ubuntu *Server* because the desktop versions of Ubuntu still use the old NetworkManager by default.) Later in this chapter, we'll work with AlmaLinux.

So, let's start by providing a brief explanation of networkd and resolved.

Check out the following link to see the Code in Action video: `https://bit.ly/31mmXXZ`

Understanding networkd and resolved

The traditional NetworkManager has been around for quite some time, and it's still the most appropriate solution for most Linux desktops and laptops. The main reason that Red Hat developed it was to enable Linux-powered laptops to instantly switch back and forth between wired and wireless networks, or from one wireless domain to another. NetworkManager also still works well for just normal Linux servers. All RHEL-type distros and all desktop versions of Ubuntu still use NetworkManager by default.

> **Note**
> I'm not always going to type `systemd-networkd` or `systemd-resolved`. Unless I'm typing actual commands, I'm just going to shorten the names to `networkd` and `resolved`, which is what most people do anyway.

You already know that I have this creepy habit of reading your mind. So, I know that you're thinking, *But Donnie, if NetworkManager is so good, why do we need networkd and resolved?* Ah, I'm glad you asked. It's just that you can do certain things with `networkd` and `resolved` that you can't do quite as easily with NetworkManager. For example, you can use networkd to set up a bridged network for running containers. This allows you to directly assign IP addresses to your containers so that they can be directly accessed from the outside world. With resolved, you can set up split DNS resolution, obtain DNS server addresses from either a DHCP server or an IPv6 router advertisement, and use DNSSEC, MulticastDNS, and DNS-over-TLS. On the other hand, NetworkManager is still the best solution for normal desktop and laptop usage, due to its ability to instantly switch between networks whenever needed.

On a system that's running a pure networkd environment, the network configuration would be stored in one or more `.network` files in the `/etc/systemd/network/` directory. However, as I've already said, the RHEL distros don't use networkd by default, so at this point, there are no `.network` files on the AlmaLinux machine to show you. Ubuntu Server does use networkd by default, but the Ubuntu engineers have done something that makes things a bit more interesting. Instead of configuring either networkd or NetworkManager in the normal way, they created Netplan, which we'll look at next.

Understanding Netplan on Ubuntu

Netplan is the new network configuration tool for Ubuntu. On a desktop machine, it doesn't do much except tell the system to use NetworkManager. On a server, you would create the networkd configuration in a `.yaml` file in the `/etc/netplan/` directory. Netplan will take this `.yaml` file and translate its contents into networkd format.

Viewing installer-generated Netplan configurations

To begin, I'd like to show you the default configuration on an Ubuntu desktop machine. (Yeah, I know. I didn't tell you that you'd need an Ubuntu desktop virtual machine, but that's okay. This is the only time we'll need it, so you can just look at what I'm showing you here.) In the `/etc/netplan/` directory, we have the default configuration file that was created when I created the virtual machine:

```
donnie@donald-virtualbox:~$ cd /etc/netplan/
donnie@donald-virtualbox:/etc/netplan$ ls -l
total 4
-rw-r--r-- 1 root root 104 Feb  3  2021 01-network-manager-all.
yaml
donnie@donald-virtualbox:/etc/netplan$
```

Inside the `01-network-manager-all.yaml` file, we have this:

```
# Let NetworkManager manage all devices on this system
network:
  version: 2
  renderer: NetworkManager
```

Here's the breakdown:

- The `network:` line is flush with the left-hand side of the screen, which means that this is a new node. The next two lines are indented by one space, which means that they are part of this node definition.
- What the `version: 2` line means is unclear. The `netplan` man page says that it's a *network mapping*, but doesn't explain it further, other than to indicate that it *might* have something to do with the version of YAML that Netplan uses. Or, it could be the syntax version of the `netplan` configuration. It's hard to say for sure because there appears to be no documentation that clears up the mystery. At any rate, the man page does indicate that this `version: 2` line always has to be present in the definition for a `network:` node.
- The `renderer:` line tells the system to use NetworkManager, and all the other configuration is done within the normal NetworkManager files. Since this is a desktop machine, most people would just use the GUI management utilities to reconfigure the network. (Most GUI-type utilities are self-explanatory, so we won't say anything more about them.) If no `renderer:` line is present, then the system will use networkd instead of NetworkManager.

> **Note**
> When creating or editing `.yaml` files, remember that proper indentation is very important. If the indentation isn't correct, things won't work. Also, tab characters aren't allowed in `.yaml` files, so you'll need to use the spacebar to do the indentation.

In contrast, Ubuntu Server is configured to use networkd. So, the Netplan configuration that was created by the Ubuntu Server installer looks like this:

```
donnie@ubuntu2004:/etc/netplan$ ls
00-installer-config.yaml
donnie@ubuntu2004:/etc/netplan$ cat 00-installer-config.yaml
# This is the network config written by 'subiquity'
network:
  ethernets:
    enp0s3:
      dhcp4: true
  version: 2
donnie@ubuntu2004:/etc/netplan$
```

The `network:` node is always the top-level node. Under that, we see the `ethernets:` node, which defines the network interface. (In this case, the interface's name is `enp0s3`.) The `dhcp4:  true` line tells the system to obtain an IPv4 address from a *DHCP* server. (In this case, the DHCP server is built into my internet gateway router.)

When the network starts, Netplan will take this `.yaml` file and translate it into networkd format. However, it doesn't store a permanent copy of the `.network` file. Instead, it creates a transient `.network` file in the `/run/systemd/network/` directory, as we see here:

```
donnie@ubuntu2004:/run/systemd/network$ ls -l
total 4
-rw-r--r-- 1 root root 102 Aug 13 15:33 10-netplan-enp0s3.
network
donnie@ubuntu2004:/run/systemd/network$
```

Inside this file, we can see this:

```
[Match]
Name=enp0s3

[Network]
DHCP=ipv4
LinkLocalAddressing=ipv6

[DHCP]
RouteMetric=100
UseMTU=true
```

At long last, we get to see what an actual networkd configuration file looks like, and we see that's it's divided into the `[Match]`, `[Network]`, and `[DHCP]` sections. As I mentioned previously, though, this isn't a permanent file. It will disappear when you shut down or reboot the machine, and reappear when the machine boots back up. (On a non-Ubuntu machine that doesn't use Netplan, you would have a permanent copy of this file in the `/etc/systemd/network/` directory.) Most of this file is self-explanatory, but there are a couple of interesting things. Under the `[Network]` section, we see that IPv6 **LinkLocalAddressing** is enabled, even though there's nothing about it in the Netplan `.yaml` file. Under the `[DHCP]` section, we see that the value for the *Maximum Transmission Unit* for this network link will be obtained from the DHCP server. (Most of the time, that value will be set to `1500`.) `RouteMetric=100` defines the priority that will be given to this network link. (Of course, there's only one network link here, so this isn't doing anything for us.)

To show what a static IP address configuration looks like, I created a new Ubuntu Server machine and told the installer to create a static configuration. The Netplan `.yaml` file on that machine looks like this:

```
donnie@ubuntu2004-staticip:/etc/netplan$ cat 00-installer-config.yaml
# This is the network config written by 'subiquity'
network:
  ethernets:
    enp0s3:
      addresses:
      - 192.168.0.49/24
      gateway4: 192.168.0.1
      nameservers:
        addresses:
        - 192.168.0.1
        - 8.8.8.8
  version: 2
donnie@ubuntu2004-staticip:/etc/netplan$
```

The generated transient `.network` file looks like this:

```
donnie@ubuntu2004-staticip:/run/systemd/network$ cat
10-netplan-enp0s3.network
[Match]
```

```
Name=enp0s3

[Network]
LinkLocalAddressing=ipv6
Address=192.168.0.49/24
Gateway=192.168.0.1
DNS=192.168.0.1
DNS=8.8.8.8
donnie@ubuntu2004-staticip:/run/systemd/network$
```

This time, all we have is just the `[Match]` and `[Network]` sections. Since we're not using DHCP on this machine, there's no `[DHCP]` section.

Now, keep in mind that you don't have to use the default Netplan configuration that was created when you installed the operating system. You can edit or replace the default `.yaml` configuration file as your needs dictate. Let's look at that next.

Creating Netplan configurations

Now, let's say that we want to convert our first Ubuntu Server machine from DHCP addressing into static addressing. The first thing I'll do is rename the current `.yaml` file to keep it as a backup in case I ever want to revert back:

```
donnie@ubuntu2004:/etc/netplan$ sudo mv 00-installer-config.
yaml 00-installer-config.yaml.bak
[sudo] password for donnie:
donnie@ubuntu2004:/etc/netplan$
```

Next, I'll create the new `00-static-config.yaml` file, like this:

```
donnie@ubuntu2004:/etc/netplan$ sudo vim 00-static-config.yaml
donnie@ubuntu2004:/etc/netplan$
```

Let's make this new file look like this:

```
network:
  ethernets:
    enp0s3:
      addresses:
      - 192.168.0.50/24
      gateway4: 192.168.0.1
```

```
      nameservers:
        addresses:
        - 192.168.0.1
        - 8.8.8.8
        - 208.67.222.222
        - 208.67.220.220
  version: 2
```

Okay, I'll confess that I cheated a bit by copying and pasting this from the other virtual machine. I then changed the IP address and added the addresses for two other DNS servers. For the record, the DNS servers I'm using here are:

- `192.168.0.1`: This is the address of my internet gateway router. This router has been configured to use the DNS servers that are run by my ISP, which is TDS Telecom. So, the `192.168.0.1` address isn't the real DNS server.
- `8.8.8.8`: This is one of the addresses for Google's DNS servers.
- `208.67.222.222` and `208.67.220.220`: These addresses are for the DNS servers that are maintained by the OpenDNS organization.

So, the more the merrier when it comes to `nameservers:` addresses. If one nameserver goes down, we'll just use another one, which eliminates one single-point-of network failure.

After saving the new file, you need to *apply* it, like so:

```
donnie@ubuntu2004:/etc/netplan$ sudo netplan apply
```

Be aware that if you do this from a remote terminal, you might not ever see the command prompt come back, which will make you think that things got stuck. It's not that, it's just that if you assign a different IP address from what the machine had to begin with, you'll break the SSH connection. (In fact, that's what just happened for me.) So, in real life, you might want to do this from the server's local terminal instead of remotely.

When you use the apply operation, you're generating the new networkd configuration and restarting the networkd service. The generated networkd configuration should now look something like this:

```
donnie@ubuntu2004:/run/systemd/network$ cat 10-netplan-enp0s3.
network
[Match]
Name=enp0s3

```

```
[Network]
LinkLocalAddressing=ipv6
Address=192.168.0.50/24
Gateway=192.168.0.1
DNS=192.168.0.1
DNS=8.8.8.8
DNS=208.67.222.222
DNS=208.67.220.220
donnie@ubuntu2004:/run/systemd/network$
```

Now, let's try something else. Let's pretend that our virtual machine has multiple network interfaces, and we want to make doubly sure that this network configuration always gets applied to the correct interface. We'll do that by assigning this configuration to the MAC address of the desired interface. First, we'll use `ip a` to get the MAC address, like this:

```
donnie@ubuntu2004:~$ ip a
. . .
. . .
2: enp0s3: <BROADCAST,MULTICAST,UP,LOWER_UP> mtu 1500 qdisc fq_
codel state UP group default qlen 1000
    link/ether 08:00:27:f2:c1:7a brd ff:ff:ff:ff:ff:ff
    inet 192.168.0.50/24 brd 192.168.0.255 scope global enp0s3
       valid_lft forever preferred_lft forever
    inet6 fe80::a00:27ff:fef2:c17a/64 scope link
       valid_lft forever preferred_lft forever
. . .
. . .
```

As you likely already know, the hardware address of a network interface goes by many names. Most of us know it as the *MAC address*. It's also known as the *physical address*, the *hardware address*, or, as we see here, the *link/ether* address. Anyway, let's copy that address so that we can paste it into the `.yaml` file. Under the `enp0s3:` node of the configuration file that we just created, we'll insert a new `match:` node with the `macaddress:` property of the desired network interface. The modified file should now look like this:

```
network:
  ethernets:
    enp0s3:
      match:
```

```
        macaddress: 08:00:27:f2:c1:7a
      addresses:
      - 192.168.0.50/24
      gateway4: 192.168.0.1
      nameservers:
        addresses:
        - 192.168.0.1
        - 8.8.8.8
        - 208.67.222.222
        - 208.67.220.220
  version: 2
```

This time, instead of using an `apply` operation, we'll try a `try` operation, like this:

```
donnie@ubuntu2004:/etc/netplan$ sudo netplan try
Warning: Stopping systemd-networkd.service, but it can still be activated by:
  systemd-networkd.socket
Do you want to keep these settings?

Press ENTER before the timeout to accept the new configuration

Changes will revert in 110 seconds
Configuration accepted.
donnie@ubuntu2004:/etc/netplan$
```

The `netplan try` command does the same thing as `netplan apply`, except that it gives you a chance to revert back to the old configuration if the new one doesn't work.

Okay, I've shown you a few examples of how to set up networking with the combination of Netplan and networkd. There's a lot more to this, of course. If you want to see some more complex network setups, your best bet is to consult the `netplan` man page. Toward the bottom, you'll see some really good examples.

Okay, let's move on and learn how to use networkd in the Red Hat world.

Understanding networkd and resolved on RHEL-type machines

We've already established that all RHEL-type machines, such as our AlmaLinux machine, use NetworkManager by default. Now, let's say that we have an AlmaLinux server and that we need the added capabilities of networkd. The `systemd-networkd` package isn't installed by default, and it isn't in the normal Alma repositories. However, it is in the third-party EPEL repository, so we'll install it by doing:

```
[donnie@localhost ~]$ sudo dnf install epel-release
```

Now, we can install the `systemd-networkd` package, which includes both networkd and resolved:

```
[donnie@localhost ~]$ sudo dnf install systemd-networkd
```

Next, disable NetworkManager and enable networkd and resolved. Note that I'm not stopping NetworkManager or starting networkd and resolved just yet (I'm logged in remotely and don't want to break my network connection. Besides, I still haven't created a networkd configuration):

```
[donnie@localhost ~]$ sudo systemctl disable NetworkManager
. . .
[donnie@localhost ~]$ sudo systemctl enable systemd-networkd
systemd-resolved
```

When configuring networkd, we can't use the `systemctl edit` command because it will create the `.network` files in the wrong location. Instead, we'll just `cd` into the `/etc/systemd/network/` directory and use a normal text editor. Let's name this file `99-networkconfig.network` and add the following content:

```
[Match]
Name=enp0s3

[Network]
DHCP=yes
IPv6AcceptRA=yes
```

The networkd `.network` files are set up the same way as any other systemd unit file. Instead of having to worry about proper indentation as you would with the Netplan `.yaml` files, you just place all the parameters into the proper sections. In the `[Match]` section, we have the name of the network adapter. In the `[Network]` section, we're saying that we want to get an IP address from DHCP and accept IPv6 router advertisements.

The next step is to get rid of the static `/etc/resolv.conf` file and create a symbolic link to the one that gets generated by resolved. We'll do that with these two commands:

```
[donnie@localhost ~]$ cd /etc
[donnie@localhost etc]$ sudo rm resolv.conf
[sudo] password for donnie:
[donnie@localhost etc]$ sudo ln -s /run/systemd/resolve/resolv.
conf /etc/resolv.conf
[donnie@localhost etc]$
```

If you do an `ls -l /etc/resolv.conf` command at this point, it will appear that the symbolic link is broken. That's because we haven't started `systemd-resolved.service` yet. So, resolved still hasn't generated the dynamic `resolv.conf` file in the `/run/systemd/resolve/` directory.

The final step is to reboot the machine and then test for proper network operation.

Now, let's say that we want to convert this machine into a static configuration, and we also want to add a few features. Let's edit the `/etc/systemd/network/99-networkconfig.network` file and make it look like this:

```
[Match]
Name=enp0s3
MACAddress=08:00:27:d2:fb:23

[Network]
Address=192.168.0.51/24
DNSSEC=yes
DNSOverTLS=opportunistic
Gateway=192.168.0.1
DNS=192.168.0.1
DNS=8.8.8.8
DNS=208.67.222.222
```

```
DNS=208.67.220.220
IPv6AcceptRA=yes
```

In the `[Match]` section, I've added the `MACAddress=` equal line to ensure that this configuration will always apply to this specific network adapter. As I did previously, I obtained the MAC address by doing an `ip a` command.

In the `[Network]` section, I assigned the IP address with its netmask, the default gateway address, and four DNS server addresses. I'm also forcing this machine to use `DNSSEC`, as well as to use `DNSOverTLS` whenever it's available. Once you save this file, either reboot the machine or do a `sudo networkctl reload` command. Then, verify that the networking works. (Note that you don't need to do a `daemon-reload` when configuring networkd.)

Before we move on, I want to talk about those two strange DNS options that you can see here. **DNS Security Extensions** (**DNSSEC**) is a fairly new feature that helps prevent DNS cache poisoning attacks. It does this by attaching a cryptographic signature to DNS records so that the DNS resolver on your local machine can verify them before accepting them. If you choose to set this parameter to `yes`, be sure to test things thoroughly to ensure that you can access everything that you need to access. So far, it's working well here. That surprises me because most websites still aren't set up with DNSSEC cryptographic keys. However, the public DNS root servers and the top-level domain servers are set up with DNSSEC keys, so we can at least verify the responses from them.

> **Note**
>
> To get a good idea of how widely DNSSEC is used on the public internet, go to `https://dnssec-analyzer.verisignlabs.com/` and enter a domain name of a website. This will show you a simple graphic of what uses DNSSEC and what doesn't.

The **DNSOverTLS** feature aims to ensure that all the queries and responses to and from DNS servers are encrypted with the same type of TLS that websites use. It's supposed to protect user privacy, but it's also somewhat controversial. Yeah, it can prevent people from sniffing your DNS queries, and it can prevent an attacker from intercepting the queries and sending back wrong responses. However, in an enterprise environment, it makes it difficult or impossible for network administrators to monitor the websites that employees visit, as well as control access to those websites. Most public DNS servers aren't set up to use TLS, so I set this to `opportunistic`, which allows this machine to use it if it's available. (Your IT team will need to get together with company management to determine if the advantages of **DNSOverTLS** outweigh the disadvantages.)

When you use networkd without Netplan, there will be no dynamic `.network` file in the `/run/systemd/network/` directory, as you saw on the Ubuntu machine. However, resolved will create a dynamic `resolv.conf` file in the `/run/systemd/resolve/` directory. We don't need to go there to see it because we created a symbolic link for it in the `/etc/` directory. Let's see what's in it:

```
[donnie@localhost etc]$ cat resolv.conf
. . .
. . .
nameserver 192.168.0.1
nameserver 8.8.8.8
nameserver 208.67.222.222
# Too many DNS servers configured, the following entries may be ignored.
nameserver 208.67.220.220
[donnie@localhost etc]$
```

Oh, dear. It appears that resolved only wants to see up to three DNS servers in its configuration. For now, that's okay. This will enable us to see something else that we need to see a bit later.

Okay, I've shown you a couple of simple examples of what you can do with networkd and resolved. If you want to be truly amazed, open the `systemd.network` man page and look at all that's there. (And yes, that is *systemd.network*, without the *d* after *network*.) You can create some very complex setups, and you can view some examples toward the bottom of the man page. What I find especially interesting is that with networkd, you can do some things that you used to have to do with either `iptables` or `nftables`. It seems to me that doing these things with networkd would be somewhat simpler. You'll also see that by adding a `[DHCPSERVER]` section, networkd can function as a simple DHCP server. Adding a `[CAN]` section allows you to control the **Control Area Network** (**CAN**) for automotive systems. Setting up a `[BRIDGE]` configuration allows you to assign normal IP addresses to containers so that the outside world can access them without having to use port forwarding. Well, the list of what you can do with networkd is quite long, and there's no way that I can cover it all here.

Finally, I'd like you to open the `netplan` man page on your Ubuntu Server machine. Even though Netplan is supposed to be a frontend for networkd, you'll see that what you can do with Netplan is only a subset of what you can do when working directly with networkd.

Now that we've seen the basics of configuring networkd and resolved, let's look at a pair of network diagnostic utilities.

Using networkctl and resolvectl

On both the Ubuntu and the Alma machines, you can try out two cool utilities that can help you see what's going on with your network configuration. To see the list of network links and their statuses, use either `networkctl` or `networkctl list`. (The `list` option is the default, so you don't have to type it.) What you will see on the Alma machine should look something like this:

```
[donnie@localhost ~]$ networkctl
IDX LINK      TYPE          OPERATIONAL   SETUP
  1   lo            loopback       carrier
unmanaged
  2   enp0s3   ether              routable
configured

2 links listed.
[donnie@localhost ~]$
```

On this machine, we only have two links. The `OPERATIONAL` status of the loopback link shows as `carrier`, which means that this link is operational but that it's not routable. `SETUP` shows that the loopback is `unmanaged`, which means that we can't reconfigure it. The `enp0s3` link is our normal Ethernet link, which shows as `routable` and `configured`.

On the Ubuntu Server machine, things are a bit more interesting. As shown here, there are a few more links:

```
donnie@ubuntu2004:~$ networkctl
IDX LINK                   TYPE       OPERATIONAL    SETUP
  1   lo                          loopback   carrier
unmanaged
  2   enp0s3                  ether         routable
configured
  3   docker0                bridge      no-carrier
unmanaged
  4   cali659bb8bc7b1 ether       degraded
unmanaged
```

```
  7    vxlan.calico              vxlan        routable
unmanaged

5 links listed.
donnie@ubuntu2004:~$
```

In addition to the two normal links, we have three links that were created when the `docker` package was installed. The `docker0` link is an `unmanaged` bridge that's currently in a `no-carrier` `OPERATIONAL` status. I don't have any containers running, so nothing is using it. The bottom two links are for Kubernetes, which is an orchestration manager for Docker containers. (The *calico* reference comes from *Project Calico*, the maintainer of this Kubernetes networking code.) The `cali659bb8bc7b1` link is listed as `degraded`, which means that it is online with a `carrier`, but it's only valid for link-local addresses.

The `status` option shows you the links with their associated IP addresses, the default gateway address, and the addresses of the DNS servers that we want to use. Here's what that looks like on the Ubuntu Server machine:

```
donnie@ubuntu2004:~$ networkctl status
●    State: routable
   Address: 192.168.0.50 on enp0s3
            172.17.0.1 on docker0
            10.1.89.0 on vxlan.calico
            fe80::a00:27ff:fef2:c17a on enp0s3
            fe80::ecee:eeff:feee:eeee on cali659bb8bc7b1
            fe80::648c:87ff:fe5f:94d5 on vxlan.calico
   Gateway: 192.168.0.1 (Actiontec Electronics, Inc) on enp0s3
       DNS: 192.168.0.1
            8.8.8.8
            208.67.222.222
            208.67.220.220
. . .
. . .
```

Of course, we've already seen how to reload a modified network configuration. On Ubuntu with Netplan, you'd do either `sudo netplan apply` or `sudo netplan try`. On the Alma machine, you'd do `sudo networkctl reload`.

To look at DNS server information, we'd use `resolvectl`. The main thing to note here is that the output is divided into sections. First, there's the `Global` section, which shows the settings from the `/etc/systemd/resolved.conf` file. On the Alma machine, these settings look like this:

```
[donnie@localhost ~]$ resolvectl
Global
       LLMNR setting: yes
MulticastDNS setting: yes
  DNSOverTLS setting: no
      DNSSEC setting: allow-downgrade
    DNSSEC supported: yes
          DNSSEC NTA: 10.in-addr.arpa
                      16.172.in-addr.arpa
. . .
. . .
```

After the `Global` section, each link has its own settings, which can override the `Global` settings. Here are the settings for the `enp0se` link on the Alma machine:

```
. . .
. . .
Link 2 (enp0s3)
      Current Scopes: DNS LLMNR/IPv4 LLMNR/IPv6
       LLMNR setting: yes
MulticastDNS setting: no
  DNSOverTLS setting: opportunistic
      DNSSEC setting: yes
    DNSSEC supported: yes
  Current DNS Server: 192.168.0.1
         DNS Servers: 192.168.0.1
                      8.8.8.8
                      208.67.222.222
                      208.67.220.220
```

Look carefully, and you'll see a few `Link` settings that override the `Global` settings. Previously, we saw that the `resolv.conf` file for this machine has a warning about how we've listed too many nameservers, and that resolved might ignore the fourth one. But we see all four nameservers here, so everything is good.

There are lots more options for both networkctl and resolvectl. I'll let you read about them in the `networkctl` and `resolvectl` man pages.

Next, let's take a brief look at the networkd and resolved unit files.

Viewing the networkd and resolved unit files

Before we go, I'd like you to take a quick look at the unit files for networkd and resolved. Here's the list of them:

```
[donnie@localhost system]$ pwd
/lib/systemd/system
[donnie@localhost system]$ ls -l *networkd*
-rw-r--r--. 1 root root 2023 Jun  6 22:26 systemd-networkd.
service
-rw-r--r--. 1 root root  640 May 15 12:33 systemd-networkd.
socket
-rw-r--r--. 1 root root  752 Jun  6 22:26 systemd-networkd-
wait-online.service
[donnie@localhost system]$ ls -l *resolved*
-rw-r--r--. 1 root root 1668 Aug 10 17:19 systemd-resolved.
service
[donnie@localhost system]$
```

I'm not going to take the time to trace through them for you because by now, you should be able to do that yourself. I mean, it's mainly a matter of looking everything up in the `systemd.directives` man page, as we've done quite a few times before. Once you've done that, we'll wrap this baby up.

Summary

As always, we've covered a lot of ground in this chapter. We started by comparing NetworkManager to systemd-networkd and systemd-resolved. Next, we looked at how to deal with the Netplan tool on Ubuntu. The RHEL-type distros use NetworkManager by default and don't use Netplan, so we looked at how to convert your Alma machine over to use networkd and resolved. After that, we worked with a couple of diagnostic utilities, and then wrapped things up by briefly looking at the networkd and resolved unit files.

Now, it's time to talk about *time*, which we'll do in the next chapter. I'll see you there!

Questions

Answer the following questions to test your knowledge of this chapter:

1. Which of the following statements is true?

   A. NetworkManager is better for servers because it can instantly switch between networks.

   B. NetworkManager is better for servers because it's more versatile.

   C. NetworkManager is better for desktops and laptops because it can instantly switch between networks.

   D. networkd is better for desktops and laptops because it can instantly switch between networks.
2. True or False: If there's no `renderer:` line in a Netplan `.yaml` file, the system will default to using NetworkManager.
3. On an Ubuntu Server machine, which of the following would you do after you've edited the network configuration file?

   A. `sudo netplan reload`

   B. `sudo networkctl reload`

   C. `sudo netplan restart`

   D. `sudo networkctl restart`

   E. `sudo netplan apply`
4. What does it mean when a `networkctl` command shows a link as `degraded`?

   A. The link is offline.

   B. The link is online, but not operating at full speed.

   C. The link is online, but is only valid for link-local addresses.

   D. The link is unreliable.

Answers

1. C
2. False
3. E
4. C

Further reading

Configuring the network with Netplan on Ubuntu:

- `https://ubuntu.com/server/docs/network-configuration`
- How to configure networking on Ubuntu 20.04 with Netplan:
- `https://www.serverlab.ca/tutorials/linux/administration-linux/how-to-configure-networking-in-ubuntu-20-04-with-netplan/`
- YAML Tutorial:
- `https://www.tutorialspoint.com/yaml/index.htm`
- YAML for Beginners:
- `https://www.redhat.com/sysadmin/yaml-beginners`
- `systemd-resolved`: Introduction to split DNS:
- `https://fedoramagazine.org/systemd-resolved-introduction-to-split-dns/`
- Multicast DNS: Name resolution on a small scale:
- `https://www.ionos.com/digitalguide/server/know-how/multicast-dns/`
- DNS over TLS: An improved security concept:
- `https://www.ionos.com/digitalguide/server/security/dns-over-tls/`
- Project Calico:
- `https://www.tigera.io/project-calico/`

16 Understanding Timekeeping with systemd

On modern computer systems, it's vitally important to maintain accurate time. To do that, our computers obtain the current time from a time server while using some implementation of the **Network Time Protocol** (**NTP**). In this chapter, we'll look at these various implementations and discuss the pros and cons of each.

In this chapter, we will cover the following topics:

- Understanding the importance of accurate time
- Comparing NTP implementations
- Understanding chrony
- Understanding `systemd-timesyncd`
- Understanding the **Precision Time Protocol** (**PTP**)

All right, it's time to get started!

Technical requirements

Timekeeping is done differently in the Ubuntu and RHEL worlds. So, we'll be using both Ubuntu Server and *two* AlmaLinux virtual machines to look at both of these.

Check out the following link to see the Code in Action video: `https://bit.ly/3Dh4byf`

Understanding the importance of accurate time

Accurate timekeeping on computers wasn't always real important. My very first computer job involved working with a pair of transistorized computers that were each the size of a refrigerator, and that had orders of magnitude less processing power than a modern smartphone. There was no hardware clock, and there was no NTP. Every time we rebooted these beasts, we just looked at our notoriously inaccurate wall clock and manually entered the time from it. Things didn't change much with the early personal computers. I mean, you still had to set the time manually, but they did eventually come with battery-powered hardware clocks that would still keep time when you shut the computers down.

Nowadays, it's critically important for computers to maintain accurate time. Scientific computing, log keeping, database updating, and financial transactions all require it. Certain security protocols, such as Kerberos, DNSSEC, and **Transport Layer Security** (**TLS**) also require it. Modern stock exchanges use automated trading bots that require it. For these reasons and others besides, mankind invented the NTP.

The basic concept of NTP is easy to understand. Every modern operating system includes an NTP client. Every time you boot your computer, the NTP client obtains the correct time from a highly accurate NTP server that's someplace on the internet. To ensure even greater time accuracy, some organizations might use a local time source, which could be either a local server or something such as a GPS clock.

There are several software implementations of NTP. Let's do a quick comparison of them.

Comparing NTP implementations

The **Original Guy** (**OG**), or *reference implementation*, of the NTP world is `ntpd`. It was created way back in the 1980s and served us well for a long time. You can use it on client machines to keep their time synchronized, or you can set it up as a time server. However, it does have several shortcomings, including numerous security problems that were found during a code audit in 2017.

The `chrony` implementation, which can also be used as either a client or a server, was created from scratch to fix the shortcomings of `ntpd`. Unlike `ntpd`, `chrony` has the following features:

- It works well on computers that have unstable network connections or that get turned off for long periods.
- It works better with virtual machines.
- It can adjust itself better when the speed of the hardware clock oscillator fluctuates due to a temperature change.
- It can achieve sub-microsecond accuracy by using hardware timestamping and a hardware reference clock.

RHEL 7 and its clones were the first Linux distros to ship with `chrony` instead of `ntpd`. The RHEL 8 and SUSE distros also use `chrony` by default.

Another alternative is `systemd-timesyncd`, which is part of the systemd ecosystem. Unlike `ntpd` and `chrony`, `systemd-timesyncd` is an implementation of the lighter-weight **Simple Network Time Protocol** (**SNTP**), instead of the full-blown NTP. SNTP requires less processing power, which makes it better for low-resource computers. The downside is that SNTP and `systemd-timesyncd` lack some of the bells and whistles that NTP has. For example, you can't use them to set up a time server, and you can't use them with either hardware timestamping or hardware reference clocks. So, you can forget about getting that good sub-microsecond accuracy with `systemd-timesyncd`. On the other hand, SNTP and `systemd-timesyncd` might be all you need for most situations. Ubuntu uses `systemd-timesyncd` by default, and it will work fine for you most of the time. If it doesn't, it's easy to switch your machine over to `chrony`.

The **Precision Time Protocol** (**PTP**) isn't an implementation of NTP. Rather, it's an entirely different protocol that's designed for extreme – and I do mean extreme – timekeeping accuracy. To use it, you must have a precision time source on the local network, and you must have switches and routers that can work with it. It uses hardware timestamping and hardware reference clocks to achieve picosecond accuracy.

Okay, that does it for our overview. Now, let's talk a bit about `chrony`. We'll look at it on the AlmaLinux machine since Alma uses it by default.

Understanding chrony on the AlmaLinux machine

There are two components in the chrony system. We have chronyd as the daemon and chronyc as the user interface. The chronyd component can run in either client or server mode. First, let's look at the unit file for chonyd.

The chronyd.service file

There are a few interesting things to look at in the /lib/systemd/system/chronyd.service file. In the [Unit] section, we have this:

```
[Unit]
Description=NTP client/server
Documentation=man:chronyd(8) man:chrony.conf(5)
After=ntpdate.service sntp.service ntpd.service
Conflicts=ntpd.service systemd-timesyncd.service
ConditionCapability=CAP_SYS_TIME
```

The Conflicts= line indicates that we can't run multiple NTP implementations together on the same machine. If systemd detects that either ntpd or systemd-timesyncd is running, then chronyd will fail to start. The ConditionCapability= line indicates that this service runs under a non-privileged account, even though no non-privileged user account is configured in either this unit file or in the /etc/chrony.conf file. Instead, chronyd is hardcoded to run under the non-privileged chrony account. We can confirm this with a simple ps aux command, like so:

```
[donnie@localhost ~]$ ps aux | grep chrony
chrony       727  0.0  0.1 128912  3588 ?        S    15:23
0:00 /usr/sbin/chronyd
donnie      1901  0.0  0.0  12112  1092 pts/0    R+   16:44
0:00 grep --color=auto chrony
[donnie@localhost ~]$
```

Because chronyd does run under a non-privileged user account, we need to set the CAP_SYS_TIME capability for that non-privileged user account so that it can set the system time.

Next, let's look at the `[Service]` section of the `chronyd.service` file:

```
[Service]
Type=forking
PIDFile=/run/chrony/chronyd.pid
EnvironmentFile=-/etc/sysconfig/chronyd
ExecStart=/usr/sbin/chronyd $OPTIONS
ExecStartPost=/usr/libexec/chrony-helper update-daemon
PrivateTmp=yes
ProtectHome=yes
ProtectSystem=full
```

The `ExecStart=` line starts `chronyd` with options that it obtained from the file that's referenced in the `EnvironmentFile=` line. If we go there, we'll see that no options have been configured:

```
[donnie@localhost system]$ cd /etc/sysconfig/
[donnie@localhost sysconfig]$ cat chronyd
# Command-line options for chronyd
OPTIONS=""
[donnie@localhost sysconfig]$
```

The `chrony-helper` program that's referenced in the `ExecStartPost=` line is a shell script that obtains the addresses of NTP servers from either a DHCP or a DNS server. At the moment, this line doesn't do anything for us. This is because `chronyd` is currently configured to contact a pool of NTP servers that is listed in the `/etc/chrony.conf` file, as shown here:

```
[donnie@localhost sysconfig]$ cd /etc/
[donnie@localhost etc]$ cat chrony.conf
# Use public servers from the pool.ntp.org project.
# Please consider joining the pool (http://www.pool.ntp.org/
join.html).
pool 2.cloudlinux.pool.ntp.org iburst
. . .
. . .
```

At the bottom of the `[Service]` section, we can see the `PrivateTmp=yes`, `ProtectHome=yes`, and `ProtectSystem=full` lines, which add a measure of security.

Finally, there's the `[Install]` section of the `chronyd.service` file:

```
[Install]
WantedBy=multi-user.target
```

Okay, there's nothing exciting here. It's just the standard `WantedBy=` line that makes this service run in multi-user mode.

Next, let's look at the `chrony.conf` file.

The chrony.conf file

Most `chronyd` configuration is done in the `/etc/chrony.conf` file. (The only exception would be on those rare occasions where you might want to configure some options in the `/etc/sysconfig/chronyd` file.) I'm not going to cover every option in the file because you can read about them by going to the `chrony.conf` man page. However, I will point out a couple of things that you might need to reconfigure.

By default, `chrony.conf` is configured to obtain the current time from a pool of time servers that are out on the internet, as we see here:

```
pool 2.cloudlinux.pool.ntp.org iburst
```

The `iburst` option at the end allows `chronyd` to update the clock a bit faster when you first boot up the machine. Large organizations might have local timeservers to prevent all machines on their network from going out to the internet to obtain the time. In those cases, you would need to configure this line with the IP address of the local timeserver. (We'll look at this a bit later when we set up a time server.)

For increased timekeeping accuracy, you can enable hardware timestamping by removing the # symbol from the beginning of the following line:

```
#hwtimestamp *
```

The only catch is that the network interface adapters in your computer must support hardware timestamping. To verify that, use the `ethtool -T` command, followed by the name of your network interface adapter. Here's what that looks like on one of my old 2009-model Hewlett-Packard machines:

```
donnie@localhost:~> sudo ethtool -T eth1
Time stamping parameters for eth1:
Capabilities:
  software-transmit      (SOF_TIMESTAMPING_TX_SOFTWARE)
```

```
  software-receive       (SOF_TIMESTAMPING_RX_SOFTWARE)
  software-system-clock (SOF_TIMESTAMPING_SOFTWARE)
PTP Hardware Clock: none
Hardware Transmit Timestamp Modes: none
Hardware Receive Filter Modes: none
donnie@localhost:~>
```

Well, that's not good. There's no PTP hardware clock, and there's no hardware timestamping. Let's see if things look any better on my Dell Precision workstation, which is several years newer:

```
donnie@siftworkstation: ~
$ sudo ethtool -T enp0s25
[sudo] password for donnie:
Time stamping parameters for enp0s25:
Capabilities:
        hardware-transmit     (SOF_TIMESTAMPING_TX_HARDWARE)
        software-transmit     (SOF_TIMESTAMPING_TX_SOFTWARE)
        hardware-receive      (SOF_TIMESTAMPING_RX_HARDWARE)
        software-receive      (SOF_TIMESTAMPING_RX_SOFTWARE)
        software-system-clock (SOF_TIMESTAMPING_SOFTWARE)
        hardware-raw-clock    (SOF_TIMESTAMPING_RAW_HARDWARE)
PTP Hardware Clock: 0
Hardware Transmit Timestamp Modes:
        off                   (HWTSTAMP_TX_OFF)
        on                    (HWTSTAMP_TX_ON)
Hardware Receive Filter Modes:
        none                  (HWTSTAMP_FILTER_NONE)
        all                   (HWTSTAMP_FILTER_ALL)
        ptpv1-l4-sync         (HWTSTAMP_FILTER_PTP_V1_L4_SYNC)
        ptpv1-l4-delay-req    (HWTSTAMP_FILTER_PTP_V1_L4_DELAY_REQ)
        ptpv2-l4-sync         (HWTSTAMP_FILTER_PTP_V2_L4_SYNC)
        ptpv2-l4-delay-req    (HWTSTAMP_FILTER_PTP_V2_L4_DELAY_REQ)
        ptpv2-l2-sync         (HWTSTAMP_FILTER_PTP_V2_L2_SYNC)
        ptpv2-l2-delay-req    (HWTSTAMP_FILTER_PTP_V2_L2_DELAY_REQ)
        ptpv2-event           (HWTSTAMP_FILTER_PTP_V2_EVENT)
        ptpv2-sync            (HWTSTAMP_FILTER_PTP_V2_SYNC)
        ptpv2-delay-req       (HWTSTAMP_FILTER_PTP_V2_DELAY_REQ)
donnie@siftworkstation: ~
$
```

Figure 16.1 – Hardware timestamping on my Dell Precision T3610 workstation

Yes, this does look better. We see a PTP hardware clock and hardware timestamping. The bad part is that at the moment, I can't take advantage of this, because this machine is running Lubuntu Linux. Lubuntu, just like Ubuntu, runs `systemd-timesyncd`, which can't take advantage of hardware timestamping. But that's okay for now. If I were to ever feel the need to, I could easily switch this machine over to `chrony`. (I'll show you how to do that in just a bit.)

Now, let's skip to the bottom of the chrony.conf file, where we see these lines:

```
# Specify directory for log files.
logdir /var/log/chrony

# Select which information is logged.
#log measurements statistics tracking
```

Here, we can see that it's configured to store chronyd logs in the /var/log/chrony/ directory. But if we were to go there now, we'd see nothing but an empty directory. That's because the line at the bottom, which tells chronyd what information to log, is commented out. To change that, just remove the # symbol from the beginning of the line so that it now looks like this:

```
log measurements statistics tracking
```

Then, restart chronyd:

```
[donnie@localhost ~]$ sudo systemctl restart chronyd
[donnie@localhost ~]$
```

You should now see log files in the /var/log/chrony/ directory:

```
[donnie@localhost ~]$ cd /var/log/chrony/
[donnie@localhost chrony]$ ls -l
total 12
-rw-r--r--. 1 chrony chrony 2603 Aug 24 14:29 measurements.log
-rw-r--r--. 1 chrony chrony 1287 Aug 24 14:29 statistics.log
-rw-r--r--. 1 chrony chrony  792 Aug 24 14:29 tracking.log
[donnie@localhost chrony]$
```

This pretty much covers the basics. Let's get a bit fancier by setting up a chronyd time server.

Setting up a chronyd time server

For this demo, you'll need two Alma virtual machines. We'll set up one as the time server and the other to use the time server. (Ideally, we'd want the time server to have a static IP address, but we won't worry about that for now.)

On the time server machine, edit the `/etc/chrony.conf` file. Here's the line that you'll change:

```
#allow 192.168.0.0/16
```

Remove # from the beginning of the line and change the network address so that it matches your own. For me, the network address is correct, but the netmask is wrong. So, I'll change the line so that it looks like this:

```
allow 192.168.0.0/24
```

Next, restart `chronyd`:

```
[donnie@localhost ~]$ sudo systemctl restart chronyd
[donnie@localhost ~]$
```

The final step for setting up the time server is to open the appropriate firewall ports:

```
[donnie@localhost ~]$ sudo firewall-cmd --permanent
--add-service=ntp
success
[donnie@localhost ~]$ sudo firewall-cmd --reload
success
[donnie@localhost ~]$
```

Now, switch over to the other Alma virtual machine and edit the `/etc/chrony.conf` file on it. Comment out the `pool` line and add a line that points to the IP address of the time server virtual machine. The two lines should now look something like this:

```
#pool 2.cloudlinux.pool.ntp.org iburst
server 192.168.0.14 iburst
```

Save the file and restart the `chronyd` service. When you look at the status of `chronyd`, you should see that this machine now obtains its time from your time server. It should look something like this:

```
[donnie@logserver ~]$ systemctl status chronyd
● chronyd.service - NTP client/server
   Loaded: loaded (/usr/lib/systemd/system/chronyd.service;
enabled; vendor preset: enabled)
   Active: active (running) since Tue 2021-08-24 14:59:43 EDT;
55s ago
```

```
 . . .
. . .
Aug 24 14:59:48 logserver chronyd[15558]: Selected source
192.168.0.14
Aug 24 14:59:48 logserver chronyd[15558]: System clock TAI
offset set to 37 seconds
[donnie@logserver ~]$
```

> **Note**
> Sometimes need to preface this command with sudo in order to see information about the network time sources.

That's all there is to it. Let's change gears now and look at the `chronyc` client utility.

Using chronyc

You can use the `chronyc` utility to either look at information about the `chronyd` service or to dynamically configure certain aspects of the `chronyd` service. Let's start by looking at tracking information on our time server:

```
[donnie@localhost ~]$ chronyc tracking
Reference ID    : 32CDF46C (50-205-244-108-static.hfc.
comcastbusiness.net)
Stratum         : 3
Ref time (UTC)  : Tue Aug 24 19:16:00 2021
System time     : 0.000093940 seconds fast of NTP time
Last offset     : -0.000033931 seconds
RMS offset      : 0.000185221 seconds
Frequency       : 10909.050 ppm fast
Residual freq   : +0.002 ppm
Skew            : 0.344 ppm
Root delay      : 0.016927114 seconds
Root dispersion : 0.018588312 seconds
Update interval : 128.6 seconds
Leap status     : Normal
[donnie@localhost ~]$
```

Rather than go over everything here, I'm going to let you read about it by going to the `chronyc` man page. However, I do want to talk about the `Reference ID` line at the top.

The `Reference ID` line just tells us the hostname or the IP address of the remote time server that this local timeserver is synchronized to. We see that this local time server is synchronized to a remote time server that's operated either by Comcast or by an organization that uses Comcast hosting. Note that this remote time server is a member of the pool that's configured in the `chrony.conf` file.

Now, let's look at the Alma machine that we set up as a client of this local time server:

```
[donnie@logserver ~]$ chronyc tracking
Reference ID    : C0A8000E (192.168.0.14)
. . .
. . .
[donnie@logserver ~]$
```

As expected, we see the IP address of the local time server.

The `sources` command will show you all of the time servers that our machine can access. Here are the time servers that are in the default pool for the Alma machines:

```
[donnie@localhost ~]$ chronyc sources
210 Number of sources = 4
MS Name/IP address                    Stratum Poll Reach LastRx
Last sample
===============================================================
================
^* 50-205-244-108-static.hf>    2   9   377   349   -551us[
-384us] +/-   43ms
^+ clock.nyc.he.net                  2   8   377    13
+1084us[+1084us] +/-    51ms
^+ t2.time.gq1.yahoo.com         2   9   377    92   +576us[
+576us] +/-   49ms
^+ linode.appus.org                  2   8   377   23
+895us[ +895us] +/-   70ms
[donnie@localhost ~]$
```

As before, I'll let you look at the `chronyc` man page to see what all the fields are.

So far, we've been able to look at everything with normal user privileges. Looking at other types of information might require sudo privileges, as we see here on the time server:

```
[donnie@localhost ~]$ sudo chronyc clients
[sudo] password for donnie:
Hostname                     NTP   Drop Int IntL Last     Cmd
Drop Int  Last
===============================================================
================
192.168.0.7                   29      0   8   -   129       0
0    -    -
localhost                      0      0   -   -     -       8
0    8   287
[donnie@localhost ~]$
```

Very cool. We see the IP address of the virtual machine that we set up as a client of this local time server.

Just for fun, let's see how much work our local time server has been doing:

```
[donnie@localhost ~]$ sudo chronyc serverstats
NTP packets received       : 84
NTP packets dropped        : 0
Command packets received   : 20
Command packets dropped    : 0
Client log records dropped : 0
[donnie@localhost ~]$
```

This shows the number of NTP packets and command packets that were received from the clients.

There's a whole lot more to this command than what I can show you here. Your best bet is to read all about it by going to the chronyc man page.

That's about it for chronyd and chronyc. So, let's shift over to the Ubuntu machine and look at systemd-timesyncd.

Understanding systemd-timesyncd

Ubuntu uses systemd-timesyncd by default. It's a simple, lightweight system that's easy to configure. Before we get to that, let's take a quick look at the systemd-timesyncd.service file.

The systemd-timesyncd.service file

The `[Unit]` section of the `/lib/systemd/system/systemd-timesyncd.service` file looks like this:

```
[Unit]
Description=Network Time Synchronization
Documentation=man:systemd-timesyncd.service(8)
ConditionCapability=CAP_SYS_TIME
ConditionVirtualization=!container
DefaultDependencies=no
After=systemd-sysusers.service
Before=time-set.target sysinit.target shutdown.target
Conflicts=shutdown.target
Wants=time-set.target time-sync.target
```

Note the `ConditionVirtualization=!container` line. The `ConditionVirtualization=` part checks to see if the operating system is running in a virtualized environment. In this case, it wants to see whether it's running in a container. The `!` in front of `container` denotes a negation. In other words, if systemd detects that this operating system is running in a container, then the `systemd-timesyncd` service won't start.

In the `[Service]` section, you'll see a lot more security-related parameters than you saw in the `chronyd.service` file on the Alma machine. There are so many that I can only show you some of them here:

```
[Service]
AmbientCapabilities=CAP_SYS_TIME
CapabilityBoundingSet=CAP_SYS_TIME
ExecStart=!!/lib/systemd/systemd-timesyncd
LockPersonality=yes
MemoryDenyWriteExecute=yes
NoNewPrivileges=yes
. . .
. . .
SystemCallFilter=@system-service @clock
Type=notify
User=systemd-timesync
WatchdogSec=3min
```

This makes sense, considering that Ubuntu uses AppArmor as its mandatory access control system instead of SELinux, which is what the Alma machine uses. A default configuration of AppArmor doesn't provide near as much protection as a default configuration of SELinux, so it makes sense to include more security directives in this service file. Also, note the `User=systemd-timesync` line, which configures the non-privileged user account for this service.

The `[Install]` section is a bit different from what we're used to:

```
[Install]
WantedBy=sysinit.target
Alias=dbus-org.freedesktop.timesync1.service
```

Instead of getting started as part of `multi-user.target`, `systemd-timesyncd` gets started as part of `sysinit.target`. So, it gets started much earlier in the boot process.

Next, let's briefly look at how to configure `systemd-timesyncd`.

The timesyncd.conf file

When I said that we'll *briefly* cover this, I really did mean *briefly*. That's because there's not a whole lot to configure. Here's the entirety of the `/etc/systemd/timesyncd.conf` file:

```
[Time]
#NTP=
#FallbackNTP=ntp.ubuntu.com
#RootDistanceMaxSec=5
#PollIntervalMinSec=32
#PollIntervalMaxSec=2048
```

Everything is commented out, which means that everything is set with its default values. The first thing to notice is that there's nothing set for the `NTP=` line and that the `FallbackNTP=` line points to a pool of time servers at `ntp.ubuntu.com`. So, this machine will only obtain its time from one of the time servers that's in that pool. The remaining three parameters are set with sane values that you'll likely never have to change. (I'll let you read about them in the `timesyncd.conf` man page.)

That's enough about this file for now. Now, let's look at a couple of `timedatectl` options.

Using timedatectl

Two `timedatectl` viewing options are specific to `systemd-timesyncd`. The `timesync-status` option looks like this:

```
donnie@ubuntu2004-staticip:/etc/systemd$ timedatectl timesync-
status
       Server: 91.189.94.4 (ntp.ubuntu.com)
Poll interval: 32s (min: 32s; max 34min 8s)
         Leap: normal
      Version: 4
      Stratum: 2
    Reference: 8CCBCC4D
    Precision: 1us (-23)
Root distance: 45.074ms (max: 5s)
       Offset: -336.094ms
        Delay: 101.668ms
       Jitter: 1.560ms
 Packet count: 214
    Frequency: -500.000ppm
donnie@ubuntu2004-staticip:/etc/systemd$
```

At the top, we see the remote time server that this machine accesses, and we see that it's a member of the `ntp.ubunutu.com` pool. Further down, we see that `Rootdistance` from the time servers comes in at 45.07 milliseconds, which is well within the five seconds that's set in the `timesyncd.conf` file.

The other `timedatectl` option is `show-timesync`, which looks something like this:

```
donnie@ubuntu2004-staticip:~$ timedatectl show-timesync
FallbackNTPServers=ntp.ubuntu.com
ServerName=ntp.ubuntu.com
ServerAddress=91.189.89.198
RootDistanceMaxUSec=5s
PollIntervalMinUSec=32s
PollIntervalMaxUSec=34min 8s
PollIntervalUSec=32s
```

```
NTPMessage={ Leap=0, Version=4, Mode=4, Stratum=2,
Precision=-23, RootDelay=1.129ms, RootDispersion=30.349ms,
Reference=11FD227B, OriginateTimestamp=Tue 2021-08-24
17:16:48 EDT, ReceiveTimestamp=Tue 2021-08-24 17:16:48
EDT, TransmitTimestamp=Tue 2021-08-24 17:16:48 EDT,
DestinationTimestamp=Tue 2021-08-24 17:16:48 EDT, Ignored=no
PacketCount=1, Jitter=0 }
Frequency=-32768000
donnie@ubuntu2004-staticip:~$
```

This shows the same information that's in the `timesync-status` option, except that it's now in a machine-readable format.

Next, let's edit the `/etc/systemd/timesyncd.conf` file so that this machine will obtain its time from our local AlmaLinux time server. We'll just uncomment the `#NTP=` line and add the IP address of the Alma machine. It should now look something like this:

```
NTP=192.168.0.14
```

After restarting the `systemd-timesyncd` service, we should see that this machine now obtains its time from our local time server, as we see here:

```
donnie@ubuntu2004-staticip:~$ timedatectl timesync-status
       Server: 192.168.0.14 (192.168.0.14)
Poll interval: 32s (min: 32s; max 34min 8s)
         Leap: normal
      Version: 4
      Stratum: 3
    Reference: 32CDF46C
    Precision: 1us (-25)
Root distance: 27.884ms (max: 5s)
       Offset: -279.517ms
        Delay: 470us
       Jitter: 0
 Packet count: 1
    Frequency: -500.000ppm
donnie@ubuntu2004-staticip:~$
```

There's an excellent chance that `systemd-timedatectl` is all you'll ever need. But what if you really need the extra features and precision that come with `chrony`? Well, let's see if we can switch our Ubuntu machine over to `chrony`.

Configuring Ubuntu to use chrony

The first step is to stop and disable `systemd-timesyncd`, like this:

```
donnie@ubuntu2004-staticip:~$ sudo systemctl disable --now systemd-timesyncd
Removed /etc/systemd/system/dbus-org.freedesktop.timesync1.service.
Removed /etc/systemd/system/sysinit.target.wants/systemd-timesyncd.service.
donnie@ubuntu2004-staticip:~$
```

Now, install the `chrony` package, like this:

```
donnie@ubuntu2004-staticip:~$ sudo apt install chrony
```

Since this is Ubuntu, the `chronyd` service will be enabled and started automatically when the installation completes. The only difference from what you saw on the Alma machine is that the `chrony.conf` file on Ubuntu is in the `/etc/chrony/` directory.

Sometimes, you just need to be precise. So, let's talk a bit about PTP.

Understanding the Precision Time Protocol

For many financial, scientific, and enterprise applications, you've just got to have the most accurate time possible. In these instances, getting the time from a remote time server on the Internet just doesn't meet your needs. So, you need something better. With proper hardware, **PTP** can keep your network time synchronized to picosecond accuracy. The whole explanation of PTP is rather complex, so allow me to simplify things a bit.

An overview of PTP

Unlike NTP, PTP cannot obtain its time from a remote time server that's out on the internet. Instead, PTP can only be used within a **Local Area Network** (**LAN**) and will obtain its time from a local source. This local time source, which is usually called the *Grandmaster Clock*, will most likely obtain its time from a **Global Positioning System** (**GPS**) satellite, and will then synchronize the clocks on the other network devices to the GPS time. To do this, the Grandmaster Clock sends `sync` messages out to the network. The client devices will respond by sending back `delay request` messages, and the Grandmaster Clock will respond with `delay response` messages. The network packets that carry these messages all have timestamps that will be used in the calculations for figuring out how to adjust the time on the network devices. To make this all work, your network must be set up with switches and routers that can transfer these messages.

In addition to the Grandmaster Clock, there are three other types of clocks that can be found on a PTP network:

- **Ordinary clocks**: These clocks are on the end user devices such as servers, desktop clients, IoT devices, and so forth.
- **Transparent clocks**: These are the network switches that transfer the messages between the Grandmaster Clock and the ordinary clocks. Transparent clocks can't send messages beyond their VLAN boundaries.
- **Boundary clocks**: These are optional and are only needed if you need to divide your network into different VLANs. Instead of just transferring messages between the Grandmaster and the ordinary clocks, a boundary clock synchronizes with the Grandmaster, and then sends out sync messages to the ordinary clocks on its VLAN. The advantage of using boundary clocks is that it helps prevent the Grandmaster from getting overwhelmed with `delay request` messages.

It is possible to set up a Linux server as a boundary clock, but you probably won't. Most likely, your organization will obtain its transparent clocks and boundary clocks from its preferred network equipment vendor, such as Cisco or Juniper. So, how would you use PTP with Linux? Mostly, you'd just set up PTP on your servers, desktop machines, and IoT devices so that they would obtain their time from a PTP server rather than from an NTP server. Let's check it out.

Installing PTP

To set up either a Linux server, a Linux desktop, or a Linux IoT device to obtain its time from a PTP source, you'll have to install the `linuxptp` package. On the Alma machine, you'd do:

```
[donnie@logserver ~]$ sudo dnf install linuxptp
```

On the Ubuntu machine, you'd do:

```
donnie@ubuntu2004:~$ sudo apt install linuxptp
```

Next, stop and disable whichever timekeeping service your machine is running. If your machine is running `chroynd`, the command would be:

```
[donnie@logserver ~]$ sudo systemctl disable --now chronyd
```

If your machine is running `systemd-timesyncd`, the command would be:

```
donnie@ubuntu2004:~$ sudo systemctl disable --now systemd-
timesyncd
```

Installing the `linuxptp` package installs two different services, which are the `ptp4l` service and the `phc2sys` service. Before we can enable or start the PTP services, we'll need to configure them. Let's look at how to do this on the Alma machine.

Configuring PTP with software timestamping on AlmaLinux

The first step is to edit the `/etc/sysconfig/ptp4l` file. When you first open the file, you'll see this:

```
OPTIONS="-f /etc/ptp4l.conf -i eth0"
```

This default configuration is for a master server, and it has the wrong network adapter name. We'll add the `-s` option to make this run in client mode and change the network adapter's name. You won't have hardware timestamping available on your virtual machines, even if it is available on the network adapter of your host computer. To deal with that, we'll also add the `-S` option to make it use software timestamping. The edited line should look something like this:

```
OPTIONS="-f /etc/ptp4l.conf -S -s -i enp0s3"
```

(Of course, use your own network adapter's name in place of mine.)

Now, enable and start the `ptp4l` service:

```
[donnie@logserver ~]$ sudo systemctl enable --now ptp4l
```

The service does run, even though there's no PTP time source on my network. Regardless, the last line of the `systemctl status` output shows that the `ptp4l` service has selected the best master clock. I have no idea where that clock is, but it doesn't matter. In a real-life scenario, you would know because you'd be dealing with a real clock:

```
[donnie@logserver ~]$ systemctl status ptp4l
● ptp4l.service - Precision Time Protocol (PTP) service
   Loaded: loaded (/usr/lib/systemd/system/ptp4l.service;
enabled; vendor preset: disabled)
```

```
   Active: active (running) since Wed 2021-08-25 18:16:26 EDT;
8s ago
 Main PID: 1841 (ptp4l)
    Tasks: 1 (limit: 4938)
   Memory: 276.0K
   CGroup: /system.slice/ptp4l.service
           └─1841 /usr/sbin/ptp4l -f /etc/ptp4l.conf -S -s -i
enp0s3
. . .
. . .
Aug 25 18:16:33 logserver ptp4l[1841]: [5697.998] selected
local clock 080027.fffe.94a66f as best master
[donnie@logserver ~]$
```

Okay, we're good with the software timestamping. Now, let's look at hardware timestamping.

Configuring PTP with hardware timestamping on AlmaLinux

Using hardware timestamping gives you the most precise timekeeping that you can get. The only catch is that the network interface adapters on your machine have to be capable of doing hardware timestamping. Fortunately, that shouldn't be a problem with newer computers. (In the *Understanding chrony* section, I showed you how to verify whether your network adapter does support hardware timestamping.)

The first step is to edit the `/etc/sysconfig/ptp4l` file, as you did previously. This time, leave out the `-S` option so that the edited line looks like this:

```
OPTIONS="-f /etc/ptp4l.conf -s -i enp0s3"
```

Next, you'll need to configure and enable the `phc2sys` service so that the computer clock can synchronize with the PTP hardware clock that's in the network adapter. The first step is to configure the `/etc/sysconfig/phc2sys` file. By default, the file looks like this:

```
OPTIONS="-a -r"
```

Change that line so that it looks something like this:

```
OPTIONS="-c CLOCK_REALTIME -s enp0s3 -w"
```

Here's the breakdown:

- `-c CLOCK_REALTIME`: The `-c` option specifies the clock that is to be synchronized. `CLOCK_REALTIME` is the normal computer clock.
- `-s enp0s3`: In this file, `-s` specifies the device that will be used for synchronization. In this case, we're using the PTP hardware clock that's in the `enp0s3` network adapter to synchronize the normal system clock.
- `-w`: This tells the `phc2sys` service to wait until the `ptp4l` service is in a synchronized state before attempting to synchronize the system clock.

The final step is to restart the `ptp4l` service and to enable and start the `phc2sys` service. Note that this will fail on your virtual machine because the VirtualBox network adapter doesn't have a PTP hardware clock. When you've seen what you need to see, disable the `ptp4l` and `phc2sys` services and re-enable the `chronyd` service.

Next, let's look at how to do all of this on Ubuntu.

Configuring PTP with software timestamping on Ubuntu

There are no supplementary PTP configuration files on Ubuntu, so you'll need to edit the `ptp4l.service` file. Start by doing:

```
donnie@ubuntu2004:~$ sudo systemctl edit --full ptp4l
```

In the `[Service]` section, you'll need to change the `ExecStart` line, which looks like this:

```
ExecStart=/usr/sbin/ptp4l -f /etc/linuxptp/ptp4l.conf -i eth0
```

Change it so that it looks something like this:

```
ExecStart=/usr/sbin/ptp4l -f /etc/linuxptp/ptp4l.conf -S -s -i
enp0s3
```

Finally, enable and start the `ptp4l` service, as you did previously on the Alma machine.

Now, let's wrap this up by configuring hardware timestamping on Ubuntu.

Configuring PTP with hardware timestamping on Ubuntu

Again, start by editing the `ptp4l.service` file. This time, enable hardware timestamping by leaving out the `-S` option so that the `ExecStart` line will look like this:

```
ExecStart=/usr/sbin/ptp4l -f /etc/linuxptp/ptp4l.conf -s -i
enp0s3
```

Next, edit the `phc2sys.service` file by doing:

```
donnie@ubuntu2004:~$ sudo systemctl edit --full phc2sys
```

In the `[Service]` section, make the `ExecStart` line look something like this:

```
ExecStart=/usr/sbin/phc2sys -c CLOCK_REALTIME -s enp0s3 -w
```

The final step is to restart the `ptp4l` service and to enable and start the `phc2sys` service. Alas, that will also fail this time, due to not having the PTP hardware clock in the VirtualBox network adapter. When you've seen what you want to see, change the virtual machine back to whichever timekeeping service that you were using before.

All right, that's it for timekeeping. I think it's time to wrap this baby up.

Summary

As always, we've covered a lot of ground and had a bit of fun in the process. We started by discussing why accurate timekeeping is so important and then did a quick overview of the various implementations of timekeeping software. We then took a detailed look at `chrony` and `systemd-timesyncd`. We wrapped up with a quick look at PTP.

In the next chapter, we'll look at systemd's relationship with boot managers and bootloaders. I'll see you there.

Questions

Answer the following questions to test your knowledge of this chapter:

1. In the `chrony.conf` file, which of the following lines will allow `chronyd` to function as a time server?

   A. `network 192.168.0.0/24`

   B. `allow 192.168.0.0/24`

   C. `permit 192.168.0.0/24`

   D. `listen 192.168.0.0/24`

2. How would you set up `systemd-timesyncd` to function as a time server? (We will assume that we're on the `192.168.0.0/24` network.)

   A. Add a `network 192.168.0.0/24` line to the `timesyncd.conf` file.

   B. Add a `permit 192.168.0.0/24` line to the `timesyncd.conf` file.

   C. Add an `allow 192.168.0.0/24` line to the `timesyncd.conf` file.

   D. You can't.

3. For dealing with PTP, which of the following clock types allows messages to flow between the PTP master clock and the client machines on the same VLAN?

   A. Boundary clocks

   B. Grandmaster clocks

   C. Router clocks

   D. Transparent clocks

4. When dealing with PTP, which service causes a machine's system clock to synchronize with the PTP hardware clock in the network adapter?

   A. phc2sys

   B. ptp4l

   C. ptp

   D. clock

Answers

1. B
2. D
3. D
4. A

Further reading

To learn more about the topics covered in this chapter, take a look at the following resources:

- GPS clocks: `https://timetoolsltd.com/category/gps-clocks/`
- `chrony` versus `systemd-timesyncd`: `https://unix.stackexchange.com/questions/504381/chrony-vs-systemd-timesyncd-what-are-the-differences-and-use-cases-as-ntp-cli`
- `chrony` versus `ntp`: `https://chrony.tuxfamily.org/comparison.html`
- PTP versus NTP: `https://www.masterclock.com/support/library/network-timing-ntp-vs-ptp`
- Red Hat's official `chrony` documentation: `https://access.redhat.com/documentation/en-us/red_hat_enterprise_linux/8/html/configuring_basic_system_settings/using-chrony-to-configure-ntp`
- Introduction to the Precision Time Protocol: `https://youtu.be/ovzt3IUFbyo`
- Precision Time Protocol Clock Types: `https://youtu.be/rbb9DcIGLKY`

17
Understanding systemd and Bootloaders

A bootloader is necessary for any operating system, including Linux. In this chapter, we'll look at the GRUB2 and systemd-boot bootloaders, and we'll discuss the differences between them. Becoming familiar with the material in this chapter can help you choose which bootloader is best suited for your needs, and to troubleshoot things that might go wrong.

In this chapter, we will cover the following topics:

- Understanding the basic computer architecture
- Understanding GRUB2
- Understanding systemd-boot
- Understanding Secure Boot

Note that there are several different bootloaders in use, some of which are specific to embedded and IoT devices. In this chapter, we'll only concentrate on GRUB2 and systemd-boot, which are used on servers and normal workstations.

Now, let's get started!

Technical requirements

We'll start with the same Ubuntu Server and Alma virtual machines that we have been using throughout. We'll use these to look at a normal BIOS-based GRUB2 configuration.

To see how the GRUB2 bootloader works on an EFI-based machine, you'll need to create another pair of Alma and Ubuntu Server virtual machines with the EFI feature enabled. To do that, create the initial VirtualBox setup for the Alma and Ubuntu machines as you always do. Then, before you start up the machines to install the operating system, open the **Settings** dialog box. Under the **System** menu, click the **Enable EFI** checkbox, as shown here:

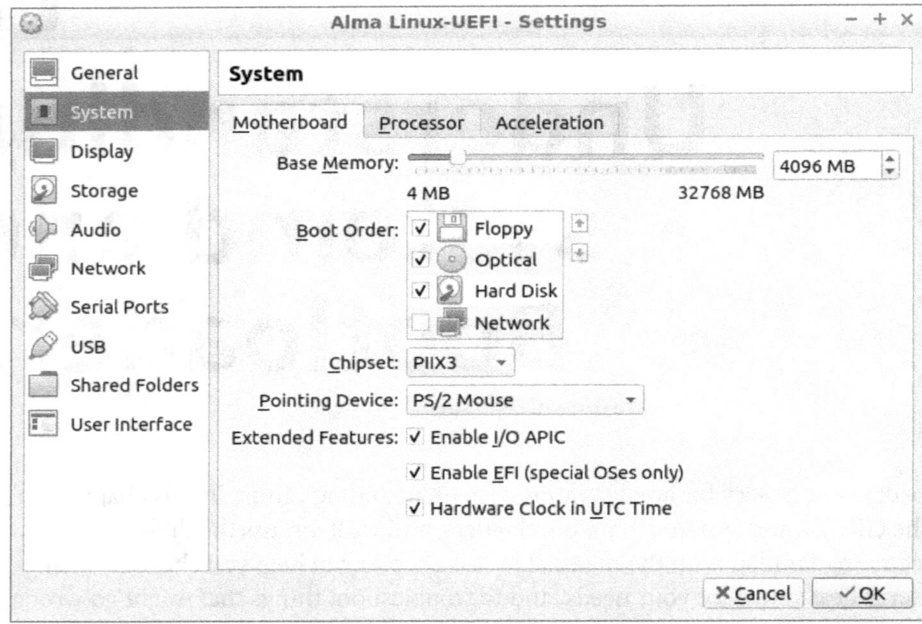

Figure 17.1 – Checking the Enable EFI box

Then, install the operating system as you normally would.

To look at a systemd-boot environment, you'll need to create a virtual machine with Pop!_OS Linux. Enable the EFI feature as you did for the Alma and Ubuntu machines, and install the operating system as you normally would.

> **Note**
>
> Pop!_OS Linux is built from Ubuntu source code by the System76 computer vendor. Pop!_OS is the only Linux distro I know of that uses systemd-boot by default. You can set up Clear Linux and Arch Linux with either GRUB2 or systemd-boot, but installing either of them involves more complexity than we want to deal with now.
>
> You can download Pop!_OS from here:
>
> `https://pop.system76.com/`

Now that you have your virtual machines, let's briefly define a few terms that we need to know about.

Check out the following link to see the Code in Action video: `https://bit.ly/3pkVA8D`

Understanding the basic computer architecture

Before we can talk about bootloaders, we need to define a few terms that describe the basic computer architecture:

- **Bootloader**: The bootloader is the first software program that runs when a computer is booted. Its job is to load the Linux kernel and to start the `init` system.
- **Boot manager**: When you first power on your computer, a boot manager will present you with a boot menu. If you have multiple operating systems installed, the boot manager will allow you to choose which one to boot. If a Linux distro has multiple kernels installed, the boot manager will allow you to choose which kernel to boot.
- **BIOS**: The **Basic Input/Output System** (**BIOS**) is firmware that resides in a chip on a computer motherboard. It contains the basic instructions that start up a computer. After the computer is started, the BIOS will perform a **Power-on Self Test** (**POST**) to verify that the hardware is working properly. Then, the BIOS will start the bootloader. It worked well for its time but is now outdated. One problem is that it can't deal with drives of more than two terabytes in size. I mean, if you were to install a three-Terabyte drive in a BIOS-based machine, you'd be able to use the drive, but one Terabyte of drive space would go to waste. BIOS also can't deal with the Secure Boot feature.
- **EFI/UEFI**: This was originally called the **Extensible Firmware Interface** (**EFI**), but the name was changed to **Unified Extensible Firmware Interface** (**UEFI**) for the Version 2 variant. It has replaced BIOS on newer computers. Unlike BIOS, EFI/UEFI works very well with very large drives. It also works with the Secure Boot feature.

- **MBR**: There are two general categories of partition types. The **Master Boot Record** (**MBR**) type is the older type. Its main flaw is that it doesn't work with partitions that are larger than two terabytes. Even if you have an EFI/UEFI-based machine that can work with large drives, MBR still limits you to these smaller partitions. What's a bit confusing is that the term *MBR* also refers to the first 512-byte sector of a drive, which is where the bootloader gets installed on BIOS-based machines.
- **GPT**: The **GUID Partition Table** (**GPT**) type of partition has replaced the old MBR type. It works well with partitions that are larger than two Terabytes. (The exact maximum partition size depends on which filesystem you've used to format the partition.) On EFI/UEFI machines, you need to install the bootloaders in a GPT partition instead of in an MBR. (I'll explain why I've said *bootloaders* instead of *bootloader* later.)
- **GRUB2**: The **Grand Unified Bootloader Version 2** (**GRUB2**) is currently the most popular bootloader on laptops, desktops, and servers. It works well on machines with multiple installed operating systems. It's not part of the systemd ecosystem, but it can be used on systemd machines.
- **systemd-boot**: This bootloader is part of the systemd ecosystem. It isn't widely used just yet, but it could be someday. It's lighter-weight and simpler to configure than GRUB2, and it also works well for machines with multiple operating systems installed.

Okay, now that we have the terminology nailed down, let's look at GRUB2.

Understanding GRUB2

The original GRUB, which is now referred to as *GRUB Legacy*, first came on the scene in 1995 as a replacement for the old LILO bootloader. It was easy to work with because it was easy to configure and it was implemented consistently on all Linux distros that used it. Unlike LILO, it can boot non-Linux operating systems. So, you can install Windows and Linux on the same computer, and GRUB lets you choose which one to boot up. GRUB Legacy worked well on the old BIOS-based computers, but it doesn't work with the newer EFI/UEFI computers. (Well, actually, the Fedora team did create a forked version of GRUB Legacy that would work with EFI/UEFI, but they abandoned it in favor of GRUB2 in 2013.)

GRUB2 isn't an update of GRUB Legacy. Instead, it's a whole new bootloader that was created from scratch. Now, I have to tell you that there are both good things and bad things about it. The good thing is that it can work with the new EFI/UEFI computers. The bad things are that it's a lot more complicated to configure, and different Linux distros implement it differently. So, things can get a bit confusing when you have to work with multiple distros.

Almost all Linux distros, including the Ubuntu and Alma distros that we've been using, use GRUB2. On a BIOS-based machine, GRUB2 gets installed into the primary drive's MBR, which is the first 512-byte sector of the drive. On an EFI/UEFI machine, GRUB2 gets installed into a special EFI partition, which always has to be a GPT-type partition. (This special partition is referred to as the **EFI System Partition** or **ESP**.)

Now, here's where things get a bit confusing. As I said, unlike GRUB Legacy, GRUB2 isn't implemented in the same way across all Linux distros, as we'll see in a bit. To see how this all works, let's begin by comparing the GRUB2 setup on our BIOS-based and EFI/UEFI-based AlmaLinux virtual machines.

Comparing GRUB2 on BIOS and EFI/UEFI systems

On both BIOS-based and EFI/UEFI-based machines, the Linux kernel and the `initramfs` files get installed in the `/boot` partition. But this is where the similarities end. Let's see how it's done with BIOS.

GRUB2 on a BIOS-based Alma 8 machine

On a BIOS-based machine, the `/boot` partition is normally `/dev/sda1`, as we see here:

```
[donnie@alma-bios ~]$ mount | grep 'boot'
/dev/sda1 on /boot type xfs
(rw,relatime,seclabel,attr2,inode64,logbufs=8,logbsize=32k,
noquota)
[donnie@alma-bios ~]$
```

We also see that the `/boot` partition is formatted with just a normal Linux filesystem. On RHEL-type machines, this would normally be `xfs`. On Ubuntu machines, this would normally be `ext4`.

The Master Boot Record, where the bootloader is installed, isn't a partition. Rather, the MBR is just the first 512 bytes of the drive. The GRUB2 configuration file (`grub2.cfg`) is in the `/boot/grub2/` directory. On RHEL-type machines, the `/etc/grub.cfg` symbolic link points to the actual configuration file, as we see here:

```
[donnie@alma-bios etc]$ sudo ls -l grub2.cfg
lrwxrwxrwx. 1 root root 22 Mar 15 14:28 grub2.cfg -> ../boot/
grub2/grub.cfg
[donnie@alma-bios etc]$
```

Understand though, that if you ever need to reconfigure GRUB2, you'll never edit this `grub.cfg` file. Instead, you'll edit the `/etc/default/grub` file. Then, you'll rebuild the `grub.cfg` file by doing:

```
[donnie@alma-bios ~]$ sudo grub2-mkconfig -o /boot/grub2/grub.cfg
```

There is an `efi/` directory within the `/boot/` directory, but it isn't used. It contains a nest of subdirectories, but there are no files, as we see here:

```
[donnie@alma-bios ~]$ sudo ls -l /boot/efi/EFI/almalinux
total 0
[donnie@alma-bios ~]$
```

Whenever we boot the machine, we see a boot menu with our different boot-up choices:

```
AlmaLinux (4.18.0-240.22.1.el8_3.x86_64) 8.3 (Purple Manul)
AlmaLinux (4.18.0-240.15.1.el8_3.x86_64) 8.3 (Purple Manul)
AlmaLinux (4.18.0-240.el8.x86_64) 8
AlmaLinux (0-rescue-3a17f34dc2694acda37caa478a339408) 8

Use the ↑ and ↓ keys to change the selection.
Press 'e' to edit the selected item, or 'c' for a command prompt.
```

Figure 17.2 – The GRUB2 boot menu on AlmaLinux

The configuration files for these menu choices are in the `/boot/loader/entries/` directory. This directory requires root privileges to enter. So, let's make things easier on ourselves by going to the `root` shell:

```
[donnie@alma-bios ~]$ sudo su -
[sudo] password for donnie:
Last login: Sat Aug 28 18:09:25 EDT 2021 on pts/0
[root@alma-bios ~]# cd /boot/loader/entries/
[root@alma-bios entries]#
```

Now, let's see what we have:

```
[root@alma-bios entries]# ls -l
total 16
-rw-r--r--. 1 root root 388 Apr  5 12:09
3a17f34dc2694acda37caa478a339408-0-rescue.conf
-rw-r--r--. 1 root root 368 Apr  5 13:20
3a17f34dc2694acda37caa478a339408-4.18.0-240.15.1.el8_3.x86_64.
conf
-rw-r--r--. 1 root root 368 Apr 11 18:23
3a17f34dc2694acda37caa478a339408-4.18.0-240.22.1.el8_3.x86_64.
conf
-rw-r--r--. 1 root root 316 Apr  5 12:09
3a17f34dc2694acda37caa478a339408-4.18.0-240.el8.x86_64.conf
[root@alma-bios entries]#
```

These configuration files are known as `BootLoaderSpec` (`BLS`) files. Whenever you boot your machine, GRUB2 will take information from these `BLS` files and use it to populate the boot menu. A new `BLS` file will be generated automatically every time a new Linux kernel is installed, even if it's a kernel that you've compiled yourself. If you do a system update and `dnf` removes any older kernels, the `BLS` files for those older kernels will be deleted. Let's peek inside one of these files to see what's there:

```
[root@alma-bios entries]# cat 3a17f34dc2694acda37caa478a339408-
4.18.0-240.22.1.el8_3.x86_64.conf
title AlmaLinux (4.18.0-240.22.1.el8_3.x86_64) 8.3 (Purple
Manul)
version 4.18.0-240.22.1.el8_3.x86_64
linux /vmlinuz-4.18.0-240.22.1.el8_3.x86_64
```

```
initrd /initramfs-4.18.0-240.22.1.el8_3.x86_64.img $tuned_
initrd
options $kernelopts $tuned_params
id almalinux-20210409120623-4.18.0-240.22.1.el8_3.x86_64
grub_users $grub_users
grub_arg --unrestricted
grub_class kernel
[root@alma-bios entries]#
```

As we see here, this file defines which kernel and `initramfs` images to load, along with the various kernel options. But we don't see specific kernel options here. Instead, we see variable names preceded by a `$`. This just means that the kernel option information will be pulled in from the `/boot/grub2/grub.cfg` file and the `/boot/grub2/grubenv` file.

If you install Linux alongside an already existing installation of another operating system, the boot menu entry for that operating system should also be created automatically. (This works even if the other operating system is Windows.) The `/etc/grub.d/30_os-prober` script is what finds the other operating systems for you.

> **Note**
> This is different from what you might be used to. Older Linux distros, such as the RHEL 7-type distros, don't use `BLS` files. Instead, all boot menu information is listed in the `grub.cfg` file. Red Hat first introduced `BLS` files in Fedora 30, and they're now used in all RHEL 8-type distros. (As we'll see later, even the newest Ubuntu distros still don't use them.)

Now, let's look at an EFI/UEFI machine.

GRUB2 on an EFI/UEFI-based Alma machine

On our EFI/UEFI machine, the `/boot/` partition is mounted on `/dev/sda2`, while the `/boot/efi/` partition is mounted on `/dev/sda1`, as we see here:

```
[donnie@alma-efi ~]$ mount | grep 'boot'
/dev/sda2 on /boot type xfs (rw,relatime,seclabel,
attr2,inode64,logbufs=8,logbsize=32k,noquota)
/dev/sda1 on /boot/efi type vfat (rw,relatime,fmask=0077,
dmask=0077,codepage=437,iocharset=ascii,shortname=winnt,
errors=remount-ro)
[donnie@alma-efi ~]$
```

The `/boot/efi/` partition is where the bootloaders reside. We can also see that the normal boot partition is formatted with the normal `xfs` Linux filesystem, but that the `/boot/efi/` partition is formatted with the `vfat` filesystem. The `efi` partition must always be formatted with `vfat` because nothing else works.

Next, we see that the symbolic link in the `/etc/` directory has a different name and that it points to the `grub.cfg` file in a different location:

```
[donnie@alma-efi etc]$ sudo ls -l grub2-efi.cfg
lrwxrwxrwx. 1 root root 34 Mar 15 14:28 grub2-efi.cfg -> ../
boot/efi/EFI/almalinux/grub.cfg
[donnie@alma-efi etc]$
```

As before, the directories that we want to explore require root privileges to enter. Let's make things a bit easier by going to a `root` shell:

```
[donnie@alma-efi ~]$ sudo su -
Last login: Sat Aug 28 17:52:08 EDT 2021 on pts/0
[root@alma-efi ~]#
```

There's still a `/boot/grub2/` directory, but the only thing it contains is a symbolic link that points to the GRUB environmental settings file:

```
[root@alma-efi ~]# cd /boot/grub2/
[root@alma-efi grub2]# ls -l
total 0
lrwxrwxrwx. 1 root root 28 Mar 15 14:28 grubenv -> ../efi/EFI/
almalinux/grubenv
[root@alma-efi grub2]#
```

Almost everything else of importance is in the `/boot/efi/` directory:

```
[root@alma-efi ~]# cd /boot/efi
[root@alma-efi efi]# ls
EFI
[root@alma-efi efi]# cd EFI/
[root@alma-efi EFI]# ls
almalinux  BOOT
[root@alma-efi EFI]#
```

At the bottom of this nest, we see the /boot/efi/EFI/almalinux/ and /boot/efi/EFI/BOOT/ directories. Let's look in the BOOT/ directory:

```
[root@alma-efi EFI]# ls -l BOOT/
total 1568
-rwx------. 1 root root 1237503 Mar 15 14:44 BOOTX64.EFI
-rwx------. 1 root root  362968 Mar 15 14:44 fbx64.efi
[root@alma-efi EFI]#
```

The BOOTX64.EFI file is part of the shim system, which allows Linux to boot on machines that have the Secure Boot feature enabled. (We'll talk about Secure Boot at the end of this chapter.) The fbx64.efi file is the fallback bootloader. Its job is to recreate the boot manager options that are built into the firmware in case they somehow get deleted. It does this by scanning the BOOTX64.CSV files that are in the subdirectories for any operating systems that are installed.

Now, here's what we see in the almalinux/ directory:

```
[root@alma-efi EFI]# ls -l almalinux/
total 5444
-rwx------. 1 root root     122 Mar 15 14:44 BOOTX64.CSV
drwx------. 2 root root    4096 Mar 15 14:28 fonts
-rwx------. 1 root root    6572 Aug 26 18:13 grub.cfg
-rwx------. 1 root root    1024 Aug 28 17:51 grubenv
-rwx------. 1 root root 1900112 Mar 15 14:28 grubx64.efi
-rwx------. 1 root root 1171320 Mar 15 14:44 mmx64.efi
-rwx------. 1 root root 1240144 Mar 15 14:44 shimx64-almalinux.
efi
-rwx------. 1 root root 1237503 Mar 15 14:44 shimx64.efi
[root@alma-efi EFI]#
```

In addition to the normal GRUB2 files that we'd see on a BIOS-based machine, we see several files that are specific to EFI/UEFI machines:

- grubx64.efi: This is what makes GRUB2 work on an EFI/UEFI machine.
- shim64-almalinux.efi and shimx64.efi: These files go along with the BOOTX64.EFI file to make Alma work on a Secure Boot machine.
- mmx64.efi: This is part of the *Machine Owner Key* system, which also helps out with Secure Boot.

- `BOOTX64.CSV`: This file works with the fallback bootloader and contains a boot menu entry for this installation of Alma. (If multiple operating systems were installed, they would all have their own `BOOTX64.CSV` files.) If you peek inside this file, you'll see this:

```
[root@alma-efi almalinux]# cat BOOTX64.CSV
��shimx64.efi,AlmaLinux,,This is the boot entry for AlmaLinux
[root@alma-efi almalinux]#
```

> **Note**
>
> Something to keep in mind is that the `BOOTX64.CSV` file is not an ASCII text file as most Linux configuration files are. (That would explain those two funny-looking questions marks that you see in this code.) Instead, it's a UTF-16 Unicode file, as we see here:
>
> ```
> [root@alma-efi ~]# cd /boot/efi/EFI/almalinux/
> [root@alma-efi almalinux]# file BOOTX64.CSV
> BOOTX64.CSV: Little-endian UTF-16 Unicode text, with no line terminators
> [root@alma-efi almalinux]#
> ```
>
> Normal text editors save files in ASCII format. So, if you ever need to manually create or edit a `BOOTX64.CSV` file, you'll need to convert it into UTF-16 format. Let's say that you've created a `boot.csv` file in your home directory. You can convert it with the `iconv` tool, like this:
>
> ```
> [donnie@alma-efi ~]$ iconv -t UTF-16 < ~/boot.csv > BOOTX64.CSV
> [donnie@alma-efi ~]$
> ```
>
> Now, you're ready to copy the file to its proper location.

Next, we have the `BLS` files for the boot menu choices, just as we had on the BIOS machine:

```
[donnie@alma-efi ~]$ sudo ls -l /boot/loader/entries/
[sudo] password for donnie:
total 8
-rw-r--r--. 1 root root 388 Aug 26 18:10 5a1e1f5e83004e9eb0f6e2e0a346d4e7-0-rescue.conf
-rw-r--r--. 1 root root 316 Aug 26 18:10 5a1e1f5e83004e9eb0f6e2e0a346d4e7-4.18.0-240.el8.x86_64.conf
[donnie@alma-efi ~]$
```

When we boot an EFI/UEFI machine, we'll see that the boot menu looks somewhat different than what it does on a BIOS machine:

```
AlmaLinux (4.18.0-240.el8.x86_64) 8
AlmaLinux (0-rescue-5a1e1f5e83004e9eb0f6e2e0a346d4e7) 8
System setup
```

Figure 17.3 – The boot menu on an EFI/UEFI machine

We now see a **System setup** choice, which takes us into the EFI management utility we see here:

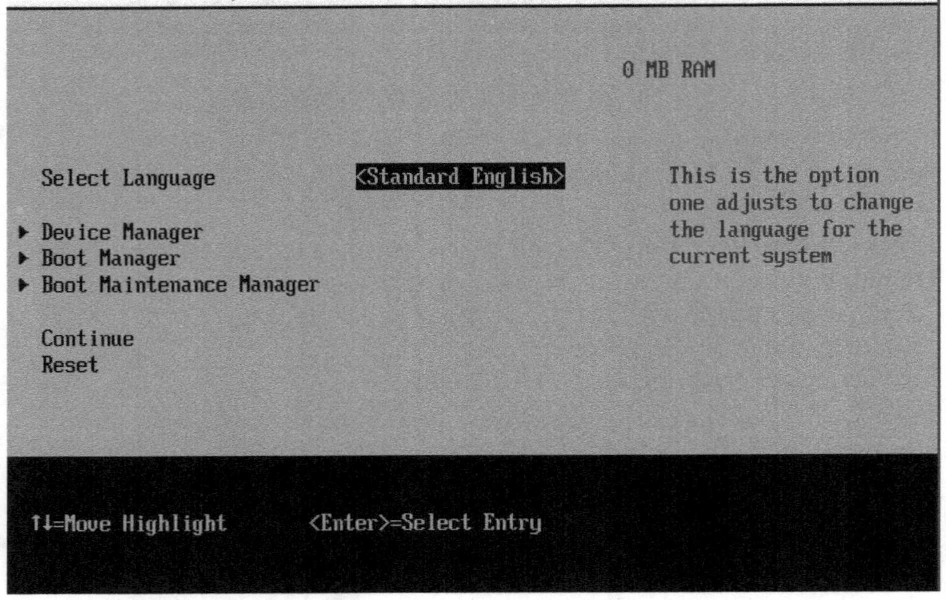

Figure 17.4 – The EFI management utility

This can do several things for us. If we select **Boot Maintenance Manager**, we'll see the **Boot Options** option. If we select that, we'll see that we can add or delete boot options, or change the default boot order:

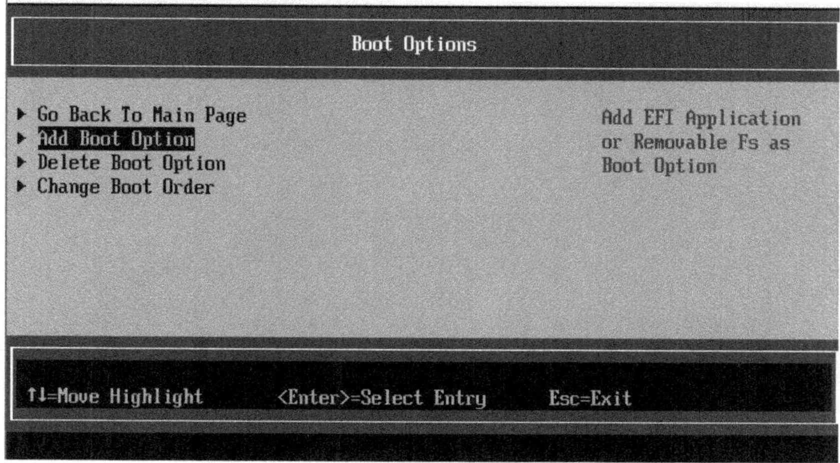

Figure 17.5 – The Boot Options screen

This could come in handy if we ever need to boot from a DVD or USB device rather than from the default device.

Under the **Boot Manager** option, we see the **EFI Internal Shell** option:

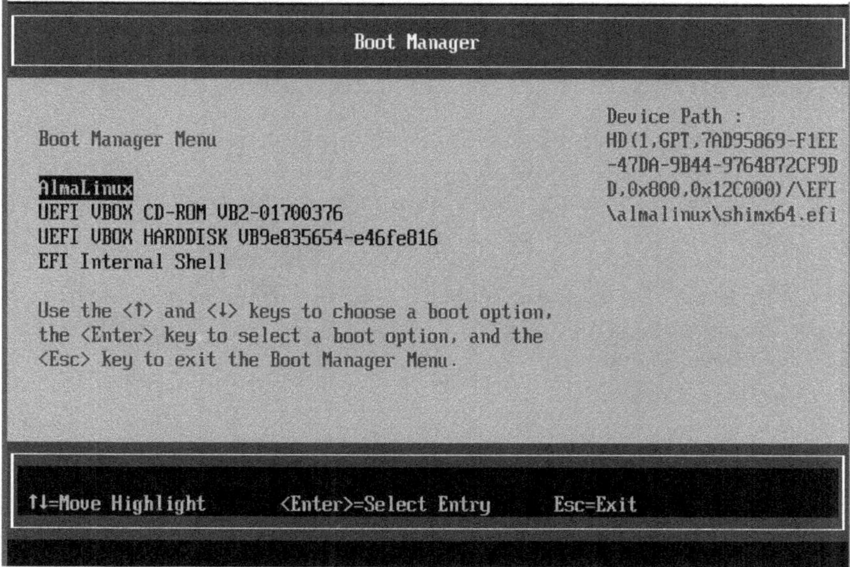

Figure 17.6 – The Boot Manager screen

This internal shell can help you troubleshoot boot-up problems and looks like this:

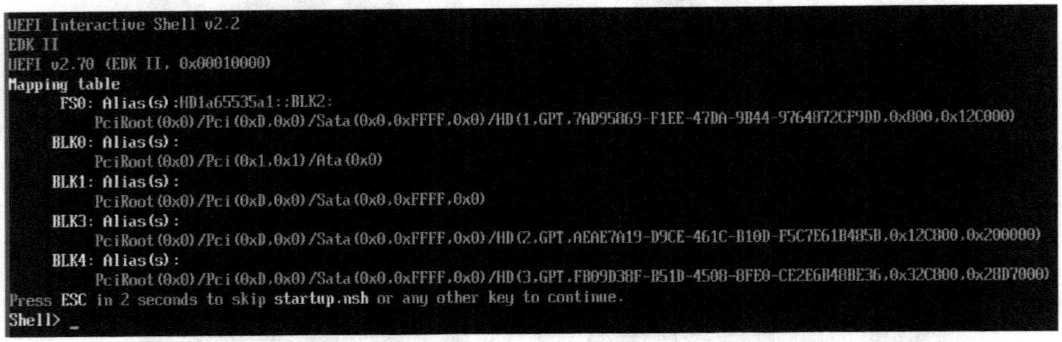

```
UEFI Interactive Shell v2.2
EDK II
UEFI v2.70 (EDK II, 0x00010000)
Mapping table
      FS0: Alias(s):HD1a65535a1::BLK2:
          PciRoot(0x0)/Pci(0xD,0x0)/Sata(0x0,0xFFFF,0x0)/HD(1,GPT,7AD95869-F1EE-47DA-9B44-9764872CF9DD,0x800,0x12C000)
     BLK0: Alias(s):
          PciRoot(0x0)/Pci(0x1,0x1)/Ata(0x0)
     BLK1: Alias(s):
          PciRoot(0x0)/Pci(0xD,0x0)/Sata(0x0,0xFFFF,0x0)
     BLK3: Alias(s):
          PciRoot(0x0)/Pci(0xD,0x0)/Sata(0x0,0xFFFF,0x0)/HD(2,GPT,AEAE7A19-D9CE-461C-B10D-F5C7E61B485B,0x12C800,0x200000)
     BLK4: Alias(s):
          PciRoot(0x0)/Pci(0xD,0x0)/Sata(0x0,0xFFFF,0x0)/HD(3,GPT,FB09D38F-B51D-4508-8FE0-CE2E6B48BE36,0x32C800,0x28D7000)
Press ESC in 2 seconds to skip startup.nsh or any other key to continue.
Shell> _
```

Figure 17.7 – The EFI internal shell

To see the commands that you can run from this shell, just type `help`. I'm not going to cover this shell in detail because it's not something that you'll use very often. However, I've linked to a good tutorial in the *Further reading* section.

Okay, that covers it for GRUB2 on the AlmaLinux machine. Now, let's look at how things are a bit different on the Ubuntu machine.

GRUB2 on BIOS-based and EFI/UEFI-based Ubuntu machines

The biggest difference is that Ubuntu doesn't use `BootLoaderSpec` files, as the RHEL 8-type distros do. Instead, all menu entries are defined within the `/boot/grub/grub.cfg` file. To see these menu entries, open the file and search for stanzas that begin with `menuentry`. Here's a snippet from one such menu entry:

```
menuentry 'Ubuntu' --class ubuntu --class gnu-linux --class gnu --class os $menuentry_id_option 'gnulinux-simple-34969a2a-6e3f-4806-8260-e62b948678e3' {
        recordfail
        load_video
        gfxmode $linux_gfx_mode
        insmod gzio
. . .
. . .
```

```
        linux    /boot/vmlinuz-5.4.0-81-generic
root=UUID=34969a2a-6e3f-4806-8260-e62b948678e3 ro
        initrd   /boot/initrd.img-5.4.0-81-generic
}
```

The only other real difference is that there's no symbolic link to the `grub.cfg` file in the `/etc/` directory.

Next, let's reboot to get to the good stuff. Let's look at *systemd-boot*.

Understanding systemd-boot

The first thing to note here is the name, *systemd-boot*. It's shocking, I know. We have a systemd component whose name does *not* end in the letter *d*. But seriously, systemd-boot is a component of systemd that has some cool features. Compared to GRUB2, it's lighter-weight, easier to configure, boots faster, and works well with the modern implementations of Secure Boot. Contrary to popular belief, systemd-boot is a *boot manager*, not a *bootloader*. It can automatically probe for other operating systems on the machine and add them to the boot menu. (GRUB2 only does this when you first install the operating system, while systemd-boot does this each time you boot the machine.) Once you've booted the machine and have chosen your desired boot option, systemd-boot hands the boot operation over to a *real* bootloader.

So, why isn't it more widely used? Well, it's just that systemd-boot *only* works on EFI/UEFI systems. There are still a lot of older BIOS-based computers in use, and all of them would become unusable if all operating systems were to switch to EFI/UEFI-only bootloaders.

> **Note**
>
> You can read about the various features of systemd-boot on the `systemd-boot` man page.

For our demos, we'll use **Pop!_OS** Linux, which is a product of the System76 company. System76 is a computer vendor, so it made sense for them to produce an operating system that would only run on newer machines. It's based on Ubuntu, so you can use the same Ubuntu commands that you're used to using, other than any commands that deal with the bootloader. (At the time of writing, it was based on Ubuntu 21.04.)

When I created the Pop!_OS virtual machine, I just accepted the installer's default partition setup. Here's what it looks like:

```
donnie@pop-os:~$ mount | grep 'sda'
/dev/sda3 on / type ext4 (rw,noatime,errors=remount-ro)
/dev/sda2 on /recovery type vfat (rw,relatime,fmask=0077,dmask
=0077,codepage=437,iocharset=iso8859-1,shortname=mixed,errors=
remount-ro)
/dev/sda1 on /boot/efi type vfat (rw,relatime,fmask=0077,dmask
=0077,codepage=437,iocharset=iso8859-1,shortname=mixed,errors=
remount-ro)
donnie@pop-os:~$
```

Here, we see that `/dev/sda1` is mounted as `/boot/efi/`, which is the EFI system partition where the bootloaders reside. We also see a `/recovery/` partition, which is something I've never before seen on any Linux machine. This `/recovery/` partition contains a live version of Pop!_OS. Boot from this partition if you ever need to repair or even reinstall the operating system without losing users' files.

Unlike GRUB2, systemd-boot does not have any configuration files in the `/etc/` directory. Instead, they're all in the `/boot/efi/` directory. As we did previously, we'll make things easier by going to a `root` shell:

```
donnie@pop-os:~$ sudo su -
[sudo] password for donnie:
root@pop-os:~#
```

Here's what's inside the `/boot/efi/` directory:

```
root@pop-os:~# cd /boot/efi
root@pop-os:/boot/efi# ls -l
total 8
drwx------ 7 root root 4096 Aug 27 14:15 EFI
drwx------ 3 root root 4096 Sep  1 17:11 loader
root@pop-os:/boot/efi#
```

Let's look in the `loader/` subdirectory first:

```
root@pop-os:/boot/efi/loader# ls -l
total 12
drwx------ 2 root root 4096 Sep  1 15:45 entries
```

```
-rwx------ 1 root root   23 Sep  1 17:11 loader.conf
-rwx------ 1 root root  512 Aug 27 14:15 random-seed
root@pop-os:/boot/efi/loader#
```

We'll come back to the two files in just a bit. First, let's look into the `entries/` subdirectory:

```
root@pop-os:/boot/efi/loader/entries# ls -l
total 12
-rwx------ 1 root root 256 Sep  1 15:48 Pop_OS-current.conf
-rwx------ 1 root root 274 Sep  1 15:48 Pop_OS-oldkern.conf
-rwx------ 1 root root 299 Aug 27 10:13 Recovery-9C63-930A.conf
root@pop-os:/boot/efi/loader/entries#
```

These three `BootLoaderSpec` files represent the three choices that will come up on the boot menu when you boot up your machine. (I know that you haven't seen the boot menu yet, but that's okay. We'll fix that shortly.) Just for fun, let's peek inside the `Pop_OS-current.conf` file:

```
root@pop-os:/boot/efi/loader/entries# cat Pop_OS-current.conf
title Pop!_OS
linux /EFI/Pop_OS-bc156c8a-fcb8-4a74-b491-089c77362828/vmlinuz.
efi
initrd /EFI/Pop_OS-bc156c8a-fcb8-4a74-b491-089c77362828/initrd.
img
options root=UUID=bc156c8a-fcb8-4a74-b491-089c77362828 ro quiet
loglevel=0 systemd.show_status=false splash
root@pop-os:/boot/efi/loader/entries#
```

Unlike GRUB2, there are no other files for storing the kernel options. So, they all have to be stored here. What you might think of as a bit unusual is that the kernel file that this `BLS` file calls in has a `.efi` filename extension. I'll explain why that is in just a few moments.

The `/boot/efi/loader/random-seed` file stores a random seed value. (I bet you would never have guessed that.) This allows the machine to boot with a fully initialized entropy pool, which allows the `/dev/urandom` device to create better random numbers. This makes security better by allowing the system to create security keys that are harder to crack. (Note though, that this feature doesn't work on virtual machines.)

Next, let's look at the /boot/efi/loader/loader.conf file:

```
root@pop-os:/boot/efi/loader# cat loader.conf
default Pop_OS-current
root@pop-os:/boot/efi/loader#
```

Wait a minute. That's all there is to it? Well yeah. (Didn't I tell you that systemd-boot is much easier to configure than GRUB2?) I do see a slight problem here, though. It's just that the boot menu won't show up unless you quickly press the proper key after you turn on the machine. Let's edit this file to have the boot menu show for five seconds. The edited file should look like this:

```
default Pop_OS-current
timeout 5
```

Okay, that was tough. I just hope that you were able to handle it. Seriously, though, there are a few more options that you can read about on the loader.conf man page and they're all very easy to configure. (By the way, don't reboot the machine just yet. We'll make one more change in just a bit, and then you can reboot.)

In the /boot/efi/EFI/ directory, we see these subdirectories:

```
root@pop-os:/boot/efi/EFI# ls -l
total 20
drwx------ 2 root root 4096 Aug 27 14:15 BOOT
drwx------ 2 root root 4096 Aug 27 14:15 Linux
drwx------ 2 root root 4096 Sep  1 15:45 Pop_OS-bc156c8a-fcb8-
4a74-b491-089c77362828
drwx------ 2 root root 4096 Aug 27 14:13 Recovery-9C63-930A
drwx------ 2 root root 4096 Aug 27 14:15 systemd
root@pop-os:/boot/efi/EFI#
```

The Linux/ subdirectory is empty, so we won't bother looking into it. In the BOOT/ subdirectory, we only see one file:

```
root@pop-os:/boot/efi/EFI/BOOT# ls -l
total 92
-rwx------ 1 root root 94079 Jul 20 14:47 BOOTX64.EFI
root@pop-os:/boot/efi/EFI/BOOT#
```

As we saw on the Alma and Ubuntu machines, we have the `BOOTX64.EFI` file, which makes this machine work with Secure Boot. However, we don't have the fallback bootloader file.

In the `systemd/` subdirectory, we see the executable file that makes systemd-boot work:

```
root@pop-os:/boot/efi/EFI/systemd# ls -l
total 92
-rwx------ 1 root root 94079 Jul 20 14:47 systemd-bootx64.efi
root@pop-os:/boot/efi/EFI/systemd#
```

Finally, let's look inside the `Pop_OS-bc156c8a-fcb8-4a74-b491-089c77362828/` subdirectory:

```
root@pop-os:/boot/efi/EFI/Pop_OS-bc156c8a-fcb8-4a74-b491-
089c77362828# ls -l
total 240488
-rwx------ 1 root root       167 Sep  1 15:48 cmdline
-rwx------ 1 root root 108913836 Sep  1 15:48 initrd.img
-rwx------ 1 root root 107842809 Sep  1 15:48 initrd.
img-previous
-rwx------ 1 root root  14750528 Sep  1 15:48 vmlinuz.efi
-rwx------ 1 root root  14739488 Sep  1 15:48 vmlinuz-previous.
efi
root@pop-os:/boot/efi/EFI/Pop_OS-bc156c8a-fcb8-4a74-b491-
089c77362828#
```

This is much different than what you saw on the GRUB2 machines. Here, we're using the *EFI Stub Loader* feature that's built into the Linux kernel. The `vmlinuz.efi` file is just a copy of the `/boot/vmlinuz-5.11.0-7633-generic` file, which is the newest installed Linux kernel. By renaming this kernel file with a `.efi` filename extension, systemd-boot effectively turned this kernel file into its own bootloader. (Pretty slick, eh?) The `vmlinuz-previous.efi` file is a copy of the `/boot/vmlinuz-5.11.0-7620-generic` file, which is the second oldest installed kernel. Every time we install a new kernel on this systemd-boot machine, the original copy will go into the top-level `/boot/` directory, and a copy with the `.efi` filename extension will go into this directory.

Another thing to note here is that there are no `shimx64*.efi` files, as we saw on the Alma and Ubuntu machines. That's because systemd-boot doesn't need the shim system to work with Secure Boot. (I'll explain this in more detail in the *Understanding Secure Boot* section.)

Okay, we don't need the root shell anymore, so type `exit` to get back to your normal user shell.

The final systemd-boot component I want to show you is the `bootctl` tool. To see the status of systemd-boot, run the command without any options:

```
donnie@pop-os:~$ sudo bootctl
System:
     Firmware: UEFI 2.70 (EDK II 1.00)
  Secure Boot: disabled
   Setup Mode: user
 Boot into FW: supported

Current Boot Loader:
      Product: systemd-boot
247.3-3ubuntu3.4pop0~1626806865~21.04~19f7a6d
     Features: ✓ Boot counting
               ✓ Menu timeout control
. . .
. . .
```

Use the `list` option to view all of the boot menu entries:

```
donnie@pop-os:~$ sudo bootctl list
Boot Loader Entries:
        title: Pop!_OS (Pop_OS-current.conf) (default)
           id: Pop_OS-current.conf
       source: /boot/efi/loader/entries/Pop_OS-current.conf
        linux: /EFI/Pop_OS-bc156c8a-fcb8-4a74-b491-
089c77362828/vmlinuz.efi
       initrd: /EFI/Pop_OS-bc156c8a-fcb8-4a74-b491-
089c77362828/initrd.img
      options: root=UUID=bc156c8a-fcb8-4a74-b491-089c77362828
ro quiet loglevel=0 systemd.show_status=false splash
. . .
. . .
title: Reboot Into Firmware Interface
           id: auto-reboot-to-firmware-setup
       source: /sys/firmware/efi/efivars/LoaderEntries-
4a67b082-0a4c-41cf-b6c7-440b29bb8c4f
```

Use the `set-default` option to permanently change the default boot option, or the `set-oneshot` option to set the default boot option for only the next boot-up. Take the ID of the boot option that you want to use from the list output and specify it with either option, like this:

```
donnie@pop-os:~$ sudo bootctl set-oneshot Pop_OS-oldkern.conf
donnie@pop-os:~$
```

Now, go ahead and reboot the machine. This time, you'll see the boot menu come up. After the five-second menu timer expires, you'll see the machine boot up on the alternate kernel that you chose with this `bootctl set-oneshot` command.

There's more that you can do with `bootctl`, but I'll let you read all about it in the `bootctl` man page.

Let's wrap this chapter up by briefly look at the Secure Boot feature.

Understanding Secure Boot

Secure Boot is an EFI/UEFI feature that prevents computers from loading any operating system, operating system modules, or device drivers that haven't been signed by an authorized security key. It helps prevent computers from loading various types of malware, such as rootkits. To enable or disable it, boot your machine to its setup screen, as you see here on my late-model Acer machine:

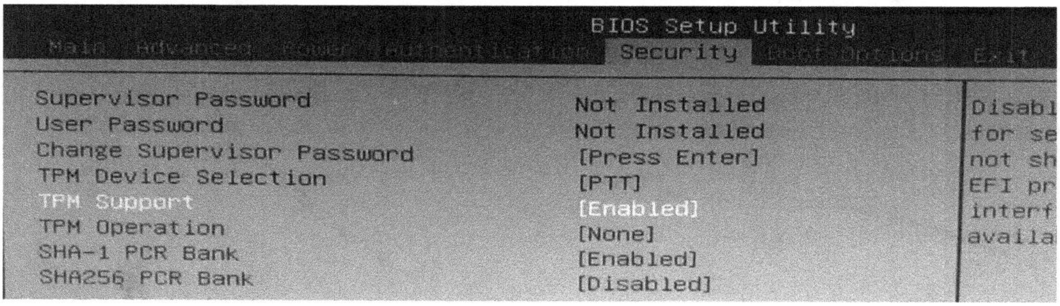

Figure 17.8 – UEFI setup screen with Secure Boot enabled

For some strange reason, it's still called the *BIOS Setup Utility*, even though this machine has a UEFI. What I want you to notice is the **TPM Support** option, which shows as **[Enabled]**. **TPM** stands for **Trusted Platform Module** and is the firmware chip on the motherboard that contains the signing keys that the Secure Boot option needs.

On a Windows machine, Secure Boot is a big deal, because Windows has traditionally been very susceptible to malware infections. Linux is much less susceptible, although Secure Boot could be useful even for it. Ever since Microsoft introduced Windows 8, all new computers that come with Windows have Secure Boot enabled by default. For now, it's possible to disable Secure Boot on a Windows machine if you need to. With Windows 11, that will no longer be an option.

When Secure Boot first came on the market, it caused much wailing and gnashing of teeth among the Linux faithful. That's because Secure Boot works by looking at the cryptographic signature of the machine's bootloader, and then compares it to the signature list that's in the computer's TPM. Okay, that doesn't sound so bad. What is bad is that the necessary signatures and signing keys are loaded into the TPM when the computer is manufactured, and Microsoft pretty much controls which signatures and keys get loaded. So, at first, Windows was the only operating system that was guaranteed to boot on a machine with Secure Boot enabled. Linux developers had to come up with a way to make Linux work with Secure Boot. The Linux faithful wailed and gnashed their teeth even more when they learned that this would have to involve letting Microsoft issue the signing keys for Linux bootloaders. (Yeah, the same Microsoft whose CEO at the time once stated that Linux is a *cancer*.)

In this chapter, although you don't realize it yet, we've seen how GRUB2 and systemd-boot handle the Secure Boot feature in different ways. GRUB2 works with the shim system, which uses pre-signed shim files. On the Alma machine, these are the `shimx64.efi` and `shimx64-almalinux.efi` files, which we saw in the `/boot/efi/EFI/almalinux/` directory. On the Ubuntu Server machine, all we have is the `shimx64.efi` file in the `/boot/efi/EFI/ubuntu/` directory. So, why do we have this shim system, instead of just signing the GRUB2 bootloader files? Well, there are two reasons. One is that GRUB2 is already rather bloated and adding the Secure Boot code to it would bloat it even more. The other reason is that the GRUB2 code is licensed under the GPL3 free-as-in-speech software license. For some reason that I don't know, Microsoft refuses to issue signing keys for anything that's under GPL3. For that reason, systemd-boot is licensed under GPL2, which Microsoft seems to like better.

When we looked at Pop!_OS Linux, I pointed out that it doesn't have any `shimx64*.efi` files. Since systemd-boot is under GPL2, Microsoft will sign its files, making the shim system unnecessary.

Okay, I'm reading your mind again, hopefully for the final time. You're thinking, *But, Donnie. What if I've created a kernel module, and I need it to load on a Secure Boot machine? And what if I install Linux on a Secure Boot machine, and then decide that I don't trust any signing keys that are issued by Microsoft? What can I do?*

Well, in both cases, it is possible to create signing keys and load them into the TPM yourself. It's a long procedure that I can't go into here, so I'll refer you to the *Managing EFI bootloaders for Linux* site that's linked in the *Further reading* section. In its *Table of Contents*, you'll see a link to the Secure Boot page, where you'll find the procedure.

And that, guys and gals, is it for the bootloader chapter. Let's summarize and then wrap this baby up in swaddling clothes.

Summary

As always, we've covered much ground in this chapter. We started by providing an overview of the computer architecture and then discussed how the GRUB2 bootloader works on both BIOS-based and EFI/UEFI-based computers. Then, we covered systemd-boot on the Pop!_OS Linux machine, and wrapped up with a discussion of Secure Boot.

In the next chapter, which will be our final one, we'll talk about systemd-logind. I'll see you there.

Questions

To test your knowledge of this chapter, answer the following questions:

1. Which of the following statements is true?

   A. Only GPT partitions can be used on BIOS-based computers.

   B. Only a GPT partition can be used to install GRUB2.

   C. Only a GPT partition can be used to install systemd-boot.

   D. Only an MBR partition can be used to install systemd-boot.

2. How does GRUB2 work with Secure Boot?

   A. It uses the shim system.

   B. Its files are directly signed by Microsoft.

   C. GRUB2 doesn't work with Secure Boot.

3. How does systemd-boot work?

   A. It uses the `grubx64.efi` file to activate the bootloader.

   B. It copies the kernel file over to a file with a `.efi` filename extension so that the kernel can act as its own bootloader.

   C. It directly calls in the Linux kernel from the `/boot/` directory.

   D. It doesn't work at all.

4. What is necessary to make Secure Boot work?

   A. Nothing. It works on all computers.

   B. That the machine has a BIOS chip, and that TPM is enabled.

   C. That the machine has an EFI/UEFI, and that TPM is enabled.

   D. Nothing. It never works.

Answers

1. C
2. A
3. B
4. C

Further reading

To learn more about the topics that were covered in this chapter, take a look at the following resources:

- The 15 best bootloaders for home and embedded systems: `https://www.ubuntupit.com/best-linux-bootloader-for-home-and-embedded-systems/`
- The UEFI Interactive Shell: `https://linuxhint.com/use-uefi-interactive-shell-and-its-common-commands/`
- What is `vmlinux.efi`?: `https://askubuntu.com/questions/330541/what-is-vmlinuz-efi`
- How to modify systemd-boot: `https://www.techrepublic.com/article/how-to-modify-systemd-boot-on-linux/`
- `Pop!_OS` recovery partition: `https://support.system76.com/articles/pop-recovery`
- Secure Boot overview: `https://www.dell.com/support/kbdoc/en-us/000145423/secure-boot-overview`
- An explanation of Secure Boot: `https://docs.microsoft.com/en-us/windows-hardware/design/device-experiences/oem-secure-boot`
- Secure Boot Linux: `https://linuxhint.com/secure-boot-linux/`

- Installing Linux with Secure Boot: `https://www.linux.org/threads/installing-linux-with-secure-boot-and-friends.29454/`
- Changing to `BootLoaderSpec` files: `https://fedoraproject.org/wiki/Changes/BootLoaderSpecByDefault`
- Managing EFI bootloaders for Linux: `https://www.rodsbooks.com/efi-bootloaders/index.html`
- Ballmer: Linux is a cancer: `https://www.theregister.com/2001/06/02/ballmer_linux_is_a_cancer/`

18
Understanding systemd-logind

Yes, it's true – there's even a new way of managing user logins and user sessions in systemd. In this chapter, we'll delve into the mysteries of `systemd-logind`, and show you some fairly nifty user management tricks. Knowing these tricks can definitely help you out in a business environment. Specific topics in this chapter include:

- Understanding the need for a new login service
- Understanding `systemd-logind.service`
- Understanding `logind.conf`
- Understanding `loginctl`
- Understanding `polkit`

All right, let's get started.

Technical requirements

We won't need anything fancy for this chapter. Just use your normal **Alma** and **Ubuntu Server** virtual machines, and it will all be good. Well, let me rephrase that. You'll want to use Ubuntu Server for the `logind.conf` demos, because restarting the `systemd-logind` service is problematic on graphical mode machines (I'll explain more about that in a bit). At the end of the chapter, there will be a couple of demos for which it will be handy to have a desktop interface, so you'll want an Alma machine with the **Gnome 3** desktop for them.

All right, let's begin by looking at the `systemd-logind.service` file.

Check out the following link to see the Code in Action video: `https://bit.ly/3EiIHSD`

Understanding the need for a new login service

I know, you're wondering, *Why do we even need a new login service?* One reason is because of the tight integration between `systemd` and `cgroups`. The `systemd-logind` service does several things for us, but its main job is to create cgroup slices and scopes for everyone who logs into a system. As we go through this chapter, we'll look at a few other things that `systemd-logind` also does for us. (To read a short description about all of the things that `systemd-logind` does, see the `systemd-logind` man page.)

Understanding systemd-logind.service

There's a considerable difference in how this unit file is set up on RHEL-type systems and Ubuntu. Let's first look at the RHEL-type setup on the Alma machine.

The Alma Linux systemd-logind.service file

On the Alma machine, the `[Unit]` section of the `/lib/systemd/system/systemd-logind.service` file looks like this:

```
[Unit]
Description=Login Service
Documentation=man:systemd-logind.service(8) man:logind.conf(5)
Documentation=https://www.freedesktop.org/wiki/Software/systemd/logind
Documentation=https://www.freedesktop.org/wiki/Software/systemd/multiseat
Wants=user.slice
```

```
After=nss-user-lookup.target user.slice
# Ask for the dbus socket.
Wants=dbus.socket
After=dbus.socket
```

Here's the breakdown:

- `Wants=user.slice`: This makes total sense. Due to systemd's tight integration with cgroups, a user slice must be created for every user who logs in.
- `After=nss-user-lookup.target`: The **Name Service Switch** (**NSS**) determines where the system is to look for various types of information, including user authentication information. This is configured in the `/etc/nsswitch.conf` file, which we'll discuss next.
- `Wants=dbus.socket` and `After=dbus.socket`: There's no `[Install]` section of this service file, so this service won't automatically start when we reach either the multi-user or graphical target. Instead, a `dbus` message will get generated when the first user logs in for the first time, which will automatically start the service.

Okay, let's look at the relevant lines of the `/etc/nsswitch.conf` file. Open it and look for these four lines:

```
passwd:      sss files systemd
shadow:     files sss
group:       sss files systemd
. . .
. . .
gshadow:    files
```

In the `passwd:`, `shadow:`, and `group:` lines of the file, the `sss` means that user and group information will be pulled from the **System Security Services Daemon** (**SSSD**). The `sssd` allows you to use **LDAP**, **FreeIPA**, or even **Microsoft Active Directory** as a means of user authentication. If you're not using any of these three authentication methods, then authentication information will be pulled from files, which are the `/etc/passwd`, `/etc/group`, `/etc/shadow`, and `/etc/gshadow` files. If the system can't find information about the user who's logging in in either `sss` or `files`, then it will go to `systemd`. The `systemd` setting allows the system to authenticate a dynamic user that might be configured in a service unit file, and that wouldn't have an entry in either the `/etc/passwd` or `/etc/shadow` files.

> **Note**
>
> *Dynamic users*, to which I alluded in the preceding paragraph, aren't for normal human users who would log into a computer. They're *system accounts* that are used for running services with reduced privileges. A dynamic user gets created on-the-fly whenever a service that uses one starts, and gets destroyed whenever the service stops. You'll never see an entry for a dynamic user in the `/etc/passwd`, `/etc/group`, `/etc/gshadow`, or `/etc/shadow` files.

Now, let's get back to the `systemd-logind.service` file, and look at the `[Service]` section. I can't show it all to you at once, so here's the top part:

```
[Service]
ExecStart=/usr/lib/systemd/systemd-logind
Restart=always
RestartSec=0
BusName=org.freedesktop.login1
WatchdogSec=3min
CapabilityBoundingSet=CAP_SYS_ADMIN CAP_MAC_ADMIN CAP_AUDIT_CONTROL CAP_CHOWN CAP_KILL CAP_DAC_READ_SEARCH CAP_DAC_OVERRIDE CAP_FOWNER CAP_SYS_TTY_CONFIG
. . .
. . .
```

It's mainly the standard stuff that we've gone over before, so you should have a good handle on it already. The main thing I want you to notice is the `CapabilityBoundingSet=` line, which grants a lot of root-level capabilities to this service. The second part of the `[Service]` section consists of a lot of security and resource control directives:

```
. . .
MemoryDenyWriteExecute=yes
RestrictRealtime=yes
RestrictNamespaces=yes
RestrictAddressFamilies=AF_UNIX AF_NETLINK
RestrictSUIDSGID=yes
SystemCallFilter=@system-service
SystemCallErrorNumber=EPERM
SystemCallArchitectures=native
LockPersonality=yes
```

```
FileDescriptorStoreMax=512

# Increase the default a bit in order to allow many
simultaneous logins since we keep one fd open per session.
LimitNOFILE=16384
```

As always, I'll leave it to you to look these directives up in the `systemd.directives` man page.

All right, that's it for the `systemd-logind.service` file on the Alma machine. Let's look at the one on the Ubuntu machine.

The Ubuntu Server systemd-logind.service file

The `systemd-logind.service` file on the Ubuntu machine is considerably different from the one on the Alma machine. Let's look at the `[Unit]` section first:

```
[Unit]
Description=Login Service
Documentation=man:systemd-logind.service(8) man:logind.conf(5)
Documentation=https://www.freedesktop.org/wiki/Software/
systemd/logind
Documentation=https://www.freedesktop.org/wiki/Software/
systemd/multiseat
Wants=user.slice modprobe@drm.service
After=nss-user-lookup.target user.slice modprobe@drm.service
ConditionPathExists=/lib/systemd/system/dbus.service

# Ask for the dbus socket.
Wants=dbus.socket
After=dbus.socket
. . .
```

The first difference we see is that the `Wants=` line calls in the `modprobe@.service` to load the **Direct Rendering Manager** (**DRM**) (`drm`) kernel module. I'm not sure why that is, because this seems like something that should get loaded when you boot the machine. In fact, this seems to be the case on the Alma machine, as we see here:

```
[donnie@localhost ~]$ lsmod | grep drm
drm_kms_helper         233472  1 vmwgfx
```

```
syscopyarea             16384  1 drm_kms_helper
sysfillrect             16384  1 drm_kms_helper
sysimgblt               16384  1 drm_kms_helper
fb_sys_fops             16384  1 drm_kms_helper
drm                    569344  4 vmwgfx,drm_kms_helper,ttm
[donnie@localhost ~]$
```

For some reason that I don't know, the Ubuntu developers decided to load the `drm` module when the `systemd-logind` service starts, instead of at boot-up.

The `[Service]` section on the Ubuntu machine is much larger, because it contains more security directives than what you saw on the Alma machine. Why? Well remember, the Alma machine is running **SELinux**, which gives comprehensive system protection right out of the box. Ubuntu Server is running **AppArmor**, which isn't nearly as good, at least not in its out-of-the-box configuration. So, the extra security directives in the `systemd-logind.service` file give us some good *Mandatory Access Control* protection that AppArmor doesn't give us. Here's a snippet of the `[Service]` section, which shows some of the extra directives for Ubuntu:

```
[Service]
BusName=org.freedesktop.login1
CapabilityBoundingSet=CAP_SYS_ADMIN CAP_MAC_ADMIN CAP_AUDIT_
CONTROL CAP_CHOWN CAP_DAC_READ_SEARCH CAP_DAC_OVERRIDE CAP_
FOWNER CAP_SYS_TTY_CONFIG CAP_LINUX_IMMUTABLE
DeviceAllow=block-* r
DeviceAllow=char-/dev/console rw
DeviceAllow=char-drm rw
DeviceAllow=char-input rw
...
...
# Increase the default a bit in order to allow many
simultaneous logins since
# we keep one fd open per session.
LimitNOFILE=524288
```

As always, I'll let you read about these security directives in the man pages.

Next, let's look at the configuration file for `systemd-logind.service`.

Understanding logind.conf

The `/etc/systemd/logind.conf` file is the configuration file for the `systemd-logind` service. Now, before we get too far, I want to recommend that you use a text-mode virtual machine for this section. The demos will have you make several changes to the `logind.conf` file, and you'll need to restart the `systemd-logind` service after each one. If you do that on a graphical mode machine, you'll get logged out of the desktop, and will have to log back in. The desktop doesn't always come back up correctly, and you'll end up having to restart the machine. With a text-mode machine, that isn't a problem. So, since the Ubuntu Server machine is already in text mode, we'll use it for the demos.

The good news is that the `logind.conf` file is identical on both the Ubuntu machine and the Alma machine. Here's what it looks like:

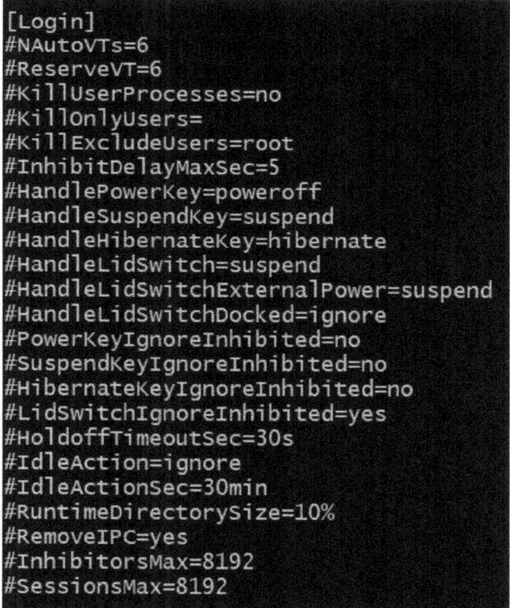

```
[Login]
#NAutoVTs=6
#ReserveVT=6
#KillUserProcesses=no
#KillOnlyUsers=
#KillExcludeUsers=root
#InhibitDelayMaxSec=5
#HandlePowerKey=poweroff
#HandleSuspendKey=suspend
#HandleHibernateKey=hibernate
#HandleLidSwitch=suspend
#HandleLidSwitchExternalPower=suspend
#HandleLidSwitchDocked=ignore
#PowerKeyIgnoreInhibited=no
#SuspendKeyIgnoreInhibited=no
#HibernateKeyIgnoreInhibited=no
#LidSwitchIgnoreInhibited=yes
#HoldoffTimeoutSec=30s
#IdleAction=ignore
#IdleActionSec=30min
#RuntimeDirectorySize=10%
#RemoveIPC=yes
#InhibitorsMax=8192
#SessionsMax=8192
```

Figure 18.1 – The logind.conf file

As is the case with all of the configuration files in `/etc/systemd/`, all directives are commented out. The values shown are the default ones that are compiled into the `systemd-logind` executable. You can probably figure out what many of these directives do just by looking at their names, and you can consult the `logind.conf` man page to read about the ones that aren't so obvious. So, rather than cover each directive in detail, I just want to go over a few of the more interesting ones. Let's start with the *virtual terminals* setting.

Virtual terminals

At the top, we see the `#NAutoVTs=6` line. This sets the number of available *virtual terminals*. Virtual terminals don't do much for you on a desktop machine, because you can just open multiple terminal emulators from the **Start** menu. But, they're extremely handy on a text-mode machine. In fact, I use them all the time here on one of my text-mode, Linux-powered GPU mining rigs. While the mining software is running in the default virtual terminal, I can do a *Ctrl* + *Alt* + *Function* key sequence to bring up another terminal so that I can do something else there. So, to bring up virtual terminal 2, I would do *Ctrl* + *Alt* + *F2* and log into a new session. I can bring up a total of six virtual terminals by using function keys *F1* through *F6*. (Doing *Ctrl* + *Alt* + *F1* gets you back to the default terminal.) That's cool because while the mining software runs in the **F1** terminal, I can have a text-mode cryptocoin wallet running in the **F2** terminal, edit a file in the **F3** terminal, and `ssh` into my other GPU mining rig from the **F4** terminal. On a graphical mode desktop machine, one virtual terminal is reserved for the desktop. (It's usually the **F1** terminal, but that could vary with different distros.) You can try this on your virtual machine, but there's a bit of a trick to it. If your host machine is running **Windows**, just do the *Ctrl-Alt-Function* key sequence from your normal keyboard, as you'd do on a bare-metal Linux machine. But, if your host machine is running Linux, you'll need to open the **VirtualBox Input/Keyboard** menu and bring up the **Soft Keyboard**:

Figure 18.2 – The VirtualBox Soft Keyboard

Then, do your *Ctrl-Alt-Function* key sequence by clicking on the soft keyboard. If you try to do it the normal way with your normal keyboard, the key sequence will be intercepted by the host machine.

You'll likely never edit this line, because six virtual terminals are enough for most people. But if you ever do need more, you can add them here. For example, let's say that you need to have eight virtual terminals instead of just six. Just change the `#NAutoVTs=6` line to `#NAutoVTs=8`. Then, restart the `systemd-logind` service:

```
donnie@ubuntu20-04:/etc/systemd$ sudo systemctl restart
systemd-logind
donnie@ubuntu20-04:/etc/systemd$
```

You can see the extra two virtual terminals by doing *Ctrl* + *Alt* + *F7* and *Ctrl* + *Alt* + *F8*.

Next, let's see how users can keep processes going after they log out.

Keeping user processes going after logout

These next three lines work together:

```
#KillUserProcesses=no
#KillOnlyUsers=
#KillExcludeUsers=root
```

If you're an old-timer like me, you'll likely remember how this worked in the old SysV days. You'd log into a Linux server, start a process from the command line, and then log out while the process was still going. The problem was that the process would stop as soon as you logged out. If you logged in remotely and started a process, it would stop if you accidentally closed the remote terminal of your local machine or if the local machine were to reboot. In order to keep the process on the remote machine going if any of those things happened, you'd need to start the process with either `screen` or `nohup`. Now though, you don't have to worry about that as long as these three lines stay as you see them here. To demonstrate, create an account on the text-mode Ubuntu machine for Frank, if you haven't done so already:

```
donnie@ubuntu20-04:~$ sudo adduser frank
```

Then, have him remotely log in. Have him create the `loop.sh` shell script in his own home directory, like this:

```
#!/bin/bash
i=0
```

```
for i in {0..100000}
do
        echo $i >> number.txt
        sleep 5
done
exit
```

It's a silly little loop that does nothing but create an entry in a text file every five seconds. That's okay though, because it serves our purpose. (Also, note that I didn't upload this script to **GitHub**, because it would take longer for you to download it than it would to just type it yourself.) Next, have Frank set the executable permission on the `loop.sh` file:

```
frank@ubuntu20-04:~$ chmod u+x loop.sh
frank@ubuntu20-04:~$ ls -l
total 4
-rwxr--r-- 1 frank 83 Sep  9 16:29 loop.sh
frank@ubuntu20-04:~$
```

Now, have Frank start the script as a background process:

```
frank@ubuntu20-04:~$ ./loop.sh &
[1] 2446
frank@ubuntu20-04:~$
```

Verify that the script is running by doing `tail -f number.txt`:

```
frank@ubuntu20-04:~$ tail -f number.txt
10
11
12
13
14
15
16
17
18
```

Do a *Ctrl* + *C* to stop the `tail -f` process. Then, have Frank log out by typing `exit`.

Next, have Frank log in again, and again have him do `tail -f number.txt`. You should see that the number list keeps incrementing, which means that the process kept going after Frank logged out. To stop the process, use `ps aux` to get the `PID` number, and then use that PID number in a `kill` command:

```
frank@ubuntu20-04:~$ ps aux | grep loop.sh
frank        2446  0.1  1.5  32012 31120 ?        S    16:35
0:00 /bin/bash ./loop.sh
frank        2598  0.0  0.0   3304   736 pts/2    S+   16:46
0:00 grep --color=auto loop.sh
frank@ubuntu20-04:~$ kill 2446
frank@ubuntu20-04:~$
```

Then, have Frank log out by typing `exit`.

Now, let's say that we don't want Frank to keep his processes going after he logs out. In your own terminal, open the `/etc/systemd/logind.conf` file in your text editor. Change the `#KillOnlyUsers=` line so that it looks like this:

```
KillOnlyUsers=frank
```

Save the file and restart the `systemd-logind` service:

```
donnie@ubuntu20-04:/etc/systemd$ sudo systemctl restart
systemd-logind
donnie@ubuntu20-04:/etc/systemd$
```

Note that there's no `reload` option for this service.

Go back to Frank's terminal, and have him log back in. Have him start the `loop.sh` script in the background, as you did before. When you do a `tail -f number.txt` command this time, you should see that the number list no longer increments.

Okay, we're through with Frank for now, so go ahead and have him log out.

> **Note**
> A few days ago, the day that I started writing this chapter, Frank the cat decided to help out. He pressed some keys on my keyboard and deleted a whole paragraph, replacing it with a string of dashes. (Thank goodness for the **Undo** feature.)

Next, let's look at a few *power management directives*.

Power management directives

Further down in the `/etc/systemd/logind.conf` file, you'll see the `HandlePowerKey=`, `HandleSuspendKey=`, `HandleHibernateKey=`, `HandleLidSwitch=`, `HandleLidSwitchExternalPower=`, and the `HandleLidSwitchDocked=` power management directives. You can probably figure out what these directives do just by looking at their names, and you can see the default settings in the `logind.conf` file. To see the other settings that you can use for these directives, just consult the `logind.conf` man page. It's a good write-up, so I won't repeat any of that here. But, I will offer one example.

Let's say you have a laptop, and you need it to keep running when you shut the lid. Just look for this line:

```
#HandleLidSwitch=suspend
```

Change it to look like this:

```
HandleLidSwitch=ignore
```

I'm going to assume that you're running your laptop in graphical mode. (Doesn't everyone?) Since restarting `systemd-logind.service` doesn't work well on graphical mode machines, your best bet would be to just reboot the machine so that the new setting can take effect. Now, instead of suspending the laptop when you close the lid, it will continue running as merrily as it did with the lid open. (You can try this on your virtual machine if you really want to. But, since your virtual machine doesn't have a lid, you won't see anything happen.).

For our last example, let's do some *Idle Action*.

The IdleAction directives

`IdleAction`, eh? Boy, if that isn't an oxymoron, I don't know what is. But seriously, you can configure these next two directives to control what happens when you leave the computer sitting idle for a specified period of time:

```
#IdleAction=ignore
#IdleActionSec=30min
```

By default, the machine will just keep running until you shut it down. Just for fun, change these two lines so that they look like this:

```
IdleAction=poweroff
IdleActionSec=3min
```

Restart `systemd-logind.service`, and then just wait, without touching the virtual machine. After three minutes, you should see the machine automatically shut down. Of course, you don't want to leave the virtual machine with this configuration, so boot it up again and change these settings back to their default values. Then, restart `systemd-logind.service`.

There are still a few directives that I didn't cover, but you can read about them in the `logind.conf` man page. Let's move on to the `loginctl` management utility.

Understanding loginctl

Another bit of good news is that `loginctl` works identically on both Ubuntu and Alma. You can use it to keep an eye on what other users are doing, change certain settings for a user's login environment, or even as a security tool to get rid of malicious users.

> **Note**
>
> For this section, we'll continue with the Ubuntu Server machine. Create user accounts for Pogo, Vicky, and Frank, if you haven't already done so. Log yourself in from the local terminal, and again from a remote terminal. Do *Ctrl-Alt-F2* on the virtual machine to get to the second virtual terminal, and have Vicky log in there. Then, have Pogo and Frank log in from their own remote terminals.

Before we get into the real meat of the matter, we need to define a couple of terms:

- **session**: A *session* gets created whenever a user logs into the system. Each session is assigned a decimal number as its ID.
- **seat**: A *seat* consists of all of the hardware that is assigned to a specific workstation. Each seat has an assigned text-string name that consists of from 1 to 255 characters. A user who logs into a computer at the local console will always be assigned a seat. Users who log in remotely will *not* be assigned a seat. In a default setup, `seat0` is the only seat that you will ever see. Creating new seats involves configuring `udev` rules, which is beyond the scope of this book.

Doing either `loginctl` without any options or `loginctl list-sessions` shows you who is logged in and where they've logged in from:

```
donnie@ubuntu20-04:~$ loginctl
SESSION  UID USER   SEAT  TTY
     10      1001 frank               pts/1
     14      1003 vicky   seat0    tty2
     16      1004 pogo                pts/2
      3       1000 donnie  seat0    tty1
      6       1000 donnie             pts/0

5 sessions listed.
donnie@ubuntu20-04:~$
```

You see that Vicky and I are the only ones with assigned seats, while Frank and Pogo have to remain standing. (Yeah I know, bad joke.) But seriously, Vicky and I were assigned to `seat0` because we're both logged in at the local terminal. I logged in from `tty1`, which is the default virtual terminal. Then, I did *Ctrl-Alt-F2* to get to the second virtual terminal (`tty2`), and had Vicky log in there. It's probably not real likely that you'll have two people log into two different virtual terminals of the same local machine, but it could happen. I did it now to show you that more than one user can be assigned to the same seat. You also see that I have two sessions going for myself, because I'm logged in from both the local terminal and from a remote `ssh` session on the `pts/0` terminal. Frank and Pogo are only logged in remotely, which is why they don't have seats. Also, note that every session has its own assigned ID number in the first column.

> **Note**
>
> I've just shown you how the `list-sessions` option works on Ubuntu. On a RHEL 8-type distro such as Alma, the `SEAT` and `TTY` columns will both be empty for any users who have logged in remotely. (I have no idea why.) However, you will see the `pts` information for a user when you use either a `user-status` or a `session-status` option, which I'll explain next.

Use the `user-status` option to see detailed information about a user. If you don't specify a username, you'll see information about your own user account. Right now, let's see what kind of mischief our intrepid opossum, Pogo, is up to:

```
donnie@ubuntu20-04:~$ loginctl user-status pogo
pogo (1004)
           Since: Sat 2021-09-11 16:50:45 EDT; 24min ago
```

```
           State: active
        Sessions: *16
          Linger: no
            Unit: user-1004.slice
                  ├─session-16.scope
                  │ ├─2211 sshd: pogo [priv]
                  │ ├─2302 sshd: pogo@pts/2
                  │ └─2303 -bash
                  └─user@1004.service
. . .
Sep 11 16:50:45 ubuntu20-04 systemd[2226]: Startup finished in 125ms.
donnie@ubuntu20-04:~$
```

To see slightly less information, we'll look at Pogo's `session-status`. We see that he's in session number `16`, so the command and output will look like this:

```
donnie@ubuntu20-04:~$ loginctl session-status 16
16 - pogo (1004)
           Since: Sat 2021-09-11 16:50:45 EDT; 39min ago
          Leader: 2211 (sshd)
             TTY: pts/2
          Remote: 192.168.0.51
         Service: sshd; type tty; class user
           State: active
            Unit: session-16.scope
                  ├─2211 sshd: pogo [priv]
                  ├─2302 sshd: pogo@pts/2
                  └─2303 -bash

Sep 11 16:50:45 ubuntu20-04 systemd[1]: Started Session 16 of user pogo.
donnie@ubuntu20-04:~$
```

We've seen examples of how to get information about users and sessions. Let's look at how to get information about seats. A `list-seat` command shows you all of the available seats:

```
donnie@ubuntu20-04:~$ loginctl list-seats
SEAT
seat0

1 seats listed.
donnie@ubuntu20-04:~$
```

Unless you've configured one or more `udev` rules, `seat0` is the only one you'll ever see. Now, use the `seat-status` option to see the hardware that this seat includes:

```
donnie@ubuntu20-04:~$ loginctl seat-status seat0
seat0
        Sessions: *14 3
         Devices:
                  ├─/sys/devices/LNXSYSTM:00/LNXPWRBN:00/input/
input0
                  │ input:input0 "Power Button"
                  ├─/sys/devices/LNXSYSTM:00/LNXSLPBN:00/input/
input1
                  │ input:input1 "Sleep Button"
                  ├─/sys/devices/LNXSYSTM:00/LNXSYBUS:00/
PNP0A03:00/LNXVIDEO:00/input/input4
                  │ input:input4 "Video Bus"
                  ├─/sys/devices/pci0000:00/0000:00:01.1/ata2/
host1/target1:0:0/1:0:0:0/block/sr0
                  │ block:sr0
. . .
```

There are several more options for getting information about users, sessions, and seats, but you get the idea. Besides, you can get more information from the `loginctl` man page.

Next, let's say that for whatever reason, you want to kick Frank out of his session. Just use the `terminate-session` option, followed by Frank's session ID number, like this:

```
donnie@ubuntu20-04:~$ sudo loginctl terminate-session 10
[sudo] password for donnie:
donnie@ubuntu20-04:~$
```

Here, you see that Frank's session really has been terminated:

```
frank@ubuntu20-04:~$ Connection to 192.168.0.49 closed by
remote host.
Connection to 192.168.0.49 closed.
donnie@siftworkstation: ~
$
```

If a user is logged into multiple sessions and you want to shut down all of their sessions, use the `terminate-user` option, like this:

```
donnie@ubuntu20-04:~$ sudo loginctl terminate-user pogo
donnie@ubuntu20-04:~$
```

There are a few other management commands that you might find useful. They're easy to understand, and there's a good write-up about them in the `loginctl` man page.

Next, let's cover a cool tool that can replace `sudo` in *some* instances.

Understanding polkit

PolicyKit and **polkit** aren't part of the systemd ecosystem, but `systemd-logind` does provide access to `polkit` functionality. PolicyKit was a **Red Hat** innovation that came on the scene quite a few years ago, and it could be used on various Unix-like operating systems. In 2012, a new version was released with the brand new name, *polkit*. The developers changed the name as a reminder that this is a whole new code base that isn't compatible with the older version.

The polkit service is similar to sudo in that it allows a normally non-privileged user to perform certain privileged tasks. There is, however, a big difference between the two.

The sudo utility is quite easy to configure, and you can easily grant pretty much any admin privilege or privileges to any user. When you install the operating system, you'll have full sudo privileges for yourself, and nobody else will have any. On the other hand, polkit comes pre-configured with a set of administrative tasks for which it can grant root privileges. You can add more tasks, and there might be times when you'll want to. Keep in mind though, that writing rules and actions for polkit is more complex than writing rules for sudo. So, you'll want to study the examples that are already on the system and read the documentation before you try to write your own. Before we look at these rules and actions, let's see how polkit grants root privileges.

We'll start with the Alma Linux machine. We need root privileges to peek into some of the polkit directories, so let's just go to the root shell:

```
[donnie@localhost ~]$ sudo su -
[sudo] password for donnie:
[root@localhost ~]#
```

Now, look in the /etc/polkit-1/rules.d/ directory:

```
[root@localhost ~]# cd /etc/polkit-1/rules.d/
[root@localhost rules.d]# ls
49-polkit-pkla-compat.rules  50-default.rules
[root@localhost rules.d]#
```

The file we want is the 50-default.rules file, which looks like this:

```
[root@localhost rules.d]# cat 50-default.rules
/* -*- mode: js; js-indent-level: 4; indent-tabs-mode: nil -*-
*/

// DO NOT EDIT THIS FILE, it will be overwritten on update
//
// Default rules for polkit
//
// See the polkit(8) man page for more information
// about configuring polkit.

polkit.addAdminRule(function(action, subject) {
```

```
    return ["unix-group:wheel"];
});
[root@localhost rules.d]#
```

Take note of the final stanza:

```
polkit.addAdminRule(function(action, subject) {
return ["unix-group:wheel"];
```

This means that if `polkit` detects someone trying to perform an administrative task without using `sudo`, it will look in the wheel group to see if anyone is there. If there is someone in the wheel group, then it will prompt the user to enter the password of that person. If the wheel group has no members, that means that the root user has an assigned password. If that's the case, `polkit` will prompt for the root user password.

On the Ubuntu machine, the files we need to see are in the `/etc/polkit-1/localauthority.conf.d/` directory, and we don't need root privileges to enter it:

```
donnie@ubuntu20-04:~$ cd /etc/polkit-1/localauthority.conf.d/
donnie@ubuntu20-04:/etc/polkit-1/localauthority.conf.d$ ls -l
total 8
-rw-r--r-- 1 root 267 Aug 16  2019 50-localauthority.conf
-rw-r--r-- 1 root root  65 Aug 16  2019 51-ubuntu-admin.conf
donnie@ubuntu20-04:/etc/polkit-1/localauthority.conf.d$
```

The `50-localauthority.conf` file looks like this:

```
donnie@ubuntu20-04:/etc/polkit-1/localauthority.conf.d$ cat
50-localauthority.conf
# Configuration file for the PolicyKit Local Authority.
#
# DO NOT EDIT THIS FILE, it will be overwritten on update.
#
# See the pklocalauthority(8) man page for more information
# about configuring the Local Authority.
#
[Configuration]
AdminIdentities=unix-user:0
donnie@ubuntu20-04:/etc/polkit-1/localauthority.conf.d$
```

There's only one important line here, which looks for the root user. (That's the `unix-user` with UID `0`.) The other file looks for members of the `sudo` or `admin` groups:

```
donnie@ubuntu20-04:/etc/polkit-1/localauthority.conf.d$ cat 51-ubuntu-admin.conf
[Configuration]
AdminIdentities=unix-group:sudo;unix-group:admin
donnie@ubuntu20-04:/etc/polkit-1/localauthority.conf.d$
```

The biggest difference between the Red Hat and Ubuntu worlds so far is that on Red Hat-type systems, members of the wheel group have full sudo privileges. On Ubuntu systems, members of either the sudo group or the admin group have full sudo privileges. Now, let's see how this works.

On the Ubuntu machine, try to reload the `ssh` service without using sudo:

```
donnie@ubuntu20-04:~$ systemctl reload ssh
==== AUTHENTICATING FOR org.freedesktop.systemd1.manage-units ===
Authentication is required to reload 'ssh.service'.
Authenticating as: Donald A. Tevault (donnie)
Password:
==== AUTHENTICATION COMPLETE ===
donnie@ubuntu20-04:~$
```

As you see, polkit asks for my password because I'm the only member of the sudo group. Now, let's try using polkit to look at the firewall configuration:

```
donnie@ubuntu20-04:~$ iptables -L
Fatal: can't open lock file /run/xtables.lock: Permission denied
donnie@ubuntu20-04:~$
```

It failed, because polkit isn't configured to work with the `iptables` command.

Next, let's see what happens if Pogo tries to use polkit. For it to work though, his password will need to be different from your own password. If it's the same, change it to something else:

```
donnie@ubuntu20-04:~$ sudo passwd pogo
New password: Retype new password:
passwd: password updated successfully
donnie@ubuntu20-04:~$
```

Now, let's have Pogo try to reload `ssh`:

```
pogo@ubuntu20-04:~$ systemctl reload ssh
==== AUTHENTICATING FOR org.freedesktop.systemd1.manage-units
===
Authentication is required to reload 'ssh.service'.
Authenticating as: Donald A. Tevault (donnie)
Password:
polkit-agent-helper-1: pam_authenticate failed: Authentication
failure
==== AUTHENTICATION FAILED ===
Failed to reload ssh.service: Access denied
See system logs and 'systemctl status ssh.service' for details.
pogo@ubuntu20-04:~$
```

As before, polkit asks for my password, because I'm a member of the sudo group and Pogo isn't. Pogo doesn't know my password, so he can't perform this command.

While we're still on the Ubuntu machine, let's see what some of these rules look like. We'll `cd` into the `/usr/share/polkit-1/rules.d/` directory and peek inside the `systemd-networkd.rules` file:

```
// Allow systemd-networkd to set timezone, get product UUID,
// and transient hostname
polkit.addRule(function(action, subject) {
    if ((action.id == "org.freedesktop.hostname1.set-hostname"
||
         action.id == "org.freedesktop.hostname1.get-product-
uuid" ||
         action.id == "org.freedesktop.timedate1.set-timezone")
&&
```

```
        subject.user == "systemd-network") {
        return polkit.Result.YES;
    }
});
```

Here, we're assigning root privileges to the `systemd-networkd` system user account so that it can perform these three tasks without prompting for a password. (The `return polkit.Result.YES;` line is what prevents it from asking for a password.)

For something a bit more complex, let's `cd` into the `/usr/share/polkit-1/actions/` directory and peek inside one of its files. We'll choose the `com.ubuntu.languageselector.policy` file, since it's the shortest. The only part that we need to look at is the `action id=` section, which looks like this:

```
. . .
 <action id="com.ubuntu.languageselector.
setsystemdefaultlanguage">
    <description gettext-domain="language-selector">Set system
default language</description>
    <message gettext-domain="language-selector">System policy
prevented setting default language</message>
    <defaults>
      <allow_any>auth_admin</allow_any>
      <allow_inactive>no</allow_inactive>
      <allow_active>auth_admin_keep</allow_active>
    </defaults>
  </action>
. . .
```

The `<default>` stanza at the bottom is where we define who can perform this action. Here's the breakdown:

- `<allow_any>`: This tag sets authorizations for any client machine. The `auth_admin` setting requires the user to enter the administrative password before the action can be performed.
- `<allow_inactive>`: This tag sets authorizations for clients in inactive sessions on the local console. It's set to `no` here, which prevents these clients from having any authorization.

- `<allow_active>`: This is for clients in an active session on the local console. The `auth_admin_keep` value requires that the user enter the admin password. It also allows the user to maintain authorization for a short period of time.

The other action files are set up in a similar manner, and I'll leave it to you to peruse through them. For more details on the rules and actions, see the `polkit` man page.

The polkit service is activated by a `dbus` message whenever someone tries to perform an administrative action that's configured in `polkit`, as we see by the `Type=dbus` line in its unit file:

```
donnie@ubuntu20-04:~$ cd /lib/systemd/system
donnie@ubuntu20-04:/lib/systemd/system$ cat polkit.service
[Unit]
Description=Authorization Manager
Documentation=man:polkit(8)

[Service]
Type=dbus
BusName=org.freedesktop.PolicyKit1
ExecStart=/usr/lib/policykit-1/polkitd --no-debug
donnie@ubuntu20-04:/lib/systemd/system$
```

Okay, that does it for the Ubuntu machine. Things are pretty much the same on the Alma machine, except that you need root privileges to `cd` into the `rules.d/` directory, as we see here:

```
[donnie@localhost system]$ cd /usr/share/polkit-1/
[donnie@localhost polkit-1]$ ls -l
total 8
drwxr-xr-x. 2 root     4096 Jul 23 15:51 actions
drwx------. 2 polkitd root  287 Jul 12 17:51 rules.d
[donnie@localhost polkit-1]$
```

Now, let's shift over to the local graphical terminal of the Alma virtual machine. If you're still in the root shell, type `exit` to get back to your own shell. Now, try to reload `sshd`, and you'll see a dialog box pop up to ask for the admin password:

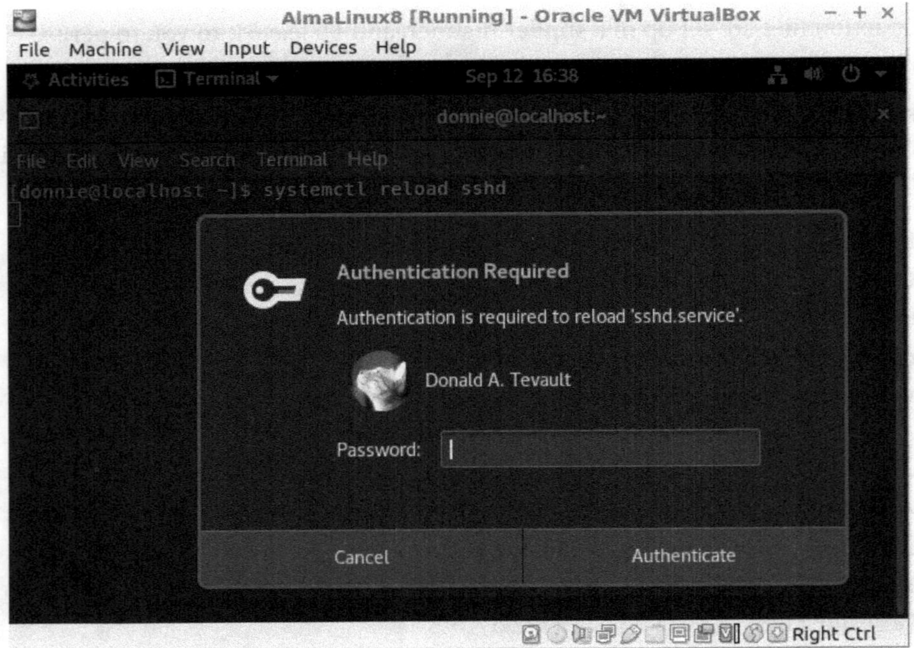

Figure 18.3 – The graphical polkit password dialog box

Okay, I think that that's about it for polkit. Let's summarize what we've learned and wrap things up.

Summary

As always, we've seen some cool stuff in this chapter. We began with a discussion about the `systemd-logind.service` file, and saw how it's set up differently on the Ubuntu and Alma machines. We then looked at the `logind.conf` file, and played with some of its configuration options. After that, we played with `loginctl` and wrapped up with a discussion of polkit.

And that, guys and gals, wraps things up not only for this chapter, but also for the whole book. I hope that you've enjoyed our journey through the idyllic *land of systemd* as much as I have. Take care, and I hope to see you again soon.

Questions

1. How does the `systemd-logind` service get activated?

   A. As part of the multi-user target

   B. As part of the graphical target

   C. When it receives a `dbus` message

   D. As part of the `sysinit` target

2. What happens when two different users remotely log into a Linux server?

   A. They both get assigned to `seat0`.

   B. One gets assigned to `seat0` and the other gets assigned to `seat1`.

   C. They both get assigned to `seat1`.

   D. Neither of them gets an assigned seat.

3. In which of the following files does `systemd-logind` look to find out how to do user authentication?

   A. `/etc/nsswitch.conf`

   B. `/etc/default/nsswitch.conf`

   C. `/etc/sysconfig/nsswitch.conf`

   D. `/etc/authenticate.conf`

4. Which of the following statements is true about polkit?

   A. In its default configuration, it works with only a pre-defined set of administrative commands.

   B. In its default configuration, it works with all administrative commands, just as sudo does.

   C. It only works with the root user password.

   D. It can only be used on text-mode machines.

Answers

1. C
2. D
3. A
4. A

Further reading

- The SSSD home page: `https://sssd.io/`
- An explanation of seats and sessions: `https://www.man7.org/linux/man-pages/man3/sd-login.3.html`
- The polkit reference manual: `https://www.freedesktop.org/software/polkit/docs/latest/polkit.8.html`

Index

Symbols

A

B

C

D

E

M

N

O

P

R

S

T

U

V

X

Other Books You May Enjoy

If you enjoyed this book, you may be interested in these other books by Packt:

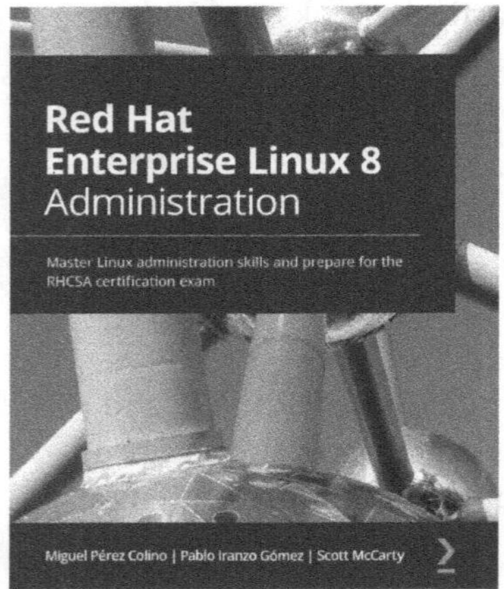

Red Hat Enterprise Linux 8 Administration
Miguel Pérez Colino, Pablo Iranzo Gómez, Scott McCarty
ISBN: 978-1-80056-982-9

- Deploy RHEL 8 in different footprints, from bare metal and virtualized to the cloud
- Manage users and software on local and remote systems at scale
- Discover how to secure a system with SELinux, OpenSCAP, and firewalld
- Gain an overview of storage components with LVM, Stratis, and VDO
- Master remote administration with passwordless SSH and tunnels
- Monitor your systems for resource usage and take actions to fix issues
- Understand the boot process, performance optimizations, and containers

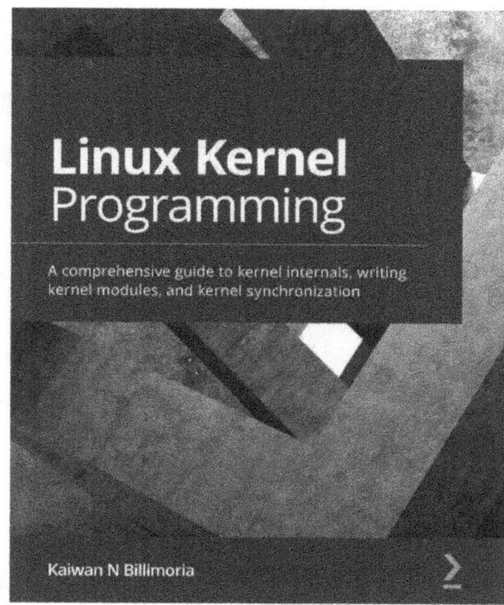

Linux Kernel Programming

Kaiwan N Billimoria

ISBN: 978-1-78995-343-5

- Write high-quality modular kernel code (LKM framework) for 5.x kernels
- Configure and build a kernel from source
- Explore the Linux kernel architecture
- Get to grips with key internals regarding memory management within the kernel
- Understand and work with various dynamic kernel memory alloc/dealloc APIs
- Discover key internals aspects regarding CPU scheduling within the kernel
- Gain an understanding of kernel concurrency issues
- Find out how to work with key kernel synchronization primitives

Packt is searching for authors like you

If you're interested in becoming an author for Packt, please visit `authors.packtpub.com` and apply today. We have worked with thousands of developers and tech professionals, just like you, to help them share their insight with the global tech community. You can make a general application, apply for a specific hot topic that we are recruiting an author for, or submit your own idea.

Share Your Thoughts

Now you've finished *Linux Service Management Made Easy with systemd*, we'd love to hear your thoughts! Scan the QR code below to go straight to the Amazon review page for this book and share your feedback or leave a review on the site that you purchased it from.

`https://packt.link/r/1801811644`

Your review is important to us and the tech community and will help us make sure we're delivering excellent quality content.

www.ingramcontent.com/pod-product-compliance
Lightning Source LLC
Chambersburg PA
CBHW060921060326
40690CB00041B/2904